Selling Intervention and War

Selling Intervention and War

The Presidency, the Media, and the American Public

Jon Western

The Johns Hopkins University Press
Baltimore and London

© 2005 The Johns Hopkins University Press
All rights reserved. Published 2005
Printed in the United States of America on acid-free paper
9 8 7 6 5 4 3 2 1

The Johns Hopkins University Press
2715 North Charles Street
Baltimore, Maryland 21218-4363
www.press.jhu.edu

Library of Congress Cataloging-in-Publication Data

Western, Jon W., 1963–
    Selling intervention and war : the presidency, the media, and the
American public / Jon Western.
        p.   cm.
    Includes bibliographical references and index.
    ISBN 0-8018-8108-0 (hardcover : alk. paper) — ISBN 0-8018-8109-9 (pbk. :
alk. paper)
        1. United States—Foreign relations—1945–1989—Public opinion.
2. United States—Foreign relations—1989—Public opinion.   3. United
States—Military policy—Public opinion.   4. Intervention (International
law)—Public opinion.   5. War—Public opinion.   6. Public opinion—
United States.   7. United States—Foreign relations—Decision making—
Case studies.   8. Public relations and politics—United States—Case
studies.   I. Title.
    E840.W44 2005
    327.73′009′045—dc22

                                                                    2004019605

A catalog record for this book is available from the British Library.

To Jenifer Urff

Contents

Preface and Acknowledgments

This book is a study of the politics behind American decisions on the use of force. We frequently hear claims that politics stops at the water's edge—or at least that it is supposed to—especially in matters concerning the use of force. This book argues that such claims are a myth. Matters of war and military intervention are almost always politically contested. Political debates and disagreements occur because American political and opinion leaders, as well as the American public, differ widely in their beliefs about the nature and severity of international threats, about when and where the United States should use force, and about the efficacy of military force. Although all American leaders pledge that U.S. troops will only be used in defense of American "national interests" and in ways consistent with "American values," the empirical record shows wide variation in the use and meanings of these terms.

This work began in my observations of the politics of war and military intervention over the past decade. I served as an intelligence analyst at the U.S. Department of State in the early 1990s; there I closely observed many of the political debates over whether or not the United States should use military force in the Persian Gulf War, Somalia, Haiti, and Bosnia. I was also aware of the prevailing intelligence assessments of each crisis and intrigued by how those assessments frequently were framed, leaked, used, and often distorted by advocates of various beliefs in the administration, Congress, and the news media in an effort to influence public and political opinion either for or against intervention and war.

As I began my research, I discovered that the contentious debates I witnessed were not new, nor were the politics and advocacy campaigns surrounding those decisions. Indeed, since the ascendancy of the United States as a superpower following World War II, the competition among foreign policy elites has been particularly intense as they have sought to frame events and sell to the public their views of the need for, or reasons against, the deployment of U.S. combat troops. With these observations in mind, I focused my research on the nexus between public opinion and elite beliefs on the decisions to use force, with a particular attention to the roles of elite belief groups, the presidency, and the media. The chapters that follow present detailed case studies demonstrating the direct influence of this competition and advocacy on decisions to intervene and not to intervene. The cases examined are the decisions not to intervene in Indochina in 1954 and Bosnia in 1992 and the decisions to intervene in Lebanon in 1958, Grenada in 1983, Somalia in 1992, and Iraq in 2003.

It is frequently claimed that the terrorist attacks on September 11, 2001, fundamentally altered American foreign policy. Because my argument was constructed and much of this book was written before those attacks and the promulgation of the Bush Doctrine on preemption, I had an interesting vantage point from which to observe and analyze the political debates in the run-up to the war in Iraq in 2003 and was able to situate the Bush administration's efforts to sell the war within broader trends. I concluded that much about the campaign for war on Iraq was not new. The hardline views on Iraq and intense efforts to sell war on Iraq long predate the events of September 11, 2001. To be sure, as discussed in Chapter 6, the Bush administration used some extraordinary measures to gain public and political support, but in many respects that campaign is only the latest chapter in a long historical pattern of selling war.

My intent throughout has been twofold. I wrote this book to satisfy my own curiosity and to develop some additional, albeit modest, theoretical insights into American decisions on the use of force. I develop a model drawn from liberal theory of international relations which allows us to analyze systematically the domestic determinants of American foreign policy behavior. Also, I wrote this book for my students, hoping to provide a useful tool for undergraduate and graduate entry-level courses in American foreign policy and to introduce students to a theoretical approach supported by sufficient historical and empirical understanding. Therefore, each chapter contains a detailed historical background, to provide the reader with a broad historical and comparative context in which to understand the decision in each case.

Throughout the process of writing this book, I have benefited from the support of many people. My greatest intellectual debt is to Robert Jervis and Jack Snyder, who mentored the project from its inception and who have read and reread many earlier versions. I also owe a very special thanks to my colleague at Mount Holyoke College Vincent Ferraro, with whom I have spent many long hours discussing and debating the complexities and history of American foreign policy. He is truly a gifted and generous teacher and scholar.

Others who deserve thanks for comments and suggestions are Mark Blythe, Tim Crawford, Page Fortna, James Goldgeier, Bruce Jentleson, Colin Kahl, Peter Liberman, Patrice McMahon, Jodi Nelson, Aaron Seeskin, and Leslie Vinjamuri. I am also very grateful to Henry Y. K. Tom, Claire McCabe, and Anne Whitmore at the Johns Hopkins University Press.

I am indebted to the staff at the National Archives and Records Administration in College Park, Maryland, and at the Center for Legislative Archives in Washington, D.C. Daniel Holt and David Haight guided me through the resources at the Eisenhower Presidential Library in Abilene, Kansas.

The United States Institute of Peace Jennings Randolph Program for International Peace and the institute's Balkans Initiative program provided me with generous financial assistance and a place to write much of this book. I especially want to thank Sally Blair, Harriet Hentges, Joe Klaits, John Menzies, and Daniel Serwer.

My colleagues at Mount Holyoke College and the Five Colleges, Incorporated—Amherst College, Hampshire College, Smith College, and the University of Massachusetts at Amherst—have provided a very stimulating environment in which to work. I am particularly grateful to Joseph J. Ellis, Sohail Hashmi, and Kavita Khory for their comments on parts of the manuscript and to Linda Chesky Fernandes, who helped me keep some sense of organization in my work.

Portions of Chapters 5 and 6 are extracted from articles published earlier and are used with the permission of *International Security* and *Security Studies*. I thank them for allowing me to use that material here.

Finally, I could not have completed this book without the support of my family. My parents, Wayne and Barbara Western, and my parents-in-law, Richard and Arlene Urff, have been very generous with their time and support. My sons Charley and Alex patiently endured my long hours in the office and my research trips and always greeted my returns with smiles and laughter. And, finally, Jenifer Urff, my wife, balancing her own professional career, took care of our children and always found the time and energy to read and comment on my work along the way. I am forever amazed and grateful. I dedicate this book to her.

Selling Intervention and War

CHAPTER ONE

Liberal Theory and the Politics of Selling War

Beliefs . . . in religions or propagandas are usually presented as historical facts; but, in so far as both the facts and the deductions from them are controversial within any population, they lack the status of truth.
—QUINCY WRIGHT

Public opinion is primarily a moralized and codified version of the facts.
—WALTER LIPPMANN

Introduction

The United States stands unrivaled, indeed historically unparalleled, among nations. It currently possesses the capabilities to deploy a massive array of fire power to distant portions of the globe within days, if not hours, of a presidential decision to undertake such an act. This capacity, coupled with a likely proliferation of regional and civil violence in the coming decades, the ongoing war on terror, and the continued potential for the unlawful proliferation of weapons of mass destruction, suggests that the United States will face increasing demands and opportunities for military intervention and war. Most Americans believe that American troops will see more combat in the future.[1]

With the prospect of even more frequent U.S. military actions looming on the horizon—and especially in the wake of the Bush administration's proclamation of a doctrine of preemption and the subsequent war in Iraq—scholars, pundits, and policymakers are engaged in extensive and heated debates about what should constitute American doctrine on intervention and war. Foreign policy and national security experts are debating these questions: When will the United States need to use military force? Under what conditions should the United States use force? *How* should the United States decide to use force? What are the limits to the effectiveness of the use of force?

One of the most striking characteristics of these debates is the wide disparity of views and ideas among scholars, pundits, and policymakers about what constitutes the proper use of force. Also striking is the intensity and passion with which they express their views. Some, like President George W. Bush and his administration, see the world in stark terms of good versus evil. They see threats lurking in almost every corner of the globe. In a world where rogue states and terrorist organizations may conspire in the proliferation of weapons of mass destruction, they argue, the United States cannot stand by idly while dangers form; for them, if a threat is plausible it is probable. They argue that the United States must be prepared and willing to use force to confront those challenges—unilaterally and preventively, if necessary.

Others similarly view the world as a highly dangerous environment and likewise advocate considering the use of force when vital American geostrategic or economic interests are at stake. However, this group tends to hold a narrower, more selective view of what constitutes a threat to vital national interests. It is less inclined to support the use of force in a seemingly unlimited crusade to rid the world of evil. Advocates of this position further contend that not every *potential* danger should be considered a vital danger to the United States. Ultimately, they believe, the application of force should be guided by caution and prudence and American security is best enhanced with the active support of traditional allies who can share the burdens of the near-term and long-term costs of war.

Still others assert that the United States must become more of a global citizen. They argue that the world today is highly interdependent and that America's long-term security is inseparable from the well-being of others in the international community. This group rejects American unilateralism and advocates aggressive efforts to develop multilateral responses to threats to international and regional peace and security. They advocate the use of force not only when American geostrategic and economic interests are endangered but also in response to serious humanitarian crises and other major threats to international law and order.

Finally there are those who believe that using force in any form is a risky and dangerous enterprise and so should be saved for truly exceptional and rare circumstances. This group sees many threats in the world, but it considers the United States at greatest risk when it sends its young men and women into combat situations without the full support of the public and when there is no clearly defined mission, objectives, and exit strategy. This group routinely warns of the dangers of what it sees as an American tendency to imperialism and overcommitment.

Despite the daily appearance of these divergent viewpoints in the op-ed pages of American newspapers, there is a curious puzzle about these debates and the arguments contained within them: given the intensity and passion of concern about when and where the United States should use force, why do most conventional theories of international relations and American foreign policy generally not acknowledge the importance of these debates? This omission raises some interesting questions: Do these passionate debates in Washington today and the advocacy groups that participate in them have any relevance to policy formation and to the ultimate decisions on whether or not to send troops into combat? If, as most international relations theories suggest, these debates are irrelevant, why have the leading academic and policy journals devoted so many pages to their arguments? Furthermore, an empirical examination of historical cases suggests that many of the current arguments about when, where, and how the United States should use force were also part of U.S. intervention decisions during the Cold War. Did these debates affect American decisions on intervention and war then?

In considering these questions, this book explores:

- why and under what circumstances the United States has used military force to intervene or go to war in regional and civil conflicts and crises;
- why and under what circumstances the United States has chosen *not* to use military force and *not* to intervene or go to war in regional and civil conflicts and crises;
- what influence, if any, the ideas found within debates over intervention have had on American foreign policy actions; and
- what the interplay is between the advocacy of ideas and beliefs for and against military intervention and war and the decision-making process.

The Argument

It is an axiom of political life in Washington, D.C., that on virtually any domestic and foreign policy issue there is a variety of opinion and that much of daily life in Washington is spent competing for political power. It is further axiomatic in Washington that to gain political power one uses a mix of institutional, informational, and propaganda resources to mobilize public support. Hence, over the past five decades, political elites in Washington have dedicated extensive resources to developing advocacy resources and strategies and public relations structures to spin news and information in their heated battles for public and political support.[2]

These political battles crop up in almost every aspect of policymaking in Washington. They are especially evident when a U.S. president weighs the costs and benefits of sending military forces to war. In nearly every instance when a president has considered using American force in overseas combat missions, intense political debates have ensued among America's foreign policy elites about whether or not force should be used and extensive efforts have been designed to mobilize public and political support.[3]

Despite conventional acknowledgment that this is the norm within the Washington policy community, very little explicit theorizing has been generated about how these policy battles influence American foreign military activities. In this chapter I develop a model to explain the wide variation in when and where the United States has intervened militarily. I begin by introducing the basic assumptions of liberal theory of international relations and then I derive a theoretical model to establish specific links between, on the one hand, elite beliefs, informational and propaganda resources, and organizational capacity and, on the other, how these factors influence public opinion, the political pressure generated by them, and, ultimately, decisions for or against intervention and war.

My basic argument is this: Elite political groups hold diverse beliefs about the world and the nature of the international system, and these views lead to similarly diverse ideas and expectations about the nature and severity of a given threat to the country and the costs and benefits associated with the use of military force. In response to international crises or other triggering events, these groups form positions for or against the use of force depending on their ideological predispositions. These elites then coalesce into one of four major advocacy groups, which actively promote their views for or against the use of force. I hypothesize that the decision to use force or not is the result of the competition among these advocacy groups and their relative abilities to captivate and mobilize public and political support for their views. The view held by the president and his or her core advisors will often enjoy a privileged position in mobilizing public and political support, because of such advantages as extensive control over national security decision-making resources and presidential prestige. However, advocacy groups whose views are not shared by the president can influence presidential action by increasing public and political opposition to the president's views.

I argue that public and political support is a function of two critical elements: information flows and the public's predispositions. How the public perceives a crisis initially and in the near future depends on the information it receives about the nature and severity of the crisis or threat. Advocacy groups who hold different views on security and threat compete for information and propaganda advantages in order to frame (i.e., contextualize) the conflict for the public. The factors determining the outcome of this advocacy process include: (1) the beliefs of the president and the degree of cohesion within his administration, (2) the relative distribution of information and collective action assets among the opposition groups, (3) the role of the news media, and (4) the duration of the crisis. The arguments put forward by the groups must, however, resonate within the political space afforded them by the public's general mood (latent public opinion). Any argument for or against war must strike a chord with Americans' attitudes toward the country's standing in the world and the global security climate in which a particular crisis has occurred. To be successful in capturing public and political support, a group will have to address these questions: How credible are the threats to American interests and values? Is there a clear theory of victory? And, what are the long-term costs and benefits of military action?

Liberal Theory: The Assumptions

Liberal theory presupposes that a state's preferences—which precede its actions—are a function of state-society relations.[4] Unlike other prevailing theories of international relations, liberal theory does not assume that states are unitary actors or that their interests can be assumed from a set of fixed preferences or the configuration of their material capabilities. Depending on the nature of the state-society relations and the specific domestic institutional and social context, state preferences will vary. Liberal theory distinguishes regime types, asserting that liberal democracies are different from nonliberal regimes.

With respect to its assessment of liberal democracies, liberal theory starts with three core assumptions.[5] First, state action is the result of the push and pull of societal actors operating within a particular liberal ideological and institutional context. These societal actors behave rationally in pursuit of their material and ideal welfare. Second, homogeneity of opinion is extremely rare. Within a segmented and diverse population, the societal groups that emerge to contest in any policy arena will have differing conceptions of security, sovereignty, and wealth and differing ideas about how best to protect and promote them. This diversity will inspire frequent and ongoing debates within society about the effect of international events on the state's interests and values. Third, representative institutions provide the vehicles by which competing preferences and social power are transformed into state policy. Indeed, the hallmark of liberal democracies is that state action is the product of a dynamic and complex interaction between elite groups and the public.

From these three assumptions, the analysis begins with the following questions:

1.   Who are the principal societal groups and what are their preferences?
2.   What are the institutional parameters within which they operate?
3.   What are the respective capabilities of each group to influence outcomes within those institutional parameters?

I address these questions in order. I identify the major societal actors within liberal democracies, and the United States in particular, and their views concerning war and peace. I then detail the particular relationship between elites and the public that forms the basic parameters for considerations of, and ultimately the decisions about, war in the United States. Last, I identify how competing elite groups compete via informational and institutional resources to generate public and political support in an attempt to influence policy outcomes.

Warring Ideas: Preferences for and against War

Questions of war and peace generate a seemingly profound paradox within liberal democracies. Scholars and policymakers have long debated whether or not democracies are more pacific, more hesitant to go to war, than nondemocracies. The empirical record shows that democracies do demonstrate remarkable reluctance to battle other democracies. However, the record also reveals that democracies are often more than willing to go to war, indeed even to initiate hostilities against nondemocracies. Yet, the classical liberal theorist Immanuel Kant provided insights into this seeming paradox by elucidating both the constraints against and the motivations for war.

Constraints against War in a Democracy

More than two centuries ago, Kant wrote in his essay "Perpetual Peace" that democratic states are different when it comes to considerations of war. His propositions form the basis of much of the democratic peace literature written over the past two decades and are now well known to most scholars.[6] Because citizens participate in the development of their laws and policy, democracies face an initial constraint on going to war—the public's *expectations* of the material costs of war. The most common reference to this proposition comes from Kant's declaration that

> if the consent of the citizens is required in order to decide that war should be declared (and in this constitution it cannot but be the case), nothing is more natural than that they would be very cautious in commencing such a poor game, decreeing for themselves all the calamities of war. Among the latter would be: having to fight, having to pay the costs of war from their own resources, having painfully to repair the devastation war leaves behind, and, to fill up the measure of evils, load themselves with a heavy national debt that would embitter peace itself and that can never be liquidated on account of constant wars in the future.[7]

Citizens, and hence democracies, strive to protect their material well-being—their lives, their property, and their wealth—and so are reluctant to go to war unless the threat to their interests outweighs the expected costs of war.

But this is only part of liberal theory's story. For Kant there is also a normative, value-based constraint associated with republics and war. This constraint is embedded within Kant's proposition on the pacific nature of a "federation of peace": Republican states coexisting in a world of republics will lead to peace. Individuals are equally endowed with reason and rationality and desire to live free from coercion and repression. Free and autonomous individuals, as citizen self-legislators, will not make laws that violate the fundamental freedoms each cherishes. The outcome is a shared set of values of justness and tolerance and a governing authority—the state—that is ancillary to individual freedom and is limited to protecting life, liberty, property, and wealth. The logic then holds that if citizens recognize others as living in another *republic*, they will presume them to be legitimate, tolerant, and just.[8] Political scientist Michael Doyle sums up the process: "As culture progresses, an understanding of the legitimate rights of all citizens and of all republics comes into play; and this, now that caution characterizes policy, sets up the moral foundations for the liberal peace. . . . Domestically just republics, which rest on consent, presume foreign republics to be also consensual, just, and therefore deserving of accommodation."[9]

The logic here suggests that one republic's going to war against another republic would violate the basic principles and values held most dear by citizens of a republic. Because of the need to mobilize public support of a war, legitimacy and its normative bases are a prerequisite for war. This forms an inherent bulkhead against war. Waging a war that contradicts liberal values would be illegitimate, and hence unlikely.

This leaves us with two basic liberal propositions constraining war:

Proposition #1. Democracies are reluctant to wage war when costs defined in terms of material interests are high.

Proposition #2. Democracies are reluctant to wage war when costs defined in terms of values are high.

Motivations for War in a Democracy

But, we know that democracies are not pacific. In fact they go to war frequently. Kant and other liberal theorists have long recognized multiple reasons democracies go to war. For Kant, the central problem in the international system—and hence the tendency toward war and no doubt the motivation for his essay on peace—was the pervasiveness of nonrepublics. Republican forms of government operating in a world with nonrepublics face constant threats from the nonrepublics because

in a constitution which is not republican, and under which the subjects are not citizens, a declaration of war is the easiest thing in the world to decide upon, because war does not require of the ruler, who is the proprietor and not a member of the state, the least sacrifice of the pleasures of his table, the chase, his country houses, his court functions, and the like. He may, therefore, resolve on war as on a pleasure party for the most trivial reasons, and with perfect indifference leave the justification which decency requires to the diplomatic corps who are ever ready to provide it.[10]

This condition provides the first liberal motivation for war: defense against attack. The existence of nonrepublics makes attack possible at any moment, the timing depending on the whims of the despot. Since a republic can never be certain of the intentions of its nonrepublican neighbors, republics pursuing their material well-being and security must remain ever vigilant and prepared for war. Furthermore, the general perception within a liberal community is that despotic regimes are particularly threatening because, when subjects living under a despot see free and equal citizens prospering under a republic, they will demand their own freedom.[11] Because despotic leaders cannot tolerate this demand, they are particularly hostile and violent toward republics. As a result, liberal states often find themselves in a situation where they believe they must fight either to repel or to prevent an attack from a despot. In other words, democracies often go to war to protect their material interests in the face of constant threat in a hostile world.

Motivation for war in a liberal republic can also have a strong normative component. Legitimate authority is authority that is restricted from coercing individuals. Repressive and despotic regimes are by this definition illegitimate. They also violate the basic equality of individuals. As a result, not only do republics wage war against nonrepublics in defense of their security, but they may do so to transform the despotic regime into a republic. In addition, if one accepts Kant's broader arguments on the categorical imperative and the universality of the republican constitution—his first definitive article—then intervention and war to help the victims of despotism and tyranny is just.[12] While Kant himself rejected the justness of such wars, he nonetheless recognized a liberal inclination toward them; and we have seen that liberal states routinely fight wars "to promote freedom, to protect private property, or to support liberal allies against nonliberal enemies."[13]

These conditions provide the second motivation for war: liberal democracies may go to war to protect and promote liberal values.

Proposition #3. Democracies may resort to war when interests are threatened.

Proposition #4. Democracies may resort to war when values are threatened.

American Elite Beliefs on Intervention and War

These Kantian propositions form the parameters within which societal groups debate and advocate for or against war. In the United States, groups emerge with particular combinations and interpretations of what constitutes a threat to American interests or a threat to American values and what might be the costs of American military action.

These liberal theoretical parameters are implicit in the historical cleavages among American foreign policy elites. For the past thirty years, scholars have demonstrated that foreign policy elites hold fundamentally differing views on the role of the United States in the international system, on American priorities in the world, and about what constitutes a threat to the United States.[14] Using extensive survey data, scholars have revealed that these cleavages have led to fundamentally different views about when and where the United States should use combat troops to intervene in overseas conflicts.[15]

These various viewpoints can be plotted on a matrix, along lines that measure threat versus cost and interests versus values, in a manner consistent with Kantian logic. (See Figure 1.1.) When examining global events, some elites are predisposed to emphasize what they perceive as threats to interests; others are predisposed toward concerning themselves with the potential costs of going to war; others tend to see how global crises pose a threat to American values; while still others are predisposed to believe that using force in response to some international crisis often contradicts (or imposes a high cost on) American values.

Within this framework, there are four major distinct groups that define the range of foreign policy elite beliefs.

Selective Engagers

Selective engagers are those who adhere to many of the tenets of the theory of realism and the view that the world is highly competitive.[16] Selective engagers define American interests in traditional realist terms: the protection of American security (homeland security); stability among the great powers and within the global liberal economic order; and protection of geostrategically important resources, with particular attention to the stability of global oil production and distribution. To advance these interests, selective engagers believe that the United States must seek to maintain its primacy in the international

	Threat to U.S.		Costs of War
U.S. Interests	Hardliners		Reluctant Warriors
		Selective Engagers	
			Neo-Isolationists
		Liberals	
			Pacifists,
U.S. Values	Humanitarianists		Anti-Imperialists

Figure 1.1. Relative Importance of Foreign Policy Elites' Concerns

system and be willing and able to use the full weight of its military and foreign policy resources to advance American interests.

But, selective engagers are, by definition, selective and prudential in the use of force.[17] Compared to hardliners (described below), they pay greater attention to the potential costs of military action—both direct costs to material capabilities and indirect costs to American prestige, credibility, and values. They remain wary of the potential for over commitment of resources and the possibility that unilateral or overly aggressive American action might generate a backlash of opinion at home and abroad.[18]

During the Cold War, selective engagers in the United States focused intently on the competitive international struggle with the Soviet Union. They promoted a strong and forceful American foreign policy to deter and contain Soviet expansion. For them, use of force was a vital component of that policy. However, they perceived the Soviet Union not merely as an ideologically driven superpower but as a superpower motivated also by traditional great power preferences. As a result, even within the highly competitive Cold War environment, selective engagers actively courted the People's Republic of China to serve as a counterweight to the Soviet Union. They also saw détente and arms control negotiations as means to ease the escalating and costly arms race with the Soviet Union.

In the post–Cold War era, selective engagers continue to advocate for American primacy. They advocate a strong U.S. international posture and the capability to deploy U.S. forces rapidly in conjunction with allies when strategic material interests are directly threatened. They believe that coordinated action with key allies is imperative to controlling the costs to American military capabilities and international prestige in responding to international threats. They have actively resisted unilateralism, the new isolationism, and the expansion of U.S. use-of-force doctrine to include threats to American values.

Hardliners

Hardliners advocate a more assertive American military presence in the world.[19] They generally diverge into two strains: traditional conservatives and neoconservatives. Both strains, like selective engagers, believe the world to be highly competitive, but hardliners are quicker to see dangers, to advocate the use of force, and to discount potential costs in the face of dangers.

During the Cold War they were steadfastly committed to intense struggle with the Soviet Union. They strongly supported the use of force to contain Soviet expansion in Southeast Asia, Africa, Latin America, and the Middle East. In particular, they opposed the policies of détente and arms control as endangering American interests. They believed that the Soviets would exploit any American concessions and thereby increase America's vulnerability.

In the post–Cold War era, hardliners continue to advocate expanding U.S. military presence, to ensure American material primacy in the international system. They assert that the United States must not yield its leadership position to others. They see particularly grave dangers lurking in the world, and as a result, they believe it is imperative that the United States be prepared to act, unilaterally if necessary, to avert those dangers. In the run-up to the war in Iraq, for example, both traditional conservatives and neoconservatives believed it was vital to remove Saddam Hussein from power.

Reluctant Warriors

Reluctant warriors are found predominantly in U.S. military institutions. They oppose American involvement in limited wars.[20] Persuaded by the military stalemate in Korea and the failed war in Vietnam, this group believes that strict conditions must be met before American forces are deployed into ambiguous regional and civil conflicts. It holds to the belief that since the American military trains principally for major conventional war, any military deployment must be conditioned on the deployment of overwhelming force and massive mobilization of American political and economic resources.

Frequently aligned with the reluctant warriors are *neo-isolationists*, who historically have been opposed to overseas commitments.[21] This group takes a much more restrictive view of national defense. Intensely patriotic, its primary concern is the preservation of American cultural and economic autonomy and the promotion of conservative religious values. This group comprises mainly prairie populists and southern evangelical conservative Christians. They believe that the use of force should be limited to those rare cases of imminent and direct threat to U.S. political independence and territorial integrity. During the Cold War, neo-isolationists supported the American nuclear strategy to deter a Soviet attack on U.S. territory. In the wake of the Cold War, this group believes, the United States should reorient its foreign and defense postures to enhance homeland security and has advocated dramatically scaling back American commitments overseas.[22]

Liberals

Liberals argue that American foreign policy should be oriented toward an expansion of the post–World War II liberal order, with its emphasis on the United Nations and the global liberal economic order.[23] They believe that the world has become increasingly interdependent—economically, militarily, and politically—since the end of World War II, and they advocate greater development of multinational institutions. During the Cold War, liberals tended to seek accommodation with the Soviet Union on arms control and on facilitating greater economic and cultural exchange; but many initially supported war in Korea and Vietnam, to block international communism and to promote democratic political and capitalist economic structures. They turned against those efforts, however, when they concluded that American actions would not lead to democracy and free markets.

A subset of liberals is *humanitarianists*, who are staunch believers that American foreign policy should be guided chiefly by the promotion of the right to self-determination, individual liberties, and human rights.[24] This group supports American-led multilateral intervention in response to significant violations of international norms and laws and to stop or prevent atrocities perpetrated against civilians. They oppose the use of force for purely material or selective-engagement purposes, particularly when the intervention would contribute to the strength and support of antidemocratic political forces and regimes. During the Cold War, this group opposed American military intervention in Vietnam, the Dominican Republic, Latin America, and elsewhere by arguing that these interventions to prop up dictatorial regimes contradicted American values.

In the post–Cold War era, liberals have remained committed to promoting international security institutions. They, like selective engagers, have supported U.S. military intervention principally as part of international forces. Under the label of "assertive multilateralism," they have differed from selective engagers in that they have been more inclined to support intervention when the liberal conception of world order—multilateral institutions—has been undermined by ongoing conflict. Humanitarianists, meanwhile, have added their voice as strong advocates for humanitarian military interventions in response to the extreme violence in the Balkans, the Great Lakes region of Central Africa, and the Middle East. They see an expanded role for the American military, with its tremendous resource capacity and logistical infrastructure, in supporting and providing humanitarian intervention and relief in a wide variety of regional and civil conflicts.

The Institutional Framework within Which Groups Act

While the existence of competing beliefs among policy elites is well established, critical questions remain: Do belief groups matter? Do they influence decisions on intervention and war? And, if so, how?[25] To understand the impact of these competing ideas and beliefs, liberal theory suggests, we need to identify the relationships among these groups and their relative strengths of political influence. This requires an analysis of how political decisions concerning the use of force are made, the range of competing beliefs, and the relative political resources of each group.

Elite Sensitivity to Public and Political Support

In republics, while citizens participate in self-governance, they do so through representative institutions. The decision to send troops into a combat situation is one of the most difficult decisions a president must make. In the United States, Congress is empowered by the Constitution to declare war, but both historical precedent and domestic law have given the president considerable authority to deploy troops without explicit congressional consent.[26] Nonetheless, while decisions concerning military intervention and war are not made by public referendum, both the president and Congress do understand that they are ultimately beholden to the voters for their political success. In addition, while the public may be inattentive to most matters of foreign policy, they are highly sensitive to questions of war.[27]

It is precisely because of the citizenry's heightened interest in matters of war and peace that foreign policy elites tend to be particularly sensitive to the views of the populace.[28] For example, political scientist Philip Powlick interviewed more than seventy senior officials in 1988 and 1989 and found that senior National Security Council members consistently weighed the expectation of public support or disapproval of a particular policy initiative and that the assessment of the public's attitudes set the initial parameters in national security policy formulation.[29] Similarly, political scientist Ronald Hinckley concluded that on matters of using force, presidents and their advisors have been particularly sensitive to how the public will respond to a particular policy approach.[30] These findings and others suggest, however, that elites carefully monitor public attitudes and factor the public's considerations of the political space for intervention and war into their deliberations.

Public Susceptibility to Elite-Based Information

How does the public come to understand the nature of a foreign regional or civil conflict and whether or not a vital interest or value of the United States is threatened and what the costs of military intervention might be? Scholars have long been divided over whether public opinion emanates from bottom-up rational approaches by the public or top-down manipulative actions by elites.[31] While this debate cannot be resolved here, both bottom-up and top-down theories agree that a key determinant of public attitudes is access to information. Opinions are formed by a blend of information and predispositions.[32]

When the public begins to form its views and attitudes about a particular conflict or crisis, information about that event is essential. Benjamin I. Page and Robert Y. Shapiro concluded that American public opinion ultimately relies on the "information systems" that convey data to the public.[33] John Zaller argues that citizens form their attitudes in response "to the arguments they encounter only to the extent that they are knowledgeable about political affairs" or they are presented with credible alternative information by informed elites.[34]

Dependence on elite information sources is particularly the case in matters of national security, because the average person has neither the inclination nor the ability to monitor closely events from around the world. Consequently, masses are beholden to elites—government officials, journalists, and foreign policy and regional affairs experts—for information.

Selling War: Information and Propaganda Advantages

Recognition of the public's susceptibility to elite information flows gives elites the incentive to employ their instruments of persuasion—information and propaganda—to cultivate public and political support. Decision makers and advocates for a particular position routinely seek to control and spin information in a way that is consciously designed to maximize support for their position.[35] Because most foreign policy crises do not speak for themselves, the public must rely on elites to interpret a context for the event or to present a range of historical analogies that provide insights into the event.

When one group of elites holds, or is able to capture, an advantage in the control and dissemination of information, American attitudes frequently become biased toward those with "the information advantage."[36] If information is presented in a one-sided and biased manner, the "rational public" may support policies that are largely "irrational."[37] Conversely, when information is highly available, widely disseminated, and openly contested by a wide range of elites, public opinion will reflect the underlying predispositions of the majority of the public—or *latent public opinion*.

The research on liberal theory and elite-public relationships reveals that four factors shape the scope and breadth of information and propaganda advantages held by an advocacy group or coalition of groups:

1. the group's ties to the president;
2. opposition groups' organizational and material resources capacity;
3. the role of the news media, its expertise on a particular regional or civil conflict, and its relationship to the executive branch; and
4. the duration of the crisis.

The Role of the Presidency

Any analysis of the mobilization of public opinion and participation in the decision to use military force must begin with an examination of the leading national security institution, the presidency.[38] Having direct ties to the president can facilitate a group's ability to organize and to mobilize public and political support in a number of ways. It provides groups and actors with significant institutional resources. Those who control the presidency often are able to set the agenda for national action. Furthermore, the national security decision-making apparatus often affords those who control it greater autonomy, because access to executive structures often conveys with it advantages in early analysis, evaluation, and interpretation of threats and crises in another country. The vast resources of official overseas missions, intelligence collection assets, and privileged stature in international diplomatic channels allow the president extraordinary advantages in access to information emanating from other countries. This in turn allows the president to have the first take on what the threat or crisis means for the United States. The initial analytic impression projected by an elite is often of paramount importance in creating broad-based support for a policy. Since ideas and impressions are hard to change once they take root, the group that gets the jump on characterizing the situation creates the initial conventional wisdom.[39] And, because much of this information is processed through a closed national security apparatus that does not allow for extensive external debate, the opportunities for mobilized opposition against the governing group's position may be significantly disadvantaged without some independent ability to confirm or refute the veracity of executive information.

Control of the presidency also often affords huge advantages in presenting and packaging the message to the public. Since the president ostensibly is endowed with the public trust, public opinion is often very responsive, at least initially, to issues presented by the president.[40] The organizational advantage also allows the group in power to fund mass organizations and think tanks and thereby generate a pool of policy advocates who are sympathetic to the administration's views but who very often are not perceived as having explicit ties to the executive.

However, while controlling the presidency bestows privileges, other factors can temper those advantages. Most notably, when elites within the executive branch have been divided in their views with respect to a crisis, information collected within the administration has frequently been leaked. This has given competing advocacy groups access to information that might otherwise have been restricted. Furthermore, when there have been divisions within it, the administration has often been unable to present a firm or unified policy line. Such an inability allows competing advocacy groups and the media opportunities to criticize the president or frame the crisis in different terms.

Opposition Resources and Mobilization Capacity

Because of the relatively open U.S. political institutional framework, groups not in control of the presidency have the ability to garner their own resources and influence political outcomes. These opposition groups can exert pressure on the policymaking process by engaging in their own efforts to mobilize public support.

An essential feature of successful social organization and oppositional mobilization is the ability to collect credible and timely information that demonstrates that the existing policy will not lead to a credible solution and/or that another policy is likely to be more successful.[41] This requires, foremost, that the opposition have resources to collect independent information and not be dependent on information emanating from the administration.

At times, opposition groups may be able to ally with likeminded elites in the Congress or in the bureaucracy who may have information resources such as institutional oversight mechanisms, privileged channels of communication and policy deliberation, or additional intelligence collection assets. In other instances, opposition groups may rely on the resources of the news media, think tanks, lobbying groups, or nongovernmental organizations that may have their own information collection assets on the ground in the country in crisis.

The Role of the Media: Independent (and Not So Independent) Brokers

In democratic states an independent news media may facilitate social mobilization by groups outside of government. The media can provide a forum for the collection and dissemination of information that critically assesses the views presented by the presidency. However, even with a thriving independent media, there are times when a group in control of the executive will be able to rely on the media to advance its information advantages.[42] The remote location of some foreign conflicts, the secretive and technical dimensions of foreign threats, and the restricted societies of many countries can preclude exhaustive reporting from the ground, at least initially.[43] Consequently, lacking resources, expertise, and access to the conflict, the media often focuses its early attention on the U.S. policy response and reporting from Washington.[44] Furthermore, because of institutional and competitive pressures and the fear of losing access to the information, most correspondents are reluctant to challenge executive sources openly, especially in the early stages of a foreign policy crisis. This has often resulted in correspondents' accepting and reporting the "assumptions and consensus" of the foreign policy establishment. They have also tended to accept the "official definition of national interest, designation of goals, and selection of strategies."[45]

In addition, at the beginning of a crisis or conflict, the U.S. government exerts considerable influence by coordinating with foreign leaders and/or American publishers and editors to set limits on media access. During the early stages of the U.S. deployment to Vietnam, 1962–65, there were remarkably few critical journalistic analyses of the war.[46] The U.S. media frequently gained access to Vietnamese officials through U.S. diplomatic channels, which ultimately propagated a line very similar to that of the U.S. government. Also, in the early 1960s, many of the most influential news outlets were sympathetic to the administration's position on Indochina. For example, Henry Luce of *Life* magazine referred to South Vietnamese dictator Ngo Dinh Diem in a highly favorable light, going so far as to portray Diem as the "Churchill of Southeast Asia" and ignoring that Diem "had just received 605,025 votes from 450,000 registered voters in Saigon and was consolidating his dictatorship."[47] Such biased reporting assisted the administration in framing the conflict so as to generate widespread public support for American intervention.[48] Without an independent ability to corroborate or disprove the official line, opposition groups are seriously hindered in their ability to refute the ruling group's position.

While the media does at times simply endorse the views of the group in power, it can also be extraordinarily critical.[49] The determining variable seems to be whether or not the media has a significant presence of correspondents with regional and language training in the field. Correspondents who have extensive experience reporting from a country prior to the outbreak of a crisis often have established a strong cadre of contacts independent of U.S. government sources. In a study of the U.S. role in the Cuban revolution, historian Thomas Patterson found that a critical deterrent to the Eisenhower administration's providing more extensive support to Fulgencio Batista in the face of Fidel Castro's insurgency movement in 1958 was the extensive reporting by *New York Times* correspondent Herb L. Matthews, *Chicago Tribune* correspondent Jules Dubois, and *Washington Post* reporter Karl Meyer.[50] All three journalists had extensive knowledge of and experience in Cuba. They consistently challenged the Eisenhower administration's portrayal of Batista as a leader ultimately committed to democracy who was simply trying to ensure internal security. The reporting of journalists with expertise in the affairs of the country provided critical information to members of Congress and to social organizations and helped mobilize a very strong opposition to the administration's efforts to provide overt (and even covert) military assistance to Batista.

Duration of the Crisis

The length of a crisis can also affect relative information and propaganda advantages. Having more time enables groups outside of the executive to develop resources and cultivate information sources to challenge or verify the administration's viewpoints. Unexpected crises inherently give the executive the information advantage: there generally are limited sources of information—few correspondents or independent analysts—so the media and competing advocacy groups must rely on information gathered and disseminated by the administration. Furthermore, in the early periods of crises, the executive branch has often invoked national security claims to justify restricting media access to the (potential) theater of military operations, thereby curtailing independent reporting of events. For example, during the initial U.S. deployment to Grenada in 1983, the press was kept off the island for more than forty-eight hours. In Panama in 1989, the press was confined to U.S. military bases during the initial assault. And, during the Persian Gulf War, American journalists could observe and report only on events selected by the U.S. military, which strictly confined press movements to press pools.

Arguments That Sell: Latent Public Opinion and the Need for a Credible Threat and a Theory of Victory

Not all arguments are equally capable of resonating with the public. Public judgment—that which obtains after reasoned and deliberative debate—emerges as a combination of reason and manipulative persuasion.[51] The public does tend to hold a rational (consistent) set of views about the necessity and appropriateness of various foreign policy instruments. In order to mobilize support around a threat to American interests or values, arguments must be plausible. An argument that flies in the face of the public's experience or otherwise strains credulity is not likely to be given much weight—no matter how much the information is controlled or spun.

Conversely, direct attacks like those that occurred on December 7, 1941, and September 11, 2001, were clear and unambiguous. Not only was it not difficult for President Roosevelt and President George W. Bush to mobilize broadbased support for American military action in World War II and the war in

Afghanistan, respectively; it would have been difficult for either president to argue against going to war in the face of those attacks.

Latent Public Opinion

In the case of the decision whether to use military force, latent opinion is the public's initial impression of the threat posed or the potential costs of military action. It is often associated with the most recent similar case. For example, the efforts to mobilize opinion for war against Iraq in 2002–2003 resonated with the American public. While no Americans were eyewitness to the existence of weapons of mass destruction in Iraq, a decade of demonization of Saddam's regime, his prior use of such weapons, and the proximity in time to the events of September 11, 2001, all made the Bush administration's position on Iraq credible to a significant portion of the Congress and the public. Clearly, a sufficient portion of opinion found the threat plausible in terms of specificity and proximity, given the events of September 11.

Conversely, similar attempts by hardliners throughout the 1990s to generate support for U.S. military action in Iraq to overthrow Saddam Hussein were not successful. Despite a rigorous campaign, those efforts failed to convey a specific and proximate threat to the United States; the message that Saddam Hussein posed an imminent threat to American interests and values simply did not resonate with the public during those years.

A second critical component of an argument that will sell is whether or not there is a clear theory of victory. In order to support war, Americans, by and large, must be convinced that the war will be won within an acceptable cost range. This requires a plausible argument that the military capabilities that the United States would bring to bear could in fact achieve the desired objectives. For example, President Reagan, despite his high personal approval ratings and his intense efforts to win public support, was unable to mobilize and sustain widespread support for increasing American financial and military assistance to El Salvador or the Contras in Nicaragua. Most Americans believed that Reagan's policies would be only the first step in what would likely become a gradually escalating war that could not be won against the Sandinistas in Nicaragua and the leftist guerilla movements in El Salvador. With the specter of another Vietnam hovering, Reagan could not come up with a credible theory of victory.

In sum, while the public is susceptible to elite manipulation, it is also discerning. Arguments either for or against war, if they are to be successful, must demonstrate that the threats or costs of war are specific and proximate. Ambiguous or distant threats—especially those without precedent—or vague claims of the costs of war are more difficult to sell.

Testing the Argument

To examine and test my argument and the leading competing explanations of U.S. military intervention, I use a comparative case method. Five cases are presented in four separate chapters and are used to construct several tests of covariation. I employ a combination of measurement strategies—historical observation, process tracing, and qualitative content analysis—to determine the validity and strength of the arguments.[52]

The Dependent Variable

This study examines the most overt type of American military intervention in foreign conflicts: deployment of combat operational forces to influence another country's domestic or foreign policies.[53] I define military intervention as the overt deployment of more than 500 combat military forces. By establishing a threshold of 500 combat personnel I exclude those cases in which American military forces have been deployed for the explicit purpose of providing protection and evacuation support for U.S. civilians and government personnel. Using this standard also excludes from consideration cases in which the United States rattles its sabers but does not explicitly intervene, such as the deployment of naval forces off the coastline of another country for signaling purposes.

Nonintervention is defined as a situation in which the president and his advisors have considered and deliberated or there has been extensive public and political discussion of the deployment of more than 500 combat personnel, but force has not been deployed.

The Independent and Intervening Variables

Advocacy Groups and Their Preferences

The typology of groups specified in this argument is deduced from liberal theory and discussed above. Deciphering accurate boundaries for each group requires detailed historical evaluation, so in each chapter I present an analysis

Figure 1.2. Process of Decision to Go to War

of each group's beliefs and positions before investigating its participation in a case. The groups' positions have been determined by examining their public statements and private consultations as revealed in archival and secondary sources and through interviews with key figures within the groups.

Measuring the Intervening Variable Cluster

I use two strategies to determine the intervening variables (the information advantages and latent public opinion). First, I measure the variables directly. I examine the degree of latent public opinion by reviewing published public opinion survey data. I examine the opposition groups' resources and institutional capacity and the media's resources at a given conflict site by reviewing archival and other primary data on the number of personnel and resource assets that were on the ground. In addition, I examine the extent of the public relations campaign waged by the various organizations that constitute each of the advocacy communities discussed. Second, I employ a detailed process-tracing method to determine the influence of the causal variables by conducting a systematic review of policy debates and deliberations concerning the relative balance of advantages in information control and dissemination.

Case Selection

Cases were selected on two criteria. The first criterion was variation in the dependent variable. In reviewing the current literature on intervention and war I found many arguments for why the United States *has* intervened, but very few systematic works address cases of nonintervention. A satisfactory explanation of why the United States decides to intervene or go to war in a regional conflict must ensure that those same conditions do not also hold in cases of nonintervention.[54]

I collected a broad range of cases of intervention and nonintervention since World War II. From this universe of cases I made selections based on the second criterion, variation in the independent and intervening variables. I chose two cases from the Eisenhower administration—Dienbienphu in 1954 and Lebanon in 1958. The benefit of these two is that the Eisenhower administration is the most recent one for which there is open access to the historical archives, and this allowed me to conduct a comprehensive archival and primary source investigation. Grenada, Somalia, Bosnia, and Iraq were all cases in which there was extensive disagreement among elites about whether or not the United States should intervene. They also vary both within and across each of the core intervening variables: executive cohesion, opposition resources, the role of the media, and latent public opinion. As the reader will see, each chapter contains multiple decision points, or mini cases.

An additional benefit of the chosen sample is that the cases vary in time and location. They come from the pre-Vietnam Cold War, post-Vietnam Cold War, and post–Cold War periods and from Africa, the Middle East, Southern Europe, Asia, and the Caribbean. If my argument can hold up when applied to multiple cases of intervention and nonintervention across time and place, the strength of the theoretical insights will have been demonstrated.

Outline of the Book

The five case studies are presented in four succeeding chapters. Each chapter begins with a brief introduction to the case, followed by a detailed discussion of the prevailing political context in which that particular crisis emerged and the range of foreign policy beliefs that existed prior to the outbreak of the crisis. I then trace the decision-making process, paying close attention to the relevant causal mechanism that influenced the outcomes. In addition, although each case study serves as a stand-alone test of the argument, I have interwoven a broader historical narrative into each chapter, to present a richer context that reflects both the continuity and the change in elite beliefs, the American presidency, the media, and the role of advocacy in American foreign policy over the past five decades. The book concludes with a review of the empirical findings, a discussion of the theoretical and broader political implications of the patterns by which elites have engaged in the process of selling war and intervention during the past fifty years, and thoughts on what we might see in the future.

CHAPTER TWO

Saying No to the French at Dienbienphu

America must stop the communists now!

It is criminal that our country should be furnishing the war material to kill thousands of natives to assist France in maintaining her colonial empire.

I am sick and tired of our men being sent all over the world to be slaughtered for the interests of other countries.

Who the Hell do they think they're kidding on this Indo-China business? Do they think we're all morons?

—LETTERS TO THE SENATE ARMED SERVICES COMMITTEE

Introduction

During the decade following World War II, the Soviet Union acquired the atomic bomb and the ability to directly destroy American cities; communist military and political advances severed Europe and the Korean peninsula and engulfed China; and by 1950, more than half of the world's population was subject to communist control. In the United States, the Red Scare and fears of fifth columns dominated daily political discussions in Washington and on Main Street. It is almost uncontested that during this period American foreign policy objectives focused primarily on containing communist expansion. For all these reasons, scholars and pundits routinely proclaim that the 1950s were a golden era of bipartisan consensus in American foreign policy.[1]

Despite the appearance of an overarching foreign policy consensus, however, the empirical record reveals a vastly more complex U.S. political environment. While there may have been a general consensus to contain Soviet expansion, there were vastly differing interpretations as to what containment meant and, consequently, what policies should be implemented. Although most analysts and decision makers were seriously concerned about communist expansion throughout the world, they remained deeply divided, both on whether or not the United States should lend support to others in their fights against communism and on when and how much that support should be. Throughout the late 1940s and early to mid-1950s, there were extensive debates within U.S. policymaking circles about U.S. support for Greece, Turkey, Iran, Czechoslovakia, West Germany, Hungary, Korea, and Indochina.[2] These debates were not simply a matter of differences over the magnitude of support, over how much the United States should help. These debates often went to the very heart of the nature of U.S. support—should the United States help at all.

Early in the Cold War, intense debate was generated about whether or not the United States should intervene to rescue beleaguered French forces who were fighting communist-led Vietminh troops in Indochina in 1954. In December 1953, Ho Chi Minh's Vietminh forces surrounded a French outpost at Dienbienphu in northern Vietnam, imperiling 12,000 elite French troops. Over the next five months, as the Vietminh tightened their noose, French officials twice requested U.S. air and naval military support to ease the siege at Dienbienphu. On both occasions the United States seriously considered intervention, and on both occasions it refused. Two months after the second refusal, the French acquiesced in Indochina and withdrew in military and political defeat. The resulting Geneva Accords, signed in July 1954, formally ended the conflict and split Vietnam into two countries, with Ho Chi Minh's Vietminh communist forces in control of an independent, pro-Soviet North Vietnam. As in China in 1949, Communists had taken control of another region of Southeast Asia.

Why did the United States not intervene in Indochina in 1954? Why, at the height of the Cold War, did President Eisenhower decide not to help one of America's longtime allies in its battles against international communist forces? Perhaps, the first explanation was developed and published by reporter Chalmers Roberts. In a June 1954 *Washington Post* story titled, "The Day We Didn't Go to War," he suggested that the primary influence was congressional opposition voiced at an April 3, 1954, congressional briefing by Secretary of State John Foster Dulles and Chairman of the Joint Chiefs of Staff Admiral Arthur W. Radford.[3] Roberts reported that members of Congress simply did not believe that American blood should be spilled for French colonialism and that they would consent to intervention only if certain conditions were met. He argued that Eisenhower was a hands-off president who deferred foreign policy decisions to his secretary of state, who in turn, on the questions of Indochina, was constrained by an angry Congress.

For the two decades that followed the Eisenhower presidency, this view represented the orthodox explanation for the Dienbienphu decision. It corresponded with the general interpretation of Eisenhower's executive style and his image as a president who was more interested in golf than governing.

Beginning in the late 1970s, as secret government documents were declassified and made available to researchers, scholars changed their views on Eisenhower.[4] Most scholars, after studying the first wave of declassified archival materials, found Eisenhower to be an enormously skilled politician who was very much in control of the decision-making process and who was, himself, highly reluctant to intervene. They concluded that, as an experienced military leader, he well understood the limits of military force and the risks and likely human costs of American intervention in the jungles of Southeast Asia. He was also concerned about the financial costs of another war amid growing deficits and domestic budgetary constraints. This military awareness, coupled with his savvy political skills, effectively ensured that the United States would not get sucked into a costly land war in Asia.

For other scholars, a review of Eisenhower's public and private discussions and policy decisions concerning Indochina throughout the spring of 1954 reveals that his personal position on this issue was conflicted.[5] He was clearly wary of unilateral intervention in support of France and he believed that any American intervention would be costly. But, he also consistently from January through May of 1954 stressed that American force might well have to be used to prevent a communist victory in Southeast Asia. And, while he publicly stated his opposition to American military involvement, he simultaneously argued in private to his closest advisors that the loss of Indochina to international communism would be unacceptable. On three separate occasions from January through May 1954, he ordered the Joint Chiefs to develop contingency plans for U.S. military intervention. In February and again in March he ordered elements of the Seventh Fleet to preposition in case they were needed for the defense of Indochina.

As the French position deteriorated in late March and April and as the prospects increased that all of Indochina might be lost to international communism, Eisenhower studied the Joint Chiefs' proposals for an American-led multilateral intervention in Indochina. These proposals, however, contained three specific conditions: that the Associated States of Indochina "invite" international intervention, that the intervention be multilateral, and that Congress and the public support the action.[6] The ultimate key to understanding Eisenhower's decision not to intervene in Indochina is to decipher why these conditions were developed and how they influenced American behavior.

The Argument

The decision not to intervene in Indochina was the product of intense political competition that pitted Eisenhower and his selective engager and hardliner advisors against liberals and noninterventionists. The selective engagers, led by President Eisenhower, strongly believed that Indochina constituted a vital geostrategic interest to the United States. Throughout the crisis at Dienbienphu, Eisenhower searched for ways that the United States could forestall a communist victory. Liberals and noninterventionists both adamantly opposed American involvement. Liberals opposed it because they morally objected to sending U.S. soldiers to fight and die for what they saw as defending French colonialism. Reluctant warriors opposed any action that might lead to another protracted land war in Asia.

From the outset, selective engagers trying to generate public and political support for direct American military involvement were fighting an up-hill battle. First, the crisis in Indochina came less than a year after the conclusion of the war in Korea, and latent public opinion was overwhelmingly opposed to another American military deployment to Asia. Second, Eisenhower was unable to frame the nature of the Indochina crisis as part of the global struggle against international communism. Instead, most public and political commentary portrayed the French military struggles as the inevitable result of a French attempt to reimpose colonial rule on the indigenous populations of Southeast Asia. The inability of the administration to contradict this portrayal stemmed from several factors. First, Eisenhower and his administration were deeply divided. While the president and several of his selective engager and hardliner advisors were inclined to support the French requests for military assistance, many senior Army and Air Force officials were adamantly opposed to American military action in Indochina. Furthermore, throughout the first two months of the Dienbienphu crisis, virtually every high level deliberation on military intervention was leaked to the press. Second, Eisenhower's opponents had extensive access to their own independent information concerning the crisis; they were not dependent upon the executive branch for hard data. From 1949 onward, the American media and policy liberals had extensive resources in Indochina and had consistently portrayed the war principally as an indigenous rebellion against French colonialism. Finally, the crisis at Dienbienphu extended over a six-month period, and this allowed opponents to American military involvement ample time to mobilize and campaign against American intervention. All of these variables combined to shut the political space for any consideration of American military intervention, even if such a response meant a communist victory in Indochina.

Elite Views on Indochina before the Dienbienphu Crisis

Selective Engagers

During the early Cold War years, foreign policy elites who held selective engagement views dominated much of the foreign policy establishment. President Truman and his advisors carved out an international position for the United States after World War II that committed the United States to maintaining global leadership. Dwight Eisenhower inherited this commitment and policies that roughly paralleled his own selective engagement perspective. He and his primary advisors, such as Secretary of State John Foster Dulles, Defense Secretary Charles E. Wilson, National Security Council Advisor Robert Cutler, and Treasury Secretary George Humphrey, viewed the international system as a highly competitive environment.[7] They saw the United States as being in an intense battle with the Soviet Union and they unquestioningly embraced a policy of actively containing Soviet expansion and maintaining U.S. overseas commitments. In 1952 Dulles warned, "Already one-third of the world is dominated by an imperialist brand of communism, . . . ; already the free world has been so shrunk that no further substantial parts of it can be lost without danger to the whole that remains."[8] During his first televised speech as secretary of state, Dulles displayed a map of Eurasia and declared that 800,000,000 people were controlled by "our proclaimed enemies." He later stated, "If Soviet communism is permitted to gobble up other parts of the world one by one, the day will come when the Soviet world will be so powerful that no corner of the world will be safe."[9]

However, for the selective engagers in the Eisenhower administration a major goal for the United States was to maintain its security and its global position without bankrupting itself in the process. As Robert Divine writes, "on his way back from the pre-inauguration trip to Korea, Ike made clear his determination to solve 'the great equation' of maintaining a strong national defense at a bearable cost to the nation."[10] Dulles told the Council on Foreign Relations in January 1954 that there would be "grave budgetary, economic and social consequences" if the United States tried to maintain readiness to fight "in the Arctic and in the Tropics; in Asia, the near East, and in Europe; by sea, by land, and by air; with old weapons and with new weapons."[11] This concern with costs and domestic budgetary priorities led the selective engagers in the Eisenhower administration to develop the New Look policy, which shifted the burden of containment to the nation's nuclear arsenal.[12] The policy called for the United States to rely on its massive nuclear weapons capabilities to retaliate against Soviet aggression anywhere in the word "at places and with means of its choosing."[13]

The New Look was not an effort by Eisenhower to end America's reliance on the use of conventional force as an instrument of statecraft in regional and civil conflicts. He merely sought to correct what he believed was an imbalance in the relationship between defense spending on conventional force structure and economic priorities. Neither Eisenhower nor Dulles believed that the sole basis of American containment policy would be to threaten to escalate every local war into nuclear war.[14] Furthermore, the United States remained well postured with conventional force deployments and with foreign military assistance packages to support conventional responses to communist aggression in a number of regions around the world. The New Look was designed to put domestic economic conditions on par with international security commitments; it was not designed to withdraw the country from those commitments.

Selective Engagers' Views toward Indochina before Dienbienphu

Throughout the Truman administration and the first year of the Eisenhower administration, selective engagers consistently believed in the vital geostrategic significance of Indochina. Of primary concern for both administrations in their efforts to contain communism in Indochina was the need to ensure the continuation of the French military campaign against Ho Chi Minh's communist insurgency. Selective engagers believed that if the French pulled out of Indochina there would be little to stop the spread of communist forces throughout Southeast Asia. In June 1952, Truman's National Security Council concluded that "the loss of a single country [in Southeast Asia] would probably lead to relatively swift submission to or an alignment with communism by the remaining countries of this group."[15]

Eisenhower's views paralleled this assessment, from the beginning of his administration. In August 1953, his National Security Council concluded: "Under present conditions any negotiated settlement [between France and the Vietminh] would mean the eventual loss to Communism not only of Indochina but of the whole of Southeast Asia. The loss of Indochina would be critical to the security of the U.S."[16] Later that month Eisenhower made a strong public case for his aid package to Indochina in a speech to a national governors conference:

> Now, first of all, the last great population remaining in Asia that has not become dominated by the Kremlin, of course, is the sub-continent of India, including the Pakistan government. Here are 350 million people still free. Now let us assume that we lose Indochina. If Indochina goes, several things happen right away. The Malayan peninsula, the last little bit of the end hanging on down there, would be scarcely defensible—and tin and tungsten that we so greatly value from that area would cease coming. But all India would be outflanked. Burma would certainly in its weakened condition, be no defense. Now India is surrounded on that side by the Communist empire. Iran on its left is in a weakened condition. . . . All of that weakening position around there is very ominous for the United States, because finally if we lost all that, how would the free world hold the rich empire of Indonesia? So you see, somewhere along the line, this must be blocked. It must be blocked now. That is what the French are doing."[17]

According to State Department documents, less than a month later, Eisenhower told his key advisors that "the solution to the Indochina problem was the first priority . . . and stated his belief that the loss of Indochina could not be insulated, and that that loss would, shortly after, cost . . . the rest of Southeast Asia. Korea on the other hand, might be an insulated loss."[18] And, in October 1953, Eisenhower reaffirmed that Indochina was "of such strategic importance to the United States that an attack on them probably would compel the U.S. to react with military force either locally at the point of attack or against the military power of the aggressor."[19]

Amidst all this debate, the United States was actually engaged in support of the French mission. Beginning in 1949, the nation provided a significant amount of financial and military assistance to France in its war effort. During the Truman administration, American aid to the French war in Indochina increased each year. By the time Truman left office in January 1953, the United States was bankrolling nearly 60 percent of the war. By the end of Eisenhower's first year, the American contribution had increased to more than 80 percent of the cost of the war.

However, by 1953, selective engagers were faced with several dilemmas regarding Indochina. First, to effectively alter the course of the war, they believed, the French would need to wage a much more aggressive military campaign on the ground. Senior American officials were frustrated with the way the French military was conducting its activities, and they deplored France's cautious, defensive military strategy. To facilitate a more aggressive campaign, Eisenhower in October 1953 found an additional $400 million in discretionary funding for the French war effort. Second, selective engagers believed that until France developed an indigenous Vietnamese military motivated to fight, the population of Vietnam would be highly suspicious of any U.S. or international military action. Furthermore, congressional debates on authorizing additional American assistance to France for Indochina during the summer of 1953 resulted in extensive liberal criticism of France's colonial status in Indochina. In response, Eisenhower pledged to press the French to move toward independence for the Associated States.

But herein lay the critical dilemma for the selective engagers and for the French: If France were to grant independence, it would no longer have any motivation to continue the struggle in Indochina. French public opinion would demand an immediate suspension of the conflict and the complete French withdrawal from Indochina—which would likely lead to the loss of the territory to communist forces. Eisenhower and his aides were also struggling to convince the French to ratify the European Defense Community (EDC) Treaty, which would pave the way for the rearmament of West Germany and even greater European stability. The selective engagers in the administration feared that excessive pressure on Paris would lead the French to balk at the EDC Treaty.

Given these circumstances, the deterioration of the French position in early 1954 created numerous headaches for the selective engagers. Eisenhower and his advisors were committed to resisting a communist takeover in Indochina. They hoped to persuade France to alter its military strategy, while they continued to press Congress for additional material support for the French.

Hardliners

Although the Eisenhower administration was dominated by selective engagers, there were many powerful hardliners, both in and out of government. Doctrinaire hardliners such as Vice President Richard Nixon, Chairman of the Joint Chiefs Admiral Radford, and members of Congress like Walter Judd, Paul Douglas, George Malone, and William Jenner all advocated a strong and forceful demonstration of American military power in the face of international communist expansion. Several influential columnists and media personalities, among them Joseph and Stewart Alsop and *New York Times* national security correspondent Hanson Baldwin, advocated aggressive American responses to international challenges.

While most hardliners believed in the necessity of the postwar American commitment to Western Europe, they remained bitterly opposed to American acceptance of the "secret understandings" at Yalta, Teheran, and Potsdam, which they believed had been a capitulation by Roosevelt and Truman to Soviet domination of Eastern and Central Europe. In the 1952 presidential campaign, hardline Republicans inserted into the foreign policy plank of the GOP platform a specific repudiation of the Yalta, Teheran, and Potsdam agreements. This group was also angered by the loss of China in 1949 and demanded unconditional U.S. support for Taiwan. They also sharply criticized the failure of the Truman administration and later the Eisenhower administration to escalate the American effort in Korea and secure a victory. In the 1952 GOP platform, hardliners accused Truman's administration of waging the war in Korea "without will to victory" and charged that they "by their hampering orders had produced stalemates and ignominious bartering with our enemies."[20] Hanson Baldwin of the *New York Times* commented: "Korea was the right war in the right place at the right time if we wished to stop the spread of Asiatic Communism."[21]

Hardliners' Views toward Indochina before Dienbienphu

For hardliners, Indochina was the key to all of Southeast Asia. They argued that if it were lost, the United States would be deeply imperiled. This geostrategic importance of Southeast Asia was conveyed by Senator Paul Douglas in 1951 in perhaps the first speech to describe the "domino theory" of communist expansion:

Indochina is now in grave danger of falling to the Communists. Not only is there a strong internal Communist movement, but a Chinese Communist army is poised at their gates and is ready to strike. If this happens, Burma, Thailand, Malaysia, and Indonesia will be sitting ducks and will fall very quickly. Ceylon will then be in great danger. India, already facing the Russian Communists from the northwest through a thin strip of Afghanistan, will find herself suddenly faced with terrific pressure from the east in a Communist-held Southeast Asia. To the west of India are only the weak, semi-neutral, feudal countries of Afghanistan, Iran, and Saudi Arabia.

Sitting in the jaws of a nutcracker, with Russia as one jaw, a Communist-held Southeast Asia as the other jaw, . . . India, whether Prime Minister Nehru recognizes it or not, will surely fall. . . . With India gone, the countries of the Middle East, lacking our help, or even the threat—as against Communist aggressors—of our help, will also go to the Communists. Then Africa and so on.[22]

During congressional debates in the summer of 1953 on whether or not to increase U.S. aid for the French war effort, the views of the hardliners were summed up by Republican senator Alexander Wiley of Wisconsin, who argued that "we ought to give some of our bombs to the French pilots, including small A-bombs."[23] Alexander Smith, one of the Senate's experts on Asia, warned: "The avenues of conquest in Southern Asia lead through Indochina. . . . It is well to remember that the attack on the United States [at Pearl Harbor] was not launched until after the enemy had secure control of Indochina. That is why continued resistance to the Communist advance is so essential to us as well as to other free nations."[24]

Long before the crisis in Indochina intensified, in early 1954, hardliners had concluded that the geostrategic importance of Indochina and the need to contain communist expansion warranted a full consideration of all available means within the U.S. military arsenal to prevent another China and another Korea. As the crisis worsened and the French faltered at Dienbienphu, the selective engagers and the hardliners began to debate direct U.S. military intervention.

Liberals

Contrasting the views of selective engagers and hardliners was a group of influential congresspeople, members of religious and civic organizations, and media personalities who believed that selective engagers and hardliners consistently (and often recklessly) overstated the nature of international threats to the United States. While these liberals opposed international communism—on the grounds that it was antithetical to democracy and liberty—they also tended to believe that instability in the Third World was the product of internal inequalities, perpetual poverty, and social and political forces that refused to transfer sovereignty to the people. They argued that threats to the values of liberty, justice, and democracy were the real threats to the United States.[25] They also believed that American foreign policy had a tendency toward excess when it moved under the banner of anticommunism. In particular, they opposed American behavior that violated basic norms of human rights and humanitarian conditions. They especially opposed supporting colonialism, whatever the broader purpose might be.

Among the liberal critics of America's selective engagement and hardline policies were the following members of Congress: Claude Pepper, Glen Taylor, Mike Mansfield, J. William Fulbright, John F. Kennedy, Guy Gillette, and Wayne Morse. These individuals consistently voiced their opposition to the selective engagers' claims concerning the Cold War.[26] All of them favored expanding notions of international justice and law and curtailing what they viewed as American overreaction to the Soviet Union. They often challenged the other groups' views on whether or not a particular regional crisis was actually inspired by external communist forces or by indigenous forces seeking greater equality.

Liberals' Views toward Indochina before Dienbienphu

Throughout the early Cold War years, liberals repeatedly raised questions about the direction of American foreign policy. For example, in early 1947, President Truman proclaimed that two of America's European allies, Greece and Turkey, were in imminent danger from communist infiltrators and he proposed a massive military and financial assistance program for both governments. During the ensuing congressional debate on the aid packages, several liberal members of Congress, along with liberal religious and civic organizations, strenuously voiced their opposition to American assistance to what they viewed as corrupt "antidemocratic" regimes in both countries.[27] Several liberal critics suggested that the Truman administration was so focused on the Soviet Union that it was failing to see that the dictatorial policies of the Greek and Turkish governments were the root of the internal instability in those countries. In the end, President Truman, pledging his commitment to the long-term democratization of both countries, was able to mobilize widespread support for American financial assistance, but liberals did serve notice that they would demand that the aid be consistent with American principles.

Perhaps no other foreign policy issue galvanized liberals more in the early 1950s than the question of American support for what liberals interpreted as French colonialism in Southeast Asia. Even during World War II, when the outcome of the war with Japan was not yet certain, liberals—including President Franklin Roosevelt—opposed American support for French rule in Indochina. In February 1945 the French requested American military assistance to overtake the Japanese forces that had invaded Indochina. In response, Roosevelt told his Joint Chiefs of Staff that he was "in favor of anything that is against the Japanese in Indochina provided we do not align ourselves with the French."[28]

After Roosevelt's death, Truman changed course on American policy and began supporting the French and acquiescing to French resumption of colonial control over Indochina. For the next several years, American policy reflected the views of selective engagers. However, several members of Congress and national groups continued to speak up in opposition to colonial rule by America's European allies. Following his first trip to Indochina, in 1953, Senator Mike Mansfield, who had been a staunch supporter of aid to France's war effort there, concluded that France was not likely to prevail if it continued to cling to notions of imperial control.[29] This view corresponded to the views expressed by Senator John F. Kennedy in a travel report following his 1951 visit to the region: "In Indochina, we have allied ourselves to the desperate effort of a French regime to hang on to the remnants of empire. There is no broad, general support of the native Vietnam Government among the people of that area. . . . The task is . . . to build strong native non-Communist sentiment within these areas and rely on that as a spearhead of defense rather than upon the legions of General de Lattre."[30] Kennedy further opined that independence was both moral and prudent, in that it alone would provide the inspiration for the creation of an effective resistance to communist expansion. By the summer of 1953, several liberal members of Congress were questioning American financial support for the French war effort. Kennedy introduced legislation calling for a 25 percent reduction in U.S. assistance to the French in Indochina and tied the residual monies to a French commitment to, and announcement of a specific date for, independence for the Associated States of Indochina.[31]

Liberal press organizations also kept themselves apprised of the situation in Indochina. The *Christian Science Monitor* proclaimed in April 1953, "Unless American aid is used to promote Indochina independence rather than to defend French prerogatives it might as well be stopped tomorrow."[32] And, throughout the country, dozens of religious and private organizations devoted to international issues expressed their support for the development of multi-lateral and international norms and laws.[33] In August, photojournalist David Douglas Duncan published a highly critical profile of American policy on Indochina in *Life* magazine. Duncan spent two months traveling throughout Indochina to research the story.[34] He included quotes from American officials on the ground who complained that the French had developed a highly cor-rupt leadership and that the country was "all but lost."

Noninterventionists and Reluctant Warriors

Finally, there were those who remained committed to American noninter-vention in regional conflicts. Even as the Cold War intensified, the old guard isolationist wing of the Republican Party maintained its stalwarts.[35] Senator Robert Taft had long trumpeted his opposition to American overseas commit-ments. Although Taft died a year before the Dienbienphu crisis of 1954, his iso-lationist legacy continued. Prominent Republican members of the Senate and House of Representatives, such as populists Bill Langer and Usher Burdick from North Dakota, Hugh A. Butler of Nebraska, Henry Dworshak of Idaho, and southern nationalist Walter George from Georgia, actively opposed ex-panding U.S. military and financial assistance packages to other countries and used many forums to publicly deride presidential requests on these matters.[36] John Bricker from Ohio introduced the Bricker Amendment resolution, a con-stitutional amendment to curtail executive authority on treaty-making. The midwest populist and southern nationalist movements, often aided by well-known media moguls such as Colonel Robert R. McCormick, also mobilized, holding public forums for religious and citizens' groups on the question of what they regarded as excessive expenditures on helping populations around the world.[37]

In response to the military stalemate in Korea and the protracted peace negotiations over that conflict, a new group rose to prominence that was highly reluctant to intervene in limited wars. Several Army commanders complained bitterly that the politically inspired restrictions on operational plans during the Korean conflict had constrained them from implementing their "optimal" military strategies.[38] Among the sharpest critics of limited wars were Army Generals Matthew B. Ridgway and Mark Clark, Air Force Chief of Staff Nathan Twining, and Navy Vice Admiral C. Turner Joy.[39] They vowed that never again would they support U.S. military action that would limit the ability of military commanders to achieve victory.

Noninterventionists' and Reluctant Warriors' Views toward Indochina before Dienbienphu

From as early as 1950, isolationist members of Congress warned against American involvement in Indochina. Bruce Barton, a former member of Congress from New York, publicly argued that American support of the French and the Vietnamese emperor Bao Dai would lead to greater American presence in the area and to disaster. In 1951, the notoriously isolationist McCormick and Scripps-Howard newspapers began extensive editorializing that the United States was involved in a gradual escalation of its commitments in Indochina; they publicly opposed increased U.S. assistance to Indochina. Perhaps no clearer statement of the noninterventionist position on Indochina was made than that of Robert Taft. A note found on his desk shortly after he died read, "No Indo-China-Except in case of emergency invasion by the Chinese."[40] Finally, as American troops withdrew from Korea in the summer of 1953, senior Army strategists and planners led by Army Chief of Staff General Ridgway committed themselves to ensuring that the United States would not soon find itself in another land war in Asia.[41]

The Four Stages of the Crisis at Dienbienphu

Ultimately, the decision not to intervene in Indochina in 1954 was not one but four related decisions, made by President Eisenhower at four distinct stages in the crisis. The setting for each decision was: (1) the deterioration of the French position in the winter and spring of 1954 and the debate over deploying military technicians, (2) the visit by French Army Chief of Staff Paul Ely and the collapse of defensive positions around Dienbienphu in mid-March, (3) the effort to establish the United Action policy in early April, (4) the collapse of French forces at Dienbienphu and policy reconsideration in May. In order to understand the dynamics surrounding the American decision, all four of these must be evaluated.

Stage 1: Deterioration of the French Position

By the fall of 1953, French public opinion had dramatically turned against the war effort. French Prime Minister Joseph Laniel announced that his government would seek to include the Indochina question on the agenda at the international conferences with the Soviet Union and the United States and their allies set for April 1954 in Geneva. Within the administration, Eisenhower and his closest selective engagement advisors adamantly opposed including Indochina on the agenda at Geneva. They feared that the French would compromise with the communist forces and then quit Indochina altogether. In response, Eisenhower focused on various strategies the United States could develop to beef up the French war effort.

The general feeling in the administration was that French setbacks stemmed from inappropriate military tactics in a battle that could be won.[42] Both selective engagers and the hardliners felt that with additional financial support a more aggressive military strategy, and an expansion of training programs for indigenous Vietnamese forces, the French could turn the course of the battle in Indochina. In the fall of 1953, Eisenhower found an additional $400 million in discretionary executive funds to support a new French military initiative developed by famed French general Henri Navarre, commander in chief of French forces in Indochina. The administration hoped that France would stay the course while General Navarre worked on a new military strategy to alter the course of the war.

However, a critical question deeply divided the Eisenhower administration: What would the United States do in the event of a French defeat or withdrawal? Leading the advocates for a forceful American response if the French military floundered were hardliners such as Chairman of the Joint Chiefs of Staff Admiral Radford and Vice President Nixon. The hardliners felt that it was imperative that the United States take strong and decisive military action to prevent a French defeat or withdrawal. In internal NSC discussions on Indochina, both Nixon and Radford argued that the United States needed to prepare for direct American military support in the event of a catastrophic French failure in Indochina.[43] Admiral Radford demanded that any contingency planning include an assessment of direct American military intervention in support of the French. In December 1953, Radford assembled a special Joint Chiefs committee that recommended that the United States be prepared to use its own troops in Indochina and provide such additional support to the forces of the Associated States as seemed feasible.[44]

In contrast to the views of Admiral Radford and Nixon, the senior Army leadership was much more cautious. In particular, General Ridgway, the Army chief of staff, argued that the defense of Indochina would be virtually impossible. In December 1953, the Plans Division of the Army Staff predicted that seven U.S. Army divisions and one U.S. Marine division would be needed to replace French forces should they withdraw from Indochina. Given the existing American global defense commitments and defense posture, the Army Staff concluded that if the United States found itself intervening in Indochina, "the effects on the overall U.S. defense posture would be severe."[45] General Ridgway and his staff argued that the United States needed to reconsider "the importance of Indochina and Southeast Asia in relation to the possible cost of saving it."[46]

The selective engagers, including Eisenhower and Dulles, found themselves caught between the hardliners and the noninterventionists. Eisenhower and Dulles believed that in the event of a French collapse or withdrawal, the United States might be required to provide air and naval power in support of French and regional ground forces, to forestall a communist victory. They were both sincerely concerned about the geostrategic implications of a French defeat, but they were also wary of the prospects of involving U.S. forces in Indochina.

As the debate over developing contingency plans intensified in December 1953 and January 1954, General Navarre deployed 12,000 French troops to Dienbienphu, a remote valley in northwest Vietnam at the crossroads of supply routes between Vietnam and Laos. Navarre believed that the deployment of such a large force would entice the Vietminh into a large battle. He also believed that the high mountains surrounding the valley would provide sufficient defensive fortifications for his forces to easily overwhelm a much larger invading force. Navarre miscalculated, however, and his plan backfired. In early January 1954, the Vietminh successfully advanced nearly 50,000 troops to the valley and surrounded the entire French position.

The deterioration of the French position generated intense concern and attention within the Eisenhower administration. In view of the declining French public support for the military campaign and political pressure on the Laniel government to negotiate with the communists at Geneva, and the faltering French military position, Eisenhower and his advisors now increased their focus on developing strategies to forestall a French defeat.

The critical questions for the administration were: What could be done to convince the French to continue fighting against communist expansion in Southeast Asia, and What could the United States do? To address these issues, Eisenhower appointed a special committee on Indochina headed by his long-time friend W. Bedell Smith to explore various ways in which the United States could press the French to break their resistance to large-scale training of in-digenous forces. Over the next two months, the committee met regularly.

Latent Public Opinion

Constraining all policy discussions and development of options was the critical issue of American public and political opinion. Eisenhower and his political advisors were acutely aware that the American public was not likely to stomach another land war in Asia. By the end of the Korean conflict, much of the public had grown extremely weary of the war effort, and Eisenhower him-self had campaigned on a peace platform during the 1952 presidential election. From the beginning of his administration, Eisenhower and his political advi-sors closely monitored public opinion polls and political commentary on the situation in Indochina.[47] In the summer of 1953, his staff recruited famed poll-ster Alfred Politz to evaluate public opinion on Indochina. Politz found that even if the communists had directly invaded Indochina only 47 percent of Americans would have supported any U.S. aid to defeat the communists, and less than 30 percent favored using U.S. troops under such circumstances. An interesting follow-up question revealed that only 10 percent favored U.S. in-volvement if it meant that the United States would be lending support to French colonial policies.[48] Polls taken throughout the summer and fall of 1953 consistently found that less than 15 percent of Americans supported fighting in Indochina on behalf of the French.[49] In fact, the outcome of a September poll reflected such overwhelming opposition to American intervention that George Gallup took the exceptional step of footnoting the findings of one of his polls: "The size of the disapproval vote is unusually significant. *Rarely in polling annals has opinion divided in such a lopsided fashion as it does in the case of the troops to Indochina issue.*"[50]

Information and Framing the Issue of Indochina

The analyses presented to Eisenhower on Indochina consistently revealed that the American public and most of the political commentators viewed the crisis in Indochina as a French struggle to reimpose colonial rule on the indige-nous populations in Southeast Asia. In mid-1953 the administration recognized that it needed to shift the public's perception of the crisis—to portray the con-flict as part of the geostrategic struggle against communism—or popular and political sentiment would balk at additional U.S. financial and material assis-tance for France.[51] During a high-profile visit by the French prime minister,

René Mayer, in March 1953, Eisenhower told his advisors that he believed it was imperative that Mayer address the American public on radio and television to "counteract the familiar belief" that the war was fueled by French colonialism.[52] Eisenhower told the French premier that it was essential for the French leadership to take the case to the American public and present the conflict in Indochina as, at core, a struggle against communism. He stressed this to Mayer, "because, unfortunately many Americans continue to think of the war in Indo-China as a French colonial operation rather than as a part of the struggle for the free world against the forces of Soviet Communism."[53] Over the course of the next nine months, Eisenhower and Dulles used every occasion when speaking on Indochina to emphasize the valiant and heroic battles waged by France to preserve freedom for the Indochinese people.

As the crisis surrounding Dienbienphu unfolded in early January 1954, the president and his advisors stepped up their efforts and aggressively attempted to alter the public perception of the conflict. They concluded that an essential element of any increased American assistance was to convey to the American public the importance of Indochina to U.S. national security. Eisenhower urged absolute secrecy on White House deliberations and sanctioned release of only information that supported the administration's view.[54] He also ordered the Joint Chiefs to develop a comprehensive American strategy to assist the Navarre Plan, a key component of their design to increase the pace and scope of the U.S. information program "to increase the willingness of the people of [both] France and the U.S. to support the prosecution of the war."[55] In short, there was a clear recognition from the beginning of the crisis that if the United States were to take more assertive action in Indochina, it would need to redefine the conflict from one about colonialism to one focused on the global struggle against communism.

Executive Fragmentation and Media Leaks

Despite the administration's efforts during the early phase of the crisis, political commentary and press reports on Indochina continued to portray the Indochinese conflict as being fueled primarily by popular Vietnamese resentment to French colonial policies.[56] Several factors contributed to this. First, as mentioned above, the executive itself was deeply divided on American military action in Indochina. While Eisenhower and his selective engager and hardline advisors were actively contemplating American military action, senior Army commanders adamantly opposed any form of American action. On several occasions, critical information on the administration's deliberations on Indochina was leaked to the press. For example, on January 21, the French government requested an additional thirty-five B-26 bombers and 400 American support personnel to help break the crisis at Dienbienphu. Both selective engagers and hardliners supported sending all available B-26s and personnel, and a week later the president agreed to send twenty-two B-26s and to send 200 U.S. technical support personnel.

The decisions to send this aid were leaked to the press.[57] The disclosure of the deployment of the 200 American military personnel and additional aircraft without any congressional notification or approval generated an immediate negative response from noninterventionists and liberals. From mid-1953 onward liberals and noninterventionists had warned the administration publicly that any deployment of American military personnel to Indochina would have to be approved by Congress.[58] That the administration had, without congressional consent, deployed military personnel—albeit military technicians— angered liberals and noninterventionists. Senator John Stennis of the Senate Armed Services Committee demanded that the American technicians be withdrawn immediately. Liberals argued that the deployment of American military personnel in support of French colonialism set a dangerous precedent that would undermine American credibility around the globe. These arguments were coupled with a flurry of media reports from Indochina, Paris, and Washington suggesting that America was moving toward a hot war in Indochina.[59]

Within days of this leak, sources within the administration also leaked the news that the president had formed the special committee on Indochina headed by Smith. This immediately exposed the administration to further criticism. Several major news organizations sharply criticized the escalation in Indochina. For example, the *Washington Post* complained that while "factual information" was "extremely hard to come by," the war had "a taint of colonialism."[60] The editorial also warned the administration, "Before there is any thought of unilateral intervention by this country the matter ought to be taken before the UN for whatever collective remedy could be devised."[61] The press leaks and the subsequent public frenzy against the administration's policies caught the White House off guard and angered the president.[62] The morning after the press reports, Sherman Adams, Eisenhower's top political advisor, called Secretary of Defense Wilson and "raised hell."[63]

In response to this and other leaks Eisenhower demanded that his staff better control the information flow on the crisis and produce fewer written directives and memoranda. On February 8, National Security Council Advisor Robert Cutler circulated a memo to the NSC disclosing the penalties for security leaks. Cutler included a copy of a November 23, 1953, NSC memo titled "Prevention of Unauthorized Disclosures of Classified NSC Information," which stated that leaks would not be tolerated and that the president had the authority to "direct the Federal Bureau of Investigation to conduct investigations to identify the sources thereof in order that appropriate administrative action may be promptly taken."[64] Eisenhower also told his advisors that, to avoid further leaks, he would prefer to rely on oral directions as much as possible.[65]

Particularly frustrating to both selective engagers and hardliners was the fact that the administration had virtually no ability to control the information coming out of Indochina and the interpretation given to that information by American-based correspondents and columnists. Vice President Nixon expressed his concern: "What should really concern us is the constant stream of bad news from the battle areas. This is developing a defeatist attitude in the United States as well as in France. The recent Alsop columns were proof. Furthermore, there was a very defeatist atmosphere on Capitol Hill about the usefulness of any further American aid for Indochina."[66] Nixon recommended that the United States deploy "*the very best men* in the information and propaganda fields" to correct the problem.[67]

Mobilized Opposition

A second factor undermining the administration's ability to frame the Indochina crisis according to their view was the fact that liberals and noninterventionists were well positioned to collect and disseminate credible information to challenge the administration's line. Throughout the late 1940s and early 1950s, dozens of religious organizations had established more than one hundred missions throughout Indochina. Beginning in 1950, as the Vietminh began their assaults on the French positions, missionaries in Indochina reported to their commissioning organizations that the French had alienated much of the population of Southeast Asia by reimposing colonial rule on the Associated States. American religious organizations acted on this information, launching a series of letter writing campaigns to Congress and the White House in 1952 and 1953 during the annual congressional debates on appropriations for the

French war effort. The religious leaders argued that any American financial assistance to France should be tied to immediate and unconditional guarantees by the French of independence for the Associated States.

In addition, several liberal senators and members of the House who had been skeptical of French "promises" of eventual consideration of independence traveled to Indochina in 1952 and 1953 to gain first-hand information about the French war effort.[68] During the summer 1953 congressional debates, these liberals issued testimonials and reports of their "fact-finding" trips to their colleagues in which they expressed deep concerns about France's colonial efforts. As a result, both the House of Representatives and the Senate required more explicit action from France toward granting independence to the Associated States as a condition of additional U.S. assistance.

Noninterventionists, for their part, had become highly mobilized during the Korean conflict. Leading political figures representing southern evangelical Christians and midwestern prairie populists argued that Indochina was destined to be a similar war. And, many of the leaks to the press on the deliberations by the Eisenhower administration referred to "anonymous senior U.S. military officials," many of whom were expressly opposed to intervention in Indochina.

Finally, the American news media had an extensive presence in Indochina. In 1953 and early 1954, more than 100 American journalists were either stationed in or traveled to and reported extensively from Indochina.[69] Furthermore, with their experiences of the war in Korea, many journalists had developed East Asian regional expertise and were acutely aware of the internal political dynamics in Indochina. Many had also established close contacts with Vietnamese civilians and municipal officials who had extensive and detailed knowledge of French colonial administrative practices that frequently contradicted official French press statements.[70]

Effect on Eisenhower

The existence of these factors had a direct effect on Eisenhower's policy decisions. In response to the extensive criticism of his decision to deploy the 200 military technicians, and specifically in response to a warning from Senator Leverett Saltonstall that the president would face trouble in both the Appropriations Committee and the Armed Services Committee if he did not suspend the deployment, Eisenhower ordered his staff to find some alternative to the overt use of American military personnel. His diary entry on the subject reads in part:

I telephoned to the secretary of defense to tell him of Chairman Saltonstall's anxiety about the plan for sending two hundred technicians into Indochina. Chairman Saltonstall says that the opposition in the Senate Committee is so great that it may affect appropriations for the area. He believes this opposition would diminish if there were an unequivocal statement on the part of the administration that the technicians will be removed from Indochina by June 15, regardless of French capacity to meet the requirement.

I instructed Mr. Wilson to devise the necessary plan, even if it meant the hiring of technicians under the aid program to replace the air force technicians in Indochina.[71]

In early February, amid the frenzied initial reaction to the decision to deploy the military technicians, Eisenhower and his staff regrouped and devised an aggressive public relations strategy.[72] The plan called for senior administration officials to stress two points on Indochina.[73] First, they were to deemphasize the severity of the crisis at Dienbienphu in hopes of mitigating public concern and war anxiety. While Eisenhower was increasingly anxious about the position of the French, he was not yet convinced that their situation in Dienbienphu was totally desperate. Based on intelligence reports, he and Dulles believed that the French troops probably would be able to hold out past the onset of the rainy season, in April. That would give the troops a reprieve from a full-scale Vietminh attack until the season ended in the fall. Since the situation was thought to be not yet dire, Eisenhower and his staff decided to tone down any discussion of direct American military action in the region. Second, they attempted to redefine the conflict as a struggle in which the French were actually spilling blood to protect the populations of Indochina from intolerable communist aggression.

To sell this strategy, senior administration officials participated in dozens of public forums, press conferences, and congressional hearings. For example, Admiral Radford, in a highly unusual move, personally contacted Senator Saltonstall, chairman of the Senate Armed Services Committee, and asked if he could be allowed to come before the committee to explain the situation.[74] In his subsequent testimony, Radford warned that failure to support the French would mean almost certain communist control of all of Southeast Asia. On February 10, Secretary of Defense Wilson addressed reporters on the situation in Indochina. He deliberately downplayed the threat to American military personnel in Indochina. He also declared that a French victory in Indochina was "possible and probable."[75] The same day, the president asserted that the situation in Indochina was stable and that "no one could be more bitterly opposed to ever getting the United States involved in a hot war in that region than I am; consequently, every move I authorize is calculated, so far as humans can do it, to make certain that that does not happen." He further reiterated, "So what we are doing is supporting the Vietnamese and the French in their conduct of that war; because, as we see it, it is a case of independent and free nations operating against the encroachment of communism."[76]

A week later, during a press conference on February 17, the president again attempted to redirect the emphasis from French colonialism to a struggle against communism. In response to a question on whether there was any way to distinguish anticommunist forces in Indochina from those in support of colonialism, the president proclaimed: "There is no colonialism in this battle at all. France has announced several times, and most emphatically last July, that they are fighting to give the three associated states their freedom, their liberty; and I believe it has been agreed they would live inside the French Union, but as free and independent states. Now, as I see it, the Vietnamese are fighting for their own independence, and I have no trouble at all making the distinction that you speak of."[77]

Despite these efforts, the selective engagers and hardliners faced an up-hill battle against a mobilized coalition of liberals and noninterventionists. In its report to Eisenhower on March 2, the President's Special Committee on Indochina specified a series of steps to improve the French military position, but the report declared that it was imperative that the United States develop "a specific domestic and foreign information campaign . . . to de-emphasize 'hysteria' publicity, and to bring widespread recognition of and appropriate attention to [the fact that] France, in supporting the fight of the Associated States of Indo-China against Communist domination, is the principal nation now shedding its blood for the freedom of others."[78] Clearly, unless there was some dramatic change in the way the American public perceived the conflict in Indochina, the policy options would be tightly constrained. It was apparent to the White House that Americans did not want to go to war in Asia and that they were especially opposed to any type of intervention of American combat troops that would be called upon to fight and die for French colonial policy.[79]

By the time the Vietminh tightened the noose around Dienbienphu on March 13, the administration's arsenal of feasible policy options had already been reduced. The selective engagers in the administration were not willing to abandon Indochina, but under intense political pressure neither could they fully commit to its defense. Over the next few weeks, the selective engagers would need to become more creative in developing a policy that supported their underlying normative beliefs about what needed to be done in Indochina but could be sold within the existing constraints.

Stage 2: The Siege of Dienbienphu

On March 13, 1954, Vietminh forces directly attacked the French defensive perimeter at Dienbienphu. For the first time since the initial encirclement in December, the French forces appeared in imminent danger of defeat. Within days of that event, France requested direct American military intervention in support of its troops.[80] On March 20, President Eisenhower directed elements of the Seventh Fleet stationed in the Philippines to steam to the Gulf of Tonkin and be prepared to conduct air and naval combat operations on short notice.[81]

That same day, the French Army chief of staff, General Paul Ely, arrived in the United States to brief U.S. officials on the status of the French forces. Ely submitted a request for an additional twenty-five B-26 bombers with American pilots. Ely was immediately championed by Admiral Radford, who paraded him around the Pentagon, the State Department, and the White House in hopes of persuading Eisenhower, Dulles, and other advisors to make a stronger American commitment to the defense of Dienbienphu.[82] In Radford's report to the president at the conclusion of Ely's visit he summed up his fears in these words: "I am gravely fearful that the measures being taken by the French will prove to be inadequate and initiated too late to prevent a progressive deterioration of the situation. The consequences can well lead to the loss of all of S.E. Asia to Communist domination. If this is to be avoided, I consider that the U.S. must be prepared to act promptly and in force possibly to a frantic and belated request by the French for U.S. intervention."[83]

The selective engagers also became increasingly concerned and frustrated. Eisenhower clearly believed that the United States had to do something. He reiterated that "the collapse of Indochina would produce a chain reaction which would result in the fall of all of Southeast Asia to the Communists."[84] In response to Ely's visit, Eisenhower agreed to provide an additional twenty-five B-26 aircraft for use in France's air operations in Indochina. Nonetheless, the domestic political environment was unmistakable—any direct American military action would be politically risky.

At this point, the selective engagers within the administration began work on a new two-pronged policy strategy. First, the administration's Indochina experts and much of the bureaucracy mobilized to determine what the United States could actually do to reverse the military trends in and the crisis in Indochina. On March 25, the president met with his national security advisors and extensively discussed American military intervention. Dulles and Secretary of Defense Wilson both supported the development of specific contingency plans for intervention. Eisenhower concurred that it was time to examine "the extent to which we should go in employing ground forces to save Indochina from the Communists."[85] But he added that he could not envision the United States or anyone else intervening in Indochina without the support of the Associated States or the United Nations. Furthermore, fully aware of the political and public mood, he stressed that any American action had to receive congressional support. "It was simply academic to imagine otherwise," he said.[86] He then added, "This might be the moment to begin to explore with the Congress what support could be anticipated in the event that it seemed desirable to intervene in Indochina."[87] By the end of the meeting, Eisenhower was apparently convinced that three conditions would need to be met for American intervention: (1) that the intervention be multilateral, (2) that the Associated States request the American intervention, and (3) that there be congressional and public approval. These became the new working preconditions for any decision on American intervention. Still absent from these conditions, however, was the specific request that France grant the Associated States immediate independence.

The second aspect of the administration's strategy was to begin the delicate maneuvers to develop support from the American public and a reluctant Congress for greater American involvement in Indochina. From January until March 18, public discussions of American military intervention had been largely theoretical; most in the administration believed that the French would hold out at Dienbienphu. Consequently, throughout the first three months of 1954, while the administration lauded the French soldiers for their brave and gallant struggle for world freedom, it did not publicly advocate intervention, believing that the French could win as long as the United States continued to fund their war effort.

The breakdown of defensive fortifications at Dienbienphu changed that stance. It appeared that the French might very well lose the war. As a result, both selective engagers and hardliners agreed that their theme had to become more deliberate and concentrated. The focus had to be on the fact that the

French were fighting a valiant struggle against global communist domination *and* the United States might well have to participate in a *multilateral* military action to resolve the situation.[88] In mid-March, Secretary of Defense Wilson, Admiral Radford, and Dulles held several telephone discussions to coordinate their public statements on Indochina.[89] They agreed that the administration needed to stop sounding optimistic about Dienbienphu and start conveying to the media, the public, and Congress the gravity of the situation. As part of this strategy, over the next several weeks, senior administration officials, including the president, regularly invited leading journalists into the White House, the State Department, and the Pentagon for off-the-record briefings on Indochina. Meanwhile, presidential press secretary James Hagerty and the president's specialist on propaganda, C. D. Jackson, regularly conferred with Dulles, Radford, and Wilson and their staffs to ensure a consistent theme—that the war was about the French struggle against communist aggression.[90] For example, during Dulles's press conference on March 23, he repeatedly emphasized that the French soldiers were fighting for the "Free World."[91] That same day, Eisenhower stressed the valiant effort by the French and declared that Southeast Asia was of the "most transcendent importance."[92]

During the cabinet meeting on March 26, however, Dulles, who was receiving almost daily briefings on public opinion and political commentary, warned the president and the rest of the Cabinet that among the American public there was still a "general misunderstanding" about the Indochina war.[93] According to State Department public commentary reports assembled in the Office of Public Affairs, much of the political commentary and public opinion polls continued to reflect opposition to any direct use of American combat personnel and continued to see the mission as being in support of French colonialism.[94] In fact, as of mid-March only 9 percent of the public supported the use of U.S. troops whereas 45 percent favored seeking a negotiated settlement. Dulles explained the situation to the Cabinet and outlined the geostrategic and political implications of Dienbienphu, warning that unless the United States garnered the wherewithal to take decisive action, the "Reds" would "cut our defense line in half" in Southeast Asia.[95]

Eisenhower and Dulles then agreed that the secretary should make a public speech on Indochina. Over the next few days, Dulles assembled his public relations advisors to assess the latent public opinion on Indochina and to coordinate effective language to generate greater support.[96] Dulles's senior policy planning advisor, Robert Bowie, who was widely recognized as the State Department's leading expert on American domestic opinion, told the secretary that he did not believe the American public would be willing to go along with a tough program in Indochina.[97] In drafting the speech, Dulles and his advisors decided that he should acknowledge the colonialism issue but stress that the French had made significant strides by granting autonomy to the Associated States and that the United States government was vigilantly encouraging the French toward granting total independence.[98]

On March 29, Dulles delivered his speech, at the Overseas Press Club conference in New York to a national television audience. He led off by emphasizing that the French had already committed to full independence of the Associated States but that the communists were "attempting to prevent this orderly development to independence and to confuse the issues in the eyes of the world." In conclusion he asserted that the real issue was "imposition on Southeast Asia of the political system of Communist Russia and its Chinese Communist ally, by whatever means," and that this "would be a grave threat to the whole free community." He announced, "The United States feels that the possibility should not be passively accepted but should be met by *united action*. This might involve serious risks. But these risks are far less than those that will face us a few years from now, if we dare not be resolute today."[99]

While the initial political response to the speech was positive, the overall political results were interrupted by further deterioration of the situation in Indochina. Two days after Dulles's speech, the largest remaining French defensive post on the outskirts of Dienbienphu fell to Vietminh forces. The French airlift of supplies to the 12,000 troops was suspended and Dienbienphu was considered to be only days from defeat.

Eisenhower and Dulles immediately assembled the National Security Council and again raised the question of American intervention. Eisenhower and his selective engager and hardliner advisors now agreed that the situation warranted a strong American response and that the administration needed to quickly determine the magnitude of public and political support they could develop.[100] The NSC agreed that Dulles and Radford needed to brief members of Congress as soon as possible, to get a sense of whether or not Congress would be willing to support a more forceful American action, given the perilous events at Dienbienphu. They also agreed on language for a joint resolution to be presented to Congress which would authorize Eisenhower to "employ the naval and air forces of the United States to assist the forces which are resisting aggression in Southeast Asia, to prevent extension and expansion of that aggression, and to protect and defend the safety and security of the United States."[101]

On April 3, Radford and Dulles, with the draft joint resolution in hand, briefed members of Congress at the State Department. Radford began by providing a detailed briefing on the "perilous state" of French forces and the "critical importance of Southeast Asia."[102] Dulles added that if nothing was done about the situation by the United States all of Southeast Asia would fall to the communists and the United States "could ultimately be forced back to Hawaii, as before World War II."[103]

Despite the hard sales tactics, the members of Congress remained unconvinced. Several noninterventionists argued that Korea had demonstrated the high costs of intervention. Veteran isolationists were not willing to countenance another military adventure in Asia. They believed that the United States had been "burned in Korea, and they had no desire to see it burned again."[104] Meanwhile, the liberals addressed their comments to criticizing French colonial policies in Indochina.[105] Several liberals argued that any large U.S. intervention must be accompanied by a firm French guarantee of total independence to their colonial wards. At the end, the congressional response was one of skepticism but concern: the United States should not alone intervene or bear the burden of the war, and France must be willing to free the peoples of Indochina of colonial subjugation, a proposition that Dulles and Radford knew could not be met in time to forestall defeat at Dienbienphu.

The administration, however, refused to relent; and two days later, on April 5, Dulles and Radford concluded that a more dramatic message was needed to alter the public perception of and political commentary on the conflict.[106] After a discussion with Radford, Dulles testified to the House Foreign Affairs Committee that he had just received a "fresh, top-secret United States intelligence report that Chinese Communists had been identified in actual combat alongside the Communist-led Vietminh in Indo-China." He told members that the Chinese actions constituted "a form of undisguised aggression" and that open aggression by the Chinese would have "grave consequences which might not be confined to Indo-China."[107]

Liberal and Noninterventionist Opposition

While the administration stepped up its campaign to sell the American public the need for greater U.S. involvement in Indochina, a broad-based coalition of liberals and noninterventionists organized a countercampaign.[108] Non-interventionists and liberals outside the government wrote letters to members of Congress and to the editors of major newspapers urging that the United States stay out of the war in Indochina.[109] Noninterventionist media organizations such as the McCormick press and Scripps-Howard newspapers argued that without granting some form of independence to the peoples of Indochina, France would not be able to generate a motivated fighting force to challenge the Vietminh. In its lead editorial the day after Dulles's speech to the Overseas Press Club, the *Chicago Tribune* wrote, "The plain implication is that, no matter how great the risks, how much the costs, or how long the struggle, the Indo-China war is now America's baby," and it warned, "There can be no question that Dulles is talking war."[110] Editorials in newspapers throughout the Midwest and the South expressed the opinion that American military forces should not be sent to fight for the interests of others.[111] Much of the editorializing and other public commentary expressed bitter opposition to intervention. John T. Flynn, former editor of the *New York Globe*, announced on his weekly radio show that if Dulles wanted war, the country should give him "a gun and [send] him over there."[112] Others argued that Dulles was intent on risking "the final war of our civilization."[113]

In addition to those who believed the United States had no business in Indochina, another large cadre of individuals and organizations expressed their opposition to fighting in Indochina on behalf of French colonialism.[114] Religious organizations and religiously affiliated publications, in particular, argued against American support for French colonialism. Catholic bishops, the National Council of Churches, the Presbyterian Ministries, and several other Protestant ministries issued statements to their members urging them to write to their members of Congress condemning the war in Indochina as unjust and as likely to lead to a much larger and "regrettable" war and to press the French to grant "complete independence now for Indochina."[115] The famed theologian, Reinhold Niebuhr argued that America's moral authority had been eroded in Indochina because of its failure to press the issue of independence for the peoples of the region. He warned, "Atomic bombs cannot remedy this defect in the moral authority of our cause."[116] Furthermore, several women's organizations sponsored rallies and letter-writing campaigns. The League of Women Voters of the United States, the Women's International League for Peace and Freedom, and the Organization of Methodist Women, representing more than

1,700,000 Methodist women, all urged that the United States seek a negotiated solution to the crisis in Asia and to grant independence to Indochina.[117]

Most of the letters were sent to the national newspapers, key members of Congress on the military and foreign relations committees, and the White House. Among letters expressing various viewpoints to the Senate Armed Services Committee, those in opposition to direct American military involvement in Indochina overwhelmingly dominated.[118] The primary reason given for opposition to the war was the public's moral opposition to risking American lives in support of French colonialism.[119]

Throughout this public activism, noninterventionist and liberal members of Congress intensified their public criticism. On the same day Secretary Dulles warned of massive communist Chinese infiltration into the battle, Senator Guy Gillette, a noted liberal, issued an impassioned speech in the Senate. He challenged the administration's framing of the underlying causes of the conflict in Indochina:

> There is war in Indochina because of nationalism, because of the passionate desire and determination of the people to be rid of foreign rule and to govern themselves without interference from any outside source, and because of French refusal to grant independence in time and to the degree the Indochinese demand.
>
> . . . In Korea, the moral position of the United States was unassailable. . . . If the Indochina crisis is not brought before the United Nations, on what legal or moral grounds can the United States base any decision to intervene in force or to urge our associates in the free world to join in united action to prevent Communist conquest?[120]

This alternate analytical narrative was further advanced on April 6 by Senator John Kennedy, who argued that "without political independence for the Associated States, the other Asiatic nations have made it clear that they regard this as a war of colonialism." Kennedy also challenged the claims by the administration officials on the status of French commitment of independence to the Associated States:

> All of this flies in the face of repeated assurances to the American people by our own officials that complete independence will be granted.
>
> . . . Every year we are given three sets of assurances: First, that the independence of the Associated States is now complete; second, that the independence of

the Associated States will soon be completed under steps "now" being undertaken; and, third, that military victory for the French Union forces in Indochina is assured, or is just around the corner, or lies 2 years off.[121]

In addition, the American media, both in its daily reporting and in its editorial pages, consistently warned of the difficulties of fighting on behalf of the French.[122] Its analysis of the French failure in Indochina suggested that the French had applied overwhelming firepower and material resources but that they were fighting for a corrupt and archaic political structure that was destined to fail. For example, *U.S. News and World Report* posited that the Vietnamese population would not support the French because of the inequalities they believed were likely to come with French victory.[123] Liberal writers such as Graham Greene, writing from Indochina, disclosed how the French and American propaganda machines continually, to no avail, encouraged French and American reporters not to mention the issue of colonialism.[124]

Stage 3: United Action

The coordinated campaign of the liberals and noninterventionists weighed heavily on Eisenhower. Nonetheless, he was still not willing to write off Indochina. On April 5 Eisenhower met with his advisors secretly in the president's family chambers at the White House; they conferred again at a special NSC meeting on April 6. Presidential political advisor Sherman Adams recalls that Eisenhower was very sensitive to the criticism that "American intervention in Indo-China might be interpreted as protection of French colonialism." According to Adams, it was this domestic pressure that finally forced Eisenhower to add to his March 25 set of preconditions for intervention the condition that any American action could "only be tied to future independence for the Indo-Chinese states of Vietnam, Laos and Cambodia."[125] At the NSC meeting, the president articulated his acute awareness of the political and public issues intersecting policy deliberations on Indochina. He emphatically told his advisors: "There was no possibility whatever of U.S. unilateral intervention in Indochina, and we had best face that fact. Even if we tried such a course, we would have to take it to Congress and fight for it like dogs, with very little hope of success."[126]

Eisenhower decided that the best course was to formalize Dulles's call for united action and build a coalition of the United States, Great Britain, France, the Associated States, Australia, New Zealand, Thailand, and the Philippines, for the defense of Southeast Asia "against Communist efforts by any means to gain control of the countries in this area." The United Action policy, he said, might "give us the needed popular support of domestic opinion and of allied governments."[127] As Radford and his staff reworked contingency plans for some form of military intervention—including the option of using two air-craft carriers to assist the French at Dienbienphu—Dulles was dispatched to the European capitals to solicit allied support for the new coalition strategy.[128] Meanwhile, the hardliners prepared to make their pitch one more time. On April 16, Vice President Nixon told the American Society of Newspaper Editors, "If, to avoid further Communist expansion in Asia and Indochina we must take the risk now by putting our boys in, I think the Executive has to take the politically unpopular decision and do it."[129]

Nixon's comments, however, generated a storm of protests. Congress immediately demanded to know if Nixon's speech signaled a shift in policy of the executive branch. Liberal members of the Senate Foreign Relations Committee called for special hearings and for testimony from Dulles and others on the matter. And, Senator Edwin Johnson from Colorado proclaimed that Nixon was "whooping it up for war" and referred to "Mr. Nixon's war."[130] As historian Norman Graebner recounts, "so violent was the reaction to Nixon's speech among Republican [noninterventionist] editors that the administration demurred. Four days after the Vice President's speech Dulles admitted that the administration believed it unlikely that American troops would be employed in Indochina, and on April 28 he declared more emphatically that the United States would avoid sending troops to fight in Indochina or anywhere else if it could."[131] Public opinion polls in early and mid-April revealed a steady—and overwhelming—majority, nearly 8 out of 10, in opposition to direct military intervention. Eisenhower lamented to his close friend General Alfred M. Gruenther that American action without an unequivocal French pledge of independence for the Associated States "would lay [the United States] open to the charge of imperialism and colonialism, or—at the very least—of objectionable paternalism."[132]

Stage 4: The Defeat at Dienbienphu and No Blank Check from Congress

During the next month, Dulles and Radford both traveled to Europe in an effort to persuade the British and others to support the United Action policy. Both failed. In particular, the British were unwilling to commit their own troops. A significant factor in their rejection was frustration and anger at Radford's patronizing attitude that Indochina could be secured on the cheap, and because they distrusted Radford's deeper motives. Marquis Childs, a journalist, longtime Dulles friend, and British political observer, reported to Dulles at the conclusion of Radford's trip to London that the British saw Radford "coming over to London and trying to pressure the Cabinet and the chiefs of staff to come into Indo-China with sea and air power. They knew that this wouldn't work, said Eden, because it would require land forces as large as Korea. The British had a suspicion that Radford wanted to use this as a means of launching what Eden said was 'Radford's war against China.' They felt that that would be disastrous and they couldn't go along with it."[133]

On May 7, French forces surrendered at Dienbienphu. Now the issue became whether the defeat at Dienbienphu would signal a total defeat of the French in Indochina. With the British emphatic in their opposition to participating in any international military response, Eisenhower and the selective engagers again urgently assembled to recalculate their position.[134] In a meeting that day with Secretary of State Dulles, Eisenhower stated that he would be willing to ask for formal congressional authorization to "intervene with combat forces" as long as France was willing to grant "genuine freedom" to all of its Indochinese possessions: Laos, Cambodia, and Vietnam.[135] While he continued to hope for multinational effort, he dropped participation by the British as a precondition for U.S. intervention. On May 10, a second draft congressional resolution was prepared and circulated in the State Department, the Justice Department, and the Defense Department.

But the reality was that the French were still unwilling or unable to grant complete independence, because of their domestic political dynamics. If the French could not reap the rewards of their colonial possessions, they were not prepared to continue the fight. Conversely for the American administration, unless the French were willing to make this reversal, Eisenhower and his foreign policy team could do little, because the taint of colonialism persistently limited the selective engagers' options. Even more than before, the president's advisors consistently warned against any action that would give the appearance that the United States was supporting colonialism. For example, Arthur Flemming, Director of Defense Mobilization, cautioned that if the president ultimately needed to mobilize for war, the administration "must not even give the appearance of associating ourselves with other nations in order to protect colonialism and to stand in the way of movements for independence."[136] On May 5, Eisenhower lamented the extreme dilemma of Indochina for the United

States. While still concerned that the French defeat would seriously harm American interests, he nonetheless had concluded that "intervention by the U.S. . . . would place a colonial stigma on the U.S. and . . . it would exhaust us eventually."[137] On May 10, Nixon expressed his frustration with liberal members of Congress especially bitterly. During the president's weekly meeting with the Republican congressional leadership, he sharply criticized "Democratic partisanship" on Capitol Hill about Indochina and suggested that opponents of American intervention "merely criticized" the administration, "not one of them [trying] to contribute to forming a policy on S.E. Asia."[138]

On May 19, Eisenhower and Dulles reached the conclusion that without an unequivocal French pledge of independence the United States could do very little to help in Indochina amid the French collapse.[139] The French were unwilling to grant independence; they were also unwilling to continue the fight and desperately wanted some resolution at the international negotiations in Geneva. The selective engagers had vehemently opposed a settlement and had fought for four months for some other avenue, but the American domestic constraints proved too difficult to overcome. Dulles and Eisenhower agreed to withdraw the congressional resolution. In a memorandum by Dulles of his conversation with Eisenhower about the decision, he wrote:

> We were hamstrung by the constitutional situation and the apparent reluctance of Congress to give the President discretionary authority. I showed the President a rough draft of a Congressional resolution which I had discussed with Knowland on Monday, and against which Senator Knowland had reacted strongly in opposition, saying it would amount to giving the President a blank check to commit the country to war.[140]

Once again, private internal discussions concerning intervention came back to congressional and public support, of which there was very little.[141]

Over the course of the next several weeks, French troop positions faltered badly throughout Indochina. In mid-June, the French and communist Vietminh met in Geneva and reached an agreement ending the war. The French began their withdrawal from Indochina, and in the course of the next several months, the Vietminh won recognition and control over all of the newly created North Vietnam. Seemingly justifying the adamant views held by Eisenhower and Dulles, let alone Nixon and Radford, the communists secured a victory in Indochina. The United States did not intervene.

Summary

Significant cleavages existed among foreign policy elites on the issue of military intervention in Indochina. The reluctant warriors, who included General Ridgway and his staff and several members of Congress, vehemently objected to American intervention. Liberals believed that the United States could not in good conscience support an effort that would prop up a beleaguered and archaic colonial rule. Senators such as Kennedy, Fulbright, Morse, and Gillette argued that American values required the United States to push more forcefully for the independence of the Associated States.

Hardliners, and ultimately selective engagers, in the Eisenhower administration, however, believed that the loss of Indochina would be a significant blow to vital American interests in Southeast Asia. To be sure, Eisenhower was hesitant to commit American forces to Indochina, but he was equally concerned with losing Indochina to communism and the potential consequences that might have for the rest of Southeast Asia. His early expression of opposition to intervention must be considered in the context of his belief, in January and February 1954, that American intervention was not needed for an effective resolution of the situation. As the crisis intensified, so did Eisenhower's consideration of U.S.-led multilateral military action.

However, from the outset, selective engagers and hardliners were constrained by intense public and political opposition to any form of direct American military involvement in support of the French. The crisis in Indochina came less than a year after the conclusion of the war in Korea, and latent public opinion, well documented in polls regularly reported to the president, was overwhelmingly opposed to another American military deployment in Asia.

Furthermore, Eisenhower simply failed at framing the nature of the Indochina crisis convincingly. The administration's deep divides led to frequent leaks of policy deliberations. In addition, opposition groups were well established in Indochina and well versed in their own perception of the French war effort. They were able to present a credible analytical narrative of the crisis. The selective engagers and the hardliners were not. These factors combined to shut the political space for any consideration of American military intervention.

One final aspect of this case needs to be addressed. Knowing what we know about the history of the Vietnam War, scholars often praise Eisenhower for his skill and wisdom in avoiding American intervention in Indochina in 1954.

They submit that Eisenhower weaved his way through the difficult machinations of the Cold War politics at home to avoid entangling Americans in the jungles of Southeast Asia. In making their arguments, however, many of these scholars seem perplexed by how Eisenhower was able to "lose" Vietnam without any real punishment at home. For example, Leslie Gelb and Richard Betts state: "The most striking point about the failure of American diplomacy was the ease with which it was explained away at home. One day the administration simply changed its tune. . . . A number of senators made speeches about the 'terrible defeat,' but no one broke stride."[142] Melanie Billings-Yun concluded that Eisenhower was able to escape "indictment for standing by at Dien Bien Phu while yet another Asian territory fell to communism" because he "went to great lengths to conceal his role in keeping U.S. forces out of the French-Indochina War."[143]

Yet, what I find striking about both of these accounts is their failure to understand the mobilized opposition to intervention. Eisenhower was not "indicted" for his "failure" to intervene because for most Americans the failure in Indochina was a failure of French colonialism—it was wrong and it was ineffective. Groups holding such a view were not about to indict Eisenhower for upholding American values and interests. The argument here explains why Eisenhower was able to "lose Indochina" without any political ramifications. The mobilized public and congressional opposition to intervention not only endorsed, but significantly shaped, Eisenhower's policy.

Furthermore, the key factor ensuring nonintervention by the United States on behalf of the French in the spring of 1954 was the very presence of the French colonialists. Once colonialism was removed and Americans found themselves proselytizing for democracy in South Vietnam, liberals joined with selective engagers and hardliners in support for a much stronger U.S. presence in the country. In 1964 when Johnson requested a congressional resolution authorizing him to respond to the events in the Gulf of Tonkin, only two senators dissented, and this time America *would* be headed to war in Indochina.[144]

CHAPTER THREE

Intervention in Lebanon

> In this case, if there has to be a public debate about the course of action, there would be no use in taking it at all.
>
> —DWIGHT D. EISENHOWER

Introduction

On July 15, 1958, President Eisenhower ordered American troops to intervene in Lebanon to stem violence being perpetrated against the pro-Western government of President Camille Chamoun in an insurrection. This intervention receives only a footnote from most historians of American foreign policy.[1] This is because the Lebanon intervention continues to be understood as an enormous political and military success—Eisenhower's "finest hour."[2] Only one American was killed in a combat-related incident during the American intervention. And, unlike many other U.S. military actions, the intervention in Lebanon was short; the Marines were completely withdrawn by mid-October of 1958.

While it is easy to assert *post hoc* that this intervention was low risk, it is striking how lucky the United States was. American forces narrowly avoided open hostilities, not only with the groups leading the insurrection, but also with the Lebanese Army. In the hours following a coup in Iraq that toppled the Western-leaning government in Baghdad, Lebanese president Chamoun issued an emergency plea to the United States to help him stabilize Lebanon from what he described as an "externally driven" insurrection. Unaware of the impending coup in Iraq, the U.S. Sixth Fleet, loaded with combat Marines, had been floating in the eastern Mediterranean for two months monitoring the escalating instability in Lebanon and preparing for deployment there if necessary.

Despite this nearly two-month posturing, when the Marines were deployed to Beirut they possessed remarkably limited tactical and political intelligence about the conditions in the city.[3] They had no information about who might or might not be a "rebel" nor did they know which areas or districts of the city were controlled by rebel forces. Had their landing vessels not become hung-up on a sand bar that surprised Marine logisticians, the first two Marine companies would have landed and immediately advanced to the Beirut Harbor, taking a path right through the center of the rebel-controlled Basta District—a route that most certainly would have generated open fighting.[4] As it turned out, the one-day delay in deployment of the heavy equipment enabled U.S. embassy officials to intercept the Marines and instruct them to take an alternate route to the harbor and avoid areas under the control of rebel forces.

The Marines also did not realize that in the hours just prior to their landing the Lebanese Army chief of staff, General Fuad Chehab, had told U.S. ambassador Robert McClintock that several of his officers opposed the American intervention and were planning to resist it. An operational communications blackout, designed to improve the safety and security of the mission, prevented McClintock from warning the Marines. From the perspective of many Lebanese military officials, the American landing, despite having been requested by their president, was external interference in what they believed to be a purely domestic crisis between Chamoun and his political opponents. According to historian Fahim Qubain:

> The Lebanese military authorities were neither consulted nor informed of Sham'un's request. Moreover, the Lebanese army regarded its primary function as the defense of the country against foreign invasion. In line with this concept, it did not fully support the government, and had tried to remain neutral in a conflict which it regarded as primarily domestic in nature. In addition, the practical intentions and functions of the American forces were not clear then. Would they take military control of the country? Would they fight against the opposition? Were they in Lebanon to bolster the Sham'un regime? These were questions no one could answer at the time. But, since Sham'un requested the landing and

since UAR [United Arab Republic] and Soviet propaganda had been forecasting an Anglo-American invasion since the crisis began, the tendency was to answer such questions in the affirmative.[5]

Hence, the American Marines were on the beaches of Lebanon with the full approval of President Chamoun but not of the Lebanese Army.

On the second day of the intervention, this issue almost proved cataclysmic. On the morning of July 16, a Marine battalion, including several tanks, while moving into Beirut was stopped by Lebanese Army forces, who refused to allow the Americans to advance. It was quickly apparent to American officers on the scene that the Lebanese Army was "deadly serious" about blocking the American entry into Beirut. General Chehab warned Ambassador McClintock that if the Marines advanced, "Lebanese tanks would open fire."[6] As American and Lebanese military forces stared each other down with their tanks, rifles, and artillery, high-level U.S. and Lebanese diplomats and military officials conducted negotiations on the spot. After two tense hours, the Lebanese Army acquiesced on the condition that they lead the American troops into Beirut. Ambassador McClintock recorded that "real disaster was averted by a hair's breadth."[7]

This brief description of the near-misses that could have engulfed American forces in an intensely hostile, long-term guerrilla war in the Middle East illustrates, contrary to conventional views, how dangerous this deployment was.[8] Indeed, in the weeks before the decision to intervene was made, President Eisenhower repeatedly expressed his concern about the potential dangers of the mission, and special intelligence estimates on Lebanon predicted that American forces would find themselves in open and unpredictable hostilities with Egyptian- and Syrian-controlled subversives and with local Muslim populations who opposed President Chamoun.[9] After the order to enter Lebanon had been given, some in the administration had second thoughts about the intervention.[10] Eisenhower himself warned Vice President Nixon that American forces would probably meet significant resistance: "The trouble is that we have a campaign of hatred against us. . . . The people are on [Egyptian president] Nasser's side."[11]

The Argument

So why did Eisenhower decide to intervene in such a potentially risky situation? The argument presented in this chapter is that in the hours after the

Baghdad coup began Eisenhower believed the strategic threat to the United States from the actions in the Middle East warranted extraordinary measures—even if such measures entailed significant risks. The critical variable, however, was that in Lebanon, unlike in the crisis in Indochina four years earlier, Eisenhower and his advisors calculated that, based on their two-month long campaign to mobilize public sympathy for President Chamoun, they would be able to control the domestic political debate on the need for American action and to sell the conflict to the American public.

For two months prior to the July coup in Iraq, Lebanon had been engulfed in political turmoil. During this period, selective engagers in the Eisenhower administration developed alliances with selective engagers in Congress and the media to control the flow of information on the situation. In a deliberate campaign, the administration and its allies presented the Lebanese crisis in a simple good versus evil, right versus wrong dichotomy in which President Chamoun was the innocent victim of massive Egyptian and Syrian aggression. Furthermore, selective engagers consciously vilified Egyptian president Gamal Abdel Nasser as a puppet of the Soviet Union. By mid-June, Eisenhower's public relations campaign had engendered a small majority of support for U.S. military action in the region. Following the coup in Baghdad, Eisenhower and his advisors used the president's executive authority and the urgency of the crisis to act decisively in Lebanon and to launch an all-out effort to sell the military operation to the public.

Liberal, humanitarian, and noninterventionist opponents to American military intervention had expressed their opposition to American military action in support of Chamoun as early as late May, when the Lebanese crisis first surfaced. But, their efforts to organize and mobilize public and political opposition were hindered by their inability to collect independent information with which to challenge the administration's views on the credibility of President Chamoun. They were also unable to independently dispute the administration's claims about the magnitude of the external infiltration into the Lebanese conflict by Egypt, Syria, or the Soviets. Eisenhower's awareness of his opponents' inability to mobilize public and political opposition was integral to his decision to intervene in Lebanon.

The following sections summarize the views and strengths of the various advocacy communities prior to the conflict and discuss in detail the three stages in the decision-making process during the 1958 crisis in Lebanon.

Background of the Crisis

From the time Lebanon gained independence in 1943, its stability rested on a tenuous power-sharing agreement among Christians and Sunni and Shiite Muslims. The centerpiece of the agreement was the National Pact, which balanced the deep religious and cultural aspects of Western-oriented Christians, who had assimilated much of the language, culture, economics, and politics of imperial France, and Muslims, who remained closely aligned with Arab culture and traditions. To accommodate one another, Christians and Muslims agreed to recognize and respect each other's heritage while living within a single political state. To further stabilize the balance, Muslims agreed to renounce claims to Arab union, while the Christians renounced any direct alliance with the West and pledged to forego Western protection.[12] The constitutional provisions set the form of the governing institutions, in which the president would be a Maronite Christian—elected by the parliament—the prime minister would be a Sunni Muslim, and the speaker of the house would be a Shiite Muslim. The executive and legislative branches were to closely approximate proportional representation—a 6:5 ratio in favor of the Christians.[13]

This balance was extremely delicate. Attempts by Chamoun's predecessor, Bishara Khoury, to assert his control and domination over Lebanon by altering the constitution ended when Muslim and Christian moderates forced him to step down in 1952. As one commentator suggested, it was "virtually axiomatic in Lebanon, for the government to function, it must be acceptable to the important population blocs."[14] Chamoun's recognition of this facilitated his ascension to the presidency in 1952.

Chamoun's government was well received by the United States. In the wake of the Suez Crisis and the dissolution of English and French colonial power in the region, leading American officials felt it imperative that the United States step in to fill the power vacuum. Furthermore, Chamoun became increasingly wary of Nasser's pan-Arab nationalism and repeatedly encouraged a stronger American presence in the Middle East. In addition, his foreign minister, Charles Malik, was a Harvard-educated Ph.D. who had a long-established personal relationship with several senior U.S. officials, most notably Secretary of State John Foster Dulles.[15]

Chamoun's administration was only a slight improvement on his predecessor's. Overall economic conditions in the country improved and the corruption and graft that had brought the downfall of his predecessor was sharply curtailed. Nonetheless, Chamoun's regime was hardly a model of sanctity and fairness. Over the course of six years in office, Chamoun became increasingly controversial and contentious. He personally antagonized most opposition leaders—Christian and Muslim—by giving prime government positions to his loyal Maronite Christian supporters, and consequently, government resources were frequently and unequally distributed to Christian segments of the population. In addition, Muslim dissatisfaction festered as the benefits of the economic recovery benefited principally the Christian districts, generating even greater disparities of wealth among the population. Chamoun's policies opened him and his government to the fierce attacks, leveled against it by increasingly hostile Muslim and moderate Christian opponents.

The tension between Chamoun and his domestic opponents grew in early 1957 when Chamoun endorsed the Eisenhower Doctrine, which promised Middle Eastern countries U.S. aid in resisting communism. He was the only Middle Eastern leader to do so, and, while he was quickly championed by the Eisenhower administration, he came under intense attack from both internal and external opponents. His Muslim and moderate Christian opponents in Lebanon accused him of violating the National Pact by directly aligning Lebanon with the West. Regionally, Nasser's incipient Pan-Arab national movement quickly condemned the action and labeled Chamoun and Foreign Minister Malik "traitors" and "imperialist lackeys."[16]

But it was the fiasco surrounding the 1957 parliamentary elections that ultimately triggered the conditions for the mass unrest in 1958. The parliamentary election campaign was highly contentious, because the outcome of the elections would not only produce the parliament for the next four years but also determine the successor of President Chamoun, whose term was to expire in September 1958. Both the United States and Nasser exerted considerable energy to influence the outcome. The Egyptians and Syrians launched a barrage of anti-Chamoun propaganda via their national radio networks. In turn, Chamoun received significant U.S. covert assistance. In the end, he rigged many district elections to ensure a large parliamentary majority.[17] In some instances sizable cash payments were made to voters to ensure victory for pro-Chamoun delegates. The result was a landslide victory for Chamoun in what can only be termed fraudulent elections. The opposition won only 8 seats in the newly expanded parliament. Many of the most honest and popular opposition politicians were defeated.[18]

The significance of the huge parliamentary majority was not lost on the opposition. With his "victory," Chamoun had secured well over the two-thirds majority necessary to alter the constitution, which at the time prohibited him from succeeding himself as president. The opposition refused to accept the election results and intensified its active dissent to Chamoun's government. Chamoun, meanwhile, stepped-up police crackdowns on Muslim strikes and demonstrations.

Amid this emerging crisis inside Lebanon, Nasser moved in early 1958 to form the United Arab Republic (UAR) and began a campaign to promote a pan-Arab union and reduce the influence of the West throughout the Middle East.[19] Egypt and Syria, increasingly united in purpose, intensified their anti-Chamoun rhetoric over radio waves broadcast into Lebanon. Throughout the first four months of the year, sporadic violence erupted between pro-Chamoun and opposition factions there.

As the situation deteriorated, Chamoun and Malik charged that the violence was inspired from external Arab and "communist forces" seeking to subvert Lebanon's government. Despite these pronouncements, Lebanese Army chief of staff General Chehab, also a Christian, dismissed the claims of foreign interference and refused to take a side in what he and his senior command considered an entirely internal political feud. In early April, a pro-Chamoun delegate introduced a constitutional amendment that would allow Chamoun to stand for reelection. That same day, 300 leading Muslims signed a strong declaration against any constitutional amendment. Within weeks the constitutional crisis erupted into violence.

Elite Views toward the Middle East before the Crisis

Selective Engagers

In the wake of the British and French fiasco during the Suez Crisis in 1956, selective engagers became increasingly concerned about the influence of Nasser and of the Soviet Union in the Middle East. In early 1957, Eisenhower pressed Congress to pass the Eisenhower Doctrine, which proclaimed that the United States deemed the territorial integrity and political independence of the states of the Middle East to be in the United States' vital national interest. The doctrine stated explicitly that the United States would use force to assist any state which "requested assistance against armed aggression from any country controlled by international communism."[20]

For Eisenhower and his advisors, Nasser's brand of fiery Arab nationalism was a particularly acute threat to the political stability within the Middle East—especially because it resonated throughout Jordan, Syria, and Saudi Arabia.[21] Furthermore, with Nasser receiving military equipment from the Soviet bloc, selective engagers were convinced that the Soviets would exploit any expansion of the UAR to wrestle away control of the rich oil deposits of the Middle East.

This posed a dilemma for selective engagers. While they were suspicious of Nasser and believed that his unpredictability could create enormous problems for the United States and the West, they also believed that neither Nasser nor his Arab nationalists were yet under the direct control of Soviet communism. Consequently, American actions needed to be delicate, so as not to push those countries directly to the Soviet Union in the attempt to ensure the stability of the American position in the region.

The crisis in Lebanon exacerbated this dilemma. Selective engagers recognized the critical importance in the Middle East of Chamoun and his pro-Western stance. His was the first and only Middle Eastern government to openly embrace the Eisenhower Doctrine. Nonetheless, Eisenhower and the selective engagers knew that much of the crisis inside Lebanon was of Chamoun's own doing. The selective engagers in the State Department and the White House concluded that Chamoun's charges of external infiltration were overstated. They also believed that Chamoun's continuing efforts to alter the constitution and seek reelection were triggering the internal crisis.[22] But, the more pressing questions were: If Chamoun did not seek another term, who would replace him? And would Lebanon retain its pro-American position under different leadership? The dilemma, however, was that open support for a constitutional change would fuel anti-Americanism and give credence to Nasser's propaganda campaign. Thus, the American policy at the outset of the crisis was to support Chamoun's reelection but to downplay the support.[23] With no credible pro-American alternatives to Chamoun, Eisenhower's selective engagers set the United States firmly behind Chamoun. As the crisis ignited in early May, Eisenhower and the selective engagers were committed to defending the pro-Western orientation of Lebanon—especially from the agitation posed by Nasser and the UAR.

Hardliners

Unlike the selective engagers, most hardliners were convinced that Nasser had long been entrenched in the Soviet camp and that the UAR already was under Soviet domination. Within the U.S. military, Admiral Arleigh Burke, chief of naval operations, for example, argued that Nasser was nothing more than a proxy for Moscow. In public debates, columnists such as Joseph Alsop consistently berated the weak international response to the spread of Soviet influence as evidenced by Nasser's actions in the Middle East. Hardliners championed the State Department's annual survey of Communist Party strength throughout the world, which in 1958 reported that Syria was governed by "an alliance of pro-Soviet politicians, army officers, and opportunists" and that Beirut was "a center for the preparation and dissemination of Communist propaganda in the Near East."[24]

For the hardliners, the key to Middle East stability was the United States' ability and willingness to carry out the Eisenhower Doctrine. When Chamoun publicly embraced the Eisenhower Doctrine, Lebanon was seen by hardliners as more than just a vital ally; it became the centerpiece of American interests in the Middle East. During the 1957 parliamentary elections in Lebanon, hardliners in the Eisenhower administration pressed successfully for stepped-up covert actions to ensure that Chamoun gained control of his government.

Liberals

Liberals, for their part, were hesitant to embrace Eisenhower's views on the Middle East. While they shared his anticommunism, they were nonetheless concerned about his broad interpretation of communist involvement in the region. Shortly after Eisenhower announced his new doctrine, in January 1957, Senator Fulbright introduced a substitute doctrine. In it he called for a comprehensive settlement of the Arab-Israeli conflict that recognized the self-determination of Arabs and Israelis and for freedom of navigation through the Suez Canal.[25] Fulbright warned that the broad language of the Eisenhower Doctrine granted too much authority to the president to determine when force would be used. As a result, Fulbright's substitute doctrine intentionally stopped short of authorizing use of U.S. military force, because, according to Fulbright biographer Randall Woods, the senator "well knew perceptions of who was a communist and what constituted aggression could differ dramatically."[26]

During the Senate debate on the Eisenhower Doctrine, another prominent liberal, Adlai E. Stevenson, sat in the diplomatic gallery in the Senate chamber, speaking in protest of the doctrine. He argued that it was nothing more than "another military blank check, this time the right to send our forces into the Middle East."[27] Meanwhile, Senator Wayne Morse, a leading critic of Dulles and Eisenhower, introduced an amendment to the Eisenhower Doctrine demanding that, if the president intended to use force in the Middle East, he first notify Congress and provide a complete justification for the deployment.

Outside of the debates over the Eisenhower Doctrine in 1957, however, liberals were only sporadically focused on the Middle East. Much of the limited focus was on the Arab-Israeli dispute and the question of Palestinian refugees.[28] Several religious groups and peace organizations participated in fundraising and other public campaigns to help resettle displaced Palestinians and provide other support services to both Israeli and Palestinian civilians.[29] Very few Americans understood or followed events in Lebanon.

Liberals were paying little attention to the Middle East in 1958 because their primary concern was the mobilization of public opposition to the development of the atomic bomb. In the mid-1950s, a broad-based, grass-roots campaign waged a fierce battle in support of a comprehensive nuclear test ban treaty. The test ban campaign began in earnest in 1955 and gained national prominence during the 1956 presidential election campaign after Adlai Stevenson announced his support of a limited test ban treaty.[30] The nuclear test ban treaty consumed most of the liberals' organizational resources. Despite a growing number of hot spots around the world in 1958, by the time the Lebanese crisis intensified, in May and June, the primary effort of liberals was to block further testing of nuclear weapons.[31] Liberals had very little knowledge of, or resources in, Lebanon in the months and years prior to the crisis in mid-1958.

Reluctant Warriors and Noninterventionists

Old Guard Republican isolationists remained consistent in their skepticism of American commitments overseas—including the Middle East.[32] The views expressed by many noninterventionists found their voice in the *Chicago Tribune* and in several senior editors at the *Wall Street Journal*.[33] They applauded Dulles and Eisenhower for staying out of Indochina in 1954 and for resisting calls to intervene on behalf of France, Great Britain, and Israel during the Suez Crisis in 1956. Following congressional passage of the Eisenhower Doctrine in early 1957, isolationists became increasingly fearful that the United States was pursuing an overly aggressive policy in the Middle East. Critics of the Middle East policy argued that overzealous oil companies were consciously overstating the geostrategic importance of Middle Eastern oil. At the time, the United States was producing more oil than any other country, and they argued that depending on Middle Eastern oil would be extremely harmful to America's long-term interests.

In addition to the isolationists, Army military planners, as they had in the case of Dienbienphu, worried that if American troops were ever deployed to the Middle East they would find themselves confronting a hostile civilian population.[34] In particular, Army officials closely monitored the struggles of French forces fighting in Algeria and elsewhere in North Africa and feared that if the United States were ever called on to deploy to the region it would face a similar guerrilla-style conflict, which American forces were ill-prepared to fight.[35] As late as June 1958, Army planners told the *New York Times* that Lebanon would be "the worst possible place" for American intervention.[36]

Initial Preferences of Advocacy Communities

Thus, by the spring of 1958 the views on Lebanon and the Middle East were well established. Selective engagers and hardliners were particularly concerned with the rise of Nasser and the formation of the UAR. Liberals cared about stability and security in the Middle East but feared that the Eisenhower Doctrine granted the president too much discretion to use force. And, noninterventionists saw the Middle East as yet another situation that was certain to lead to even greater American commitments.

The Crisis: Four Stages of Decision Making

As in the Dienbienphu case, the decision to intervene in Lebanon was not a single decision but evolved over weeks and resulted in several decisions about American military action. In this case, three discrete periods appear: the immediate response to the May 8–13 riots, the response to renewed attacks in Beirut between June 13 and 16, and the response to the coup in Baghdad on July 14.

The May Riots

In May 1958, two events sparked an intense political crisis that concluded on July 15 with the American intervention. First, rumors spread throughout Lebanon that, even in the face of rising domestic dissent, President Chamoun was intent on pursuing a series of extra constitutional maneuvers to strengthen his presidential powers and to amend the Lebanese constitution so that he could retain his post past the constitutionally limited single term.[37] Second, on May 8, 1958, Nassib Al Matni, the popular editor of *Al Telegraph,* a Christian, and a leading opponent of Chamoun, was assassinated in Beirut. Opposition groups believed that the government was responsible for the killing, and they launched a series of protest actions, strikes, and demonstrations against the president.[38] The demonstrations quickly took on an anti-Western attitude; the United States Information Agency libraries in Tripoli and Beirut were burned and ransacked by rioters.

Over the next several days, the rioting led to organized fighting in Tripoli and Beirut. Heavy fighting broke out between Christian paramilitary forces and various Muslim factions. Muslim forces took control of most of Tripoli and Saïda. They also gained control of the Basta district in Beirut and large portions of the Bekáa Valley that paralleled the Syrian border. Druze tribesmen quickly took control of the Chouf district.

On May 13, President Chamoun called Ambassador McClintock to inquire what the U.S. response would be if he made an urgent plea for U.S. intervention under the Eisenhower Doctrine. Chamoun charged that the primary source of the violence and unrest was the subversive actions of Syria and Egypt in concert with international communist forces. The request generated the first crisis decision for the Eisenhower administration on Lebanon.

The Selective Engagers' Dilemma

The Eisenhower administration viewed the crisis in Lebanon as a complex set of domestic, regional, and global pressures, but privately it recognized that the crisis resulted mostly from Chamoun's own political ambitions and political grievances in both the Muslim and the Christian populations which he ignited. Indeed, throughout the pre-crisis period, the question of Chamoun's successor was the focus of embassy, State Department, and CIA analysis—with most reports warning about the dangers of internal political pressures.[39]

Regardless of the cause, however, the primary concern for selective engagers was the stability of the broader Middle East environment. Both selective engagers and hardliners quickly concluded that the crisis in Lebanon was another opportunity for Nasser to expand his pan-Arab nationalism. And, while the administration did not have direct evidence that Nasser was shipping equipment or personnel into Lebanon (i.e., no direct aggression) it did have intelligence confirming that Nasser was directing Egyptian and Syrian radio to broadcast anti-Chamoun messages into Lebanon.[40] Furthermore, Eisenhower and his advisors inherently distrusted Nasser and the anti-American tone of Arab nationalism. For several months in 1957, the administration had hoped for improvement in U.S.-Egyptian relations and had been making moves to achieve them. However, with the Syrian and Egyptian propaganda in Lebanon and the eruption of violence, selective engagers and hardliners quickly concluded that the stability of the entire Middle East was threatened by Nasser and the broader Arab nationalism that he was unleashing.[41]

On May 13, following Chamoun's request to McClintock, Eisenhower convened an emergency White House meeting on Lebanon with his top national security advisors. The ensuing debate revealed a great deal of anxiety and uncertainty on how to handle the request. On the one hand, they wondered what the United States could do to cope with rising pan-Arab nationalism throughout the region.[42] Dulles and Eisenhower initially speculated that overt American intervention might ignite an anti-American frenzy throughout the Arab world and make matters considerably more difficult for the United States. Dulles suggested that it might inspire Nasser to block shipping access to the Suez Canal and cut off oil supplies to the United States and its European allies and ultimately set off a global oil crisis. They wondered if American military action would be able to effectively quell the violence and if American troops would become caught in the political and military imbroglio without any way to withdraw.[43]

On the other hand Eisenhower, Dulles, and others expressed their clear concern about increasing instability in the region and possible effects on American geostrategic interests in the face of Soviet encroachments around the world and in the Middle East in particular. They agreed that the administration already had the basic authority to intervene, in the Eisenhower Doctrine. The president pointed out that there was already "considerable Congressional excitement" over Lebanon from hardliners and selective engagers and told his advisors that Senator William Knowland had already conveyed his sense that "resolute action" should be taken to stabilize the situation.

In addition, the administration was already feeling pressure from hardliners and selective engagers in Congress and the media because of intensifying anti-American sentiments and activities in Venezuela, Cuba, Indonesia, and Burma.[44] As Eisenhower later recalled with specific reference to the Lebanese situation, "the time was rapidly approaching when we had to move into the Middle East, and specifically into Lebanon, to stop the trend toward chaos."[45]

Especially given the vast untapped oil resources in the Middle East, both selective engagers and hardliners felt it was vital that the United States maintain its influence in the region. Dulles argued that if the they were to refuse a direct request from Chamoun, not only would the United States lose Lebanon, but others would see the failure of American resolve, and the United States would likely suffer losses elsewhere as a result. Eisenhower expressed concern about an increase in Soviet and communist subversion throughout the world and a proliferation of anti-American attacks if the United States did nothing.[46] As a result of these analytical judgments, during the May 13 NSC meeting, the selective engagers and the hardliners concluded that it was necessary that the United States respond affirmatively to any request for intervention.

Latent Public Opinion

The biggest concern at this point, however, was whether or not domestic opponents in Congress and among the American public would accept intervention in Lebanon.[47] While Eisenhower was predisposed to assist Chamoun, he was also adamant that any American military action would have to be tied to an assurance of firm public and political support. Throughout the deliberations on Lebanon, he routinely solicited the views of his advisors on the nature and position of potential public support for military action. During his five-and-a-half years in office to date, Eisenhower had not used American troops to intervene overtly in a foreign crisis. And, as demonstrated in the previous chapter, on the issue of using force overseas, he was particularly sensitive to public opinion.[48]

There was no overwhelming public opposition to American intervention in Lebanon in 1958. While opinion polls conducted an entire year before the crisis at Dienbienphu had revealed overwhelming opposition to American intervention there, no similar opposition was evident in the run-up to the Lebanon crisis in May 1958. In fact, the surge of anti-Americanism throughout the world, coupled with dramatic Soviet technological advances surrounding the launch of Sputnik in the fall of 1957, had sparked considerable unease among many Americans. Senator Henry "Scoop" Jackson, a leading hawkish Democrat, reflected the views of many Americans when he called for a national week of shame following the Sputnik launch.

Consequently, by the spring and early summer of 1958, while Americans were generally hesitant about deploying force, opinion polls revealed a desire for a stronger response to potential Soviet gains throughout the world.[49] However, it was not clear how this generalized anxiety would translate into particular attitudes toward an intervention in Lebanon. Clearly Eisenhower and his advisors did not have to worry about an established opposition to intervention. There was none. But there also was nothing in the polling data to reflect that the public could not be influenced against supporting military action in the Middle East.[50]

Building a Strategy to Frame the Issue and Mobilize Public Opinion

Since Lebanon was simply not on the public's radar screen in May of 1958, support would have to be built and managed. Because of this and in the face of potential liberal and noninterventionist opposition, the administration spent a considerable amount of time during the NSC meeting on May 13 discussing potential domestic opposition and identifying domestic and international legal strategies for American intervention.[51] The basic legal issue was whether or not a formal request from Chamoun would fall within the terms and conditions of the Eisenhower Doctrine. That doctrine specified explicitly that the president was authorized to use force in the Middle East in the event of overt communist aggression. Dulles acknowledged that Lebanon was not in imminent danger of attack from a communist country, but he suggested that the administration might be able to sell a broader interpretation of the Eisenhower Doctrine by highlighting the provisions acknowledging a presidential "mandate to do something when we think that our peace and vital interests are endangered from any corner."[52] Eisenhower would recall in his memoirs that he had believed a strong argument could be made justifying intervention: "here was one case where it appeared, if the Lebanese government should call upon us for help, we might move firmly and in accord with the local government and the principles of the United Nations."[53]

Nonetheless, at the end of the meeting, Eisenhower and his advisors agreed that further groundwork for mobilizing American domestic public and political support was necessary. First, Dulles and his staff went to work developing a stronger legal basis for American intervention. If the United States was going to intervene, it would be imperative that Americans believe there to be both domestic and international legal legitimacy in the action.[54] Second, the selective engagers and the hardliners agreed that unilateral intervention, without

UN or some Arab support, could quickly become a political liability at home and abroad. The initial response of liberals in Congress and the media had been to call for United Nations involvement to ease the crisis. Consequently, the administration realized from the outset that, to mollify domestic critics, it would have to begin a strong diplomatic effort to secure international support for the action. Third, Eisenhower and Dulles acknowledged that the United States could not be seen as simply propping up a politically ambitious Chamoun. The intensity of the May violence exposed Chamoun as a significant liability, which meant that the United States would have to find a strong, pro-Western successor quickly and then press Chamoun to step down.

Recognizing these political realities, the administration agreed to inform Chamoun that the United States would be prepared to honor a request from him for U.S. troops under these conditions: (1) Chamoun had to accept UN help to resolve the crisis; (2) Chamoun had to receive support from another Arab state; and (3) because Chamoun was at the center of much of the controversy, he had to declare that he would not submit his name as a candidate for a second term.[55]

In addition to the instructions to Chamoun, Eisenhower and his staff agreed that the administration must work diligently to frame the issue in Lebanon as an externally driven threat against a pro-American government. Over the course of the next several weeks, they engaged in a deliberate strategy to present the insurrection in Lebanon as being fueled primarily by Syrian and Egyptian elements.[56] They portrayed the crisis as a direct threat to the political independence and territorial integrity of a small democratic country by the powerful, unpredictable, and hostile forces of Nasser and pan-Arabism. While the selective engagers acknowledged that it would be difficult to declare that the UAR was under the direct control of the Soviet Union, they settled on a public posture in which they repeatedly *suggested* that the Syrian and Egyptian elements were acting at the behest of the Soviet Union. In this framework, Lebanon was under attack explicitly by Egypt and Syria, and implicitly by the Soviet Union. For example, during his May 13 press conference Dulles proclaimed that Lebanon's civil disturbances were fueled by "sources which we can very well imagine."[57] In another piece of the framing strategy, the administration downplayed or, often, simply avoided any public discussion of the domestic basis of the Lebanese crisis. Administration officials deliberately ignored questions about Chamoun's political antics that they themselves privately acknowledged had facilitated the crisis. The administration also argued that the president had a clear responsibility to protect the lives and property of several thousand Americans living in Lebanon, should they be imperiled by the violence there. And finally, although the administration had already assured Chamoun that the United States was prepared to intervene if he requested and met their conditions, they withheld this information from the public. In fact, according to Alan Dowty, Dulles deliberately "misrepresent[ed] the decision actually made in order to minimize possible negative repercussions; in a telephone conversation with James Reston of the *New York Times,* who had published a reasonably accurate account of the administration's decision, Dulles claimed that nothing had been said to Chamoun 'other than the possibility of moving troops in to protect American life and property.'"[58]

Executive Cohesion

This early effort to control the framework in which the situation was presented to the public was facilitated by the preexisting information advantages held by the administration. In the run-up to the crisis, the selective engagers, who dominated the Eisenhower inner circle, the higher echelons of the State Department, and the working levels of the Bureau of Near Eastern Affairs, had a virtual monopoly of information on the deteriorating situation. American intelligence efforts in the Middle East had intensified dramatically during the Eisenhower administration, and this enabled administration officials to collect a tremendous volume of information about political, military, and economic activities in the region. Not only did the selective engagers and hardliners in the administration possess significant institutional information-collection assets, but they also benefited from a strong cohesion of views. Compared to the debate over intervention in Indochina, noninterventionists were not as vocal within the senior ranks of the administration in 1958 during deliberations about Lebanon. Four years earlier, much of the debate had been generated at the Pentagon with Admiral Radford and General Ridgway as the two principal protagonists. Almost all of the initial discussion on Lebanon happened within the State Department.

This executive cohesion gave the administration more ability to control and manage the flow of information from the White House on the crisis in Lebanon than it had had during the Indochinese situation, when there was disagreement within the administration. At the outset of the crisis in Lebanon, Eisenhower restricted information to his closest advisors on the national security team. Even his cabinet members were left largely in the dark on events in the Middle

East.[59] Another result of this cohesion was that, unlike in 1954, there were almost no leaks of information on NSC deliberations.

Limited Opposition and Media Resources

Liberals and the media had little presence in Lebanon early in 1958 and were in a weak position from which to challenge the official narrative being presented by the administration. At the outset of the crisis, there were fewer than 3,000 Americans in Lebanon; most of them were American Christian missionaries with close ties to the country's Maronite Christian population and generally supportive of them and President Chamoun.[60] Very few liberal members of Congress had expertise or experience on Lebanon prior to the outbreak of the crisis in May. Despite passage of the Eisenhower Doctrine in 1957, questions about the integrity of the 1957 Lebanese parliamentary elections, and Nasser's formation of the UAR in early 1958, no senior liberal members of Congress had undertaken fact-finding missions to Lebanon. Throughout the early stages of the crisis, congressional liberals repeatedly expressed frustration with their inability to fully understand internal Lebanese political dynamics and the magnitude of external interference in Lebanon by Arab nationalists or international communists.[61]

As for the media's coverage of the crisis in Lebanon, prior to the crisis and during the initial weeks of it there were only a handful of American correspondents reporting from Lebanon.[62] Their dispatches during the first days of the crisis were largely limited to information disseminated by the U.S. embassy in Beirut. Several factors contributed to this. First, on May 9, the second day of turmoil in Tripoli, the American Information Library was burned to the ground. American reporters and their editors back in the United States focused their reporting on the damage to American property and on the potential further threats to American property and citizens.[63] For each of the major wire services, whose reports were disseminated to newspapers throughout the United States, the principal sources of information about the rioting in Lebanon were Chamoun's government, U.S. ambassador McClintock, or unnamed U.S. embassy officials.[64]

In addition, although McClintock had been in Lebanon for only a few months, he had spent much of his first several weeks as ambassador establishing close personal relationships with many of the American correspondents working in Beirut.[65] Ironically, McClintock also had been the American chargé d'affaires in Saigon during the Indochina crisis in 1954. Because he lamented his inability to control information about the situation at Dienbienphu, he frequently entertained journalists and correspondents at the embassy in Beirut and granted extensive private interviews with them to discuss the issues. His control over embassy information was notorious. While it generated some suspicion among a few of the correspondents, he nonetheless was willing to part with critical information to ensure a strong relationship with the correspondents, and they almost universally valued their connections with him.[66]

Finally, as with most media coverage of U.S. responses to crises overseas, the majority of the news stories on Lebanon were written by Washington-based White House or national security correspondents and relied heavily on information disseminated by the administration.[67] As a result, much of the early reporting conveyed the administration's portrayal of the insurrection as a pro-Soviet–inspired movement that could lead to Soviet domination throughout the vital oil region of the Middle East. Chamoun's political shenanigans that had fueled the crisis were consistently downplayed or ignored.

The Washington- and New York–based pundits, editors, and editorialists whom Eisenhower and his inner circle read with an eye toward anticipating the public mood consistently portrayed the events unfolding in Lebanon in the stark geostrategic terms presented by the administration.[68] The *New York Times* and *Washington Post* consistently referred to Lebanon's "plight" as resulting from the two equal "subversive forces" of communism and Nasserism operating in the region.[69] Chamoun's opponents were demeaned as communists, rioters, and Nasser-sponsored criminal elements. For example, Larry Collins of United Press International described the events as "pro-Western Lebanon, torn by a *leftist* uprising," and reported that the United Arab Republic of Egypt and Syria was participating in "'massive interference' aimed at the 'destruction' of this tiny nation."[70] Collins's wire reports were subsequently reprinted in hundreds of newspapers across the country. The *New York Times* editorialized on May 20 that Nasser was attempting to "seize Lebanon with the aid of his Communist allies as he attempted to seize Jordan and he did seize Syria."[71] In one notable example, when the Lebanese government charged that 500 Syrian troops had infiltrated Lebanon, Associated Press and United Press International wire dispatches reported the incident as fact rather than as an allegation by Chamoun's government.[72] The reports then formed the basis for a *Washington Post* editorial that urged the administration to protect "the tiny republic" from Nasser's hostile "thugs."[73]

Credible Threat

Three other circumstances reinforced the credibility of the selective engagers' framing of the violence in Lebanon as being sparked by international communism. First, the Lebanon crisis corresponded with Vice President Nixon's infamous trip to Latin and South America.[74] During his multicountry tour, Nixon was harassed on several occasions by hostile crowds. In Caracas his car was attacked by rock-throwing leftist students, and American naval forces were urgently deployed off the shores of Venezuela in case the threat to Nixon intensified. Second, during the same time period, American property in Algeria came under attack from anti-American Islamic groups protesting American support for the French. The administration and many commentators lumped these two incidents together and portrayed them as further evidence of stepped-up Soviet agitation against American interests around the world. Third, coincidental to the onset of violence in Lebanon, on April 29 Nasser had begun a high-profile visit to Moscow. While State Department and CIA analysts generally concluded that Nasser would not move too close to Moscow, selective engagers and hardliners—especially in Congress—condemned Nasser's visit and described it as evidence of his movement into the communist camp.

The upshot of Eisenhower's centralizing control over the collection and dissemination of official information, coupled with widely publicized attacks by leftist (often read as communist) anti-American forces in several areas of the world and with Nasser's trip to Moscow, gave the administration a significant advantage in framing the image of the Lebanese crisis to both the press and the public. The White House and the State Department continued to portray the crisis as one fueled by external agitation—an analytical narrative that increasingly seemed both plausible and probable.[75] Before ten days had passed after the crisis erupted, even though most Americans were still unsure about the need to deploy U.S. troops to Lebanon, Eisenhower's public relations experts and his inner core of advisors had concluded that most of the public were sympathetic to the plight of Chamoun.[76]

Further Strategizing: Invoking the Eisenhower Doctrine

While Eisenhower was aware that his message was resonating with the public, he and his advisors still remained concerned about how to formulate a legal basis for U.S. action. Without a sufficient legal justification, opponents in Congress probably would not be persuaded to support an intervention. Applying the Eisenhower Doctrine in this case presented some problems. First, there was no evidence that Moscow or international communism was at all involved. In fact, intelligence analyses concluded emphatically that the Soviet Union and international communism were not involved in the crisis. Second, neither Eisenhower nor Dulles wanted to declare that the UAR was under direct control of international communism, because they did not want to do anything that might encourage Nasser's move toward Moscow. And finally, they realized that much of the media was already concluding that "it might be difficult legally to prove" that the external interference was controlled by Moscow.[77]

Dulles concluded that the administration's best bet was to expand its interpretation of the Eisenhower Doctrine. Under this expanded interpretation, American intervention could fall under the Mansfield Amendment to the doctrine, which specified that "the United States regards as vital to the national interest and world peace the preservation and integrity of the nations of the Middle East." From this viewpoint, the United States would be acting to preserve the independence of Lebanon—without specifying the specific basis of the threat.

Dulles's attempt to recast the interpretation of the Eisenhower Doctrine, however, was not widely embraced. Most notably, Senator Mike Mansfield, who had written the amendment, argued that Dulles's interpretation of it went well beyond the legislative intent.[78] Liberal and noninterventionist press editorials began to appear concluding that the events in Lebanon did not warrant invocation of the Eisenhower Doctrine and, with varying intensity, appealing to the Eisenhower administration to pursue an international resolution through the United Nations. The *Christian Science Monitor* warned that the doctrine "apparently is being extended to cover practically any situation."[79] Famed journalist Edward R. Murrow also questioned whether the Eisenhower Doctrine might have been "devised to keep friendly governments in the Middle East in office against strong internal opposition."[80] Noninterventionists such as the *Wall Street Journal* concluded that the Eisenhower Doctrine was "not supported to empower the Executive to send troops rushing in to help countries that aren't even being attacked—just, for example, to support a government we might prefer to a government that might succeed it."[81] The *Chicago Tribune* declared that the Lebanese crisis illustrated the "folly" of American foreign policy.[82]

These challenges to the administration's position were closely monitored.

Dulles tasked the State Department's Office of Public Opinion Studies to report on all new developments in the Lebanon crisis. In a report to Dulles in early June, H. Schuyler Foster, director of the office, reported that, while it might be difficult to "legally prove" external aggression in Lebanon, most of the nation's public and political commentary reflected a high degree of sympathy for Chamoun and did support a more aggressive response in Lebanon if the president deemed it necessary. In a subsequent report submitted to the White House, Foster described the prevailing view among the public, quoting some of the phrases responders had used:

> The spectacle of "massive interference from outside" Lebanon against the Chamoun government, and the "violent anti-U.S. demonstrations" accompanying it, were regarded by virtually all observers as a "new test" of America's ability to "preserve some influence" in the Middle East. Some difference of opinion developed, however, as to how far the U.S. should go in aiding the Lebanese government.
>
> [However,] most commentators declared that the Lebanese turmoil resulted from an effort by "Nasserism and Communism" to topple the "pro-Western" Chamoun regime.[83]

In late May, as the administration was intensifying its aggressive public relations campaign to gain support for military intervention if need be, Chamoun and his internal security forces seemed to regain control of the situation in Lebanon. The fierce fighting in Beirut and Tripoli subsided and some order was restored. Still, the general sense within the Eisenhower administration was that Chamoun remained extremely vulnerable. General Chehab and the Lebanese Army continued to refuse requests from Chamoun to aggressively suppress the opposition groups. Chahab believed that the army would splinter along religious lines if he ordered it to side with Chamoun in his effort to alter the constitution.

During the brief lull, the Eisenhower administration turned to a diplomatic track to encourage Chamoun to find some way to resolve the situation without the need for American intervention. They pressed Chamoun to accept a United Nations investigation into Syrian and Egyptian interference in Lebanon. On June 12, the UN Security Council voted to send an observer mission to Lebanon to monitor border activity and to report to the secretary general on whether or not Syria and Egypt were directing the Lebanese insurrection or providing men, arms, or ammunition in support of the rebel forces. Dulles and

Eisenhower were hopeful that the UN investigation would present a compelling case against Nasser. They also hoped the UN mission would stifle liberal opposition.

The June Violence

After a two-week hiatus, the violence in Beirut again flared up. Opposition forces launched a direct assault on Chamoun's presidential palace. Within hours the fighting had again spread throughout Beirut and Tripoli. On June 14, the U.S. intelligence community concluded that Chamoun's position had "substantially deteriorated" and that Lebanon was now in a "state of civil war."[84] With his presidential palace surrounded, Chamoun again asked Ambassador McClintock whether or not the United States would intervene if asked. He cited extensive Syrian infiltration and told McClintock that he had reports of 500 Syrian parachutists dropping into Lebanon; he demanded that the United Nations monitors who were in Lebanon tell the world of this violation.

Secretary Dulles and President Eisenhower again began assessing military intervention. Now, however, the United Nations monitoring team seemed to be a burden. UN ambassador Henry Cabot Lodge warned Dulles that the international community would turn against any U.S. military action "if it were done without giving the UN observers a fair opportunity to get going."[85] Dulles also sensed that some members of Congress would object, and he warned Lebanese foreign minister Charles Malik on June 15 that American intervention during the UN mission "would be looked upon as undermining and causing to fail what some might feel is a vigorous and promising UN initiative."[86] He stressed, "It would be catastrophic to lay ourselves open to such a charge" and stipulated that military intervention would be undertaken only with the concerted effort of other Arab states, such as Jordan and Iraq. Dulles also argued that the United States should not do anything "before taking certain further actions in the UN."[87]

On June 15, Eisenhower convened a second emergency White House meeting on Lebanon. His frustration seemed evident. He wanted stability in the Middle East and felt that only stronger action could ensure it. Deciding that the United States would intervene if Chamoun requested it, he was nevertheless concerned about both the military and domestic political costs of any intervention. Intelligence reports briefed to the president concluded that an intervention to save Chamoun would likely result in American forces facing open hostilities with UAR subversives as well as with Muslim and Christian opponents to Chamoun. Furthermore, the selective engagers were still keenly aware that the absence of direct and explicit external aggression limited the utility of the Eisenhower Doctrine and could enable domestic opponents to rally support against American involvement.[88]

Eisenhower and his staff remained frustrated with Chamoun's handling of the situation. Chamoun had not sacked General Chehab, who had still not engaged the Lebanese Army in opposing the opposition forces. Eisenhower lamented, "How can you save a country from its own leaders?"[89] The president commented that Chehab was symptomatic of the whole situation. There seemed nobody on whom the United States could pin its hopes. Under such circumstances, he thought, even if the United States did intervene upon a Lebanese request, it would be difficult to develop a withdrawal strategy that would enable the United States to leave behind an improved situation. "Where would it lead; where would it end?" he asked. According to minutes of the meeting, Eisenhower told his advisors that "he had little, if any, enthusiasm for . . . intervening at this time."[90]

Despite Eisenhower's obvious frustration, the staff concluded that the events in Lebanon were still fluid and that any decision on intervention would wait on further developments. The administration developed a two-track strategy. First, the selective engagers worked diligently to find a diplomatic resolution whereby Chamoun would voluntarily step down in favor of a less controversial successor. The members of the top echelons of Eisenhower's national security team remained hopeful that Chamoun would be able to resolve the crisis internally.[91] Simultaneously, in case that strategy should fail, the selective engagers continued to cultivate public support for possible action in Lebanon. Eisenhower and the other selective engagers wanted to make sure that there would be no domestic obstacles to a firm American response.[92]

The Public Relations Campaign Continues

As deliberations on intervention again intensified, the administration focused on a concerted public relations campaign to frame the issue in Lebanon as one in which the "tiny pro-Western democratic" government of President Chamoun was under attack from Nasser and communist forces.[93] On June 17, Dulles told a press conference that ensuring Lebanese democracy was a vital interest for the United States. He emphasized that the free people of Lebanon deserved American support in their battles against evil forces and that, while the administration would likely respond with American forces if the United

Nations asked for such force, as the leader of the free world, the administration might also respond to "other possible contingencies."[94] In other words, Dulles refused to rule out unilateral intervention. The following day, Eisenhower re-iterated the need to help the tiny, pro-democratic country and that he could not "make predictions on the conditions" under which the United States might use force.

In addition to a deliberate rhetorical strategy, Eisenhower stressed to his advisors the need for the administration to rely on its executive institutional advantages to ensure maximal control over the public discussion on Lebanon. Over the course of the next few weeks, the administration selectively disclosed information to key Republican allies in Congress—information that was ultimately leaked—that stressed that the U.S. had extensive intelligence revealing a high degree of Syrian infiltration into Lebanon. Eisenhower worried that the press remained ready to jump the gun on Lebanon. In mid-June he warned Dulles that the administration needed to proceed delicately on the subject of Lebanon, to avoid a press feeding frenzy on the crisis. Overt contacts with the congressional leadership might tip off the media, because of the "close watch" the press kept on Dulles. Eisenhower figured that if the press saw Dulles holding urgent meetings with members of Congress they would "make a great crisis out of it."[95]

In Beirut, Ambassador McClintock was now conducting the daily press briefings himself, having ordered that he would be the only member of the U.S. delegation in Lebanon to address the press. He also personally coordinated meetings between reporters sympathetic to the administration's policies and Chamoun's representatives. In mid-June he arranged a one-on-one interview between Chamoun and noted hardline columnist Joseph Alsop. In Alsop's column on June 19, he presented a highly sympathetic portrayal of Chamoun.[96]

Liberal and Noninterventionist Response

When the June violence erupted, liberals and noninterventionists in Congress finally began to express concern that the United States was edging closer to the brink of military action. Several liberals began researching the situation and became convinced that Chamoun's own political ambition had precipitated the crisis.[97] They further concluded that American military force probably could not remedy Chamoun's troubles, and they questioned the legal basis for American military intervention. Senators Wayne Morse and Mike Mansfield both challenged the administration's intention to invoke the Eisenhower

Doctrine.[98] And, Senator Hubert Humphrey argued that only UN action would be acceptable.

Limiting their ability to dispute the administration's assessment, however, was Congress's lack of independent information. On June 23, Dulles, while briefing members of the Senate Foreign Relations Committee, told skeptics such as Morse, Mansfield, and Fulbright that there was no doubt that the United Arab Republic was "interfering in the situation" and that the United States government had collected intelligence of "more than 100 separate incidents" in which UAR forces had "come across or sent supplies" and that UAR radio transmissions had had "a tremendous impact in the area."[99] In response to questions by liberal skeptics, Dulles emphasized that he would not "discuss those specific instances because it would have the effect of breaching sources of information which [the United States] still wanted to utilize in the future."[100] In the following days, several liberal members of the committee lamented that they still had no real information, because they had yet to receive a full and complete report on the situation in Lebanon.[101]

Press Response

Further hindering the efforts of liberals to challenge the administration's perspective was that most of the news media continued to accept the administration's line that the real threat in Lebanon came from Nasser and from international communism.[102] The *New York Times* editorial board—which had endorsed a UN strategy to cope with the crisis—had been persuaded by the administration's line that there would be no violence in Lebanon "without pressure from Cairo and Moscow."[103] On June 12, the *Washington Post* concurred, saying, "The Chamoun government is the legal government of Lebanon; and it has been subjected to unconscionable interference."[104] Four days later the paper argued in its lead editorial that if Chamoun fell, "the entire Middle East would be on notice that friendship with the West is no guarantee of independence and can be an invitation to disaster."[105] It further asserted that "any prolonged faltering by the West . . . could easily spread to a major war."[106] Columnist Drew Middleton of the *New York Times* voiced the argument that if Lebanon failed, all of the Arab states would fall to the Soviet camp, and then the West would lose all access to Middle Eastern oil and eventually to all of Africa.[107] And on June 27, Joseph Alsop, back from Lebanon, wrote that the Eisenhower administration could cause another "Munich in Beirut" if it did not immediately come to the aid of Chamoun.[108] He warned that a month of "wriggling and writhing" by the American government had allowed the rebels to "heavily" reinforce themselves and dig themselves in, thereby increasing the costs of the necessary American intervention.

In short, by mid-June, as a small group of liberals began to step up their public questioning of the administration's portrayal of Lebanon, the paradigmatic debate had already become entrenched. Most of the press and the public already believed that Chamoun, for all of his faults, was the unfortunate victim of a corrupt and devious strategy by Nasser and international communists to gain complete control over the Middle East.

The entrenchment of this narrative of the crisis was particularly evident in the wake of the UN monitoring team's report on the Lebanese crisis. After more than two weeks of inspections, the UN team stated in their preliminary report that they were unable to identify any Syrian incursion along the Lebanese-Syrian border. While the report listed a series of problems the observers faced in securing access to several border areas, it nonetheless concluded that at best the Lebanese government's charges of Syrian and Egyptian infiltration were grossly exaggerated.[109] The report declared that Lebanese government claims of capturing Syrian military officers had been fabricated for the purposes of gaining international sympathy.

While the UN observers' findings were widely reported, most major news organizations dismissed their report. Relying instead on U.S. government officials' accounts, both the *Washington Post* and the *New York Times* claimed that the report was heavily flawed on a number of grounds. They both wrote in news stories and editorials that the administration's intelligence had been collected using more "sophisticated" techniques. The *New York Times* belittled the UN report, proclaiming, "On the basis on which the United Nations observers rest their preliminary and obviously inconclusive findings they would have found no Nazi interference in [interwar] Austria either. The United States, Britain, and France with experienced observers on the spot for a longer period support the Lebanese government's charges."[110] Furthermore, said the *Times,* anonymous U.S. government officials called the UN observer team a small group of "international bureaucrats" who were not given sufficient access to the border regions.

In Washington, the administration watched the fallout over the UN mission closely. Despite an ostensibly independent United Nations investigation, Public Opinion Studies director Schuyler Foster reported to Dulles that the analysis and commentary of most of the major news editors around the country continued to reflect the administration's portrayal of the conflict as fueled principally by external agitators. Others, including those that had previously been critical of the administration, simply presented the United Nations report as "highly inconclusive."[111]

By early July, the political case for military intervention had been constructed by the Eisenhower administration. The prevailing view had become that Nasser posed a significant and credible threat to Lebanon and hence to American interests throughout the Middle East. Liberals in Congress remained skeptical that Egypt and Syria were providing men and materiel to Chamoun's opponents. They continued to question why General Chehab would not engage the Lebanese Army to confront a widespread external interference in his country.

The Baghdad Coup and the Intervention

On July 14, the crisis in Lebanon intensified dramatically. That morning, pro-Nasser Iraqi forces successfully launched a coup in Baghdad, overthrowing the pro-Western Hashemite monarchy in Iraq. When Eisenhower urgently assembled the National Security Council to discuss the range of U.S. responses, the centerpiece of the discussion was immediate American intervention in Lebanon.[112] Shortly before the meeting, Eisenhower talked to British prime minister Harold Macmillan, who told him that the British were prepared to intervene in Jordan, to stabilize the pro-Western government there, if the United States sent troops into Lebanon. The NSC concluded that, although there might be significant risks associated with the intervention, the die had been cast. Doing nothing would enable Nasser to take control of the entire Middle East; the United States would lose influence throughout the region; and ultimately, American credibility worldwide would suffer. The coup in Iraq, they felt, would only bolster the case they had already presented for intervention.[113]

Following the NSC meeting, members of Congress were briefed on the situation. Dulles presented the case in very stark terms. After outlining the risks, he told members that Chamoun would no longer be able to "preserve Lebanese independence" without direct American intervention. He warned that if the United States did not intervene, the impact from "Morocco to Indo-china—would be very harmful to us. Turkey, Iran and Pakistan would feel—if we do not act—that our action is because we are afraid of the Soviet Union. They will therefore lose confidence and tend toward neutralism." The secretary of state concluded his warning by proclaiming: "If we do not act we will have to take losses greater than if we do. We would soon be faced with a stronger Soviet Union, with a worsened and weakened situation on our side."[114]

Selective engagers and hardliners among the congressional delegation quickly embraced the option of military intervention. Senator Knowland argued, "We must respond to the appeal from Chamoun or see the whole area go down the drain piece by piece." Senator Bridges asserted that the United States had a commitment to Chamoun, and opined, "If the Middle East goes, all of Africa immediately goes as well."[115]

Liberals questioned whether or not the situation was really one of Nasser- and communist-backed insurrection or an internal civil strife. Senator Fulbright declared himself unconvinced that the Soviets were inspiring the situation. He reiterated that the United Nations had found that "the strife" was "not being supported from the outside." And Senator Mansfield queried why the administration would move before putting the issue to the United Nations.[116]

In response, Dulles and Eisenhower again relied on their institutional information advantages. Dulles told the group that the UN mission had been flawed—and besides, the situation had now, a month later, changed significantly. Eisenhower and Dulles also stressed that all the information in their possession suggested that the Soviets would benefit significantly from U.S. inaction. Dulles stated emphatically, "The situation will not permit delay, nor should the Soviets have time to create trouble."[117]

The meeting solidified Eisenhower's feeling that his administration had effectively laid the necessary groundwork to generate public and political support for the intervention. Following the meeting, he formally gave the order to intervene.

Influence of Public and Political Support on Intervention

Eisenhower was clearly concerned about public and political support as he considered intervention. In almost every meeting in which military intervention was deliberated, he questioned his advisors about the general public and political mood. In the wake of his decision to intervene, he demonstrated his confidence in his public relations campaign. In a draft of a letter that he wrote to Harold Macmillan, Eisenhower expressed his views of the importance of the prerequisites of public support for military action:

> Democracies exert a tremendous power for accomplishment when there exists an over-whelming and favorable public opinion. An informed public opinion

requires mass understanding. The evidence that our understanding is not all that it should be is found in the reluctance of Congress to appropriate money for domestic information programs, mutual security costs, and economic improvement of less developed nations. . . . there is no question in my mind the need for success in creating an informed public opinion here and possibly in your country. . . . If a vast majority of our peoples stand four-square and sturdily behind the great effort to preserve the Middle East we need not fear either the dictators in the Kremlin or a puppet in Cairo.[118]

Even after the decision had been reached, Eisenhower and his advisors explored how best to consolidate and sustain public support. They discussed two options: a formal address to both houses of Congress or a nationwide television broadcast. They were already confident of widespread public support, and they did not want to overstate the intervention and set off a broader war scare, but they decided on a nationally televised address.[119]

On the evening of July 15, 1958, Eisenhower delivered a nationally broadcasted radio and television address. He told a captivated audience that history had shown that when the free people of the world fail to challenge and punish aggression, evil forces will prevail. He cited the Nazi aggression in Czechoslovakia in 1938 and the communist victory in China in 1949 as failures of containment policies, and he pointed out how the determination of the West during the Greek crisis in 1947 and the Korean conflict in 1950 had effectively stopped communist advances. He explained that the presence of American forces in Lebanon would also provide security to the thousands of Americans living there.[120]

The related public opinion campaign highlighted that, since President Chamoun had requested U.S. intervention, the action was legally justified under Article 51 of the United Nations Charter. In fact, the administration further argued, the United States had a moral obligation to provide direct assistance to a friendly nation in need. To combat opposition by the noninterventionists, Eisenhower and Dulles warned that communist domination of Middle East oil fields would strangle the American economy and "way of life." Finally, they both referred to the U.S. action as the "stationing" of American forces in Lebanon, rather than as military intervention.

Dulles urgently assembled an off-the-record, not-for-attribution briefing for American correspondents at the home of Richard Harkness of NBC.[121] He told the reporters that the United States had received highly sensitive intelligence that a similar coup was likely in Jordan, that "it was entirely directed from Cairo and Damascus," and that extensive evidence pointed to "intervention in Lebanon and Jordan from the outside." He described the "meticulously executed coup in Iraq" as evidence of powerful external forces. The Defense Department contributed to the campaign by publishing and distributing millions of leaflets justifying the American action. The Pentagon participated in newsreels that were shown in movie theaters across the country. This extensive and choreographed activity constituted an unprecedented effort by a president to convince the American public of the need for military forces to be sent to a civil crisis.

Eisenhower's assessment of the political space for intervention proved correct. Polling conducted by Gallup on the day after the action found that more than three-fourths of Americans fully supported the decision.[122]

Summary

No one predicted at the outset of the American intervention in Lebanon that it would be either easy or short. No one knew what might be the response of those fighting Chamoun's forces or even the Lebanese Army. For these reasons, the president and the secretary of state both had significant reservations about using force and hoped to resolve the crisis diplomatically. Yet, throughout the crisis, Eisenhower and Dulles both believed that American interests and credibility were on the line. Following the coup in Baghdad, Eisenhower concluded that, on the basis of his assessments of the costs and benefits, the United States needed to take action.

For two months before the decision was made, Eisenhower and his selective engager advisors exerted control on the flow of information about the Lebanese crisis and cultivated public and political support for President Camille Chamoun. They engaged in an extensive campaign to frame the conflict as one in which a tiny democratic friend of the United States was imperiled by the evil forces of international communism. As historian Douglas Little wrote: "It was far simpler, Ike and his advisors believed, to exaggerate the communist threat in Lebanon and stretch the logic of the Eisenhower Doctrine to the breaking point than to risk defeat on Capitol Hill by seeking congressional approval for the use of U.S. troops to combat anti-Western Arab nationalists."[123] The administration's efforts were aimed at a receptive latent public opinion. Most Americans already endorsed strong U.S. action in the Middle East.

The selective engagers and hardliners in the administration consciously employed their significant advantages in information and propaganda regarding the crisis. There was extensive executive cohesion—unlike during the Indochina crisis in 1954—and, as a result, very few leaks to the press. To the extent that information did flow from Lebanon, the major U.S. news organizations had only a small handful of reporters on the ground and few of those traveled outside of the immediate Beirut area to acquire their stories. Many of the reporters relied on information from the U.S. embassy officials and, consequently, the reports presented in the U.S. media systematically portrayed the crisis exactly as the administration intended. Chamoun was consistently portrayed as a sympathetic character. There was little or no reporting of the questionable political maneuvering that Chamoun had engaged in, which had precipitated the crisis. Nor was there much discussion of the evidence (or lack thereof) of actual communist infiltration in the Lebanese revolt. To the extent that administration critics invoked the United Nations observer mission's report of minimal external interference, the administration used their institutional advantages by ambiguously referring to classified intelligence reports that contradicted the monitors' report—all of which was part of a concerted campaign to undermine the credibility of the UN monitors and to prevent critics from challenging the administration's viewpoint. Americans, firmly believing that the U.S. military action was in support of a small democratic friend who was up against a brutal communist campaign, backed the intervention.

CHAPTER FOUR

Battling the Vietnam Syndrome in Grenada

How are we going to sell this to the public? —ROBERT MCFARLANE,
NATIONAL SECURITY ADVISOR

We got away with it by establishing special ground rules, by not letting
the press in and justifying it later. —MICHAEL K. DEAVER,
DEPUTY CHIEF OF WHITE HOUSE STAFF

Grenada, we were told, was a friendly island paradise for tourism. Well, it
wasn't. It was a Soviet-Cuban colony, being readied as a major military
bastion to export terror and undermine democracy. We got there just in
time. —PRESIDENT RONALD REAGAN

Introduction

On the morning of October 25, 1983, President Ronald Reagan stepped
before the microphones at a hastily gathered press conference in the White
House and announced:

> Ladies and gentlemen, on Sunday, October 23, the U.S. received *an urgent formal
> request* from the Organizations of Eastern Caribbean States to assist in a joint
> effort to restore order and democracy on the island of Grenada. We acceded to
> the request to become part of a multinational effort with contingents from
> Antigua, Barbados, Dominica, Jamaica, St. Lucia, St. Vincent, and the United
> States.
>
> I might add that two of those, Barbados and Jamaica, are not members of the
> organization but were first approached, *as we later were,* by the OECS and asked
> to join in that undertaking. And then all of them joined unanimously in asking
> us to participate....
>
> ... when I received reports that a large number of our citizens were *seeking*

to escape the island, thereby exposing themselves to great danger, and after receiving *a formal request* for help, a unanimous request from our neighboring states, I concluded that the United States had no choice but to act strongly and decisively.[1]

With this statement, President Reagan officially informed the American public that U.S. combat forces had been deployed on their largest overseas combat mission since the Vietnam War. The American assault force descended on the tiny Caribbean island nation of Grenada a week after the Marxist prime minister, Maurice Bishop, was overthrown and executed by more fervent Marxist elements.

In the ensuing battle, American forces clashed with Grenadan soldiers and Cuban construction workers and successfully evacuated more than 1,000 American citizens from the island. Less than a week later, all hostilities had ended and American forces were firmly in control of the island. Nineteen Americans died in the action, 119 were wounded; 45 Grenadans and 24 Cubans were killed. For their actions, the 6,000 U.S. soldiers received an unprecedented number of military honors per soldier, making Grenada the most decorated military action in American history. By February 1984 almost all American troops had been withdrawn, a quasi-democratic government had been restored to the island, and the Cuban and Soviet presence had been completely eliminated. President Reagan had deployed American force and succeeded resoundingly.

The Argument

As in Lebanon in 1958, because of the quick success of the American military forces, the action in Grenada does not generate much scholarly curiosity or scrutiny. The basic historical view is that the U.S. military deployment was a case in which the president could score a quick and easy victory, the risks to the U.S. military were very low, and the resounding success was certain to generate high political benefits.[2] The details of the situation in Grenada, however, reveal that senior officials in the Reagan administration were troubled by the complex context of the risks that would be associated with military action. While no one believed that the United States would suffer a military defeat in Grenada, even at the time of the invasion senior military commanders expressed great concern about the limits of the intelligence they had been provided and their ability to secure the safety of American citizens. In addition, as will be discussed below, from the outset of the crisis, in early October 1983, senior administration officials were acutely aware of the effects of the Vietnam War and expressed significant concern about the political risks of military action. Grenada was a much riskier action than is often portrayed.

The argument presented here demonstrates that the selective engagers and hardliners who dominated the Reagan administration firmly believed that Grenada posed a significant threat to American national security. For the hardliners, the evidence of a 10,000 foot runway under construction at the new Port Salinas airport, in conjunction with the Grenadan New Jewel Movement's stated Marxist-Leninist principles and open support from Moscow and Havana were clear indications of Soviet and Cuban attempts to expand international communism in the Caribbean. For the selective engagers, the anarchy on the island, the potential for an Iran-style hostage crisis, the willingness of right-wing neighboring Caribbean states to support American military action, the expectation of low military costs, and the appeal of rolling back Marxist influence in Grenada combined to favor American military action in this case.

Once the initial preference for intervention was established by Reagan and his senior advisors, the administration moved to develop the sufficient political space for that action. President Reagan's hardline anticommunist policies in Latin America during his first two years in office had triggered sharp criticism from liberals in Congress, and he and his advisors were keenly aware of the potential domestic opposition to military action in Grenada. Anticipating this opposition, Reagan tightened his grip around the decision-making process and developed an explicit campaign to ensure public support. First, he and his advisors used their institutional resources to establish a complete block of information regarding the military plans. They also cultivated a deliberate strategy to frame the crisis as a threat to American students attending St. George's University Medical School on the island, in order to sell it to the American public once the time came to release information about the invasion. And, through intense, secret diplomatic efforts, the administration pressed the Caribbean states to publicly request American military intervention. Then the administration presented this request to the American public as though it had been made wholly independent of U.S. influence. Finally, the administration assembled a team of Justice Department and State Department lawyers to craft an international and domestic legal justification for the action that could help deflect domestic opposition by framing the action as consistent with international law. In addition to utilizing the administration's executive resources, Reagan and his team evaluated the magnitude of opposition resources. They concluded that, before and during the action, liberals had virtually no presence on the ground in Grenada. Furthermore, after the coup ousting Maurice Bishop, journalists had been expelled from Grenada; and in the immediately post-coup period, the new regime strictly censored all domestic reporting. Consequently, there was almost no information emanating from Grenada other than official U.S. government statements.[3] As a result of these factors, Reagan and his team calculated prior to their decision to intervene in Grenada that as long as they could maintain their information advantages and frame the analytical debate on the crisis, they would be able to win the battles for public opinion.

Background of the Crisis

The political events in Grenada first captured the attention of senior policymakers in Washington on March 13, 1979, when a small group of the leftist New Jewel Movement (NJM) successfully launched a bloodless coup and proclaimed the People's Revolutionary Government (PRG). Grenada had gained its independence from Great Britain in 1974 and until the NJM's coup had struggled with corruption, fraud, and repression under the leadership of Eric Matthew Gairy. Gairy's notorious security guard "the Mongoose Gang" frequently launched violent campaigns to repress his domestic opponents.[4] When the NJM successfully established the PRG government, led by Prime Minister Maurice Bishop, the public overwhelmingly supported it.[5] Bishop immediately suspended Gairy's 1974 constitution and implemented participatory democracy, ostensibly to return power to the people. Bishop proclaimed the revolution to be a victory for the people and championed a broad range of social programs to alleviate poverty and malnutrition and to improve health care and education.[6] However, despite its turn to the left, the new government maintained Gairy's pattern of suppression of organized opposition and controls on the press.

Of particular concern to the United States was the new government's anti-American rhetoric and direct solicitation of material support, arms, and training from Cuba and other Soviet bloc states. In late 1979, Bishop and Cuba's leader, Fidel Castro, concluded a deal whereby Cuba began providing skilled labor and financial resources to construct a new international airport, at Port Salinas. Six months later, Bishop welcomed a Soviet fleet to Grenada and established formal relations with Moscow. At the time, Grenada's People's Revolutionary Army was largely trained by Cuban advisors and armed with Cuban weapons.

Each of these moves was viewed with concern in Washington, and the diplomatic relationship between Grenada and the United States deteriorated. The Reagan administration came into office in January 1981 and saw the events in Grenada in highly ideological terms.[7] Very early in its tenure, the Reagan administration stepped up efforts to isolate the Bishop regime and destabilize it with international financial prohibitions. Congress and the press (as well as the Grenadan government) learned in April 1981 that the Central Intelligence Agency, under Director William Casey, had developed contingency plans for American destabilization of the Grenadan government.[8]

These disclosures fueled the paranoia of the PRG regime, which was firmly "convinced that the CIA was behind any and all forms of domestic opposition, and that an American invasion was almost always on the horizon."[9] The PRG closely monitored the American press and interpreted negative reports on the revolution as a clear sign that Washington was orchestrating a destabilization effort to overthrow the PRG.[10] Bishop often lamented that the United States "conveniently overlooked" the nature of Grenada's relationship with Cuba, which provided Grenada with significant assistance in medicine, dentistry, and education, not just arms. Consequently, Bishop and the PRG regularly launched vehement verbal attacks on the American government, invoking socialist and Marxist-Leninist rhetoric.

Despite the intensity of PRG's anti-imperialistic rhetoric, and even though it clearly had established close ties to Cuba and the Soviet Union, it did not simply become a puppet of Cuba or the Soviet Union. In 1980, it formally joined the nonaligned movement. It continued to maintain its British Commonwealth status (and continued to accept British subsidization of many of its exports). It also openly courted and received foreign assistance from several European and South American countries and from Canada.

Within Grenada, however, the economy continued to be plagued by limited growth and a weak infrastructure. The country relied heavily on unreliable foreign direct investment and aid programs. In 1982, unemployment began rising, cash flow problems and curtailment of foreign aid threatened capital investment projects in agriculture and fisheries, and the effort to collectivize the agricultural sector was met with increasingly stiff resistance by the peasantry. For the first time since the revolution, the government announced layoffs. This led to increased disenchantment with the PRG, and the public began expressing its dissatisfaction with the government's restrictions on political opposition.[11]

As the public agitation grew, conservative Marxists within the PRG led by Bishop's deputy premier, Bernard Coard, demanded greater party discipline and instituted a more centralized party structure.[12] This centralization was a direct challenge to Bishop; Coard accused Bishop of abandoning the revolution and pursuing a "petty bourgeois route." Enhancing the conservative angst was the fact that, while the PRG's popularity was declining, Bishop remained highly popular. The conservatives perceived this as a direct threat to the collective structure of the central decision-making structures and feared that Bishop might move to institute singular control of the country.

Meanwhile, Bishop, recognizing the economic imperative of international tourism, and particularly of American dollars, began attempts to improve U.S.-Grenadan relations. By the end of 1982 he had established close relationships with several members of Congress—most notably Congressman Ronald Dellums and the members of the Congressional Black Caucus. In May 1983, Bishop traveled to the United States, where he publicly expressed "a desire for improved relations" between the two countries.[13] Even though the Reagan administration spurned Bishop's visit, refusing to grant him meetings with the president or the secretary of state, he returned from the United States requesting of his supporters a reduction in the anti-American rhetoric.

However, the "reform" efforts of Bishop were met with increased scrutiny by Coard and his faction. At the PRG Supreme Central Committee meeting held in mid-September 1983, Bishop came under direct verbal attack. Coard accused him of abandoning the revolution by "selling out" in "agreements with imperialism." Coard and the other conservatives demanded that Bishop acknowledge his "petit bourgeois conduct" and relinquish his "onemanism" leadership. The deputy prime minister and his supporters accused Bishop of undermining the discipline of the party, and they voted to establish a joint leadership structure that reduced Bishop's power.

Under pressure, Bishop reluctantly accepted the new arrangement; but by early October, Bishop began to have second thoughts about the increasingly hardline direction of the party.[14] After a wave of vicious rumors circulated among the party hierarchy of a likely violent conflict between Bishop and Coard, the Coard faction came forward, accused Bishop of a "putschist plot," and on October 13 army troops loyal to the hardliners placed him under house arrest.

As news of Bishop's arrest spread, Grenadans released their accumulated anger by taking to the streets and chanting "No Bishop, No Revolution!" Coard, sensing the potential for widespread instability and in an attempt to dispel public outcry that he was responsible for an unlawful takeover of the PRG, announced his own resignation from the Central Committee. On October 19, a large crowd of Bishop's supporters descended on his house, overwhelmed the armed guards detaining him, and freed him. He and the crowd then walked to Fort Rupert above the city of St. George's. As the group demonstrated in celebration of his release, three armored troop carriers arrived and opened fire on them. Civilians were wounded and several were killed in the ensuing melee. Bishop and his key advisors were captured, escorted back to Fort Rupert and executed.

That evening, General Hudson Austin, commander of the Grenadan Army, announced that the PRG had been dissolved and an emergency governing body, the Revolutionary Military Council (RMC), had been established and was in control of the country. Austin also announced that the RMC had imposed a four-day, twenty-four-hour shoot-to-kill curfew.

Six days later, American troops landed on the island and removed Austin and the RMC from power.

Elites' Views before the Grenada Crisis

The examination of the views of the various foreign policy advocacy communities begins with a discussion of the legacy of Vietnam and its influence on U.S. foreign policy institutional structures, on U.S. public opinion, and on the relevant distribution of power among the advocacy communities. In 1981 there was a resurgence of the selective engagers and hardliners in the Reagan administration. I will discuss how they engaged in specific strategies to frame the perception of the crisis and to generate public support for the action in Grenada.

The Legacy of Vietnam

Vietnam, Watergate, the general economic and social malaise that permeated the 1970s, the rise and fall of détente, and the Iranian hostage crisis polarized divisions in the American public and among foreign policy advocacy groups. While the foreign policy elite community had always been divided on whether and why to use force in overseas conflicts, these events—the Vietnam War in particular—dramatically intensified and galvanized those divisions.

Prior to the war in Vietnam, the American public had, for the most part, accepted the dominant ideological imperatives of the Cold War: to fight and to contain international communism. But this acceptance had always been subject to certain constraints. The public and most foreign policy elites believed that containment was an appropriate strategy toward an aggressive Soviet Union as long as they believed it conformed to American material interests and to the defense of American values of liberty and democracy. Indeed, liberals, hardliners, and selective engagers all supported the deployment of American troops to Vietnam in 1965 to fight communist aggression and to support the democratization of South Vietnam.

But Vietnam had been a bitter pill for liberals. They had supported President Lyndon Johnson's request for congressional authorization to deploy troops following the incidents in the Gulf of Tonkin in August 1964. However, over the course of the first two years of the war, an increasing number of liberals came to resent Johnson's use of that resolution as his authority to escalate the war. As American involvement lingered on, a more complicated version of the underlying facts in South Vietnam was revealed. New media technologies and unrestricted media access exposed the American public to some egregious acts being committed by those for whom the United States was fighting. Journalists and news organizations who had initially endorsed the administration's official view of the war increasingly reported evidence from Vietnam that directly contradicted the administration's version. By mid-1966, it was apparent that the facts about the Gulf of Tonkin incident, the magnitude of the escalation, the costs of the war, and ultimately, the effectiveness of American military actions had routinely been distorted and manipulated in an effort to keep Americans on board in support of the war.

These disclosures compelled liberals, in particular, to reevaluate their views of the war. They had initially supported the war in the hope of promoting a free and democratic South Vietnam. By 1968, it was obvious that the American effort would not achieve that. The general public as well as the liberal foreign policy elites concluded that the South Vietnamese government would not become a model of democracy. Americans were dying in large numbers and the material costs of the war had triggered unparalleled deficits. The exposure of the military's extensive reliance on Napalm, the burning of Cam Ne, the massacre at My Lai, and other abuses committed by American forces flew in the face of core American values and sparked a crisis of conscience. The war forced many Americans to reexamine their beliefs about the role of force, the trustworthiness of the president, and America's moral exceptionalness that they had long held.[15]

By the end of the war, liberals had concluded that hardliners and selective engagers had propelled the United States into the costly war. The dominant foreign policy ideology, which professed that America could not "lose" another country to communism, had been transformed by the war into an explicit demand to "avoid Vietnam-type quagmires." Liberals and noninterventionists in Congress, in the media, and in dozens of think tanks and research institutes became more vocal during the early and mid-1970s. They pledged no longer to sit back, speaking up only when selective engager and hardline views tended toward excess.[16] They began to carve out an active agenda for reorienting American foreign policy to more closely correspond to their views and values.

Liberals and noninterventionists in Congress were particularly active in reorienting American foreign policy. After Vietnam, they used the public and congressional anger over the war to initiate passage of the 1973 War Powers Act, which placed explicit limitations on the president's ability to unilaterally deploy American forces to foreign conflicts. Furthermore, in the wake of the massive aerial bombardments of Cambodia and the public disclosure of the CIA's complicity in the assassination of Chilean president Salvador Allende, liberals in Congress launched a series of congressional investigations to rein in executive excesses.[17] The Church Commission scrutinized American covert operations since World War II and concluded that too much of American foreign policy had been conducted in secret, without proper public or congressional oversight. Within a couple of years a series of congressional oversight mechanisms had been put in place to monitor intelligence and highly sensitive national security matters.

Liberals and noninterventionists also gained significant resources in a newly emboldened media culture. Investigative journalism proliferated as a result of the presidential liberties taken in both Vietnam and Watergate. Prior to the war in Vietnam, the institutional biases of the media had tended toward supporting the president on national security issues.[18] In the wake of the excesses committed by American forces in Vietnam and the concerted disinformation campaigns waged by the military establishment during the war, reporters became much more aggressive in their pursuit of stories.[19]

Liberals in the White House

The election of Jimmy Carter in 1976 marked a major victory for liberals.[20] Carter ascended to office as the "anti-establishment candidate"—the "people's president"—whose platform rested on the phrase: "be trustworthy." Carter had found during his campaign stops that Americans responded positively to his speeches appealing for a moral basis for American foreign policy and a rejection of Henry Kissinger's amoral *realpolitik*, which had been the trademark of the Nixon and Ford foreign policies. Carter pledged to restore morality to American foreign policy. In his inaugural address he proclaimed that America could "never be indifferent to the fate of freedom elsewhere," and that America's "commitment to human rights must be absolute."[21]

Under the guidance of Secretary of State Cyrus Vance, the State Department created the Bureau of Human Rights and Humanitarian Affairs. Never before had a formal bureaucratic structure been developed within the U.S. foreign policy establishment to monitor and report on human rights and humanitarian issues. Patricia Derian, a long-time human rights activist, was appointed the first assistant secretary of state for the new bureau, which began using and expanding the annual human rights reports to document extensively the human rights abuses reported in all of those countries receiving American aid.

During Carter's first year in office, the liberal wing of his administration moved to order or signal dramatic cuts in aid to military regimes in Argentina, Chile, El Salvador, Ethiopia, Nicaragua, and Uruguay because of abysmal human rights records. Fearing similar reprisals, the military regimes in Guatemala and Brazil simply withdrew their requests for aid rather than improve their own human rights practices.

Yet, even with the success of liberal beliefs in his administration, Carter retained a large number of selective engagers within the senior decision-making apparatus. The United States was still fighting the Cold War, and during Carter's first two years, events in Southeast Asia, southern Africa, and the Middle East seemed to be turning against the United States. Selective engagers such as National Security Advisor Zbigniew Brzezinski and Secretary of Defense Harold Brown frequently clashed with the more liberal Vance. The selective engagers opposed Vance's tendency to trump values over core strategic interests. The two factions disagreed on several key issues, among them the second Strategic Arms Limitation Treaty (SALT II), the MX missile, and deployment of intermediate nuclear forces to Europe.

Almost immediately, Carter's tilt toward a liberal foreign policy generated a reaction from traditional conservatives and the new wing of the conservative movement—the neoconservatives. This new group included many Democrats who had been hardliners in the 1950s and 1960s but had broken from the emergent "new left" of the Democratic party following Senator George McGovern's nomination for president in 1972. Shortly after Carter's election, conservative and neoconservative foreign policy think tanks and hardline foreign policy elites organized under the umbrella organization Committee on the Present Danger (CPD). The CPD argued that détente was lulling Americans into believing that the world was safer.[22] In particular they argued that Carter's strategic doctrine, American force posture and foreign policies signaled weakness to the rest of the world. In a series of reports, the CPD suggested that under Carter's watch the United States was losing the Cold War; in one particularly blunt report it declared that the United States had fallen behind the Soviet Union militarily.[23] The CPD launched an extensive public relations campaign to mobilize public opposition to Carter's overall foreign policy and SALT II in particular. The CPD also sought to challenge the liberal narrative on the implications of the Vietnam War. Unlike Carter, who had concluded that U.S. actions in Vietnam had been premised on a strategic vision that was rooted in "intellectual and moral poverty," members of the CPD argued that Vietnam was not only a noble cause but that the American loss in Southeast Asia affirmed the predictions of the domino theory. Laos and Cambodia both fell to communist regimes, and as a result of America's weakness, the Soviet Union had stepped up its activities in Mozambique, Angola, northern Africa, Iraq, and Central America.[24]

Under pressure from within the administration and from these outside sources, Carter's foreign policy frequently oscillated between selective engagement and liberalism.[25] For example, he did cut off or reduce dramatically American support for dictatorships in Nicaragua, Chile, Argentina, and Brazil, but support was continued to dictatorial regimes in the Philippines, South Korea, and Indonesia. By 1979, these oscillations had triggered intense scrutiny and outright hostility from selective engagers and hardliners as the Carter administration seemed unable to sort itself out on its own strategic priorities. In addition, a series of crises erupted in 1979 which the administration was not able to control. In January, the shah of Iran was forced to flee his country. In April, Iran became an Islamic republic, with Ayatollah Khomeini as supreme leader. In July, the Somoza regime in Nicaragua finally collapsed and was quickly replaced by the Sandinistas, who announced a marked shift to the left. Then in November, student backers of Ayatollah Khomeini overran the U.S. embassy and held dozens of Americans hostage for the remainder of the Carter presidency. And finally, in December 1979, the Soviet Union invaded Afghanistan, effectively marking the end of détente and the liberal hopes of greater cooperation with the Soviet Union.

By the end of the decade, the CPD, much of the public, and selective engagers within the administration concluded that Carter's policies had failed so significantly that they were accelerating the momentum of Soviet expansion in the Persian Gulf, Africa, the Middle East, the Caribbean, and Southeast Asia. The cumulative effects of Vietnam, Watergate, the coups in Iran and Nicaragua, simultaneous oil price shocks and the subsequent domestic stagflation, and seemingly intensifying Soviet agitation around the globe triggered a dramatic erosion in public confidence in American power.

Selective Engagers and Hardliners Resurgent

Amid the collapse of Carter's foreign policy and the public erosion of confidence in America's stature in the world, Ronald Reagan emerged, in 1980, with a promise to restore American glory. Reagan's campaign rhetoric and style connected with the large segment of the American public who continued to believe in America's greatness. Reagan believed that Vietnam was an honorable endeavor and that it had been lost because naysayers within the American media and among "radicals and liberals" had undermined the country's noble mission.[26] This message resonated with a public who had become frustrated with the despair and decline that was the focus of the American press. Throughout 1980 and during his early years in office, Reagan trumpeted patriotic slogans such as "America is back!" "Stand tall!" and, by 1984, "It's morning in America."

The belief among the hardliners and selective engagers was that the public wanted a revitalization of U.S. strength overseas. People would support a strong action if only they were not inundated with images of the futility of American actions.[27] It was no coincidence that Sylvester Stallone's character in the 1982 movie *Rambo: First Blood* gained such widespread popularity; in the first sequel, Rambo returned to Vietnam and restored American pride by simultaneously defeating communists, corrupt American officials, and liberals.

In Reagan's first term, he surrounded himself with leading selective engagers and hardliners. His vice president, George H. W. Bush, was a highly experienced foreign policy figure in Washington. Bush had been CIA director and U.S. ambassador to the United Nations and was a noted selective engager, as was Reagan's chief of staff, James A. Baker III, who served as the key political handler during the first term.

However, the bulk of Reagan's team were noted hardliners. Among them were at least sixty board members of the Committee on the Present Danger.[28] The core set of advisors were decidedly hardliners: his first secretary of state,

Alexander Haig, National Security Advisor Richard Allen, CIA Director William Casey, presidential counsel Edwin Meese III, and UN ambassador Jeane Kirkpatrick. They were unanimous in their view that the United States was in a fierce geostrategic struggle with the Soviet Union and that détente had proved a colossal failure.[29]

It seemed to the staunchly ideological Reaganites, that the United States had lost much of its power and prestige in the world because of its weak military posture and its political unwillingness to directly challenge the Soviet adventurism around the globe. They believed that the Soviets had been able to secure "massive advantages" in their nuclear arsenal—especially with their deployment of intermediate nuclear weapons that directly threatened Europe. The new team immediately initiated the largest peace-time military build-up in American history.[30]

The Reagan team was also sharply critical of what they believed were foreign policy debacles of the Carter administration throughout the developing world and particularly in Iran, Nicaragua, Afghanistan, and Grenada. Reagan and his aides felt that Carter's preoccupation with human rights had undermined Washington's relationships with many of its conservative allies around the globe and harmed American interests in the competition with the Soviet Union.[31] While human rights might be a noble cause, they argued, it paled in comparison to the broader, global geostrategic competition against Moscow. As Jeane Kirkpatrick summed it up: "Get rid of rightist dictators, support the democratic left, promote reform, preempt the radicals, build democracy and development: thus went the theory that gave us the Ayatollah Khomeini and the Ortega brothers. . . . Good intentions and a mistaken theory produced results as destructive as they were unintended."[32]

Reagan's grand foreign policy strategy during his first term was threefold: (1) Challenge Soviet expansion around the world by supporting "freedom fighters" and others who resisted Soviet influence (the "Reagan Doctrine"). (2) Weaken Soviet economic and political control in Eastern Europe. (3) Ultimately, change the regime in the Soviet Union.[33]

Central and South America were of particular concern to the new team. The hardliners, especially, believed that the fall of Samoza's regime in Nicaragua and the rise of the leftist movement in El Salvador were the direct results of Soviet agitation. Reagan declared that the Soviet Union and Cuba would stop at nothing to undermine U.S. influence in the Caribbean and Central America—which were not merely "in America's backyard" (in the lexicon of the time) but in

America's frontyard. As hardline NSC staff member Constantine Menges warned: "If communist groups succeed in taking over most of Central America, this will likely produce a major communist effort to take power in Mexico. . . . This would mean that after two centuries of secure borders, for the first time the people of the United States would be face to face on land with one hundred million people under communist control and allied with Cuba and the Soviet bloc."[34] According to political scientist Tony Thorndike, the administration felt that unchecked Soviet expansion had inevitably led to "a chain reaction of leftist revolutions [which] would turn the once subservient tropical basin into a rim of hostile Marxist states taking their cues from Castro's Cuba."[35]

Upon assuming power in early 1981, the hardliners formulated an aggressive campaign, both covert and overt, to roll back leftist successes in Nicaragua and to assist all forces in the region fighting leftist insurgencies. In one of the first orders of business for the Reagan team, they reversed Carter's economic sanctions against right-wing dictatorships in Chile and Argentina, proclaimed support for those authoritarian leaders, and renewed American economic assistance. In El Salvador, the Reagan administration sought to increase military assistance programs to help the right-wing dictatorship.

Reagan's overall approach to foreign policy resonated with the American public. He received widespread congressional and public support for his requests to increase the American defense budget and in response to his hawkish statements vis-à-vis Moscow. Despite these successes and his own popularity, his hardline message as applied to Latin America was not as well received. Most Americans routinely opposed expanding U.S. military assistance to the right-wing regime in El Salvador and consistently expressed serious reservations (and often outright opposition) to U.S. financial backing of the Nicaraguan Contras. In part this was because Central America, with its dense tropical jungles and mountains, seemed eerily reminiscent of Vietnam. In addition, the administration was frequently caught "hyping" the threat in Central America. For example, in the summer of 1981, shortly after coming into office, hardliners in the State Department drafted a white paper titled "Communist Interference in El Salvador." The paper claimed that captured documents revealed that the insurgency in El Salvador was a "textbook case of indirect armed aggression by Communist powers through Cuba."[36] It concluded with the statement that the government of El Salvador was simply trying to protect itself from external influence. The white paper ignored, however, information that had been long and widely known about the right-wing regime and its abuses. Most Americans, for example, were outraged by the actions of El Salvador's political leaders and army officers in December 1980, when four American nuns were abducted and killed by El Salvadoran government security forces. Indeed, Gallup polling in March 1981 revealed that only 2 percent of Americans supported sending U.S. troops to El Salvador to help that government.[37] Within this context the white paper was widely seen—and portrayed—as a simplistic effort by ideological hardliners to sell Americans on weak policy. The *Wall Street Journal* even declared that "a close reading of the white paper indicates . . . that its authors probably were making a determined effort to create a 'selling' document, no matter how slim the background material."[38]

Reagan and the hardliners, on the other hand, believed that the only problem with their policy on Central America was that liberal and noninterventionist "obstructionists" in the media and Congress were duping the American public on Reagan's hardline approach to Latin America. As Edwin Meese later lamented: "Congressional obstructionism was an ongoing feature of the conflict. Aid to El Salvador was hedged with numerous legislative conditions—certifications of progress on human rights, 'land reform,' and democratic elections. Much energy and time, in a country wracked with warfare, terrorist violence, and threatened takeover by communist insurgents, were expended on complying with these requirements."[39]

The administration held the fundamental conviction that Soviet aggression was on the rise worldwide. In September 1983, just six weeks before the crisis erupted in Grenada, the Soviets shot down Korean airliner KAL 007, killing 269 civilians. This was part of the overall context of the selective engager and hardliner positions that dominated the Reagan administration's thinking on the Western Hemisphere in the run-up to the crisis in Grenada in the fall of 1983.

Grenada Surfaces on the Radar Screen

For the Reagan hardliners, the Marxist People's Revolutionary Government regime that had come to power in Grenada in 1979 was simply another illustration of the ruthless conduct of the Soviet Union and Cuba. During a campaign speech in March 1980, Reagan pointedly referred to his belief in Grenada's link to Soviet agitation by asking, "Must we let Grenada, Nicaragua, El Salvador, all become additional 'Cubas,' new outposts for Soviet combat brigades? Will the next push of the Moscow-Havana axis be northward to Guatemala and thence to Mexico, and south to Costa Rica and Panama?"[40]

From the time they took office in January 1981, Reagan and his team aggressively pursued a strategy of isolation and destabilization in Grenada. The United States actively sought to block all international financial assistance to Grenada and refused to recognize the government of Prime Minister Maurice Bishop. Early in 1981, administration officials pressured the International Monetary Fund (IMF) to refuse a loan of $19 million requested by Grenada.[41] It also assigned a condition to American assistance to the Caribbean Development Bank, that no money could be disbursed to Grenada. And, the administration's highly touted Caribbean Basin Initiative, designed to shore up American favor in the region, explicitly excluded Grenada.

Furthermore, the Reagan administration launched a policy of overt military and covert political intimidation against Grenada. In mid-1981 both the CIA and the Pentagon devised plans for the destabilization of and American intervention in Grenada. The United States also dramatically stepped up military aid for Grenada's eastern Caribbean neighbors, increasing funding from $100,000 to $17 million between FY 1981 and FY 1983.[42]

But perhaps no issue focused the administration's attention on Grenada more than the construction of a 10,000-foot airport runway at Port Salinas. Although dozens of nations—including Canada and Great Britain—were providing technical and financial assistance for the construction project, the fact that Cuba was underwriting much of the cost and was providing a considerable share of the equipment and skilled labor convinced the Reagan administration that Cuba and the Soviet Union had plans to use the airport for military purposes.[43]

In March 1983, in a nationally televised speech designed to highlight Soviet "aggressiveness" around the world, Reagan highlighted the case of Grenada by showing aerial pictures of the airport construction on the island. He told the American audience that the airport was designed specifically to enable the Cubans and Soviets to gain a foothold on America's doorstep and advance their international communist crusade.

Liberals' Response to Reagan

Reagan's election in 1980 and his abrupt and hardline policy shifts served as a rallying cry for liberals. Liberal Carter administration officials had left government convinced that the focus they had brought to American foreign policy was sound and that the foreign policy failures that had occurred during their tenure were the result of a series of unfortunate, and ultimately uncontrollable, global events.

Reagan's initial saber rattling toward the Soviet Union and his massive defense buildup signaled to liberals that his policies would reignite the arms race and would catapult the United States into war. They were particularly incensed with Reagan's unwillingness to meet with Soviet leaders, his decision to deploy intermediate nuclear weapons to Europe, and his decision to launch the Strategic Defense Initiative, which they argued would violate the 1972 Antiballistic Missile (ABM) Treaty. A cottage industry emerged in Washington devoted to attacking Reagan's hardline stance toward the Soviet Union.

The most acute criticism of Reagan's foreign policy, however, centered on his Central American policy. The State Department white paper on El Salvador galvanized the liberals' effort to block a course they believed would certainly lead to American military involvement in Central America. Liberals established more, and beefed up existing, organizations dedicated to scrutinizing American foreign policy with respect to Central America: the Institute of Policy Studies, the North American Congress on Latin America, the Washington Office on Latin America, and the Council on Hemispheric Affairs, among others. All assembled extensive and aggressive lobbying campaigns to challenge Reagan's Central American policies. In addition, dozens of religious organizations with extensive contacts throughout Latin America participated in fact-finding missions that reported on conditions throughout the region to parishes around the United States. These organizations dedicated themselves to distributing their own information and analyses to the public, the press, and members of Congress concerning events in Central and South America.[44] They succeeded in solidifying public opinion against Reagan's hardline campaign in Central America.

Liberals' Attitudes toward Grenada

While the rest of Latin America and Cuba commanded a lot of attention from liberals, the tiny windward island of Grenada was not viewed as having much significance. Liberals during the Carter administration had expressed their dissatisfaction with the PRG's move toward one-party rule and failure to hold democratic elections, and the administration had initiated a strategy of diplomatic and economic pressure to persuade Bishop to reorient his government. Still, the policy was one of persuasion rather than intimidation. As former National Security Council staff member Robert Pastor describes it, the Carter administration "cooled the relationship and sought to expand aid to Grenada's Caribbean neighbors as a signal that only democracy would be rewarded in the region."[45] The general thrust of the liberal strategy was to simultaneously pursue economic development, improved social policies, and political liberalization. Hence, Bishop's social agenda was quietly applauded while the administration encouraged political change.

During the first year of Reagan's presidency, liberals continued to express concern over the PRG's political orientation, and they thought that Reagan's aggressive hardline policies further entrenched Marxists in power in Grenada. For many liberals, the failure of the administration to understand the social and economic conditions that fostered leftist movements would cause the policy to fail.[46] Despite these criticisms, the liberal attention to Grenada was sporadic and ad hoc at best. The most significant liberal challenge to the Reagan administration's hardline approach to the country came from the Congressional Black Caucus and a number of African American organizations that had established personal relationships with Maurice Bishop and others in the Grenadan regime.

Congressman Ronald Dellums, for example, was particularly outspoken in his criticisms of the administration's policy. In late 1982, he traveled to Grenada on a fact-finding mission. Following his trip, he issued a report to the House Armed Services Committee that concluded that the new airport was intended for the promotion of tourism and would not be used for military purposes. Particular points of curiosity for Dellums and the few reporters monitoring events in Grenada were that the lead contractor of the airport, Plessy, Ltd., was a British company and that the Canadian, Mexican, and Venezuelan governments were participating in the financing of the project. Also, several American contractors were constructing the fuel tanks at the airport. Finally, while Reagan claimed that such a small country did not need an airport with such a long runway, at least two other small island nations—Curaçao and Martinique—also had airports with 10,000-foot runways.

Despite Dellums's report, there was only marginal congressional activity against Reagan's policies on Grenada.[47] There was no organized opposition to Reagan's pressure on the IMF to block loans to Grenada or to his decision not to include Grenada as part of the Caribbean Basin Initiative. Liberals were putting their energy and resources into challenging his policies on Nicaragua and El Salvador.[48] When Prime Minister Bishop was executed in October 1983 and the crisis over his succession escalated, liberals were simply in no position to effectively challenge the administration's take on the situation or offer independent analysis of the crisis.

Reluctant Warriors and Noninterventionists

Along with the successes of liberalism in the wake of Vietnam came the re-emergence of the noninterventionists. For noninterventionists, the war in Vietnam depicted all that was wrong with American foreign policy. The United States had gone to war and lost because it had picked a war it could not win. Among the noninterventionists, two disparate groups converged in their opposition to deployment of American force to regional and civil conflicts: pacifists, who had initiated the nuclear freeze movement, and U.S. combat military officers, who had personally experienced the political and military tragedy of Vietnam and were committed to avoiding any repetition.

The peace movement that emerged out of the Vietnam War demanded that the United States redefine its relationship with the Soviet Union. The war had been lost and yet, they concluded, the dire claims made by the selective engagers and the hardliners about American vulnerability in the wake of the "falling dominos" had not materialized. The peace movement had largely dissipated after the end of the Vietnam War and during the Carter administration. The election of Reagan, however, reignited it. In particular, Reagan's defense budget and arms control policies fueled opposition among the peace groups. They dedicated most of their resources to the nuclear freeze movement that blossomed in the first three years of the Reagan presidency.[49]

Vietnam also contributed to the dramatic rise of reluctant warriors—which included many of the rank and file of the U.S. military—and in particular, U.S. Army officers.[50] Although many military commanders had long viewed with suspicion the use of force for ambiguous regional and civil conflicts, they became particularly critical of such use in the wake of the intervention in Vietnam. The military had been called upon to undertake a political mission that it was neither prepared nor equipped to handle.[51] Furthermore, the prestige of the military, as an institution signifying honor and valor, had been deeply tarnished as it fought a war that the American people came to hate. As political scientist Richard Betts argues, "the experience of the Vietnam War had stung the American military badly and would make them more than usually chary of resorting to force. What was not yet evident was the depth, stridency, and durability of this anti-interventionist sentiment. Rather than a temporary hangover, it became a stolid orthodoxy."[52] In fact, many senior military commanders came to hate the Vietnam War and the reliance on the American military for political objectives in the Third World more than any other group in American society.

As the Cold War reignited after the Soviet invasion of Afghanistan in December 1979 and after the Reagan administration's responses to the crises in Central America, military elites openly expressed their concern about using the military to address situations that were principally limited political dilemmas.[53] At various points in the 1970s and early 1980s, for example, the Joint Chiefs of Staff objected during discussion of U.S. force deployments to the Persian Gulf, to Lebanon, and to Central America. Chairman of the Joint Chiefs under President Reagan, General John W. Vessey, Jr., argued forcefully that the U.S. military should be deployed only under very narrow conditions and when there was firm and full public support and the mission was clear.[54] Military commanders were especially leery of the Reagan administration's obsession with Central America. With its thick jungle terrain, it made for quick and easy Vietnam analogies. For many Army officers, the most explicit lesson from Vietnam was that the military could simply not stand by idly and allow itself to be drawn into another quagmire.[55] They resolved to demand explicit guarantees from the president that the mission be clear and doable, that there be a firm public consensus, and that there be an explicit commitment of sufficient resources to do the job. In the early 1980s, the prevailing view of Central America was that a supportive public consensus would be virtually impossible to achieve.

The Decision to Intervene

The backdrop of the decision-making process was the highly divided foreign policy elite community of the late 1970s and early 1980s. In the small island nation of Grenada in October 1983, an unstable situation deteriorated dramatically in the days following the overthrow and execution of Prime Minister Maurice Bishop. Before the Reagan administration could intervene militarily in Grenada, they had to ensure public and political support for their decision.

Interests Threatened and Opportunity Presented

When the crisis erupted on October 13, the National Security Council staff saw the events as clear evidence of a dramatic shift in the geostrategic balance of power in the Caribbean. Fearing that an escalated Soviet presence in Grenada would provide international communists with greater resources with which to export their "revolutionary" campaigns throughout Central America, the hardliners immediately began drafting plans for a full-scale American invasion of the island to accomplish the "restoration of democracy to Grenada."[56] For them, Grenada presented an ideal situation for a quick and decisive military action that could eliminate the Soviet and Cuban presence on the island and strike a blow against communist aggression.

While the hardliners quickly decided on intervention, several of Reagan's selective engager advisors were more circumspect—initially. Vice President George H. W. Bush and Deputy Secretary of State Lawrence Eagleburger both cautioned against a hasty reaction. In the first days following Bishop's ouster, they felt that the dynamic events did not yet signify a real danger to Americans nor would they inevitably lead to great Soviet influence on the island.

However, on October 20, the day after Bishop's execution, Reagan formed a special committee of the NSC, chaired by Bush, to monitor the situation and to evaluate American options. In its first meeting on October 20, the group focused on both the geostrategic imperatives and the security of U.S. nationals. A persistent problem had been the limited intelligence coming from the island. Because the United States had no formal U.S. presence on Grenada, it lacked its own highly credible human intelligence assets. The hardliners, however, did have an ally in their cause in Governor-General Sir Paul Scoon. Scoon, a career civil servant in Grenada, had been appointed to the ceremonial Commonwealth position by Queen Elizabeth II in 1978. He was an outspoken critic of the New Jewel Movement and the People's Revolutionary Government and was a staunch advocate for American military intervention. During the October 20 meeting, hardline NSC staffer Constantine Menges, relying on Scoon's reports, relayed that highly sensitive intelligence reports coming from Grenada were reporting that the Revolutionary Military Council leaders who had seized power were likely to detain all American citizens on the island and hold them as hostages.[57] Menges concluded his briefing by making a strong pitch for the need to end the Cuban and Soviet influence on the island. The intelligence community had questions about the reliability of Scoon's reporting, but the NSC accepted the intelligence on the potential threat to American citizens as though the reports were accurate.[58]

After the briefing by Menges and similar comments from Secretary of State George Shultz, momentum quickly built for intervention. The selective engagers ultimately accepted the intelligence reporting on potential for Americans being taken hostage—the images of the Iran hostage crisis were still less than three years old—and endorsed a strategy of intervention. The general feeling was that if the U.S. did not act, the Soviets would view it as a sign of American weakness and would become emboldened to begin a more aggressive campaign in Central America. Selective engagers and hardliners concluded that this was a situation that Reagan had specifically committed himself to forestalling.

Despite the quickly developing momentum for a military option, two critical impediments surfaced. First, the reluctant warriors at the Pentagon, the Joint Chiefs chairman, General Vessey, and Secretary of Defense Casper Weinberger expressed reservations about exercising the military option, especially in light of the weakness of the intelligence upon which it would be based. Vessey pointed out that military action might not be the optimal solution for ensuring the security of American citizens. He also informed the meeting participants that the armed forces did not have operational plans for a full-scale invasion.[59] Vessey and Weinberger demanded that any plan assume a massive deployment with overwhelming force sufficient to secure the entire island and that immediate action be delayed until the military could gain more intelligence to support such an invasion.[60]

The second problem that surfaced was the question of the political and legal feasibility of such an action. The group pondered the president's constitutional authority and the likely congressional and public response and concluded that political strategies would have to be considered. They agreed that if an intervention were to take place, more intelligence would be needed, specific operational plans would need to be developed, and specific domestic political and diplomatic efforts would have to be surveyed. For the politically savvy Reagan aides, an appropriate political and legal basis for action was imperative. As Robert Beck reports, at this point "the administration lacked plausible legal grounds for a full-scale invasion. The fear for American lives and the absence of a legitimate government were simply not enough: the group seems to have been reluctant to say that the administration had just decided to violate international law."[61]

The national security team agreed to develop a political strategy to build or ensure domestic and political support. The selective engagers and hardliners understood the inherent political risks associated with any military action—especially with the effects of Vietnam still lingering—and they were not willing to launch a major military action without strong public and political support.

This sensitivity in key Reagan advisors to the domestic political bases for policy decisions was a hallmark of the Reagan administration. For Reagan and most of his hardliner and selective engager aides there was a deep suspicion of liberals and other political opponents in Congress, think tanks and, especially, in the media.[62] From its outset, the Reagan team believed that the key to successful policy decisions, including foreign policy decisions, was maintaining control of the information and selling the public on the administration's view. They believed that Americans would strongly support the president and his views as long as they were not berated by liberal attacks.

At the beginning of his administration, Reagan had assembled a highly skilled team of public relations experts, led by Michael Deaver and David Gergen, to package him and his message to the American public. The team extensively studied the failures of Reagan's predecessors and concluded that Carter, Ford, and Nixon, among others, had not effectively presented their message in short, digestible sound-bites that fit well in daily news broadcasts. They also concluded that earlier presidents had failed to control the flow of information—allowing their opponents the opportunity to challenge a policy before it had been completely formulated.[63] They understood the power of the visual media and played to Reagan's strength—his personable style and ability to connect with the average American, who longed for a stronger America.[64]

The Reagan advisors were notorious within the press corps for their effectiveness. As Richard Cohen, senior political producer for CBS News pointed out, "Michael Deaver was the executive producer of the evening news broadcast—yes he was. Michael Deaver decided what would be on the evening news each night. He laid it out there. I mean he knew exactly who we were and what we went for. He suckered us."[65] This public relations element of the presidency was a source of considerable pride within the White House. A plaque on the desk of Reagan's press secretary, Larry Speakes, read, "You don't tell us how to stage the news, and we don't tell you how to cover it."[66]

Furthermore, unlike most recent presidential administrations, Reagan and his advisors sought to institutionalize an integrated national security message. Larry Speakes held weekly lunches with the press officers from the State Department and the Pentagon. All administration officials were required, by a presidential directive issued in early 1982, to receive clearance from the White House prior to any national security briefings with reporters. In mid-1982 President Reagan instituted new regulations making it easier to classify government documents and limit their dissemination. As one critic noted: "In short, the administration attempted to impose an unprecedented degree of censorship on government officials."[67]

In cases where this strategy failed—most notably on Reagan's Central American policy—the experience only reinforced the administration's belief in the necessity of controlling information. For example, with respect to Central America, liberals and noninterventionists in the Congress, the media, and the Washington think tanks often challenged the veracity of Reagan's claims about Nicaragua and El Salvador. These opposition groups were able to collect a tremendous wealth of material on the nature of the civil wars in those two countries.[68] Ed Meese would later recount that this was a critical lesson for the administration:

> Thrown off balance at the outset, the administration never succeeded in gaining the rhetorical initiative, despite valiant efforts by the President and some of his key supporters. Instead, the liberal Democrats and their allies in the media successfully defined the issue—the Sandinistas as the injured party, the Contras as evil "Somocistas," and the CIA conducting a "secret war" on their behalf. . . .[69]
>
> . . . Once we got behind the public opinion curve, the issue was perceived to be a loser; the polls were against helping the resistance. Association with the cause could only tarnish the President's popularity, and repeated votes on Contra aid in Congress ran the danger from a public relations standpoint, of posting "losses" instead of racking up "wins." . . . .
>
> . . . The net result was that *we did a great deal less to sell the cause of the resistance than we might have.* I personally think we should have come out fighting sooner, and much harder. . . . Calling the issue a loser became a self-fulfilling prophecy—because we didn't do what it would take to win.[70]

A second point of tension that had created early problems for the administration and which heightened Reagan's personal commitment to control the flow of information was the problem of unsanctioned leaks. During the first year and a half of the administration, the selective engagers and hardliners fought numerous battles among themselves on national security and military policy pertaining to the Soviet Union and American defense expenditures. One instrument used by the combatants during this in-fighting was carefully crafted leaks to the public of sensitive information, in the hope of influencing policy decisions as they reached the president's desk. For the public relations–savvy hardliners and selective engagers, such leaks were a "vital part of image manipulation" in Washington, where perception was often "more important than reality."[71] Early and mid-1983 had been a particularly divisive time within the Reagan White House. *Washington Post* reporter Lou Cannon published a story about U.S. plans for escalating U.S. forces in Lebanon. The leak led to the infamous "polygraph" dispute, in which several hardliners, led by Ed Meese, pushed for a formal Justice Department investigation of the NSC and its staff to determine the source of leaks that had contributed to the story.[72]

In response, President Reagan increased penalties on the leaking of classified information. He also began to systematically centralize the public relations component of the national security structures. In January 1983, President Reagan signed National Security Decision Directive 77 (NSDD 77), titled "Management of Public Diplomacy to National Security."[73] The text of NSDD 77 concluded with the claim that the directive was "necessary to strengthen the organization, planning and coordination of the various aspects of public diplomacy of the United States Government."[74] Pursuant to NSDD 77, the administration established the Office of Public Diplomacy for Latin America and the Caribbean.

The Office of Public Diplomacy was responsible for coordinating the researching, publication, and distribution of thousands of short analytical briefs, white papers, briefing books, and pamphlets for members of Congress, the press, and the public. These were explicit efforts to sell the American public on Reagan's policies in Latin America and the Caribbean. The operation was conducted as, in scholar Peter Kornbluh's description, a "huge psychological operation" that "included overt and covert propaganda, pressure on the media, and illegal lobbying tactics to manipulate public opinion" in the United States.[75] The office even brought in highly trained military psychological operations (psy-ops) personnel, experts in battlefield propaganda, to assist the effort.

Such was the intensity of the information and propaganda campaign waged by the administration to develop domestic support for American military action in Grenada.

Initial Policy Development

The administration well understood that some international legal basis was paramount as a starting point for selling military action to the American public. But, some of the senior principals of the NSC were concerned that bringing in lawyers would expand the number of individuals within government with knowledge about the secret deliberations on intervention and could be a source for leaks to the press or Congress.[76] Nonetheless, the need to find some legal justification trumped concerns about operational security. On October 21, the day after the first NSC meeting on Grenada, a team of lawyers was assembled to review all of the relevant international and domestic legal issues. The team was led by State Department deputy legal advisor Michael Kosak and included senior legal experts from the State, Justice, and Defense Departments. It addressed three key legal and political questions: Could the United States deploy a large contingent of American combat forces into a hostile situation in Grenada in a way that was consistent with Grenada's claim of international sovereignty? Could it do so in a way that was consistent with the 1973 War Powers Act? What additional domestic and international legal or political challenges might the administration face if it chose to intervene in Grenada?

The lawyers deferred the last question until they had developed responses to the first two.[77] First, they concluded that if the United States were to receive a formal request—such as from the Organization of Eastern Caribbean States (OECS)—the intervention would probably be consistent with international law. The OECS was a loosely constructed regional economic alliance with no delineated security protocols. Nonetheless, the lawyers concluded that the broad language in the OECS charter could be used as a basis for international legal justification for intervention. Second, the lawyers found that the War Powers Act would not be a domestic legal constraint because the president had the authority to act in "emergency" situations to protect American citizens. Furthermore, as long as the president met with members of Congress and told them of the actions, he would satisfy the "consultation" clause of the act. This consultation was also a political imperative; the president did not want to be seen deploying American military force while leaving Congress completely out of the loop. In short, the legal team concluded that in order to garner domestic support the president had to show that the American deployment was in response to an international request and to rescue American citizens and that he had fulfilled his necessary legal and political obligation by "consulting" with members of Congress.[78]

The OECS "Request"

The same day that the State Department lawyers were devising the legal basis for American action, October 21, the U.S. representatives to the Organization of Eastern Caribbean States secretly participated in the OECS deliberations on its collective response to the events in Grenada. At the meeting, American officials urged the Caribbean nations to authorize the use of force.[79] Four of the regional leaders—John Compton, the prime minister of St. Lucia; Eugenia Charles, the prime minister of Dominica (and chair of the OECS); Tom Adams, prime minister of Barbados; and Edward Seaga, prime minister of Jamaica—all favored a strong and forceful response to the crisis.[80] Indeed, Compton and Adams both had long been worried about leftist movements within their own countries and had actually discussed the idea of U.S. military action with U.S. diplomats the day before. However, not all members of the OECS were committed to the request. At the OECS session, the foreign minister of Antigua and Barbuda expressed reservations about issuing a formal request to the United States to intervene. At that point, U.S. ambassador to the eastern Caribbean, Milan Bish, immediately went over the head of the foreign minister and called the prime minister of Antigua and Barbuda and pressured that OECS member to change its position.[81] Without the support of Antigua and Barbuda, the OECS could not formally make a request to the United States.[82] Ultimately, with the American assistance, the OECS unanimously resolved to make the request.

By coincidence, on October 21, Henry Kissinger, serving as the chairman of the Kissinger Commission on Central America, briefed Reagan on the commission's first fact-finding mission. The commission had been the creation of leading Democratic hawk, Senator Henry "Scoop" Jackson in the summer of 1983 and, despite its nonpartisan label, was staffed by Jackson Democrats and leading neoconservatives and conservatives. Kissinger and his team had spent seven days traveling throughout Central America, including El Salvador and Nicaragua. He told Reagan that the crisis in the region was greater than previously documented and that concerted American action was necessary to forestall further communist advances in Latin America.

Maintaining Absolute Secrecy

While the events in Grenada intensified and military contingency plans were being developed, the officials working on the crisis tightly compartmentalized the information flow. At the State Department, the Latin America bureau completely excluded other bureaus, including the European bureau—which had responsibility for Soviet affairs—for fear that liberals at the staff level would either oppose the action or compromise its security.[83] At the White House, the president's political advisors, including White House counsel Edwin Meese, quickly concluded that no mention of American military intervention would be made to Congress until the decision had been made and troops were en route. It was clear to the advisors, that any discussion, even in the strictest of confidentiality, would enable liberals on Capitol Hill to leak the action to the press and politically limit the president's options.[84]

To further conceal the policy deliberations, and the action itself, all senior U.S. officials agreed to keep their previously planned schedules. Consequently, on Friday, October 21 the president and Secretary of State Shultz went ahead with a planned weekend golfing vacation in Augusta, Georgia. They realized that canceling the event would alert the press, Congress, and foreign observers that something important might be under discussion.[85] During NSC meetings, the principals made a point of arriving via different White House entrances, and several of the meetings were transferred from the White House situation room to a special operations center in the Old Executive Office Building, because of its greater distance from White House reporters.

As planned, the political advisors to the president deliberately shut off the flow of information concerning the Grenada action to the White House press office, even the president's own press officer. Larry Speakes later complained: "I was blissfully unaware that we were about to invade Grenada. Two and a half years on the job, and I was still out of the loop, not completely trusted by Jim Baker, Mike Deaver, and Dick Darmon, Baker's assistant." He further added, "It was not just Baker and Darmon, but Shultz and Weinberger—and the President himself—who wanted to keep the truth from me, the press and the public."[86] Speakes was informed of the invasion only an hour before he was to tell the public about it, on the morning of October 25.

It is important to note that this secrecy was motivated by two factors. First, there was genuine concern that any leaks would imperil the success of the mission and increase the danger involved. Not only would American soldiers in the invading force be further endangered, but such a disclosure might put the American citizens on the island at risk. Consequently, the administration officials believed that operational secrecy was imperative, to ensure the element of complete surprise and to avoid endangering the Americans on the ground.

A second, and *equally important* reason for maintaining secrecy, however, was to control the domestic political response.[87] The administration was well aware that there would have been serious opposition in Congress, especially among Democrats, who controlled the House of Representatives, if the consideration of American military deployment to Grenada had become public knowledge and the subject of extensive public debate.[88] In his memoirs, Ronald Reagan acknowledged these very concerns:

> Frankly, there was another reason I wanted secrecy. It was what I call the "post-Vietnam syndrome," the resistance of many in Congress to the use of military force abroad for any reason, because of our nation's experience in Vietnam. . . . I suspected that, if we told the leaders of Congress about the operation, even under the strictest confidentiality, there would be some who would leak it to the press together with the predictions that Grenada would become "another Vietnam." We were already running into this phenomenon in our efforts to halt the spread of Communism in Central America, and some congressmen were raising the issue of "another Vietnam" in Lebanon while fighting to restrict the president's constitutional powers as commander in chief.
>
>   . . . the operation was conducted under total secrecy. We didn't ask anybody, we just did it.[89]

Ed Meese elaborated: "The negatives arrayed against decisive action in Grenada were almost too numerous to count. . . . it flew in the teeth of fashionable opinion about the uses of American military power. From the standpoint of the 1970s ideology, Reagan was planning to throw America's weight around, using our military to stand up for our interests and our allies. This was heresy, and plenty of people were prepared to say so."[90] Retrospectively, Secretary of State George Shultz concluded: "No doubt, if the military had more time to plan the operation, they might have performed even better than they did. . . . At the same time, delay would undoubtedly have meant leaks and much more opposition."[91]

It was clear at the highest levels and from the earliest deliberations on using force in Grenada that the administration's political opponents would oppose the action if they knew of it. Reagan had taken several "hits" on his Latin America policy, and his key political aides knew that political opposition, if given the chance, would likely block the American action. The senior advisors also knew that they had the advantage. No one in Congress was paying much attention to the events in Grenada and the press had virtually no access. White House Chief of Staff James Baker had been monitoring congressional and media discussions on the crisis and felt confident that Reagan's domestic opponents—the liberals and the noninterventionists—had little or no information on the events in Grenada and, consequently, would have little or no warning of an impending

American intervention in Grenada.[92] In Grenada, itself, the RMC, declaring itself in control after Bishop's execution, completely shut down information flowing from Grenada. Independent Grenadan journalists operating on the island were barred from sending any dispatches off the island, while foreign correspondents were denied entry. Consequently, American journalists had little or no information, other than second-hand reports from individuals in the region or U.S. government statements.

The Political Case Is Refined

On Saturday morning October 22, the NSC met (the president participating from Georgia via speaker phone). The group discussed the OECS request, the military aspects of the mission, and then the legal and political basis for the action. Kissinger's report the day before had stirred the desire for a forceful response to the situation in Grenada. At the conclusion of the meeting, Reagan gave the tentative go-ahead for an intervention. The caveat remained that the final go-ahead would be made only after all additional political and legal issues were in place.

After Reagan's tentative decision to launch the American action, the Joint Chiefs continued the military planning and the NSC staff and State Department lawyers stepped up their work examining the political and legal aspects of the action. Constantine Menges spent the rest of the day drafting the results of early strategy sessions regarding the political basis for the American action; the strategy focused explicitly on the imperative to rescue the American citizens "attempting to flee" the island and the U.S. response to the "urgent formal request" from the OECS.

During the morning of the following day, Sunday, October 23, a suicide bomber attacked the Marine Corps barracks in Beirut killing 241 Marines. Here was a major emergency that required urgent attention of the president. Reagan, Shultz, and McFarlane immediately cut short their weekend golfing vacation in Augusta and returned to Washington. Back in Washington, Reagan and his top advisors held two National Security Planning Group meetings in which both Lebanon and Grenada were discussed. The first meeting included a briefing on the latest developments in Lebanon. Discussion then turned to whether or not the events of that day should affect any potential American action in Grenada. Reagan concluded that, despite the events in Lebanon, the military, legal, and political planning on the crisis in Grenada should continue.

During the second NSPG meeting, which happened later the same day, the discussion moved to more specific details of the likely military action in Grenada. The group focused on two elements of the Grenada situation—the potential for a hostage crisis to emerge during the invasion (or as a result of leaks of an invasion) and on the political risks of the action. The meeting began with an extensive discussion of the military operational and contingency plans for how to avoid a hostage situation. They reviewed the intelligence based on Governor-General Scoon's reports suggesting that failure to act immediately could trigger another hostage crisis. Largely on this basis, and with the OECS request in hand, Vice President Bush joined with the hardliners to endorse the decision to intervene. The OECS request mitigated some of the concerns of General Vessey, who was still stipulating the requirements that the military receive the necessary material support and political support for the action.

The second part of the discussion turned toward the specific political aspects of the proposed military action. On this, the NSC staff still had a high hurdle to overcome. The president's core political advisors—Baker and his deputies Richard Darman and Michael Deaver—had long been suspicious of the NSC hardliners. In particular, they were concerned from the first days of the administration that the hardliners in the NSC were intent on dragging the president into a war in Central America that "would kill him" politically. From the outset of the administration in 1981 they had an intense "feeling" that they "had to be alert and careful with these guys." Deaver later recalled his worry: "My whole attitude was to protect the President."[93] Nonetheless, following the planning group briefing Baker, Darman, and Deaver were convinced that "Grenada was an action that had been very well thought out." They "had been promised and we were convinced this was something that could be justified and easily explained to the American public."[94]

One striking element of the political discussion at this point, however, was that the public justification that had been drafted by Menges the previous day made no mention of the Soviet or Cuban influence on the island. Even though the central imperative deliberated by hardliners and selective engagers throughout the planning sessions was the geostrategic imperative, the decision to avoid any mention of the Cold War aspects of the crisis "was a deliberate effort," according to Michael Deaver. Reagan and his political advisors believed that the administration's line would be a "much more easily accepted decision if it didn't look like it had cold war overtones. That it was really a regional issue."[95]

Finally, the NSC team agreed that the public relations campaign would be greatly aided if a regional leader, preferably Prime Minister Eugenia Charles of Dominica, would fly to Washington to attend the president's announcement on the invasion. Reagan and his advisors concluded that the fact that she was a leader of the regional alliance and that she was a woman "would soften the issue."[96] Indeed, Deaver later cited Eugenia Charles's performance on October 25, standing next to the president, as "the single best point" in the selling of the intervention.[97]

The anticipated political response was well considered. During the Sunday meetings, Reagan and his advisors concluded that they had successfully controlled all information on the situation in Grenada and that Americans would see this as a potential hostage situation. Furthermore, and completely unexpectedly, the entire focus of Congress, the media, and the public on Sunday and Monday—two critical days in the decision-making process and preinvasion planning on Grenada—were almost exclusively focused on the events in Lebanon. Little, if any, attention was paid to the situation in Grenada.

Consequently, as Brigitte Nacos found in her study of the crisis in Grenada, virtually all information prior to and during the initial phase of the intervention was dominated by the Reagan administration's views and interpretations of the nature of the conflict and the reasons for the American action.[98] Nacos found that in the weeks leading up to the American action, very little attention was paid to the island. What news coverage Grenada did receive conveyed the views of the president and his advisors.

This advantage was well known to the administration officials as they considered the invasion, and it gave them confidence that their message would resonate with the American public.[99] As Michael Deaver confirmed, "We knew that no one [outside of the administration] knew much about the situation in Grenada and that this was not a place television could get to easily."[100]

On Sunday evening, after the daylong series of meetings, President Reagan reiterated his decision to go ahead with a military invasion of Grenada; and as of then, all of the political, legal, and military pieces necessary for the action were in place.

The Final Decision and the Notification of Congress

On Monday, October 24, Reagan received one last series of briefings from his top political and military advisors. The Joint Chiefs told him that the military wished they had more preinvasion intelligence but that they believed the action would go smoothly. However, they continued to express their concerns about the domestic political reaction. General Vessey suggested that because of the attack on U.S. Marines in Lebanon, there could well be a "potential public opinion downside" to the action.[101]

Baker and Deaver were also concerned about this potential downside. Upon arriving in their offices Monday morning they learned that public opinion polls conducted during the previous twenty-four hours by the administration's pollster, Richard Wirthlin, revealed a "precipitous overnight decline in Reagan's approval rating" in response to the events in Lebanon.[102] They turned to Robert McFarlane, who again reassured them that the public would readily accept that the primary motivation for the action in Grenada was the protection of American students who were endangered.

Following a Monday afternoon briefing and with the support of senior political advisors who were convinced that Grenada could be managed, Reagan formally signed the invasion order. The American military forces would hit Grenada in the early morning hours of Tuesday.

That evening, Reagan performed his constitutional obligation under the War Powers Act by "consulting" key members of Congress. In a secret meeting in the White House residence, a small group of leading Republicans and Democrats were called in to hear the president. None of the members of Congress had any idea of the subject matter—a testimony to how closely the planning had been held. At the meeting, Reagan informed the members that he had conclusive evidence that Americans in Grenada were endangered, that the Soviets and Cubans had been compiling a massive amount of weapons for the Grenadan Marxists, and that Grenada was "dominated by Castro." After a brief set of questions, the members deferred to the president, aware that the landing force was already en route and nothing could be done to stop it. Speaker of the House Tip O'Neill announced: "Mr. President, I have been informed but not consulted." He later wrote: "The invasion was already under way, so even if we opposed it there was nothing any of us could do. I had some serious reservations and I'm sure my Democratic colleagues did as well, but I'd be damned if I was going to voice my criticism while our boys were out there."[103] House majority leader Jim Wright later described the bind in which the members found themselves: "All of us were aware of Bishop's overthrow some two weeks earlier. This was the first we knew, however, of the other developments. None of us was prepared to dispute the State Department findings. We had no knowledge to the contrary on which to base an objection."[104]

The information monopoly had effectively prevented opposition in advance of the intervention. Later, as Reagan's claims concerning the magnitude of Soviet and Cuban presence on the island and of caches of weapons were exposed to multiple sources of information, Wright and his colleagues would formulate considerable criticisms of the U.S. action. Tip O'Neill recorded in his memoirs several years after the "crisis" his realization that the American students were simply not threatened and that the argument had been a ruse.[105]

Selling the Public

Throughout the remainder of Monday afternoon and evening, Menges in the NSC and Baker and Darmon in the White House continued to work on the political materials about the military action. Menges provided the substantive claims concerning the events in Grenada while Reagan's speechwriters and his most senior political handlers delicately crafted the wording for the public announcement. At 5:30 a.m., on Tuesday, October 25, as the American forces were landing on Grenada, James Baker called in White House spokesman Larry Speakes, handed him a packet of information and informed him of the U.S. action.[106] At 7:00 a.m. Speakes held his regular morning briefing for reporters and informed them that American troops had landed on Grenada and that the president would address the nation at 9:00 a.m.

Meanwhile, Prime Minister Eugenia Charles arrived at the White House. After a short meeting with President Reagan, she departed with Constantine Menges and Deputy Secretary of State Kenneth Damm, who spent the next hour coaching the prime minister on what to say to the American press. According to Menges, "we worked on the phrasing of brief yet substantive answers. (In the future I would do this quite often, helping visiting heads of state prepare for the skeptical, occasionally hostile questions of the media.)"[107]

Early Returns: A Mixed Message

In his address on the morning of the invasion, President Reagan told the press that the "overriding" motivation for the invasion was to "protect innocent lives, including up to 1,000 Americans whose personal safety is, of course, my paramount concern."[108] The presentation by Eugenia Charles furthered this view.

For the next day and a half, the selective engagers and hardliners were only partially successful in generating public support. While they were able to be the leading source of news about the crisis, a series of questions lingered: Were the students really endangered?[109] What efforts had been made to secure their release via diplomatic rather than military efforts? Was the request by the OECS truly a legal basis for the action and did it not contradict the treaty of the Organization of American States? Why was the press precluded from accompanying the troops? What were the military and the administration trying to hide?

The administration struggled to cope with these questions. Clearly the initial response to Grenada was mixed. In overnight polls conducted by Wirthlin, the American public expressed concern and outrage about Lebanon and confusion about Grenada, and Reagan's political numbers dropped. In a *Washington Post* poll, Barry Sussman found that most Americans were

> distraught over what had happened in Lebanon, puzzled over Grenada, and decidedly unhappy with Reagan's adventurism.
>
> Only a minority, forty-four percent, approved of Reagan's overall handling of foreign policy. Six people in ten took the view that "the United States is trying to do too much with its armed forces overseas." Only four in ten approved of Reagan's handling of the situation in Lebanon, and only a slim majority, fifty-three percent, approved of the invasion of Grenada, *despite its having been advertised as a mission to rescue American youngsters.*[110]

The mixed public response may reflect the inconsistency between the public justifications and the actual basic reasons for the actions. This inconsistency also left senior administration officials—even the president—often struggling to stay on message during the succeeding days. For example, despite his strong statement of the threat to American students, President Reagan at one point acknowledged that American citizens had not been in any immediate danger. During a subsequent press conference, Larry Speakes was challenged by reporters to detail the exact nature of the threat to the American students. In response, he said that there was "nothing that I know of."[111] In fact, Speakes later acknowledged that he had always been skeptical of the seriousness of the threat to the students.

> Although the leaders of the coup in Grenada had warned that anyone who went outdoors would be shot, there really was no hard proof that they intended to harm the American medical students. To do so, in fact, would have been disastrous from an economic standpoint, since the medical school was a major source of income on the island, which was also heavily dependent on the tourist trade.
>
> Moreover, *the leaders of the coup sent us an urgent message the night before the invasion that any American citizen who wished to leave was free to do so.* Neverthe-

less, at 10:15 Monday night, less than eight hours before the invasion, Shultz ordered the U.S. embassy in Barbados to notify the Grenadan military leaders that their message was being rejected because we questioned whether they constituted a legitimate government.[112]

Another question that plagued the administration was how hard the United States had tried to resolve the crisis through diplomatic, rather than military, avenues. Again, the administration's response was ambiguous and often contradictory. The reality is that very little diplomatic effort had been invested before the intervention to ensure the safety of the citizens. Prior to the American invasion, the RMC leadership had cut a deal with the medical school to open the airport on Monday, October 24, so people could fly out if they wished. Indeed the airport was opened for several hours. However, it closed early that afternoon after the pro-U.S. islands neighboring Grenada suspended all air traffic. Because of its small runway, the airport in Grenada could accommodate only small aircraft with limited fuel capacity and the neighboring airports were necessary.[113] (Later, the administration used closure of the Grenadan airport as further justification for the intervention.) Meanwhile, Canadian and British diplomats had negotiated for the evacuation of its citizens on Tuesday, October 25. However, the evacuation plans were overruled by the U.S. military forces during their assault on the island. This prompted Canadian officials to conclude that it was the American invasion, not the actions of the Grenadan leadership, that had put foreign citizens in peril on the island.[114]

Given the public's initial reaction to the invasion, and aware that the political side of the situation had the potential to unravel quickly, Reagan and his advisors decided that he should address the nation in a televised speech from the Oval Office. They knew that Reagan's strength was his personal appearance to the American public.[115] As Lou Cannon would observe in his book *President Reagan: The Role of a Lifetime*, "Reagan recognized the salesman's truth that salesmen sell themselves before they sell their products, and he used his speeches to reaffirm his personal relationships with the American audience."[116]

On the evening of Thursday, October 27, Reagan presented his case by television. In his speech, two new themes were added to the public relations campaign: the military action had swiftly accomplished its mission and the American citizens had been secured. He described that the American forces had captured massive amounts of Soviet- and Cuban-made weapons, which proved that Grenada was a "Soviet-Cuban colony being readied as a major military bastion to export terror and undermine democracy."[117] Reagan also argued that the RMC forces that had executed Bishop were particularly barbaric, that it was imperative for the United States to "restore law and order and help the people of Grenada restore functioning institutions of government," and that the United States "also had a particularly humanitarian concern." "The lack of respect for human rights and the degenerating conditions" were a serious threat to "the people of Grenada." This argument was essentially "making a tentative legal case for 'humanitarian intervention'"—an attempt by the administration to co-opt liberal opposition to the action.[118]

By all accounts the speech was masterful and had dramatic effects.[119] Public opinion polls after the speech revealed a dramatic jump in approval of the president and his handling of Lebanon, Grenada, and foreign policy in general. Before the speech, only 45 percent of Americans believed the students to have been in real danger; after the speech 58 percent felt they had been.[120]

The Influence of the Information Monopoly

The absence of public debate about Grenada allowed the interpretation of information and news about events before and during the invasion to be generated primarily by the president and his key advisors. The initial news of the intervention produced only a slight majority of American support for the action. Most of the shift in support for intervention after the president's television address on October 27 came from those who saw the speech or read about it. Among those who did not watch the speech or did not hear about it, there was very little shift in opinion.

One issue that seemed to resonate with the public was Reagan's claim of "six warehouses" containing weapons stacked to the ceiling. Two days after the speech, when public support had been firmly established, American military officials, under pressure from news organizations, allowed reporters a tour of the warehouses. Loren Jenkins of the *New York Times* reported that "there appeared to be a certain amount of hyperbole in the official descriptions." Three of the warehouses contained no weapons and the "principal arms storage shed was not 'stacked almost to the ceiling' with weaponry, but was probably a quarter full—about 190 crates of assorted guns. Some were modern Soviet-made infantry weapons, but many were antiquated, of little value to a modern army or guerilla force."[121]

Additionally, during the fighting, the U.S. military reported that several hundred Cubans had headed for the hills to fight a guerrilla campaign against the U.S. forces. These stories ran for several days following the initial American assault and became, for many Americans, further evidence of the Cuban-Soviet conspiracy to take over the Caribbean. The Pentagon later admitted that the number of Cuban combatants had been overstated and that stories of Cuban guerrillas heading to the hills were unfounded. However, neither the Pentagon nor the White House ever explained why the story had been released in the first place.

Summary

Grenada was a quick and decisive victory, but the ease with which the military objectives were secured in Grenada masks the significantly higher political risks of the mission. Vietnam greatly intensified the cleavages among policy elites over when and where the United States should use military force.

Reagan and his hardliners came into office convinced that the United States was falling behind in the Cold War. They distrusted liberals and what they believed to be Carter's naïve commitment to ideals. They doubted the professional intelligence agencies' ability to fully decipher threats and they remained wary of the professional military planners and their reluctance to use force. The actions from Moscow in the fall of 1983—the shooting down of the Korean airliner in September and the results of the Kissinger fact-finding mission— reinforced the hardliners' belief in the absolute moral baseness of Soviet totalitarianism. Therefore, they were quick to interpret the events in Grenada in worst-case scenarios. They believed that the events in Grenada were further evidence of the growing threats from Moscow and Havana; they concluded that the only plausible explanation for the construction of a 10,000-foot runway at Port Salinas airport was that it would be used for Soviet military expansion; and they relied heavily on intelligence reports from Sir Paul Scoon and his warnings of dire dangers to American medical students.

Selective engagers, for their part, were more circumspect. They concluded that Moscow and Havana would certainly seek to exploit any power vacuum in Grenada, but they were never as convinced about the influence of either Havana or Moscow on the events in Grenada. Their views evolved toward intervention in large part because of their concern that another hostage crisis might erupt. The Iranian hostage crisis had been resolved only a year and a half earlier and a similar situation was not unthinkable.

Liberals, however, tended to see the events in Grenada and the rise of the

PRG as generated by poverty and indigenous reaction to the abusive regime of Gairy. They were then, and are to this day, skeptical of the claims of the threat to the medical students and the degree of Cuban and Soviet involvement in Grenada and in the coup.

Reagan and his advisors were highly sensitive to the domestic political context, so, immediately after the coup, they tightened their control of information on Grenada. The administration was well aware that liberals and other potential opponents had no presence in Grenada and that journalists had been expelled from Grenada immediately after the coup. They well understood the significant information advantages at their disposal as they considered their options for action. Within this context, the administration deliberately constructed the analytical narrative of the crisis as the necessity to save endangered American medical students and as a neighborly response to the "urgent" request of a regional alliance. Although American diplomats and senior Reagan officials were the principal initiators of the OECS request, it was presented to the public and Congress as wholly independent of U.S. diplomacy and pressure. Finally, the administration benefited from the rapid sequence of the events. Maurice Bishop was arrested on October 13 and executed six days later. Reagan made his initial decision to intervene on October 22—three days after Bishop's execution. Three days after that, American forces landed on Grenada in the predawn hours. In such a short period, there was no time for organized opposition to discover information on the situation and to develop or mobilize a public discussion on possible courses of American action.

CHAPTER FIVE

Famine in Somalia and Ancient Hatreds in Bosnia

Somalis, as the Italians and British discovered to their discomfiture, are natural born guerillas. They will mine the roads. They will lay in ambushes. They will launch hit and run attacks.

—AMBASSADOR SMITH HEMPSTONE, JR.

Statesmen . . . do not have the right to launch their nations into large unfathomable military adventures, to risk not their lives but the lives of their countrymen purely out of humanitarian feeling.

—CHARLES KRAUTHAMMER

Introduction

On November 21, 1992, General Colin Powell's chief deputy on the Joint Chiefs of Staff, Admiral David Jeremiah, stunned the National Security Council Deputies Committee at a meeting on the humanitarian crisis caused by civil strife in Somalia by announcing, "If you think U.S. forces are needed, we can do the job."[1] Four days later President George H. W. Bush decided that U.S. forces were needed. On December 9, a force of 1,300 U.S. Marines landed in Mogadishu, and within weeks more than 25,000 U.S. soldiers were on the ground in Somalia.

Prior to the November 21 deputies meeting, virtually no one in or out of the administration expected that Bush or his top political and military advisors would support a major U.S. humanitarian mission to Somalia.[2] For more than a year, the administration, and General Powell and the Joint Chiefs of Staff in particular, had steadfastly opposed calls for U.S. humanitarian military interventions in Somalia, Liberia, Bosnia, and elsewhere,[3] arguing that none of these conflicts was relevant to U.S. vital interests.[4] They were simply humanitarian tragedies.

With respect to conditions in Somalia, senior Bush administration and military officials argued repeatedly throughout most of 1992 that the deeply historic interclan conflicts that permeated the country would make any military intervention extraordinarily risky. The basic position of the Joint Chiefs and the senior White House staff was that U.S. forces would not be able to protect themselves or the distribution of humanitarian relief because the nature of the conflict made it nearly impossible to distinguish friend from foe or civilian from combatant. In short, the administration argued, attempting to rein in roaming armed bandits fueled by ancient hatreds and intermingled with the civilian population was a recipe for disaster.

Why then did President Bush, with the firm support of all of his key advisors—including General Powell—ultimately decide to launch a massive U.S. military intervention in Somalia? Why did the Joint Chiefs of Staff reverse their July 1992 assessment—that the situation in Somalia was a "bottomless pit"—to their November proclamation, "we can do the job?"[5] Nothing changed the political, military, or logistical factors on the ground during the intervening period. The conditions in Somalia had long before reached crisis proportions. What explains the sudden change of heart within the Bush administration?

The intervention is even more puzzling if one accepts the prevailing explanation for it. This construct suggests that by November 1992 the humanitarian situation had become morally untenable. According to this view, the growing outrage felt by President Bush and his key advisors over reports of massive starvation led them to three conclusions: (1) the situation had become dire; (2) only the United States possessed the capabilities to tackle the crisis; and (3) Somalia was a case where the mission of providing security for humanitarian relief was well-defined and achievable.[6] Speaking from this context, administration officials argued that Somalia was a case that fit most of the criteria General Powell held for an achievable military mission, which came to be called the Powell Doctrine: (1) the deployment could be done with overwhelming force; (2) the political and military objectives were clearly defined; (3) the mission was doable; and (4) public and congressional support was widespread.[7]

This explanation, however, is unsatisfactory for three reasons. First, it ignores the fact that the situation in Somalia had long been one of profound need. The U.S. decision in November 1992 came nearly a full year after the famine there had been declared the world's worst humanitarian emergency.[8] In fact, as early as January 1992, the assistant administrator of the U.S. Agency for

International Development (AID) and a noted advocate for Somalia, Andrew Natsios, had begun holding regular press conferences to highlight the ongoing humanitarian catastrophe.[9] By early summer, more than 300,000 civilians had died since 1989, and in July the International Committee of the Red Cross (ICRC) reiterated its six-month-old estimates that 95 percent of the population of Somalia was malnourished and 70 percent in imminent danger of death by starvation.[10] Indeed, almost all available evidence suggests that the situation had become untenable long before November 21.

Second, contrary to the public statements by the Joint Chiefs of Staff and the president at the time of the decision, the U.S. mission was not well defined.[11] The president announced that the operation was designed to establish a stable security framework to ensure the delivery and distribution of relief aid to famine victims. Yet, a basic point of contention that had not been addressed was whether or not U.S. forces would need to disarm the tens of thousands of roaming armed bandits who were at the heart of the security challenge.[12] In fact, at the time of the president's decision, several U.S. military commanders feared that the deployment might lead to an escalation of violence that could quickly engulf the U.S. forces.[13] According to one senior Pentagon official, "if the Somali warlords did not back down quickly, as was hoped, the number of troops required to continue the operation could add up in a hurry."[14]

Third, whereas in November 1992 the Joint Chiefs and others in the Bush administration argued that a U.S. mission in Somalia was doable, throughout most of the year they had contended precisely the opposite. For more than a year before the intervention, the Joint Chiefs had consistently maintained that humanitarian emergencies were, by their nature, political events and that one side or another would balk at international assistance. This meant that intervention would ultimately require taking sides—and this inevitably would create a threat to U.S. forces. The Joint Chiefs had also insisted that intervention in Somalia would be risky. When asked in the spring and early summer of 1992 to develop contingency plans for intervention, the Joint Chiefs made three arguments in opposition at a series of interagency meetings: (1) the conflict in Somalia was fueled by age-old tribal animosities; (2) the tribal combatants were heavily armed and indistinguishable from civilian populations, making protection of U.S. forces virtually impossible; and (3) the desert terrain, although open, would create enormous operational and tactical difficulties for close air support for troops on the ground.[15] Moreover, other senior officials had come to agree with the Joint Chiefs that the crisis in Somalia was, at its core, a political issue that could not be readily resolved with the use of U.S. military force.[16]

Finally, these conventional views ignore that deliberations on the humanitarian crisis in Somalia occurred amid a frenzied public debate over the violence in Bosnia, which was happening simultaneously. Throughout the spring and summer of 1992, Serb forces had besieged Sarajevo, Bosnia's capital city, isolating nearly 300,000 civilians. Media reports, editorials, and commentaries argued that the United States should use its military force, now freed from the Cold War priorities, in an effort to solve these humanitarian crises. The Joint Chiefs' abrupt shift on Somalia came within an increasingly politicized debate over Bosnia.

The Argument

Given the administration's consistent opposition to U.S. intervention in Somalia, why did President Bush and General Powell agree in November 1992 to deploy U.S. combat forces on a mission with no clear exit strategy and no well-defined objectives? In short, why did Bush and Powell violate the Powell Doctrine?

I suggest that the U.S. intervention in Somalia resulted from political interplay among foreign policy elites who held divergent beliefs about when and where the United States should intervene, and from cumulative pressure on the administration to act in both Somalia *and* Bosnia. Selective engagers, who dominated in the Bush administration and the senior military officer corps, believed that U.S. military intervention should be reserved for those cases when U.S. strategic interests were directly threatened. Throughout 1991 and most of 1992, they opposed any form of U.S. military involvement in either Somalia or Bosnia—as well as in other humanitarian crises. The central challenge to selective engagers came from the liberals who filled the ranks of humanitarian and human rights nongovernmental organizations (NGOs) and held key bureaucratic positions at the U.S. State Department and Agency for International Development and who supported military intervention to provide relief to aggrieved populations and to stop or prevent atrocities perpetrated against civilians.

Given their advantages in access to information and executive branch political mobilization resources, selective engagers were initially able to frame both the Somalian and the Bosnian conflicts as being fueled by ancient tribal and ethnic hatreds about which the United States could do little. Relying on this portrayal, the Bush administration was successful in tempering calls for greater U.S. involvement. As both crises persisted into the late summer and fall of 1992, however, liberals and the media began to amass their own information about the conflicts. In each case, they started to challenge the selective engagers' depiction of the crisis. In addition, liberals and the media began to reframe the conflicts as highly coordinated, violent campaigns orchestrated by ruthless elites to advance their narrow political ambitions. Based on this portrayal, they argued that U.S.-led intervention targeted against these political elites would quickly mitigate the humanitarian catastrophes.

Throughout the fall of 1992, liberals escalated their advocacy efforts and mobilized political pressure on the Bush administration to take action in both Somalia and Bosnia. In addition, the neoconservative faction of the hardliners split from the more conservative hardliners and took the stance that the conflict in Bosnia posed a significant problem for American interests. They too added their support for more aggressive U.S. action in that conflict, although for different reasons than the liberals. While this pressure was building, Bill Clinton won the presidential election. President Bush and General Powell believed that liberals would dominate the new administration and use the bully pulpit of the White House to promote U.S. intervention in Bosnia. Given the shift in power in Washington and the intensity of mobilized political pressure to respond to foreign humanitarian emergencies, Bush and Powell decided that if the United States were going to intervene, it should be in Somalia—not Bosnia, that Somalia would be the easier of the two missions to achieve.

Background of the Crisis in Somalia

Somalia's first civilian government came to power in July 1960 with the joining of a British colony and an Italian colony. During its first decade, no civilian government was able to develop stable political, economic, and social conditions, and in 1969, military leader Mohammed Siad Barre successfully launched a coup and took power, naming himself president. Almost immediately, Barre declared Somalia a socialist state and introduced extensive political, economic, and social reforms. The most significant "reforms" disbanded virtually all professional and political organizations and curbed all open political dissent.[17]

Barre consolidated and held his power by garnering massive military assistance from the superpowers and by effectively exploiting clan-based cleavages to undermine any significant opposition. To ensure a stable power base, Barre provided large benefits to, and heavily armed, loyal members of his own clan. With their support and with superpower military and economic assistance, Barre successfully maintained a strong rule until the late 1980s, despite perpetual economic and social crises.[18]

By mid-1988, the two decades of harsh rule and severe economic deprivations coupled with the decline of once-extensive U.S. military support provided both the catalyst and the opportunity for the emergence of open challenges to Barre's regime. Over the next two years, increased political dissent, open demonstrations, and political cleavages within the Barre regime gradually eroded the dictator's control. Regionally based rebel clan groups surfaced and provoked open conflict with Barre's military on several occasions. Barre's chief rivals came from the Somali National Movement (SNM) in the northern territories, the Somali Patriotic Movement (SPM), which operated out of the southern regions, and the United Somali Congress (USC), which emerged in several urban areas, including Mogadishu.[19]

In November 1990, the sporadic tensions ignited into open civil war when Barre ordered his security forces to search Mogadishu, house-to-house, for all opposition leaders. Battles ensued, and a faction within the USC captured much of Mogadishu and the presidential palace. With his forces routed, Barre fled Mogadishu in January 1991.

The USC quickly established its own government in Mogadishu without consulting the two other opposition groups. The USC declared Ali Mahdi Somalia's interim president and invited the SPM and the SNM to a national conference of reconciliation to draft a new constitution. Angered by the USC's not consulting them in the selection of Mahdi, both the SPM and SNM immediately rejected the offer. The SNM, which controlled the northern territory of Somaliland, subsequently declared that territory independent from Somalia. The SPM, heavily tied to the Ogadan clan, asserted almost complete control over the southern territories. Tensions and cleavages emerged within many of the clans as well. By mid-1991 the territory of Somalia was effectively under the control of no fewer than seven rival clan-based factions.[20]

Meanwhile, within the USC, a major chasm developed between President Mahdi and the USC military chief General Mohammed Farah Aideed. After months of intense rivalry, in November 1991 fighting broke out in Mogadishu between the two USC factions. The fights soon degenerated into bitter inter-gang urban warfare. Both sides conducted extremely violent campaigns, terrorizing and killing civilians who appeared sympathetic to the rival faction.

By late 1991, the Somali state had collapsed and the battling had placed the country's seven million civilians in jeopardy. *Africa Watch* reported that the warring parties were engaged in widespread "wanton and indiscriminate" attacks on civilians.[21] In addition, the fighting in Mogadishu had forced a complete suspension of all routine economic activity, including the production and distribution of food and medicine, and other basic goods and services. Within the first two months of the fighting, there had been more than 20,000 casualties and 250,000 persons had been displaced from their homes.[22] Most displaced persons made their way to refugee camps, but the camps were ill-equipped to provide relief or security.

Shortly before Siad Barre fled, the intensity of the fighting in Mogadishu had forced the United Nations representatives and the international diplomatic corps there to withdraw. Between January 1991 and mid-1992 there was little or no UN or international presence in Somalia. The most immediate result of this international draw-down was the suspension of most international relief efforts. The humanitarian relief presence in Somalia was reduced to unarmed and ill-equipped private volunteer organizations. Although these private organizations hired local armed security personnel to escort relief supplies, their efforts were largely unsuccessful.

Battles among other factions in the countryside also disrupted the production and delivery of vital food supplies to refugees. UN reports at the time estimated that as much as 80 percent of the food in the country was being looted by armed gangs. In January 1992 the ICRC calculated that almost half of the country's 6 million people faced severe nutritional needs and that many would die by starvation without some form of immediate assistance.[23] According to UN undersecretary Mohamed Sahnoun, by the beginning of 1992, nearly 300,000 Somalis had starved to death; more than 3,000 were dying daily from starvation; more than 500,000 had fled to neighboring Ethiopia, Djibouti, and Kenya, severely taxing resources in those countries; and more than 70 percent of all livestock had perished from famine.[24] In the spring of 1992, the United Nations High Commission on Refugees (UNHCR) estimated that as many as 4.5 million of the country's 6 million civilians would be subject to death by starvation without some form of immediate assistance.[25]

Background of the Crisis in Bosnia

On June 23, 1991, the governments of the republics of Slovenia and Croatia formally announced their secession from the Socialist Federal Republic of Yugoslavia. These announcements followed nearly a decade of economic and political turmoil in Yugoslavia. In the wake of Gen. Josip Broz Tito's death in 1980, Yugoslavia had been governed by a tenuous political power-sharing arrangement that dispersed governing authority among the country's six republics and two autonomous regions. This arrangement, created by Tito and codified in the 1974 constitution, maintained the Communist Party's monopoly on power and was an attempt to ensure a balance among the republics and to prevent domination in the federation by the republic of Serbia in a post-Tito Yugoslavia.

However, a series of political and economic crises throughout the 1980s created greater fissures within the federation. Croatia and Slovenia welcomed the liberalization and decentralization of the communist world and the revolutions of 1989. In the spring of 1990 both republics held multiparty elections for the first time since the inception of the federation. Non-Communist candidates campaigned and won on platforms castigating Serbian domination of the federation and the federal policies that redistributed Croatian and Slovenian wealth to the poorer southern regions of the federation.

While Croatia and Slovenia were moving toward economic liberalization and political decentralization, the federation's largest republic, Serbia, was moving in the opposite direction. In 1987, Slobodan Milošević rode to power in Serbia by aligning himself with hardline Serb nationalists and expanding the Communist Party's control on political power. Once he had consolidated his power in Serbia, Milošević quickly moved toward greater centralization of political and economic control throughout Yugoslavia. In 1989 he unilaterally altered the 1974 federal constitution by revoking the autonomous status of Kosovo and Vojvodina, a move that greatly exacerbated secessionist forces in Slovenia and Croatia.

By mid-1990 the countervailing pressures of decentralization favored by the Slovenes and Croats and the recentralization sponsored by Milošević had led to the breakup of the federation. In July 1991, just days after Croatia and Slovenia issued their declarations of independence, Yugoslav federal authorities in Belgrade dispatched forces to Slovenia. After a six-week period of clashes between Serb-led Yugoslav soldiers and Slovenian fighters, the federal forces withdrew. Slovenia's independence from Yugoslavia was largely achieved.

Croatia suffered a different fate. Many of the federal forces that had been stationed in Slovenia withdrew into Croatia and began fighting against Croatian soldiers. Between late July 1991 and January 1992, Croatian and Yugoslav forces fought an intense war. In January 1992, international mediators achieved a suspension of the fighting. More than a third of Croatian territory was still under the control of Serb-led Yugoslav forces, but Croatia had secured its independence.

Caught amidst these conflicting forces was the Republic of Bosnia-Herzegovina. With its ethnically and religiously diverse population—44 percent Muslim, 31 percent Serbian Orthodox Christian, and 17 percent Croatian Catholic—the Bosnian government attempted initially to stay out of the fray. However, as in Slovenia and Croatia, non-Communist political forces demanded multiparty elections. In December 1990, such elections were held, and seats were won by Serbian, Croat, and Muslim nationalists. Alija Izetbegovic, head of the Muslim Party, was chosen to be president.

As the war in neighboring Croatia intensified in the fall of 1991, Izetbegovic and his Muslim-dominated SDA lobbied the Bosnian Assembly to declare Bosnian sovereignty from Serb-led Yugoslavia. When Croat representatives added their support to that of the Bosnian Muslims, together they constituted nearly 60 percent of the Assembly, and the declaration easily passed. The Serbian delegates protested the declaration by abstaining en masse from the vote and walking out of the parliamentary chamber.

On January 25, 1992, Muslims and Croats pressed for a vote in the Bosnian Assembly on a resolution to hold a public referendum on independence. Muslim and Croat representatives voted in favor; Serb delegates again boycotted the vote. The outcome of the ensuing referendum, which was held in March, was never in doubt. Ninety-nine percent of all Muslims and Croats in the republic voted in favor of independence while Serbs boycotted the referendum. The result was that 66 percent of the population of Bosnia supported independence. International recognition followed. Even as the referendum was taking place, violent skirmishes between Serbs, Croats, and Muslims erupted in Sarajevo. International mediators, led by former secretary of state Cyrus Vance, went to Bosnia in the hope of stabilizing the situation. Vance encouraged leaders from the three groups to divide Bosnia into ethnic cantons, in which local municipalities would be governed by their respective ethnic majorities. Within a week of this "Sarajevo Agreement," all three sides recanted and tensions again flared.

On March 27, 1992, the Serbian leaders in Bosnia formally proclaimed the Serbian Republic of Bosnia-Herzegovina and pledged its loyalty to the "all-Serbian State of Yugoslavia." This declaration set off a massive wave of violence in northern Bosnia. Bosnian Serb and Serb paramilitary forces that had assembled several months earlier launched a major offensive against Muslim- and Croat-populated communities. Within two months, these forces, operating with the Yugoslav Army, secured all of northern Bosnia and began perpetrating the worst atrocities against civilians in Europe since World War II.

Elites' Views before the Two Crises

This section examines two decisions on U.S. military intervention, the U.S. decision to intervene in Somalia in 1992 and the decision not to intervene in Bosnia. The research for it included extensive interviews with several of the principal decision makers and participants in the policy deliberations.

Selective Engagers and the End of the Cold War

During President Bush's first year in office, the world began a major transition. U.S.-Soviet relations continued to improve significantly. Soviet leader Mikhail Gorbachev instituted a "new thinking" for Eastern Europe. This shift ultimately led to the collapse of communist regimes throughout Eastern and Central Europe. In Latin America, the Sandinista government in Nicaragua held and lost open elections, while the brutal regimes in El Salvador and Chile began processes of internal reform.

For the selective engagers, these dramatic changes were welcomed but with some anxiety.[26] On the one hand, the end of the U.S.-Soviet rivalry clearly eased the global tensions that had existed for more than four decades. The threat of nuclear war was dramatically reduced and the arms race and U.S.-Soviet competition in the Third World dissipated. Yet, the end of the Cold War also altered well-established power alignments. Selective engagers faced a new set of issues with no clear road map. Furthermore, the internal pressures that had forced Gorbachev's hand and led him to relinquish control in Eastern Europe also threatened to tear apart the Soviet Union. The selective engagers feared that these economic and political pressures could quickly unleash uncontrollable disintegration processes and ignite a resurgence of ethnic and national conflicts throughout the Soviet Union. Consequently, from 1989 until early 1992, the United States, while lauding the collapse of the Berlin Wall, the reunification of Germany, and the emergence of new regimes in Eastern and Central Europe, kept a cautious eye on Moscow. As Bush described his role, he had "an obligation to temper optimism with prudence."[27]

The selective engagers also feared the emergence of a neo-isolationist impulse at home. Much of the rationale that had been used by selective engagers to support massive military expenditures and extensive international commitments throughout the Cold War was now gone. What purpose did NATO serve without the Soviet adversary?[28] Selective engagers argued that the perpetuation of NATO and commitments such as the U.S. presence in East Asia were essential to American vital interests. They also believed that the United States should redouble its efforts to manage "new threats"—nuclear proliferation, international terrorism, and regional conflicts in areas of American interests.[29] In short, even though the Cold War had ended, there were still numerous and serious threats to America's vital national interests, and American foreign policy needed to reflect vigilance.

Selective Engagers and Regional Conflicts

The first major test in this new environment was the Iraqi invasion of Kuwait in August 1990. Selective engagers saw the Iraqi invasion as a direct challenge to stability in the oil-rich and vitally important Middle East.[30] This threat could not go unchallenged. President Bush quickly announced that the Iraqi invasion would not stand, and Secretary of State James Baker demanded that the international community act to "prevent an individual clearly bent on regional domination from establishing a chokehold on the world's economic lifeline."[31] In response, the selective engagers mobilized a massive domestic and international coalition against the Iraqi actions.

While the selective engagers were ready to use force to protect America's material interests in the Middle East, they were not fully prepared, nor fully willing, to meet the profound humanitarian challenges emanating from similar regional conflicts elsewhere. U.S. policy toward Somalia and the former Yugoslavia in 1990 and 1991 reflected the prevailing view that the end of the Cold War had caused both the Horn of Africa and the Balkans to be of dramatically diminished strategic importance to the United States.

For selective engagers, the dissolution of Yugoslavia mattered to the extent that the unleashed ancient ethnic hatreds might create regional instability. Thus, the prudent policy choice, despite the profound transitions occurring throughout the rest of Eastern and Central Europe, was to support some form of centralized authority and to press for gradual change. From 1990 until the outbreak of war in Croatia in July 1991 and Bosnia in March 1992, the administration devoted its diplomatic energies to developing strategies to forestall the collapse of the Yugoslav federation. Once violence erupted, the policy shifted from prevention to containment.

In Somalia, U.S. policy was similarly focused. During the Cold War, the United States had contributed vast sums to President Barre in an effort to stabilize the Horn of Africa against the influence of the Soviet-backed regime of Mengistu Haile Mariam in Ethiopia. With the erosion of Soviet influence and competition, policymakers in Washington no longer considered these contributions imperative to American geostrategic interests. Without the financial backing of the United States to prop up Barre's corrupt regime, Somalia quickly disintegrated into interethnic civil conflict. But because that crisis posed little threat to U.S. political or economic interests and did not seem to endanger regional or international stability, the Bush administration throughout much of 1991 and most of 1992 viewed it as an internal problem that the Somali leadership needed to resolve.

Hardliners and the End of the Cold War

Hardliners viewed the easing and, ultimately, the ending of the Cold War with suspicion. They had come to prominence with Reagan's electoral victory in 1980, but during his second term, the administration's orientation had shifted toward that of the selective engagers. Between 1986 and 1988, Reagan's personal relationship with Gorbachev and a discernible shift in both U.S. and Soviet behavior gradually ended the Cold War. Following the Reykjavik summit in October 1986, Reagan's hardline rhetoric slowly subsided, as he and Gorbachev moved forward on a series of arms control agreements. In December 1987 Reagan and Gorbachev signed the historic INF (Intermediate-range Nuclear Forces) Treaty to eliminate intermediate- and short-range nuclear missiles, the first agreement between the two nations to remove an entire class of weapons from their arsenals. After a summit meeting in Moscow in the summer of 1988, the administration's new thinking contributed to National Security Decision Directive 311, which concluded that the contacts and recent relationships between the United States and the Soviet Union offered "an opportunity to contribute to a more stable relationship" between the two countries—one, the directive predicted, "that reduces the prospect of confrontation and the risk of military conflict."[32]

Reagan's shift generated resistance and even outright opposition from many hardliners. For example, several leading hardliners campaigned against ratification of the INF Treaty, warning that the Soviets would find a way to cheat.[33] Conservative columnist Charles Krauthammer applauded the efforts of Senate hardliners to block the INF Treaty because he concluded that their "bitching and moaning" would make it more difficult for Reagan to reach a strategic arms reduction agreement before the end of his term.[34] Richard Perle, the former aide to Senator Henry Jackson and long-time critic of arms control, resigned his post as assistant secretary of defense and remained an outspoken skeptic of Soviet motives and of the arms control negotiating process. Perle's principal deputy, Frank J. Gaffney, Jr., another former aide to Senator Jackson, quit the Reagan administration seven months after Perle, in November 1987, warning that the administration was creating a "very dangerous situation" by rushing to conclude agreement on the INF Treaty.[35]

The hardliners' suspicion of the Soviet Union and the threats facing the United States continued even after the collapse of the Berlin Wall. While acknowledging Soviet economic weakness, the hardliners argued that collapse was not irreversible. In December 1989, for example, Paul Wolfowitz, then the assistant secretary of defense for international security policy, testified before the Senate Armed Services Committee that the United States needed to remain ever vigilant because of the "incompleteness and reversibility" of Soviet moves.[36] When President Bush agreed to a series of Strategic Arms Reduction Talks (START) provisions in December 1990, Perle went so far as to accuse him and James Baker of "giving away the store."[37]

Even after the Soviet Union dissolved, in December 1991, the hardliners continued to advocate beefing up America's strategic and conventional military capabilities. For the hardliners, the United States continued to face serious threats: Russia still possessed a massive nuclear arsenal; terrorist activities threatened the United States; and China was a rising superpower.[38] Arms control and talk about a post–Cold War peace dividend were not only premature, but reckless, they warned. In 1992, Wolfowitz, then serving as under secretary of defense, in a draft of the annual Defense Policy Guidance, outlined the concept of a strategy of "no peer rivals," which stressed the need for the United States to maintain military primacy among nations. The document suggested that the United States needed to avoid limiting itself to existing alliance structures and should consider that future coalitions be ad hoc assemblies, often not lasting beyond the crisis being confronted and in many cases carrying only general agreement over the objectives to be accomplished.[39]

Hardliners and Regional Conflicts

Like the selective engagers, hardliners saw the Iraqi invasion of Kuwait as a major threat to a resource-rich strategic region. However, as discussed in Chapter 6 below, they differed from selective engagers in advocating that the United States should remove not only Iraq from Kuwait but also Saddam Hussein from power in Iraq. The post–Cold War era revealed differences within the hardliner camp, as well, on the question of how to respond to regional and civil violence. Most notably, the traditional conservative wing—the *National Review* conservatives—concluded that most regional conflicts fell outside of U.S. interests. Bosnia, like conflicts in Liberia, Chad, southern Sudan, and Somalia, was tragic perhaps but ultimately not relevant to American interests.

The neoconservative wing of the hardliners did not see all regional conflicts in the same light. A key element in the hardliners' vision for American dominance was the importance of Europe—especially the newly transitioning democracies in Eastern and Central Europe—to American interests. With lingering suspicion of Soviet and Russian revanchism, the hardliners believed that the United States needed to remain wary of conflicts that might ignite further violence. Thus, when the Yugoslav federation dissolved and warfare erupted, neoconservatives saw the crisis in more stark terms. They believed that conflicts in Europe would inevitably lead to greater European instability that would harm U.S. geostrategic interests. They also concluded that the Europeans were incapable of responding to the conflict in Yugoslavia—a situation that reinforced their views that American primacy was the principal source of international stability and competent leadership in the world. By the time war spread to Bosnia, in 1992, several leading neoconservatives, such as Jeane Kirkpatrick, Richard Perle, Max Kampelman, and Albert and Roberta Wohlstetter, publicly argued for a stronger American response to what they viewed as clear-cut Serb aggression.[40] Neoconservative hardline think tanks like the Center for Security Policy and the American Enterprise Institute were also advocating more aggressive action by the United States in response to the conflict in Bosnia.

Liberals and the End of the Cold War

The end of the Cold War was a watershed moment for liberals. They saw the reduction in bilateral competitiveness in the international environment as an opportunity to create a more expansive, multilaterally cooperative world. Liberals believed that the transitions in Eastern Europe and Russia and the dramatic economic development in China signaled the beginning of a new era, characterized by market capitalism and democracy. Since the United States would be spending less on defense, it could devote more resources and energy toward actively promoting democracy and to the development of international institutions to help monitor and manage international peace and security.[41] The United States could also shift its focus regarding military aid and assistance; it no longer needed to support ruthless right-wing dictatorships around the globe. New conceptions of international security emerged; liberals hoped that the United States would espouse the emerging humanitarian norms and develop more comprehensive strategies for global poverty reduction and mitigation of environmental degradation and resource scarcity and of escalating public health concerns.

In particular, liberals hoped to tap into their experiences of the 1980s, when human rights and humanitarian NGOs had come of age. By the end of the 1980s, Amnesty International and Human Rights Watch, which were formed in 1961 and 1973 respectively, had become major forces for the advancement of international human rights. In 1984, more than twenty humanitarian organizations joined forces as InterAction in an effort to develop best practices, not only for developing and providing humanitarian relief, but also to establish greater numerical strength in advocating for humanitarian causes in Congress and at the executive branch agencies. By the end of the decade, these organizations and their resources had grown exponentially. In addition, major improvements in communication, transportation, and computer technologies allowed these NGOs to develop highly sophisticated information collection and advocacy platforms.

Liberals and Regional Conflicts

Liberals believed that America's dominance in the world enabled it to play a leading role in responding to the devastating consequences of regional and civil conflicts. Many were initially reluctant to support the first Persian Gulf

War until President George H. W. Bush had assembled a significant international coalition to join American troops in battle. After that war, they saw an expanded opportunity for the American military—with its tremendous resource capacity and its logistics infrastructure—to support and provide humanitarian relief in a wide variety of contingencies. American power could finally be harnessed for promoting the values of democracy and market capitalism. Unlike selective engagers, liberals argued that the mitigation of humanitarian tragedies was, in and of itself, worth the commitment of American resources.

Reluctant Warriors and the End of the Cold War

To most noninterventionists, the end of the Cold War signified that the prevailing grand security strategy had changed dramatically. For the reluctant warriors, like General Colin Powell, chairman of the Joint Chiefs of Staff, the changing nature of the U.S. military mission was met with unease. The basic mission of the U.S. military throughout the Cold War had been to plan, prepare, and train for fighting a massive conventional war in Europe. With the Cold War over and calls for defense cuts on the rise, military planners scrambled for new doctrines to suit new threats. Still, most of the senior military staff discouraged any fundamental reorientation of American strategic doctrine.[42] Regarding the U.S. response to Iraq's invasion of Kuwait, despite initial reluctance, Powell and other military commanders supported the Gulf War. But their support came only after Bush and Baker had clearly demonstrated that several of their criteria for war would be met, that any military action in the Gulf would have: a clear and defined mission, widespread public support, support from political leadership, the resources to carry out a heavy mission, and a clear strategy for exiting the situation—the preconditions that had come to be known as the Powell Doctrine.

Reluctant Warriors and Regional Conflicts

Much of the world view of reluctant warriors was formed out of the failures of American power in Korea and Vietnam, both instances in which civilian leaders added a series of political constraints on how the war could be fought. In the immediate post–Cold War world, reluctant warriors expressed considerable unease with and even outright opposition to the idea that American troops could mitigate or solve humanitarian problems in regional conflicts. They believed that the purpose and mission of the U.S. military, as defined in its training and combat doctrine, was to fight and win major wars, not to serve as peacekeepers or buffers between other warring factions.

The Decisions on Somalia and Bosnia in 1992

Emergence of Simultaneous Humanitarian Emergencies

Initial Executive Branch Advantages regarding Bosnia

Prior to the outbreak of war in Bosnia in March 1992, few Americans, even foreign policy elites, had focused on the place. To the extent that attention was paid to the turmoil there during the initial months of violence, the view most widely accepted was that of the selective engagers. The Bush administration criticized the Serb leadership in Belgrade for the violence and worked diplomatically to isolate Slobodan Milošević's regime, but it nonetheless firmly believed and publicly emphasized that the conflict was the inevitable consequence of intractable and longstanding hatreds unleashed at the collapse of the communist government's tight control.[43] When speaking of Bosnia, President Bush and his advisors referred frequently to a land steeped in ethnic hatreds that dated back hundreds of years. Based on this analysis, the administration argued that the prudent policy was to avoid any U.S. involvement in a situation that could only lead to a Vietnam-style quagmire in the Balkans.[44]

Latent Public Opinion

Provided with few opposing views, most Americans came to share the administration's position. The public supported its policy to contain the conflict, to keep it from spreading to areas of geostrategic interest to the United States, in particular Kosovo, Macedonia, Albania, Greece, Turkey, and Bulgaria.[45] By and large, in 1991 and 1992, the general public mood and latent public opinion were largely ambivalent about the crisis in the Balkans. The United States was just coming off the euphoria (and the expense) of the Persian Gulf War. That war had consumed much of the "peace dividend" and, with the country in the throws of a recession, most Americans were not excited about the prospects of another costly military campaign. Furthermore, to most Americans, the Balkans seemed an extraordinarily complex place. The administration's description of the war in Bosnia as fueled by age-old ethnic hatreds in which neighbors were killing neighbors fit the public's basic understanding of the area. Terms like "balkanization" and "ancient ethnic hatreds" were easily digestible.[46]

The administration's success at initially framing the conflict was aided by its huge advantages in military operational planning. From the outset of the violence, U.S. military leaders preemptively declared that even limited military objectives to ease humanitarian suffering in Bosnia would be extremely costly. For example, on June 2, 1992, a mortar shell fired by Serbs struck a group of civilians standing in line to buy bread in Sarajevo. While liberals and the media expressed outrage at the egregious attack on civilians, selective engagers and noninterventionists responded by emphasizing the inherent complexity of the situation. Their standard line was that Bosnia was different from Desert Storm: "There's no single army to confront and defeat. This is another Vietnam or Beirut—easy to get in, damn hard to get out. The American people have no taste for that."[47]

In another example, during the summer 1992 debate on whether or not to use U.S. military aircraft in support of an emergency humanitarian airlift for Sarajevo, senior planners argued that a perimeter of thirty miles would need to be established by more than 50,000 U.S. ground troops in order to secure the airport.[48] According to Brent Scowcroft, who was national security advisor to George H. W. Bush, the Joint Chiefs "probably" inflated the estimates of what it would take to accomplish some of these limited objectives, but "once you have the Joint Chiefs making their estimates, its pretty hard for armchair strategists to . . . say they are wrong."[49]

Initially, no one was in a position to challenge the administration's paradigmatic framing of the conflict in Bosnia. In the spring of 1992, no clear precedent had been set for post–Cold War humanitarian interventions; and because the former Yugoslavia had been a relatively advanced economic and political society during the Cold War, few nongovernmental humanitarian organizations had any presence there.[50] When the war in Bosnia broke out, there were few liberal or other voices to contradict the administration's basic assessment. Furthermore, because only a handful of members of Congress had much interest in or understanding of events in Yugoslavia, most deferred to the administration's resources and expertise on the conflict. As a result, those who might have opposed the selective engagement analysis—such as a few liberals and humanitarianists in Congress who did have some interest in the region— lacked a strong organizational and political base from which to mobilize public and political opposition to the Bush administration's policy.

As for the American news media, when they did begin to focus on the war in Bosnia, they too had little regional expertise. Few major news organizations had experienced correspondents on the ground.[51] The general disinterest of the public toward foreign affairs throughout the latter half of the 1980s and the early 1990s had led to a significant downsizing in the number of American foreign-based correspondents. Consequently, as the Cold War dissipated in 1990 and 1991, journalists were assigned to cover regions of the world with which they had little or no experience.[52] Most reporters sent to Eastern Europe were there primarily to report on the democratic and market transitions in Poland, Hungary, and Czechoslovakia.[53] Of course, when war broke out in Croatia in 1991, journalists scrambled to cover the story.[54] Most reports written and broadcast about the Croatian conflict reinforced the view that violent nationalistic hatreds permeated all of the former Yugoslavia and that the outbreak of overt hostilities was the inevitable result of the collapse of authoritarian rule. Throughout the fall of 1991, American reporters and administration officials warned that, although the violence in Croatia was terrible, conditions in the more ethnically diverse Bosnia would be much worse.[55] Consequently, when violence erupted in Bosnia in March 1992, there was widespread acceptance among journalists, at least initially, that the conflict there was simply a further manifestation of the unchecked hatreds that had been widely reported.[56] In addition, because journalists and editors wanted to ensure "objective" and "balanced" reporting, stories often identified and reported atrocities as though all sides were equally culpable.[57]

Together, these circumstances produced predictable pressures and influences on the reporting, and during the first several months of the war in Bosnia it endorsed the Bush administration's position and portrayed the conflict as caused by age-old ethnic hatreds in which all sides were equally to blame.[58] The American public therefore largely supported the administration's selective engagement position. With little information contradicting the legitimacy of the administration's judgment, and in the face of a proliferation of "objective" reports from Bosnia, any influence on American public opinion suggesting a more forceful response was effectively indiscernible.[59]

Somalia Caught in the Void

As in the case of the former Yugoslavia, selective engagers in the Bush administration did not see any significant U.S. interests at stake in Somalia. Walter Kansteiner of the NSC staff recalls that no one paid any attention to Somalia, that since they perceived no U.S. interests to be involved, they saw no need to take much notice.[60] Brent Scowcroft recalls that Somalia was regarded as "another collapsed state with no effective government and no U.S. interests. This was clearly an issue for the United Nations, not for us."[61]

Nonetheless, throughout the spring and summer of 1992, conditions in Somalia worsened. International relief organizations were unable to deliver sufficient amounts of food and medicine to the starving population. Armed bandits fought openly with one another in urban areas and waged systematic campaigns to steal much of the aid relief that had been delivered to the country. The NGO community tried—with little success—to stem the widespread looting. Despite these conditions, the situation entered the administration's radar screen very slowly.

Liberals and the media pointed out that Somalia was only one of several regional conflicts that were developing into humanitarian crises. Wars in Afghanistan, Angola, Chad, Liberia, southern Sudan, Mozambique, Sri Lanka, the former Yugoslavia, and elsewhere all were producing or had produced humanitarian challenges. Yet, because these hot spots were so numerous, liberal attention and resources were diffused among them. Gathering of information was also hampered by danger. Most journalists and NGOs evacuated from Somalia in 1991 when the United Nations staff and foreign diplomats left. Consequently, even though the famine in Somalia intensified dramatically in the fall of 1991 and early 1992, there was very little reporting from Somalia and the crisis only slowly entered the public discourse in the United States, during the summer of 1992.[62]

One cell of liberals within the federal bureaucracy forged a coalition. In early 1992, Andrew Natsios, assistant administrator of U.S. AID; former ambassador to Somalia James Bishop, who was acting assistant secretary of state for Human Rights and Humanitarian Affairs; and Herman Cohen, assistant secretary of state for Africa, tried to galvanize support for a stronger humanitarian response. Natsios testified before congressional committees beginning in January, arguing that Somalia was "the most acute humanitarian tragedy in the world today."[63] He also began holding monthly press conferences in hopes of generating media attention to the crisis.

By April, this cell had secured support for a nonbinding congressional resolution calling on the administration to use all means necessary to ensure the delivery of international relief assistance, but they were less successful in persuading the administration to follow the direction of the resolution. In April, Cohen initiated an unsanctioned campaign at the UN to encourage the formation of an armed 500-person peacekeeping force to deploy to Mogadishu to provide security for food warehouses that were being looted daily.[64] When Secretary of State Baker found out about Cohen's efforts, he immediately dispatched Assistant Secretary of State John Bolton to the UN to retract American support for the effort. Baker and the selective engagers did not want to see a peacekeeping operation for Somalia on the UN agenda.[65]

The Erosion of Initial Information Advantages

The Bush administration's dilemma concerning Somalia and Bosnia intensified as both crises continued into the summer of 1992 with no prospects for improvement. Throughout the summer, the media, liberals, and humanitarians gradually dedicated more resources to their own information-gathering efforts. In June, Natsios renewed his efforts to generate public and political support for aid to Somalia. He held numerous press conferences in conjunction with the Office of U.S. Disaster Assistance and reported that, based on UN estimates, nearly 5 million people were "facing the threat of starvation due to the effects of civil strife."[66]

Later that month, U.S. ambassador to Kenya, Smith Hempstone, Jr., traveled to refugee camps on the Somali-Kenyan border for the first time. He reported his trip in a cable entitled "A Day in Hell," which presented a vivid report of the suffering. His description resonated with many liberals in the State Department who believed that the Bush administration needed to do more in Somalia, and the cable was immediately leaked to the press.[67]

Meanwhile, two leading senators, Nancy Kassebaum (R-Kansas) and Paul Simon (D-Illinois), conducted fact-finding missions to Somalia in June and July and reported horrific conditions. On their return they urged their colleagues to support sending an armed UN security mission to Somalia. And several international nongovernmental organizations mobilized grass-roots campaigns to lobby for a stronger response in Somalia, while prominent international figures such as Irish president Mary Robinson and UNICEF spokeswoman Audrey Hepburn conducted high-profile visits to Somalia to draw international attention to the crisis.[68]

Also in July, *New York Times* correspondent Jane Perlez traveled into Somalia with ICRC representatives. The *Times* published her account of the gruesome conditions on its front page.[69] This, along with the testimony of Kassebaum and Simon before the House Select Committee on Hunger on July 22, elevated public and political interest in Somalia. That same day, UN Secretary-General Boutros-Ghali repeated the six-month-old UN High Commission for

Refugees' prediction that 1 million Somali children were at immediate risk and more than 4 million adults needed food assistance urgently.[70] Other international aid organizations publicly repeated their predictions that as many as 2 million people would die within the coming few weeks.[71] In response, over the next three weeks, both the House and the Senate passed resolutions in support of the deployment of armed UN security teams to Somalia.

Despite this flurry of activity, there was no clear direction or policy momentum—and no consideration of U.S. military action. Senior administration officials—Scowcroft, Baker, Eagleburger, and Powell—remained convinced that Somalia was an issue best handled by the United Nations.[72] They remained firm in their position that the United States had no interests in Somalia. While a modest amount of pressure was emerging in Washington for stronger action, polls revealed that the public was still largely ambivalent about the situation in Somalia. According to Brent Scowcroft, nothing in the public opinion polls or the political commentary suggested that Somalia was reaching "a critical mass."[73]

This is not to suggest that the administration was blatantly indifferent to the humanitarian tragedy. They were not. Bush and the NSC staff had been moved by Hempstone's cable and Perlez's story. According to NSC staffer Kansteiner, the cable was very "compelling," that Hempstone was "an excellent writer—his background as a journalist really came through. It was a real call for assistance."[74] It is reported that when President Bush read the cable he had written in the margin, "This is a terribly moving situation. Let's do everything we can to help."[75]

However, according to both Scowcroft and Kansteiner, although Bush was "personally moved" by the news, his interest was limited to determining how the United States could assist the United Nations in dealing with the problem. According to Scowcroft, "there was no discussion of using U.S. force for any purpose at this point."[76] Indeed, Hempstone himself personally opposed any form of U.S. military action; his own prescription was to hand the Somalia situation off to the UN.

Consequently, the administration referred international policy initiatives on Somalia to the United Nations. On July 26, the United States voted in support of UN Security Council Resolution 767 authorizing an emergency airlift to provide relief to southern Somalia. The administration's position was that UN flights might be able to alleviate some of the suffering, but under no circumstances would American aircraft participate in the airlift.

The noninterventionists on the Joint Chiefs of Staff staunchly opposed any U.S. policy initiatives that might escalate into some form of U.S. military deployment.[77] They basically opposed any form of U.S. military deployment in countries with inhospitable geographies, where there were deeply rooted ethnic and nationalist foundations to the conflict, or where combatants were not readily distinguishable and identifiable. At every interagency meeting, when Somalia came up the representatives from the Joint Chiefs "opposed everything" on Somalia.[78]

At the staff level this lack of unanimity led to a bureaucratic deadlock. Some liberal policy elites put forward military options for provision of relief, but the selective engagers and the noninterventionists remained opposed, calling Somalia, "a bottomless pit." Not surprisingly, this opposition frustrated the liberals, as James Bishop later recounted:

> I went to one interagency meeting and there was this Brigadier General from the Joint Staff. We came up with this option to use helicopter gun ships to support relief delivery. This general sat there and said we couldn't use helicopters in such a dusty environment. Hell, we had just fought a massive war in the Persian Gulf desert with lots of helicopters. I was evacuated from Mogadishu in January 1991 in a Marine Corps helicopter that operated just fine. But that was their attitude. They didn't want anything to do with it and they were prepared to lie to keep [their troops] out of it. At every meeting, no matter the proposal, the Joint Chiefs opposed it.[79]

By early August, according to Bishop, "we were just churning and rumbling and rumbling—but there was no real interest from above."[80] Herman Cohen concurred, saying, "We were told to be forward leaning," but the senior principals were not serious about an American-led effort to stem the suffering and "paid even less attention" to the group as it worked.[81]

The Crises Intensify

Meanwhile conditions continued to deteriorate in both Somalia and Bosnia and the administration came under increasing criticism from liberals, particularly from Democratic presidential nominee, Bill Clinton, and his campaign team, for its handling of the crisis in Bosnia. The administration's initial advantages in framing the perception of the situation in Bosnia began to dissipate. By July, many American journalists had begun traveling outside of Sarajevo and were reporting from throughout Bosnia. As they increased their knowledge of the country, the journalists collected information that contradicted the administration's public reports. They revealed that all sides were not equally guilty of perpetrating atrocities against civilian populations.[82] Stories began to shift from suggesting that the conflict was fueled by ethnic hatreds—the result of spontaneous neighbor-on-neighbor violence—to new evidence of small bands of radical Serb nationalists and paramilitaries committing atrocities in a series of highly organized campaigns.

According to National Public Radio reporter Tom Gjelten, by early August most journalists had concluded that reporting all sides as equally complicit in the violence was "quite simply incorrect. . . . Objectivity in this sense does not mean a kind of even-handedness, giving one paragraph to the atrocities of one side, one paragraph to atrocities of the other side, one paragraph to atrocities of the third side."[83] Amid new access to information, American journalists in Bosnia began reporting on the deliberate political calculations of leaders fully in control of the violence—this was not merely the manifestation of age-old ethnic hatreds, but a clear and deliberate campaign by ruthless elites (mostly Serbs).[84]

The differences between the administration's accounts and journalists' reports from Bosnia finally erupted into an issue themselves in early August 1992 with reports of the existence of concentration camps. On August 3, Roy Gutman of *Newsday* reported that Serb forces in Bosnia were holding thousands of Muslim men in concentration-style camps. At the State Department, spokesman Richard Boucher initially confirmed the camps and told reporters that the United States was deeply concerned about reports of abuses in them. He went on, however, to add, "I should also note that we have reports that Bosnians and Croatians also maintain detention centers, but we do not have similar allegations of mistreatment at those. Our view is that all parties must allow international authorities immediate and unhindered access to all the detention centers. . . . we've made clear right from the beginning of this that there were various parties involved in the fighting; that there were people on all sides . . . that were doing bad things."[85]

Liberals around the country expressed outrage that the State Department had known of the camps but had taken no action, either diplomatically or politically, to expose them.[86] In the midst of this initial outcry, the selective engagers in the administration quickly sensed the public relations crisis at hand and attempted to backtrack from Boucher's statement. On August 4, the secretary of state's office directed the Bureau of European and Canadian Affairs to downplay the camps by suggesting that there was no "confirmed evidence" of the existence of the camps.[87] Later that day, Assistant Secretary of State Tom Niles told a stunned House Foreign Affairs Committee that the U.S. government could not confirm the existence of the camps.

The fear among the selective engagers in the administration was that a momentum for action was growing rapidly as a result of the camp disclosure. After he left office, Secretary Eagleburger told reporter Warren Strobel: "All of us were being a little bit careful . . . because of this issue of whether or not it was going to push us into something that we thought was dangerous."[88] U.S. ambassador to Yugoslavia Warren Zimmerman, who had been recalled in 1992, concluded: "Niles was sent up to the Hill basically to deny this. This deniability was not possible."[89] Deniability was impossible because it directly contradicted evidence compiled weeks earlier in the Bureau of International Organizations, the Bureau of Intelligence and Research, and the CIA—most of which had been forwarded to the Bureau of European and Canadian Affairs—of the existence of the camps and of atrocities and systematic killing going on in the camps.[90] In a particularly heated exchange, Congressman Tom Lantos, a survivor of the Nazi Holocaust, delivered a challenge to Niles with the chilling remark, "You remember the old excuse that while the gas chambers were in full blast killing innocent people, we could say, not very honestly, 'We don't know.'"[91] He concluded by declaring, "Now, either Mr. Boucher is lying or you are lying, but you are both working for Jim Baker."[92]

Liberals and the media became highly motivated by these events. Roy Gutman, who had broken the story, said that he was "outraged" by the initial denial. "It was a big lie. The facts were clear, yet they denied it. I sensed more lies—more deliberate cover-up. If they were going to deny the truth, I was committed to uncovering more explicit evidence. It motivated me to do follow-up pieces to prove the story beyond a doubt."[93] Longtime *Washington Post* reporter Don Oberdorfer wrote, "I had rarely seen the State Department press corps—or what was left of it in August—so agitated."[94]

Two days later, Gutman and two other reporters traveled to an area outside Omarska, in Bosnian Serb–controlled territory. They obtained video footage of a camp holding hundreds of Muslim prisoners. The graphic images of emaciated men incarcerated behind barbed wire fences, coupled with the administration's deliberate campaign to downplay the events, were broadcast around the country. It was obvious to most journalists and liberals that the administration had been looking for anything to mitigate criticism of its policy of nonintervention. Over the next ten days, the press launched a mass of stories that excoriated the president's Bosnia policy and gave widespread attention to liberal and hardline voices demanding forceful U.S. action. Between August 2 and August 14, forty-eight television news stories on Bosnia totaling 151 minutes and 30 seconds were broadcast on the three major network evening news shows.[95] This contrasted with only ten stories during the prior twelve days.

The effects of this firestorm on Bush and his advisors were immediate. Bill Clinton launched a new round of public criticisms and urged the administration to consider the use of punitive air strikes against the Serbs to protect the relief effort.[96] Clinton demanded: "The United States and the international community must take action. If the horrors of the Holocaust taught us anything, it is the high cost of remaining silent and paralyzed in the face of genocide. We must discover who is responsible for these actions and take steps to bring them to justice for these crimes against humanity."[97] Further upsetting to the White House was that the media gave extensive play to Clinton's visible outrage in contrast to Bush's tempered reaction.[98] On August 9, ABC *World News Tonight* ran a profile distinguishing Clinton's and Bush's approaches to Bosnia which extensively quoted Clinton on the need for strong and decisive U.S. leadership.

By unfortunate coincidence for the selective engagers, amid this flurry, on August 10, Bush saw visiting Israeli Prime Minister Yitzhak Rabin for a long-planned meeting. Rabin took the occasion to declare that the camps in Bosnia were reminiscent of the Nazi camps during the Holocaust. That same day, thousands of American Jewish protesters marched on the White House, and the Wiesenthal Center and the Jewish American Congress launched a nationwide petition drive and bought full-page ads in national newspapers to press the Bush administration to immediately launch air strikes or other military action to open the camps.

Liberals in Congress also escalated pressure on the president. With greater access to information, liberals in both the House and Senate organized a series of hearings. On August 14, the Senate Foreign Relations Committee released a scathing report that presented the Serb ethnic-cleansing campaign as a deliberate and highly coordinated politically driven campaign of violence—and not spontaneous acts of deep hatreds.[99]

Former Cold War hardliners now entered the fray. After nearly four months of what they perceived to be the total failure of Europeans to handle the situation in Bosnia, neoconservatives such as Richard Perle, longtime nuclear weapons strategist Albert Wohlstetter, Jeane Kirkpatrick, as well as former British prime minister Margaret Thatcher sensed that growing violence would spill over into Kosovo, Albania, Bulgaria, Macedonia, and ultimately Greece and Turkey and escalate geostrategic threats to the United States. In particular, the hardliners opposed the United Nations arms embargo that had been imposed in mid-1991 in the hope of mitigating the Serb-Croat war and which had been extended to include Bosnia in March 1992. Hardliners believed that the arms embargo reinforced the Serbs' military superiority in Bosnia by restricting the Bosnian Muslims' ability to acquire the capability to defend themselves against the Serb onslaught. The hardliners argued that the United States should lift the arms embargo against the Bosnian Muslims—unilaterally if need be—and commit its air power to strike Serb artillery sites, military convoys, and transportation routes.[100]

The issue of the camps also began to split the selective engagers on what to do in Bosnia. While they all opposed intervention, a number of them came to see a huge political liability in doing nothing. Senior foreign affairs columnist Jim Hoagland of the *Washington Post* wrote on August 9 that Bush's inaction in Bosnia had elevated foreign policy to a major campaign issue—one that Clinton was handling more "artfully":

> The rape of Bosnia by Serbian forces can no longer be denied by the Serbs, minimized by the international community or finessed by President Bush. The human and political costs of inaction and evasion have become horribly clear in the past two weeks.
>
> The Pentagon's all-or-nothing Invincible Force Doctrine, formulated to counteract the disasters the American military suffered in Vietnam and Beirut, was a brilliant success in the desert war against Iraq.
>
> But it has kept America on the sidelines in the Balkans and arguably prolonged human suffering there. Bush is vulnerable to the campaign charge that he has failed to develop intermediate policies to deal with an unsettled world of foreign crises that fall between the extremes of the need for Invincible Force and the possibility of doing nothing.[101]

Columnist Leslie Gelb also criticized Bush for his lack of action: "Mr. Bush pretends he's doing something, . . . and dismisses constructive ideas on the use of force as 'politics.' He speaks of the horror of the camps, but makes no commitment to eliminate them. . . . Have [the world leaders] no humanity, no sense of all they might do short of massive military intervention, no vision of the international consequences?"[102]

In the face of this firestorm, Bush assembled his national security team on August 8 at his vacation home in Kennebunkport, Maine, to discuss the matter. He held news conferences three days in a row on the subject. Nonetheless, the headlines of almost every newspaper and weekly magazine chastised the administration for allowing the reemergence of "concentration camps" in Europe. Although there is no evidence that public opinion had shifted toward greater support of direct U.S. involvement in Bosnia, on the eve of the Republican Convention, the issue struck a nervous chord among the president's political advisors.[103] Bush, who had taken tremendous pride in his foreign policy accomplishments—overseeing the fall of the Berlin Wall, the reunification of Germany, the Persian Gulf War, and the dissolution of the Soviet Union—was now being publicly castigated by highly respected foreign policy commentators. Particularly sensitive to the criticisms were four of Bush's senior political advisors—James Baker, Dennis Ross, Margaret Tutwiler, and Robert Zoellick—all of whom had moved from the State Department to the White House only one week earlier, on August 1, to take charge of Bush's failing reelection bid.

Despite the increasing political costs, the president and his military advisors remained convinced that Bosnia would be a quagmire, and they were determined to avoid taking any step that might lead to escalation. After meeting his advisors on August 8, Bush reiterated his caution: "We are not going to get bogged down in some guerrilla warfare."[104]

In an interview with Warren Strobel, Lawrence Eagleburger later recounted the sense of despair he and others had felt: "You have to understand that we had largely made a decision we were not going to get militarily involved. And nothing, including those stories, pushed us into it. . . . I hated it. Because this was condoning—I won't say genocide—but condoning a hell of a lot of murder. . . . It made us damn uncomfortable."[105]

Another concern for the noninterventionists and selective engagers was that liberals and hardliners were altering the public conception of Bosnia and making the administration look callous. Several liberal and neoconservative commentators and members of Congress suggested that intervention could be done without fear that U.S. forces would become embroiled in a Vietnam-style quagmire. They focused their attention on Serb aggression and the role of Slobodan Milošević as the primary culprit. They predicted that, if the United

States removed Miloševic or targeted a military strike against him and his radical supporters, the violence in Bosnia would quickly dissipate. For example, an editorial in the *New Republic* proclaimed:

> The Balkan war is not so politically complicated that no judgment about its morality can be made. It is not merely an ethnic conflict. It is a campaign in which a discrete faction of Serbian nationalists has manipulated ethnic sentiment in order to seize power and territory. It is an act of international aggression, an assault on a member of the United Nations. Despite the U.N.'s condemnation, there have been too many platitudes about the responsibility of all factions for the war. This lazy language is an escape hatch through which outside powers flee their responsibilities.[106]

The campaign to reframe the nature of the crisis frustrated the most senior members of the administration. Brent Scowcroft recalls his reaction to the domestic criticism unleashed at the time:

> I was very suspicious that people who had never supported the use of force for our national interests were now screaming for us to use force in Yugoslavia. We looked hard at the notion of establishing safe areas and provisioning them. We actually asked NATO for an appraisal. My recollection was that NATO estimated that between 200,000 and 300,000 troops were needed—maybe they had inflated that, I don't know. . . . Regardless, we couldn't justify it in our own minds.
>   . . . I disagreed with the humanitarianists who deliberately downplayed the intractability of the conflict, who demonized Miloševic and saw this simply as a war of aggression. . . . Miloševic was a factor, but to that extent there were also national hatreds there that couldn't be ignored.[107]

Bush ordered his team to contest the liberal view that U.S. intervention could quickly break the siege of Sarajevo with little cost in American lives. Secretary of Defense Dick Cheney told CNN, "It's tragic, but the Balkans have been a hotbed of conflict . . . for centuries." Marlin Fitzwater dismissed Clinton's criticism by stating that the Democratic nominee was "unaware of the political complications in Yugoslavia."[108] General Powell's senior deputy, Lt. Gen. Barry McCaffrey, told ABC *World News Tonight* that despite the tragedy there was "no military solution." McCaffrey also testified before Congress on August 11 that between 60,000 and 120,000 ground troops would be needed to break the siege of Sarajevo and ensure uninterrupted relief.[109] Other commanders suggested that a field army of 400,000 troops would be needed to implement a cease-fire.

The administration also initiated a series of diplomatic efforts to offset the domestic pressure. In the UN, the administration introduced a Security Council resolution to authorize force in support of relief efforts in Bosnia. However, the administration explicitly announced that it would not participate in such a force. On August 13, the UN passed a resolution authorizing the use of force to protect aid convoys.

Somalia: Bush's First Reversal

In the midst of the public furor over the camp disclosure in Bosnia, President Bush announced an abrupt shift in his Somalia policy and ordered U.S. Air Force C-130s to assist in providing relief to famine victims there. The president also reversed his opposition to funding a UN Security Council resolution calling for the deployment of 500 Pakistani peacekeepers to Somalia and, in fact, announced that the Pentagon would provide transportation for the 500-man team and its equipment.[110]

Conventional arguments suggest that it was the Cable News Network's vivid images of starving, emaciated children in Somalia that had compelled the president to act, because they had provoked a sense of moral outrage within the American populace. Among the three major U.S. television networks, however, Somalia was mentioned in only fifteen news stories in the first seven months of 1992, until Bush's August decision, and nearly half "showed only fleeting glimpses of Somalia's plight" as part of other stories.[111]

The evidence suggests that Bush's policy shift on Somalia came in response to the increasing pressure to take action and to the political backlash on Bosnia that occurred on the eve of the Republican National Convention. Bush issued a policy directive in late July, and a series of interagency meetings took place in late July and early August to address the situation in Somalia; but, according to most of the participants in those meetings, none produced any specific policy proposals. According to Assistant Secretary of State for Africa Herman Cohen, "it was impossible to obtain a consensus for new initiatives at the working level because of a reluctance on the part of many to assume yet another international burden after the tremendous costs incurred for Yugoslavia, Operation Desert Storm in the Persian Gulf, Cambodia, and elsewhere."[112] During one interagency meeting in early August, representatives from Powell's staff continued steadfastly to oppose the use of force—including an airlift—and to call Somalia a "bottomless pit."[113]

Yet, curiously, it was then that Bush jumped ahead of his bureaucracy and abruptly announced that U.S. military planes would provide airlift for relief in Somalia and would transport armed UN security forces to Somalia for humanitarian purposes.[114] Herman Cohen recalls that there had been no contingency planning for an airlift and that the "ordering of the airlift came right out of the blue."[115] Most of the relief experts in the U.S. government and in the NGO community had long believed that the core problem in Somalia was one of distribution of relief and not simply the delivery of it. Andrew Natsios, who was appointed President's Special Coordinator as part of the policy package announced on August 14, opposed the airlift because it simply was not sufficient to make any real difference: "There was no way an airlift could provide enough food—the tonnage was just not enough. We knew that before it started. We just transferred the costs from ICRC to us."[116]

At the White House, the need to respond to the domestic criticism on both Somalia and Bosnia had a cumulative effect. Natsios recalls that the pressure to ignore his advice and move toward the airlift came directly from the White House. NSC staffer John Ordway was "really pushing" the airlift, "because the White House wanted a symbol . . . to show we were doing something."[117] Scowcroft recounts that the Bosnian camp issue "did have a significant influence" on the policy toward Somalia. The administration did not want to be seen as "wholly flinthearted" and an airlift to Somalia was "a lot cheaper" than intervention in Bosnia "to demonstrate that we had a heart."[118]

The decision to launch the airlift to Somalia did divert media and liberal attention away from critical coverage and commentary on Bosnia and to sympathetic stories on Somalia. In contrast to the sporadic stories on Somalia during the seven months prior to the president's decision, over the next two weeks, the networks broadcast thirty-four nightly news segments, almost all of which were sympathetic to the American airlift policy.[119] Critical commentary during stories on Bosnia dissipated after the president's public announcement of the airlift to Somalia. Between August 14 and August 31, coverage of Bosnia dropped to twenty-eight stories totaling forty-nine minutes.[120] The airlift had given the administration a slight reprieve from the pressure on Bosnia.[121]

Pressure Builds Again

As the American presidential campaign intensified, most of the focus in the media and within the foreign policy elite community was on the campaign. To the extent that foreign policy was an issue, the media, liberals, and hardliners continued their criticism of the Bush administration's opposition to American initiatives to end the assault on civilians in Bosnia and Somalia. Regarding Bosnia, the administration continued its public strategy to downplay the magnitude of the violence and characterize the conflict as one of ancient blood feuds. On August 28, Eagleburger described the conflict as "not rational. . . . it's not for any common set of values or purposes; it just goes on. And that kind of warfare is most difficult to bring to a halt."[122] Later in a television interview on the McNeil/Lehrer NewsHour he insisted: "I'm not prepared to accept arguments that there must be something between the kind of involvement of Vietnam and doing nothing, that the *New York Times* and the *Washington Post* keep blabbing about, that there must be some form in the middle. That's again, what got us into Vietnam—do a little bit, and it doesn't work. What do you do next?"[123]

Executive Fragmentation

The exposure of the camps in Bosnia had altered the information and propaganda balance. Dissension within in the administration appeared first within the State Department and the Pentagon, where several officials began openly differing with the selective engagers' policy. On August 25, the acting Yugoslav desk officer, George Kenney, resigned in protest of the Bush administration's policy. He wrote in his resignation letter, a copy of which he delivered directly to the *New York Times,* that he could "no longer in clear conscience support the administration's ineffective, indeed counterproductive, handling of the Yugoslav crisis. I am therefore resigning in order to help develop a stronger public consensus that the U.S. must act immediately to stop the genocide in Bosnia and prevent this conflict from spreading throughout the Balkans."[124]

Kenney's resignation was largely dismissed by the administration as an inconsequential move by a junior officer.[125] But, while the resignation did not result in any explicit policy change, it did alert the American foreign policy elite community—both those in the administration and outside of it—that there was dissent within the State Department on Bosnia. Over the next several months, virtually every major policy deliberation on Bosnia was leaked to the press as soon as it occurred.[126] The leaks were explicitly intended to offset the administration's public portrayal of the crisis. According to Jim Hooper, then serving as the principal deputy to Ambassador Zimmerman, who had been appointed the secretary of state's special representative on Yugoslavia, there was widespread disdain within the rank and file of the State Department for the Bush public relations strategy on Bosnia:

The administration was deliberately controlling information—they were with-holding information and spinning information—to downplay that there were concentration camps and that genocide was occurring. The whole purpose of the policy was to avoid any responsibility. They were afraid that the public would be outraged and demand more from them. The particular spin was to portray the conflict as an intractable conflict among ancient rivals.[127]

Meanwhile, some hardliners within the Pentagon also started agitating over the noninterventionists' absolute stand on the conflict. Paul Wolfowitz and Assistant Deputy Undersecretary Zalmay Khalilzad argued strenuously in fa-vor of lifting the arms embargo and the development of contingency plans on the use of force. They argued that arming the Bosnians would "make a real dif-ference on the ground in Bosnia, increase the costs of aggression for the Serbs, possibly prevent them from obtaining their objectives, discourage them from spreading the war and decrease the possibility that Middle Eastern states and Islamic radicals might get involved."[128]

Liberal and Hardline Opposition Mobilized

By the end of September, liberals and hardliners in the bureaucracy had forged a coalition and begun a concerted effort to identify the effect of the upcoming winter on the civilian population in Bosnia. Andrew Natsios of AID warned Eagleburger in a letter, "Immediate and massive action must be taken now to avert a tragedy by the onset of the winter season."[129] A week later, a secret CIA analysis outlining the impending humanitarian catastrophe due to projected winter weather forecasts was leaked to the press. The document esti-mated that as many as 100,000 Bosnian Muslims might die from starvation and exposure.[130]

Liberals in Congress and the NGO community also stepped up their cam-paign against the administration's "do nothing" policy toward Bosnia. Con-gressman Les Aspin noted in a public speech, "Those who disagree with the all-or-nothing school are unwilling to accept the notion that military force can't be used prudently short of all-out war."[131] Meanwhile, senior professional staffers on the Senate Intelligence Committee mobilized the Committee to closely scrutinize the intelligence community's collection and analysis of war crimes and atrocities and their assessment as to whether or not Serb actions constituted genocide under the 1948 Convention on Genocide.[132]

Selective Engagers' and Reluctant Warriors' Response

As interventionist voices began to permeate Washington's political discourse, the Joint Chiefs of Staff feared an escalation toward direct American involvement in Bosnia. The Pentagon responded by strengthening its wall of resistance to use of military force in Bosnia. In meeting after meeting, military commanders blocked or opposed any discussion or proposal on the use of force. According to Ambassador Zimmerman, the Joint Chiefs "refused to even discuss airdrops, that's how gun shy they were. They would never say that they couldn't do it; they just used such inflated figures—half a million here and a half a million there—and no one could challenge it."[133]

But, according to Admiral David Jeremiah, the view among the Joint Chiefs was one of increasing frustration with the civilian policymakers: "They were supposed to be making policy and telling us what they wanted to do, but they could never make up their minds. They wanted the military to bail them out from their policy failures—they wanted us to volunteer military solutions to very complex political problems and they wanted us to do it in a way where nobody would get hurt. It was just unreasonable."[134]

The cumulative pressures for action were escalating—estimates of mass starvation and deprivation, movement toward the development of a war crimes effort, discussions of a no-fly zone over Bosnia, to protect Muslim and Croat villages from aerial attack by the Serbs and of use of American military to support delivery of humanitarian relief. In response, Colin Powell decided to embark on an unprecedented public campaign to keep American troops out of Bosnia. On September 27, the day before the Deputies Committee of the NSC heard dire predictions from the CIA on worsening of the humanitarian crises during the upcoming winter, Powell called Michael Gordon of the *New York Times* to give an unsolicited interview. According to Gordon, Powell was at times angry during the interview. He "assailed the proponents of limited military intervention to protect the Bosnians," saying: "As soon as they tell me it is limited, it means they do not care whether you achieve a result or not. As soon as they tell me 'surgical,' I head for the bunker." He further complained about civilians calling for military action in Bosnia:

These are the same folks who have stuck us into problems before that we have lived to regret. . . . I have some memories of us being put into situations like that which did not turn out quite the way that the people who put us in thought, i.e., Lebanon, if you want a more recent real experience, where a bunch of Marines were put in there as a symbol, as a sign. Except those poor young folks did not know exactly what their mission was. They did not know really what they were doing there. It was very confusing. Two hundred and forty-one of them died as a result.[135]

Amid the mounting pressure, the selective engagers began to consider ways to take more aggressive action that might mitigate some of the domestic criticism. Scowcroft and Eagleburger developed a plan for U.S. support of the implementation of a no-fly zone over Bosnia. At the time, only the Yugoslav federal army possessed military aircraft; they had used them in support of Bosnian Serb ground operations against Muslims and Croats. On October 2, President Bush collected his top national security advisors at the White House to discuss the policy initiative. Eagleburger and Scowcroft supported the policy while Powell dissented.[136] Scowcroft recalls, "It wasn't that we were that far apart. It was a narrow range on which we disagreed. But, they [the Joint Chiefs] were adamant about not getting involved. But on the no-fly we thought we could make a difference on the ground and temper some of the criticism we were getting in Washington."[137] At the conclusion of the meeting, Bush decided to implement the ban on flights. Powell and Cheney, however, concluded the meeting by warning against any gradual escalation of U.S. military involvement. They argued that it was imperative that the administration "prevent the no-fly zone from becoming a slippery slope leading to deeper involvement."[138]

When he announced the new policy, Bush declared, "This flagrant disregard for human life requires a response from the international community."[139] Scowcroft recalls that the no-fly zone idea was put forth when the administration was fighting a battle for public opinion as well as a battle to find acceptable solutions to the crisis.[140]

Two days after the no-fly zone policy was announced, the *New York Times* wrote a scathing editorial criticizing Powell and his reluctance to intervene in Bosnia.

The war in Bosnia is not a fair fight and it is not war. It is slaughter. . . .

. . . when Americans spend more than $280 billion a year for defense, surely they ought to be getting more for their money than no-can-do. It is the prerogative of civilian leaders confronting this historic nightmare to ask the military for a range of options more sophisticated than off or on, stay out completely or go in all the way to total victory.

With that in hand, President Bush could tell General Powell what President Lincoln once told General McClellan: "If you don't want to use the Army, I should like to borrow it for a while."[141]

By all accounts, Powell was livid. He dashed off a scathing op-ed rebuttal to the *New York Times* in which he again laid out his profound reluctance to engage in Bosnia.[142] He argued that the military was reviewing ways to support humanitarian efforts in Bosnia but that the conflict was "especially complex" and had "deep ethnic and religious roots" that went back "a thousand years."

By the end of September, Powell and the military were very much on the defensive. The State Department was proposing new policy initiatives that, while stopping short of outright American intervention, were seen by the military command staff as the first steps toward a much greater U.S. involvement. Congress was demanding more. Candidate Clinton was expressing outrage that the United States was simply ignoring a ruthless campaign against civilians in Bosnia. Even the selective engagers at the White House began inching their way closer to involvement by drafting a strong *démarche* to Milošević on Kosovo.[143] Finally, the media were openly questioning Powell's leadership. This was the cumulative pressure on Powell and his noninterventionist stance in early November, when Bill Clinton, who had campaigned on an activist policy in Bosnia, won the 1992 presidential election.

Somalia—Also Adrift

Throughout much of September, October, and early November, Somalia simply fell off the public's radar screen. After an initial wave of news broadcasts and printed reports on Somalia, the coverage shifted to other international stories. At the National Security Council, the focus on Africa was on the negotiations at Kempton Park leading up the elections in South Africa, on the elections in Angola and the ensuing return to war in late October, and on Mozambique. All three of these situations were seen, according to Walter Kansteiner, who by then was doubling as deputy White House spokesman, as "much bigger fish with real national security interests. Somalia was just humanitarian and very low profile."[144] The primary concern among everyone at the NSC was American strategic interests. In fact, the NSC and Scowcroft were always "very reluctant" to take on Somalia. Scowcroft consistently asked anyone proposing anything on Somalia: "What are our national interests there?"[145] Even amid reports of massive starvation, humanitarian concerns were not a sufficient reason to engage American forces, and it was not until after the elections that the attitudes on Somalia changed.

This indifference to the situation in Somalia was felt even within the interagency task force addressing the crisis. By all accounts of those monitoring the daily events in Somalia, the airlift was producing no real results. The U.S. air relief was dropping food into Baidoa, and feeding centers had been set up there, but those most in need were not able to get to the relief. Ambassador Bishop remembers "sitting at . . . task force meetings chaired by Natsios. We were all saying something needed to be done. Sure, reports were written, but I don't think anyone really paid any attention to us or to what was happening on the ground."[146] On November 6, the Office of Foreign Disaster Assistance reported that more than 25 percent of Somali children under the age of five had already died.[147]

The Election of Bill Clinton

On November 3, political power changed hands in Washington with the election of Bill Clinton. To advise him on foreign policy, Clinton had surrounded himself with liberal members of Jimmy Carter's foreign policy team, and the general belief in Washington was that the Clinton team would shift markedly toward a liberal foreign policy agenda.

Both selective engagers and noninterventionists well remembered what they saw as Carter's excessive moralism and blind commitment to human rights and humanitarian issues—at the expense of American strategic interests. Throughout the campaign, President Bush and his advisors had criticized Clinton's inexperience and naïve enthusiasm with regard to foreign policy. Among the Joint Chiefs, there was disappointment at the defeat of George Bush—in part because of the close personal relationships many of them had established with Bush, but also because of their lingering suspicions of Clinton's own evasion of military service, his apparent support for a military solution to the crisis in Bosnia, and his public commitment to reversing the ban on gays in the military.[148]

Throughout the Washington foreign policy community there was wide speculation that Clinton would take quick action on Bosnia by lifting the arms embargo and possibly using American air power to strike Serb targets. The press also suggested that Clinton was likely to lift the arms embargo. Most military officials felt that lifting the embargo would inevitably pull the United States into a military support role and lead to a gradual escalation, as had occurred in Vietnam.

The election had a discernible effect within the bureaucracies at both the State Department and the Pentagon with respect to Bosnia. At State, there was an immediate recognition that Clinton would lead a much more interventionist policy.[149] Two days after the election, staffers in the European Bureau and the Policy Planning staff began circulating an initiative to lift the arms embargo against Bosnia. Within a few weeks, every relevant bureau in the State Department had signed on to the policy proposal. Everyone "was jumping on to the Clinton bandwagon."[150]

Pressure Builds Again for Action in Somalia

After the election, liberals revived discussion of Somalia as well. In early November, InterAction, a coalition of 160 U.S.-based relief groups, wrote to the lame duck president, Bush, and detailed the extensive problems relief organizations were facing in Somalia. InterAction requested that America increase its support for the United Nations by providing security for relief operations. Andrew Natsios forwarded the letter to the National Security Council and it became a topic of much discussion in preparation for a Deputies Committee meeting on November 20. During the first three weeks of November, an interagency group, chaired by Frank Wisner, who had been appointed undersecretary of state for international security affairs, met frequently to discuss a range of policy options regarding Somalia. The question of military intervention was discussed but largely dismissed because of continued and absolute opposition from the military. The group agreed to outline a series of recommendations and forward them to the Deputies Committee for consideration at the meeting on November 20. The group's planning coincided with a formal report from UN Secretary-General Boutros-Ghali which recommended the deployment of a large UN military operation.

According to Assistant Secretary of State Herman Cohen, the Deputies Committee preparation memos were written in the "Kissinger style"—three options: Option A a little too weak, Option C a little too strong, and Option B just right. Option B proposed that the United States support Boutros-Ghali's request for U.S. logistical support for a UN-led military intervention (with no U.S. ground troops). The renewed pressure from humanitarian organizations and suggestions from the State Department opened the political space for Bush to take more decisive action if he so chose. The question remained, Was he pre-pared to do so?

Clinton's First Trip to Washington

Meanwhile, on November 18, two weeks after the election, Clinton arrived in Washington for personal briefings from President Bush and General Powell. The meeting with Bush lasted an hour longer than scheduled and focused mostly on foreign affairs—including Russia and a lengthy discussion on Bosnia. While the details of the meeting have not been fully disclosed, the *Los Angeles Times* reported that Clinton urged Bush to take a more "aggressive stance in the face of Serbian ethnic cleansing."[151]

The day after his meeting with Bush, Clinton met face-to-face with Powell. After an exchange of pleasantries Clinton immediately pressed Powell on Bos-nia by asking whether there was anything that could be done. According to Powell, Clinton started the meeting by asking, "Wasn't there some way . . . that we could influence the situation through air power, something not too puni-tive." Powell lamented in his memoirs, "There it was again, the ever-popular solution from the skies, with a good humanist twist; let's not hurt anybody." Not wanting to sound *too negative* on the first meeting, Powell and told the president-elect, "I would have my staff give the matter more thought."[152] Clin-ton reported that the meeting was somewhat tense but that Powell "laid it on the line and did not fudge one of our disagreements."[153] Apparently, Clinton refused to back down on either Bosnia or the ban on gays in the military—two issues about which Powell had particularly strong feelings.

On November 20, the NSC Deputies Committee met. The three options regarding Somalia were put on the table: Option A, increasing U.S. financial and material support for the existing UN peacekeeping forces in Somalia; Option B, coordinating a broader UN effort in which the United States would provide logistical support but no ground troops; and Option C, initiating a U.S.-led multinational military intervention into Somalia. According to those present at the meeting, "the use of ground troops was [not a] serious option."[154] From the Joint Chiefs perspective, those in attendance were again "wringing their hands and blaming the military for their limited options."[155]

The next day, however, Admiral Jeremiah stunned the deputies meeting by announcing that if force was desired, the military could do the job. He recalls that by then the frustration within the Joint Chiefs had reached a critical mass:

There was a lot of pressure on us to do something. I went in to see Powell. As far as I was concerned, this was the President's decision to be made. But, we had weeks of hand-wringing and futzing around [by the civilian policymakers] trying to figure out the right thing to do. Nobody wants to send troops . . . [where groups] . . . have been fighting for hundreds of years.

When I said it, I was frustrated because . . . everyone wanted us to volunteer but nobody was making decisions about what they wanted to do.

I presented our view that—*if you decide*—this is what it will take to do the job. Were our figures overkill? Probably, but we weren't going to go in with a weak force. We said just give us the resources and let's get on with it already.[156]

Herman Cohen remembers turning to Frank Wisner and saying, "They're ready to go to Somalia because they are afraid of Bosnia."[157] Jeremiah concurs that there was pressure to act in both Bosnia and Somalia but recalls concluding that "we could do Somalia—we could do it with a relatively moderate force—and it wasn't clear to me that we could do Bosnia. Thirty thousand wouldn't get you a running start in Bosnia."[158]

Scowcroft recalls being struck by "the alacrity with which Colin Powell changed gears," and he speculated that Bosnia had something to do with it. Scowcroft knew that the military felt that Somalia would be a quagmire because the technicals would be virtually indistinguishable from the civilians. "There was no question that he was less enamored than I with the use of force. I was strongly opposed to the Powell doctrine—which has been given a lot more attention and credit than it had back then. He picked it up from Weinberger's six points. I thought it precluded using force unless we went all out."[159]

The President's Decision

On November 25, President Bush called in his senior foreign policy advisors. Powell briefed the president on a plan for a military operation to aid Somalia. After the briefing, Bush announced that he wanted to do it. According to Scowcroft, several factors ultimately played into the president's decision: (1) that the Joint Chiefs were prepared to support the action, (2) that his military commanders now believed American military action could effectively mitigate the famine, (3) that he was moved by the famine situation and was now considering his presidential legacy, and (4) that he was still feeling the cumulative domestic pressures to do something in both Somalia and Bosnia.[160]

After the briefing, Powell and Scowcroft met to work out some of the details.

Among the principal concerns of Powell was his request that the White House do everything necessary to sell the operation to the American public.[161] Powell told Scowcroft that he had titled the intervention "Operation Restore Hope" in order to ensure widespread public support. But Scowcroft doubted that public opinion needed fostering, since one reason for intervening was the public and political pressure to do something: "from what we saw of the public commentary and political pressure prior to the decision, we felt everyone in Washington supported this one."[162]

Summary

President Bush and the selective engagers declared from the beginning that they would not be dragged into Bosnia, despite all the badgering from liberals to intervene. They were convinced that Bosnia would be a Vietnam-style quagmire. About Somalia also they initially staked out a strict opposition to the use of force. At first, Bush and his advisors faced little opposition to their policies on Somalia and Bosnia. They captured significant information advantages on both crises, and there was little or no liberal or media presence on the ground in either place to provide independent information; selective engagers effectively portrayed both conflicts as the boiling over of ancient tribal hatreds about which the United States could do little.

The shifts in the Bush administration's policy on Somalia—first in August 1992 and then again in November 1992—came only in the face of mobilized political opposition. The critical variables behind these policy changes stem from the alterations in the information and propaganda advantage that occurred once competing elites and the media developed resources on the conflict areas and dedicated them to challenging the administration's portrayal of the crises.

Three factors helped to change the information advantage—and ultimately the political dynamic leading to the U.S. intervention in Somalia. First, the long duration of each crisis compounded the political effects. As the months passed and neither crisis showed any signs of abating, the political pressures to intervene mounted. The persistence of the crises enabled the media as well as liberal and hardline opponents of the Bush administration to collect information independent of the administration's and to mobilize their own advocacy resources. In each case, the independent collection of information and the mobilized dissemination and propagation of that information, and the resultant political pressure—came several months after the violence and humanitarian crises had reached massive proportions. Had *either* crisis abated in the late summer or fall of 1992, the United States likely would not have intervened in Somalia.

Second, the breakdown of executive cohesion and the disarray within the ranks of the administration exposed alternative analytical narratives of each crisis. The prevailing (and cohesive) view among the senior Bush administration and U.S. military leaders was unwavering throughout the first year of the Somali crisis and the first five months of the Bosnian conflict. However, in August 1992, in the wake of the discovery in Bosnia of detention centers resembling the Nazi concentration camps and the corresponding media attention, dissent and fragmentation within the administration with respect to both Somalia and Bosnia escalated significantly. Midlevel and senior officials, both liberal and hardline, consistently challenged the selective engager policies in each crisis. As the crises worsened, hardliners and liberals within the ranks of the State Department and the Pentagon began to leak information to the press. These leaks gave liberal opponents of the administration additional information with which to criticize its policies and led to a dramatic opening of the political debate on intervention.

Finally, after the election of Bill Clinton on November 3, President Bush and General Powell, in particular, concluded that a full-scale power shift would occur in Washington, from the selective engager Bush administration to what they believed would be a very active liberal Clinton White House. They believed that liberals within the new administration would be intent on making a strong case for, and would likely alter public attitudes toward, U.S. intervention in Bosnia. Unable to control the spin on both crises, Bush and Powell concluded that if the United States was going to intervene in response to a humanitarian crisis, it would be in Somalia and not Bosnia.

CHAPTER SIX

The War over Iraq

> Simply stated, there is no doubt that Saddam Hussein now has weapons
> of mass destruction. There is no doubt he is amassing them to use
> against our friends, against our allies, and against us.
> —VICE PRESIDENT RICHARD CHENEY

> The run-up to our invasion of Iraq featured the President and members
> of his cabinet invoking every frightening image they could conjure, from
> mushroom clouds, to buried caches of germ warfare, to drones poised to
> deliver germ laden death in our major cities. . . . It was the exploitation
> of fear. —SENATOR ROBERT C. BYRD

> I am scared to death that they are going to convince the president that
> they can do this overthrow of Saddam on the cheap, and we'll find our-
> selves in the middle of a swamp because we didn't plan to do it the right
> way. —FORMER SECRETARY OF STATE
> LAWRENCE EAGLEBURGER

Introduction

On the evening of September 11, 2001, President George W. Bush told a
shocked national audience that the United States would respond to the terrorist attacks that occurred that day and that the United States would "make no
distinction between those who planned these acts and those who harbor
them." Later that night, he told his national security advisors that he had made
the decision "to punish whoever harbors terrorists, not just the perpetrator."
He added, "I want you to understand that we are at war and we will stay at war
until this is done."[1] He concluded, "We have to force countries to choose."

At an emergency meeting of the National Security Council the following
morning, Secretary of Defense Donald Rumsfeld argued that this might be a
prime opportunity to go after Iraq as well as the terrorist movement Al Qaeda
and its main host country, Afghanistan. Rumsfeld and his principal advisors in
the Office of the Secretary of Defense had long advocated a more aggressive

strategy to overthrow Saddam Hussein's regime. The events of September 11 and the president's speech the night before seemed to give them an opportunity to press their case. Secretary of State Colin Powell, however, responded that there was no evidence of Iraq's complicity in the attacks and that the public was focused on Al Qaeda and Afghanistan, not Iraq. He warned that any attack on Iraq would harm American efforts to assemble an international coalition for a sustained war on terrorism and would be met with domestic political resistance. That evening, President Bush pulled aside Richard A. Clarke, his top counterterrorism aide, and instructed him to revisit the intelligence data to see if Iraq was involved in any way with the events the day before.[2]

Over the course of the next five days, Bush and his advisors revisited the question of Iraq several times. Rumsfeld and Deputy Secretary of Defense Paul Wolfowitz pointed out that, while the United States should target Afghanistan, Al Qaeda would be an elusive target, given the terrain of the country. Wolfowitz argued that the United States might be better served by going after Iraq. It would be easier to hit, it was identifiable, and the regime there would likely crumble quickly. It would be a quick and decisive victory for the United States. He also expressed his opinion that there was between a 10 and 50 percent chance that Iraq was involved in the September 11th attacks.

The principal argument against attacking Iraq was political. Powell continued to press that without any evidence of direct Iraqi complicity in the events of September 11, neither the American public nor the international community would support action against Iraq. Even Vice President Cheney concluded that the first target in the war on terror had to be Afghanistan, because, with the American public and the world focused on that country, "if we go after Saddam Hussein, we lose our rightful place as good guys."[3]

On the morning of September 17, Bush agreed that Afghanistan would be the singular focus of the initial response to the terrorist attacks on the United States. Intelligence briefings that morning stated that "there was no evidence that Iraq was responsible for Sept. 11."[4] Bush took Iraq off the table for the time being. However, he told his advisors, "I believe Iraq was involved, but I'm not going to strike them now. I don't have evidence at this point."[5] The implication was that he, too, wanted to topple Saddam but that without some link between him and the events of September 11th, support for invading Iraq would be a tough sell.

Yet, less than two months after his first decision, Bush shifted his position and secretly instructed Rumsfeld and the Joint Chiefs of Staff to step up extensive planning to unseat Saddam Hussein. No new evidence had emerged linking Saddam to the terrorist attacks, but Bush was now prepared to focus on Iraq. And, less than a year later, he received the backing of nearly three-fourths of both the House and Senate for a resolution authorizing him to use force if he so chose. Six months after that, with widespread public support, Bush ordered a preventive war to oust Saddam Hussein.

The chapter examines how, in the absence of any evidentiary link between Iraq and the events of September 11, Bush was able to sell the war in Iraq, to mobilize such widespread public and political support for such an ambitious campaign.

The Argument

Much has been written already about the neoconservative hardline cabal that dominates the administration of George W. Bush and how they aggressively pushed the United States toward war in Iraq. The prevailing argument posits that the neoconservatives, such as Rumsfeld and Wolfowitz, and much of the rest of the senior civilian leadership in the Office of the Secretary of Defense and their allies at the American Enterprise Institute, had long advocated military action in Iraq and that they used the fear and anxiety in the aftermath of September 11 to push their aggressive agenda.

While the evidence clearly demonstrates the existence of a strong and concerted effort by the neoconservatives to promote their agenda on Iraq, this explanation is incomplete. First, not all members of the Bush administration fit into the neoconservative camp. Indeed, President Bush and many other traditional conservatives shared in the desire to remove Saddam Hussein. Second, this argument does elaborate on why such a small group of officials was able to mobilize widespread political support in Washington and public support throughout the country. It also does not consider the fact that in the immediate aftermath of September 11, the public, by overwhelming margins, already expressed support for the use of American force to end Saddam's oppressive rule of Iraq.

The argument presented here suggests that the decision to go to war in Iraq was the result of the emergence of a hardline coalition within the administration. Following the defeat of the Taliban regime in Afghanistan, traditional conservatives, including Bush, Cheney, White House Chief of Staff Andrew Card, and National Security Advisor Condoleezza Rice, aligned with neoconservatives in Office of the Secretary of Defense on the need to remove Saddam Hussein from power. The hardliners concluded that Iraq either posed, or would soon pose, a grave threat to American security. The events of September 11th had proven to them that the unthinkable could happen—if a threat was plausible, it should now be thought of as probable.

The hardliners believed that, even though there was no direct evidence of a link between Saddam Hussein and the events of September 11, the public was highly receptive to suggestions of expanding the war on terror to include Iraq. Gallup polling in mid-November 2001 revealed that more than three-fourths of those polled expressed support for U.S. military action against Saddam Hussein. The concern for the hardliners, however, was that while the public was eager to lash out in response to September 11th, no one knew how long that anger would be sustained or if that support for war would transfer from a hypothetical question to a real military deployment. Launching a preventive war in Iraq would involve months of planning, extensive logistical preparations, and major combat troop deployments. Given such a time frame, hardliners were worried that support would evaporate and alternatives to war would be presented by liberals and others most likely to balk at supporting military action. In short, the hardliners had the support for war in the immediate months after September 11; the question was, Could they keep it?

With the time frame as the basic political constraint, the hardliners began in November 2001 to work and rework efforts to sustain public support for war in Iraq. As anticipated, over the course of the next fifteen months, public support did recede. Nonetheless, the administration was successful in keeping the majority of Americans behind it; and when Bush made the decision to go to war in March 2003, he had a solid base of support. Several factors contributed to the hardliners' success in maintaining mobilized public support for war in Iraq. First, following the terrorist attacks, the hardliners consolidated the national security apparatus and enhanced *executive branch information advantages.* Throughout the war in Afghanistan, the administration tightened its control over the dissemination of national security information. In November, they began selectively releasing classified national security and intelligence information to strengthen their case for war in Iraq. In addition, the president's popular approval sky-rocketed to levels well above 80 percent, greatly enhancing the hardliners' ability to use the presidential bully pulpit. Their information advantages were made even greater by the lack of information from inside Iraq. Because of Iraq's closed society and because Saddam Hussein had expelled weapons inspectors in 1998, liberals and the media were almost entirely beholden to U.S. government officials or Iraqi exiles and dissidents—most of whom had a clear interest in overthrowing Saddam's regime—for information on the nature of the threat and the potential costs of war.

Second, by the end of September 2002, the administration was largely united and cohesive in its views on the need to remove Saddam Hussein from power. The widespread reporting of divisions and rivalries between Colin Powell and the senior civilian leadership at the Pentagon on the need for war had abated; reports of subsequent disputes there centered on postwar planning. Powell and the hardliners at the Pentagon were largely unified in their views of the nature of the threat and their assessments of how quickly Saddam's government would fall.

Third, by controlling the agenda and the timing of the debate, the hardliners gradually introduced the concept of regime change and preemptive war over a period of several months and then timed the escalation of their campaign to coincide with the highly emotional first anniversary of the September 11 attacks, to maximize its appeal.

The administration also framed their campaign so as to co-opt the arguments of their leading opponents. President Bush addressed the United Nations General Assembly and shifted the debate from whether or not the United States should launch a preemptive war to whether or not the UN Security Council would enforce its own resolutions. In doing so, the hardliners rhetorically neutralized the principal complaint of selective engagers, reluctant warriors, and liberals by placing the issue before the United Nations. The hardliners also effectively disrupted political opposition by timing the debate on the congressional resolution authorizing the use of force so that it fell during the run-up to the November mid-term elections and by portraying the resolution as an instrument to enhance diplomatic efforts to avert war.

Finally the administration made arguments that it knew the public was willing to accept. The September 11 assault, the subsequent anthrax attacks, and the widely reported Washington, D.C., sniper shootings in the fall of 2002 exposed American vulnerabilities and generated intense national anxiety. The nature of Saddam Hussein's regime—including a decade of Iraqi noncompliance with international arms inspections and its open support for Palestinian suicide bombers—enabled the hardliners to establish a *credible threat* in a potential relationship between Saddam Hussein and international terrorist organizations such as Al Qaeda. In addition, the quick U.S. military successes in the first Persian Gulf War, in 1991, and in Afghanistan in 2001 allowed the administration to present a *plausible prediction of quick victory.* Americans believed the threat to be real, and they believed they could effectively do something about it.

With a combination of all of these factors, the Bush administration effectively framed the case for war in Iraq, not as a war of choice, but one of necessity to meet a "grave and growing threat."

Foreign Policy Elite Beliefs before the War in Iraq

Return of the Liberals?

Contrary to the expectations described in Chapter 5, Bill Clinton's election had not led to a decided shift to liberal foreign policy. Clinton had come into office highly critical of the first Bush administration's handling of Bosnia and calling for a more compassionate foreign policy. However, from the outset, Clinton and his advisors found themselves caught between the idealistic principals they had promoted throughout the presidential campaign and their recognition of the political capital necessary to alter American foreign policy. On the one hand, Clinton had surrounded himself with leading liberals, such as his national security advisor Anthony Lake and his ambassador to the United Nations Madeleine Albright. They believed that American foreign policy needed to consolidate the gains of the Cold War. They adhered to the democratic peace thesis, that the best way to enhance America's strategic position in the new era was to reorient itself toward a more assertive multilateralism and promote democracy and human rights. With these views in hand, Lake and Albright came into office with a desire to help ameliorate the conflict in Bosnia, which they viewed as one of the world's most urgent security and humanitarian problems.

However, on the other hand, Clinton had campaigned on ending the domestic recession; his own interest and expertise lay in domestic policy, and he had high ambitions to implement sweeping changes in the health care and welfare systems. These required political capital and energy that Clinton and his domestic advisors were loath to spend on difficult foreign policy problems. Furthermore, as demonstrated in the preceding chapter, Clinton's relationship with the reluctant warriors of the Joint Chiefs was already strained, and the strain was worsened by his position on the issue of gays in the military, which dominated the administration's first weeks in office.

Further complicating the initial foreign policy agenda of the new administration was the military intervention in Somalia that it had inherited from the Bush administration. The initial troop deployment to Somalia in December 1992 had been highly successful. Nearly four million Somali civilians had obtained access to food and medicine, and the major threat of starvation had ended within a matter of weeks. However, Bush and his senior advisors had not developed a strategic plan for the immediate postintervention phase. General Powell had deferred or ignored many of the reservations expressed by several of those who had worked on Somalia throughout 1992. No one had developed a comprehensive strategy to establish the sustainable security environment needed for unimpeded delivery of humanitarian relief.

By early 1993, it was apparent that if American forces were to simply withdraw from Somalia, the situation would quickly deteriorate again. It was also clear that any long-term solution would require a real plan for dealing with the armed tribal factions that were at the heart of the security problem. Because reluctance to escalate American military presence in Somalia was the dominant mood in the Clinton administration, the Joint Chiefs, and throughout Washington, the administration hoped to improve the situation there by attempting to capture the leading warlord, Mohammed Aideed. Unfortunately, that effort led to the fateful events of October 3, 1993, in which two Black Hawk helicopters were shot down and eighteen U.S. Army Rangers were killed. The graphic images of a dead American soldier being dragged through the streets of Mogadishu triggered a vocal condemnation of Clinton's policies throughout Washington. Less than a week later, Bill Clinton announced that Americans would be withdrawn from Somalia.

The fiasco in Mogadishu triggered the first full assessment of America's approach to post–Cold War peacekeeping operations. In early May 1994, one month after the last American soldier left Somalia—and, ironically, as the genocide in Rwanda was raging—President Clinton signed Presidential Decision Directive (PDD) 25, which listed the general conditions under which the United States would participate in peacekeeping operations. The document reflected a compromise between the liberals and the selective engagers in the administration. It posited that, while peacekeeping operations would remain an instrument of American foreign policy, the United States would initiate efforts to reform the United Nations and regional organizations so those international institutions could assume a greater share of the burden of peacekeeping.

The directive notwithstanding, the administration's subsequent responses to various crises reflected more the push and pull of domestic politics than adherence to a broad doctrine. For example, the United States did not respond to the genocide in Rwanda. In fact, it actively campaigned for limiting the United Nations role there.[6] When Clinton signed PDD 25, Hutu extremists in Rwanda were killing roughly 10,000 Tutsi and Hutu moderates per day; between mid-April and mid-July of 1994, more than 800,000 civilians were killed. Three months later, however, American forces were deployed to Haiti to restore President Jean-Bertrand Aristide; and in the summer of 1995, prompted by Serb assaults on United Nations safe havens in Srebrenica, Gorazde, and Zepa, liberals finally persuaded Clinton of the need for a policy shift in Bosnia. They pressed for active air strikes and exercise of the full weight of U.S. diplomacy to end the conflict. After two weeks of U.S. air strikes on Bosnian Serb targets and two months of negotiations with the warring factions, Richard Holbrooke brokered a deal among Serbia, Croatia, and Bosnia which ended the war in Bosnia.

Liberals on Iraq

Outside of the much-debated issue of humanitarian intervention, the other major foreign policy dilemma that lingered throughout the Clinton administration's two terms was the situation in Iraq. In the immediate aftermath of the first Persian Gulf War, liberals were among those most critical of the Bush administration for encouraging a Shiite uprising in southern Iraq and a Kurdish uprising in northern Iraq and then abandoning them amidst Saddam Hussein's crackdown. But by-and-large they had supported the administration's Iraq policy in 1991 and 1992. Saddam Hussein was still in power, but the administration had assembled a genuine coalition of twenty-eight nations to fight the war, Kuwait had been liberated, and Saddam Hussein's territorial ambitions had been contained.

Shortly after Clinton came into office, however, intelligence sources confirmed reports that agents of Saddam Hussein had attempted to assassinate former President George H. W. Bush during his visit to Kuwait in April 1993. Responding to this revelation, Clinton in June ordered a series of cruise missile attacks on Iraqi targets, including the Iraqi intelligence headquarters in Baghdad. The United States also increased its over-flights of the UN no-fly zone, which was established after the first Persian Gulf War to restrict Saddam Hussein's forces from using air power to target Kurds in the north and Shiite communities in the south. Despite this military action, the Clinton administration followed containment as its broad strategic objective, relying on sanctions and the no-fly zone as its principal instruments.

The mid-1990s saw a breakdown of the international consensus for maintaining the UN sanctions, which had been imposed in 1990 and 1991 to contain Saddam Hussein. Reports that sanctions were only harming civilian populations generated an international backlash against their use. In response, the Clinton administration in April 1995 supported UN Security Council Resolution 986 establishing the oil-for-food program, which allowed Iraq to sell up to $1 billion worth of oil every ninety days if the proceeds were used to buy food for Iraqi civilians. Still, the international community differed over how to respond to repeated Iraqi violations of various Security Council resolutions. For example, in 1997 Saddam blocked UN weapons inspectors from conducting unrestricted searches on suspected Iraqi nuclear weapons program sites; and after reports that U.S. intelligence agents had infiltrated the international weapons inspections team, Iraq barred American participation in the inspections. When the entire UN team withdrew, the Clinton administration threatened to take decisive military action unless inspections resumed. In February, UN Secretary-General Kofi Annan brokered a deal to get inspectors back in, so the Clinton administration did not strike.

However, Saddam's continued intransigence and his refusal in August 1998 to allow unimpeded weapons inspections led to another showdown with the United States. In October both the House of Representatives and the Senate passed overwhelmingly (the Senate passed it unanimously) the Iraq Liberation Act of 1998, which called on the administration to identify Iraqi opposition groups trying to overthrow Saddam Hussein and to aid their efforts. And, in December, Clinton launched Operation Desert Fox in which American Tomahawk cruise missiles struck nearly one hundred targets over the course of four days.

Despite the Iraq Liberation Act and Operation Desert Fox, throughout both terms, the Clinton administration's strategy remained one of containment of Saddam Hussein rather than ouster. The 1998 congressional action calling for regime change proposed not overt U.S. military action but support of any forces within Iraq that appeared capable of a campaign against him. Although the administration hoped at some point to find opposition groups worth supporting, in 1998 there seemed to be none that could potentially overthrow Saddam Hussein.

The Hardliners' Views in the 1990s

Although not in power in Washington during most of the 1990s, the hard-liners continued to press their case. They believed that under the Clinton administration the United States was becoming increasingly hamstrung by a naïve version of multilateralism. From think tanks and as private citizens, if they lacked official positions, hardliners wrote and argued that the United States needed to commit to ensuring its global dominance and to strengthening its position vis-à-vis China. They also warned of new threats, like the proliferation of weapons of mass destruction and the existence of rogue states with the potential to acquire ballistic missiles.

In their efforts, the hardliners remained vocal critics of the U.S. intelligence agencies and military planning bureaucracies. They believed that the intelligence agencies were biased toward underreporting threats and that most of the intelligence community's regional experts were too sensitive to others' interests rather than those of the United States. Several key hardliners had served on the Committee on the Present Danger in the 1970s, which had concluded that CIA analyses had grossly underestimated the Soviet threat.

In 1998, a major feud erupted between the Clinton administration and conservative hardline Republicans in Congress and in various think tanks over the threat of international ballistic missile developments and the consequent need for a national missile defense program. As a result, conservatives added to the Defense Authorization Act of 1997 an amendment creating a special commission to present a "second opinion" on potential ballistic missile proliferation and its threat to the United States. The nine-member commission, commonly referred to as the Rumsfeld Commission because it was chaired by Donald Rumsfeld, included prominent neoconservatives such as Wolfowitz, R. James Woolsey, and William Schneider.

In an exercise similar to the 1970s activities of the Committee on the Present Danger, the Rumsfeld Commission examined information recently studied by the U.S. intelligence agencies. The commission routinely assumed the worst case scenarios based on the available evidence.[7] It concluded that military and civilian intelligence offices understated the threat facing the United States, that "the threat to the U.S. posed by these emerging capabilities is broader, more mature and evolving more rapidly than has been reported in estimates and reports by the Intelligence Community" and that "under plausible scenarios

. . . . the United States might well have little or no warning before operational deployment."[8] The commission's recommendation was that the United States accelerate its research, testing, and acquisition of key components of national missile defense systems and move to early deployment.

The hardliners were also critical of traditional military planners who, they argued, were committed to outdated and outmoded concepts of force structure and battle doctrine. In particular, the hardliners argued that the traditional military bureaucracy was incapable of reforming itself to meet circumstances in the post–Cold War world. The military needed to do a better job of integrating technology and should develop a rapid deployment force. Investing heavily in technology and privatizing and outsourcing key provisions of the logistical and postconflict security elements would improve battlefield and financial efficiency.

Lessons from Bosnia

While much of the national debate on intervention during the 1990s referred to the lessons of Somalia and why not to intervene in regional and civil conflicts, hardliners were focused on the lessons from Bosnia. For them, Bosnia confirmed both the best and worst parts of American foreign policy. First, they concluded that the noninterventionist response to the violence from 1992 to 1995 reflected what happens without American leadership. While President George H. W. Bush had failed to see the importance of Bosnia, Clinton's team was too committed to an idealistic faith in multilateralism. More than anything, for the hardliners, Bosnia demonstrated that multilateralism does not work: they saw the United Nations as incompetent and the Europeans as feckless.

Second, they believed that the events in Bosnia also confirmed their fundamental belief that power begets respect and that the firm application of American military power can resolve even the world's most intractable problems. For the hardliners, once the Clinton administration demonstrated genuine resolve backed by military force, the war was over in a matter of a few short months. The U.S.-led air strikes in August 1995 and the threat of additional military action compelled the Serbs to negotiate.

Furthermore, for the hardliners, the intelligence community, which had argued that the war was unmanageable, had got it wrong. Samuel Huntington's thesis, published in *Clash of Civilizations* at the height of the Bosnian conflict, was wrong: the war in Bosnia was not fueled by age-old ethnic and religious hatreds; it was elite-driven and it was not beyond remediation. When the leaders of the warring factions signed the Dayton General Framework Agreement, under the pressure of American leadership, the war stopped on a dime.

Finally, throughout the war, neoconservative hardliners such as Rumsfeld, Perle, Wolfowitz, and Jeane Kirkpatrick had lent their support to developing contacts with leading Bosnian Muslims and advocating on their behalf. These Bosnian Muslims and the exiles predicted that American intervention not only could work, but that Americans would be received with open arms in the country. Indeed, in the seven and a half years between America's initial deployment of peacekeepers to Bosnia in 1995 and the onset of the war in Iraq in 2003 there was not a single American combat-related fatality in Bosnia. This illustrated to the neoconservatives that an ambitious American effort could pay great dividends. And with a genuine commitment and effort, the United States could remake an Islamic society into a multiethnic democracy.[9]

Hardliners and Iraq

The lessons of Bosnia, hardliners concluded, could, and should, be applied to Iraq. As early as the first Persian Gulf War, they flirted with the idea of an open invasion of Iraq to remove Saddam Hussein from power. In the fall of 1990, then Secretary of Defense Dick Cheney authorized Paul Wolfowitz to coordinate the development of a plan, known as the Western Excursion, in which U.S. troops would bypass much of the Iraqi Army in Kuwait and enter western Iraq to assist in the liberation of Kuwait and facilitate the removal of Saddam Hussein.[10] Anticipating opposition from Colin Powell, then chairman of the Joint Chiefs of Staff, Cheney ordered planning for the Western Excursion to be conducted outside of the Pentagon's normal planning structures. Wolfowitz assembled a group of sympathetic active duty and retired officers to draft the strategy. The group was ordered not to discuss their efforts with others in the Pentagon.

When Powell learned of the plan, both he and General Norman Schwarzkopf, commander of U.S. Central Command, objected. In late October 1990, Powell went to the Middle East and to Brussels to speak with American military commanders and to brief the NATO allies.[11] With Powell out of the country, Cheney assembled a team of briefers and took his Western Excursion plan to President Bush. According to *New York Times* chief military correspondent Michael Gordon and retired U.S. Army general Bernard Trainor, Cheney's actions constituted, "an extraordinary development. Cheney had concluded that the Western Excursion had been given short shrift by Powell and had decided to take matters into his own hands—and to do so without telling Powell what he was up to."[12] President Bush, along with National Security Advisor Brent Scowcroft and Secretary of State James Baker, dismissed the plan. However, when Powell discovered Cheney's efforts, he vented his frustration to Schwarzkopf: "I can't go out of town anymore. When I go out of town things get out of control. I've got to get this thing back in the box."[13]

Throughout the 1990s, hardliners criticized the Clinton administration for its failure to address what they argued was the growing and "grave" threat posed by Iraq.[14] The Rumsfeld Commission in 1998 had concluded that Iraq, Iran, and North Korea might very well develop and deploy ballistic missiles to attack the United States "with little or no warning."[15] During the tensions with Iraq in early 1998, the Committee for Peace and Security in the Gulf—a group set up by leading neoconservative intellectuals in 1990 before the first Gulf War and co-chaired by Richard Perle—published an open letter to President Clinton demanding a "comprehensive political and military strategy for bringing down Saddam and his regime."[16] The letter was signed by nine individuals who would become senior members of George W. Bush's staff: Rumsfeld, Wolfowitz, Douglas Feith, Dov Zakheim, and Peter Rodman at the Pentagon; John Bolton and Paula Dobriansky at the State Department; and Elliot Abrams and Zalmay Khalilzad at the NSC. In the opinion of this group, Iraq was already an imminent threat.[17]

The neoconservatives' disdain for Clinton's handling of Iraq was more fully articulated in David Wurmser's book, *Tyranny's Ally: America's Failure to Defeat Saddam Hussein.* Wurmser severely criticized the administration for failing to commit itself to overthrowing Saddam, but the book is also highly critical of the administration's decision to suspend its support for Ahmad Chalabi and the Iraqi National Congress (INC) in 1995. Wurmser took particular aim at the assessments made by the U.S. intelligence community and the Middle East regional specialists who had refused to embrace the INC.

By the beginning of the 2000 presidential campaign—a campaign almost devoid of focus on American foreign policy—Governor George W. Bush had quietly assembled a set of hardline foreign policy advisors that included those most critical of Clinton's Iraq containment strategy. Indeed, foreshadowing what was to come, future national security advisor Condoleezza Rice wrote in *Foreign Affairs* in early 2000 that a Republican foreign policy team, unlike the Clinton administration, would "mobilize whatever resources necessary" to remove Saddam Hussein.[18]

Reluctant Warriors' and Selective Engagers' Views in the 1990s

Meanwhile, the reluctant warriors and selective engagers were more tempered in their criticism of the Clinton administration. While they were critical of Clinton's "assertive multilateralism," they nonetheless believed that the pillars of American foreign policy should remain the maintenance of its core alliances, most notably its relationships within NATO and with East Asian allies.[19] They disapproved of Clinton's seeming preoccupation with regional and civil conflicts—in Bosnia, Haiti, Rwanda, and elsewhere. They continued to argue that while these conflicts were tragic, they were not central to American strategic interests. And they believed that Clinton's failures in Somalia were not related to planning assumptions but to problems of "mission creep."

Selective Engagers and Reluctant Warriors on Iraq

Iraq, however, remained the most complex area for selective engagers and reluctant warriors. Throughout the 1990s, they cautioned against the use of military force by the United States to obtain regime change in Iraq. They concluded that containment was an effective policy and that the hardliners were systematically underestimating the political and military costs of direct intervention. For example, in February 1998, in response to the letter-writing campaigns of the neoconservatives, James Baker wrote in the *New York Times*, "There is nothing wrong with containment of Iraq's weapons programs as a policy, provided that it is sufficiently robust and sustained."[20] Brent Scowcroft argued similarly in the *Washington Post*: "If containment could produce a peaceful end to the Cold War on our terms, surely it can be sufficient to deal with threats posed by Saddam Hussein."[21] Furthermore, he warned, launching a preemptive strike to effect regime change would initiate "a crisis the dimensions of which we can only guess and the solution to which we cannot at this juncture even imagine."

Even after Congress passed overwhelmingly the Iraq Liberation Act of 1998, selective engagers emphasized that the resolution was nonbinding and most certainly did not mean the United States would use the legislation to undertake military action in Iraq. General Anthony Zinni, then head of U.S. Central Command, argued emphatically that the act did not in practice mean much because, contrary to the views of hardliners concerning the INC, he saw no legitimate or "viable" opposition groups to fund.[22]

The Mobilization for War in Iraq

From January until September 2001, George W. Bush's foreign policy reflected an uneasy relationship between the State Department, led by reluctant warrior Colin Powell as secretary of state, and the hardline civilian leadership at the Pentagon, the National Security Council staff, and the vice president's office, led by Rumsfeld, Rice, and Cheney, respectively. Nevertheless, in the first eight months in office, the new administration significantly broke from the previous administration by pressing hard for U.S. withdrawal from the 1972 ABM Treaty, rejecting the Comprehensive Test Ban Treaty, and seeking to revise the Treaty on Chemical and Biological Weapons. The new administration also abandoned American support for the Kyoto Protocols on global warming and took the unprecedented action of withdrawing the U.S. signature from the 1998 Rome Treaty establishing the International Criminal Court. The cumulative effect of these actions so angered important members of the international community, including several key allies, that in the summer of 2001, the United States, for the first time ever, lost its seat on the United Nations Commission on Human Rights.

On Iraq, however, the administration's policy was largely static. While the neoconservatives at the Pentagon pushed for new military planning and new thinking on Iraq, Powell and the selective engager advisors at the State Department began slowly developing plans to institute a series of "smart sanctions" to revitalize the international sanctioning of Iraq and intensify pressure on the Saddam government. There was no significant opportunity for the neoconservatives or the conservatives to fundamentally shift the administration's position of containment.

September 11, 2001

The events of September 11, 2001, changed that political environment. Less than twelve hours after the attacks, Bush told the nation that his administration would "make no distinction between the terrorists who committed these acts and those who harbor them."[23] While most accounts suggest that Bush's focus that evening was on the Taliban regime's harboring of Al Qaeda in Afghanistan, the neoconservatives at the Pentagon immediately concluded Iraq should be on the table. During a National Security Council session the next day, Secretary of Defense Rumsfeld proposed that the administration consider taking direct action against Iraq. Powell immediately responded that there was no direct link between Iraq and Al Qaeda. Powell told the NSC: "Any action needs public support. It's not just what the international coalition supports; it's what the American people want to support. The American people want us to do something about Al Qaeda."[24] Following the meeting, Powell approached General John Shelton, chairman of the Joint Chiefs of Staff, and expressed his concern: "What the hell, what are these guys thinking about? Can't you get these guys back in the box?"[25] He added, "I don't know what's going on over there, but this whole—all of this Iraq stuff is a problem."[26]

Nonetheless, the following day, Wolfowitz, in an apparent effort to "prod the president to include Iraq in his first round of targets," told reporters, "It's not just simply a matter of capturing people and holding them accountable, but removing the sanctuaries, removing the support systems, ending states who sponsor terrorism."[27] For Powell this was reminiscent of the Wolfowitz style he had first experienced with Operation Western Excursion. The State Department and the White House quickly sought to downplay the remarks and responded that the focus would be on international terrorism.

The issue did not end there, however. During the weekend of September 15 and 16, Bush assembled his "war council" at Camp David to assess the events of September 11. Wolfowitz argued that Iraq presented the United States with a better opportunity than Afghanistan for a quick military victory and if the United States was to be taken seriously in the war on terrorism, it would have to go after Saddam Hussein. He concluded that Iraq was ripe; the regime would falter quickly under a U.S. attack.

Powell again argued that priority must be given to Afghanistan, the Taliban, and Al Qaeda. The two traditional conservatives among the advisors, Cheney and Rice, sided with Powell. While they both believed Iraq would have to be dealt with, they concluded that the administration's first priority had to be on preventing another direct attack on the United States, and that required hunting down Al Qaeda. At the end of the session, Cheney, Rice, Powell, and White House Chief of Staff Andrew Card all agreed: without direct evidence, Iraq would have to wait; Afghanistan should be the initial focus.

On the morning of September 17, Bush and his advisors again addressed the question of Iraq. The latest intelligence confirmed that there was no evidence linking Saddam Hussein to the events of September 11. As a result, Bush agreed to table discussion of Iraq, although he left no uncertainty that he wanted to deal with Iraq at some point.[28]

While President Bush waited for the right political conditions, the neo-conservatives at the Pentagon continued to develop their case. On September 19 and 20, the Defense Policy Board Advisory Committee, a nongovernmental advisory group to Secretary of Defense Rumsfeld chaired by Richard Perle and comprising several former members of the Committee on the Present Danger, met for nineteen hours, during which they considered strategies for confronting Iraq. Meanwhile, influential neoconservatives outside of the administration published an open letter to President Bush urging direct action in both Afghanistan and Iraq.[29] While neither the Defense Policy Board meeting nor the open letter had any immediate effect on the president, they signified the beginning of a concerted public relations campaign to influence not only the president but Congress, the media, and the public on the need to remove Saddam Hussein. Former Speaker of the House Newt Gingrich, a member of the board proclaimed, "If we don't use this as the moment to replace Saddam after we replace the Taliban, we are setting the stage for disaster."[30]

Furthermore, under the direction of Rumsfeld and Wolfowitz, Douglas J. Feith, the undersecretary of defense for policy, set up a two-man team to reexamine intelligence on Iraq.[31] Their task was similar to that of the CPD in the 1970s and the Rumsfeld Commission in 1998—to take another look at the raw intelligence data and study CIA and Defense Intelligence Agency analyses to detect any faults and limitations of the intelligence community's estimates on Iraq. The team consisted of Michael Maloof and David Wurmser. Wurmser, as mentioned above, was the author of *Tyranny's Ally,* which had been highly critical of the U.S. intelligence agencies' assessments on Iraq, which in turn were largely disdainful of the Iraqi National Congress. Significantly, Wurmser was a friend of Ahmed Chalabi, the head of the Iraqi National Congress (Wurmser described Chalabi as one of his principal mentors), and he used information from Chalabi and the INC to refute CIA and DIA analyses. In direct contrast to longstanding professional analyses by those agencies, the two-man team concluded that terrorist organizations throughout the Middle East were beginning to align with one another and with secular governments, including that of Saddam Hussein. Their analyses relied on circumstantial and fragmentary information and were at odds with CIA and DIA conclusions. Their analyses were nonetheless reported to Feith, Wolfowitz, and Rumsfeld and to the vice president's office.[32]

The upshot of this effort was that within weeks of September 11, Iraq had become the focus of significant key elements at the Pentagon and in the vice president's office. While President Bush had deferred consideration of Iraq, it was just that—a deferral. And, clearly, Rumsfeld and his staff were already looking hard for evidence that would strengthen their case against Saddam Hussein—and laying the ground work for the second phase of the war on terrorism.

Focusing on Iraq and Building an Imminent Threat

In mid-November, Taliban forces fell at Mazar-i-Sharif in northern Afghanistan, signaling a major defeat for the Taliban and precipitating the rapid collapse of their regime throughout Afghanistan. The dramatic turn of events in Afghanistan created the conditions for a shift of attention to Iraq. On November 21, Bush instructed Rumsfeld to begin planning for war on Iraq in earnest. Until the collapse of Mazar-i-Sharif, Cheney, Rice, and White House Chief of Staff Andrew Card had withheld their support for considering Iraq, because of their initial focus on defeating the Taliban and disrupting Al Qaeda. With that task apparently nearing completion, they reassessed their position and concluded that the time was right. Iraq became the centerpiece of "Phase II" of the war on terror.

Latent Public Opinion

The events of September 11, 2001, created political space for considering an attack on Iraq. In the immediate aftermath of those attacks, Americans overwhelming supported aggressive reaction in Afghanistan, but Iraq was also seen as a logical focus of America's response. Public support for regime change had been a well established trend in polling data. During the debates in 1998 over the Iraq Liberation Act and Operation Desert Fox, polling data revealed that a solid majority of those polled expressed support for U.S. military action to overthrow Saddam Hussein. Indeed, as late as February 2001, by a margin of 52 percent to 42 percent, Americans expressed approval for using ground troops to remove Saddam.[33] For the better part of a decade, the American public had been exposed to his behavior—first the Iraqi invasion of Kuwait, then the plot to assassinate former President Bush, then repeated violations of UN Security Council resolutions and the expulsion of UN weapons inspectors. In short, Saddam Hussein was well known to Americans. As a result, when the United States was attacked by terrorists, most Americans were willing to assume Iraq's complicity, absent any compelling evidence to the contrary.

Bush's shift in focus toward Iraq in November 2001 coincided with an increase in the attention paid Iraq by leading commentators. For example, on November 20—the day before Bush asked Rumsfeld to initiate serious war plans—Eliot Cohen, a leading neoconservative scholar, whose book *Supreme Command: Soldiers, Statesmen, and Leadership in Wartime* would become the president's vacation reading in the summer of 2002, argued in the *Wall Street Journal* that Iraq posed the greatest of all global threats to American security.[34] That same day, Thomas Friedman of the *New York Times* argued that it was time to shift American policy toward real democratic reform in the Islamic world and the Middle East.[35]

Furthermore, the following weekend, Gallup released data from a November 25–26 poll that revealed that 74 percent favored "invading Iraq with U.S. ground troops in an attempt to remove Saddam Hussein from power."[36] With Afghanistan seemingly in hand, talk in Washington and around the country was turning to serious discussion of what to do next, and Iraq was a logical point for debate.

Information Management and Advocacy

While the hardliners in the administration welcomed the polling data on Iraq, they also recognized that planning for a major military action there would take time and that it would be impossible to sustain public support indefinitely. Bush and his staff, highly sensitive to the importance of public opinion if war was to be a viable option, knew that it would have to be waged on the home front long before it could be fought in Iraq. The administration would have to develop a sophisticated public relations campaign to sustain the public and political support.

In his instructions to Rumsfeld, Bush ordered very tight control over the war-planning process. He wanted only those with an absolute need to know to be privy to the plans. As he later told Bob Woodward, his concern was that too wide a sharing of information would lead to leaks, which would trigger "enormous international angst and domestic speculation. I know what would happen if people thought we were developing a potential or a war plan for Iraq."[37]

Several factors contributed to this sensitivity and awareness. First, any action would require the support of Secretary of State Powell, the architect of the Powell Doctrine, which demanded not only widespread public support as a precondition for war but broad political support from Congress as well. Powell had long believed that public opinion could be swayed by strong and coherent congressional and media opposition. Even though the public was clearly moved in the immediate weeks after September 11, Powell's initial opposition to war in Iraq was premised on his belief that such widespread support likely was an angry initial response and most certainly would not be sustained. Second, Rumsfeld too argued that retaining public support would require new and creative ways of controlling information and selling the administration's strategies. He suggested that the administration consider waging the war on terror "like a political campaign with daily talking points."[38] And, despite all of the rhetoric that September 11 had fundamentally changed everything for the United States, Bush and his senior advisors were well aware of the fate of President Johnson and the nation in the war over Vietnam. In explaining his concern for the relationship between public relations and war, Bush told Bob Woodward, "I am a product of the Vietnam era. I remember presidents trying to wage wars that were very unpopular, and the nation split."[39]

Finally, and perhaps most importantly, Bush's longest and closest advisors were Karen Hughes and Karl Rove. Rove has proven to be one of the most successful political strategists in Texas history, helping to transform a predominantly Democratic state to one of Republican dominance. Throughout Bush's tenure as governor of Texas and during the first eight months of his presidential administration, Rove and Hughes repeatedly invoked the strategies used by Ronald Reagan—effective communication was a critical determinant of policy success.[40]

Lessons from Afghanistan

While the administration was sensitive to the need for developing a sophisticated information campaign, the war in Afghanistan provided valuable insights into the domestic response the administration might expect as it turned its attention to Iraq.

First, almost no political opposition or criticism of the war in Afghanistan emanated from anywhere on the political left. After September 11, President Bush's poll numbers soared and then hovered around 90 percent approval. Bush's team understood and appreciated the advantages that came from their position.[41]

Second, what criticism there was came from highly motivated sectors of the political right. When the military progress in Afghanistan seemed to slow during the last two weeks of October, conservatives and neoconservatives criticized the Bush administration for not deploying more troops. They were also concerned that Bush had sided with Powell's position on the importance of maintaining an international coalition over what they perceived as the necessity of "absolute victory." In short, there was a vocal segment of American society ready to mobilize support for war in Iraq.

Third, in mid-October, much of the twenty-four-hour streaming news coverage and commentary began to focus on the "slow pace" of American military actions in Afghanistan, and reporters began asking whether or not American troops were bogged down in a "quagmire." Despite the oscillation of the media, the American public remained consistent in its support for the president. In other words, the media occasionally focused on negative aspects of the war, but the public seemed resilient in the face of apparent setbacks.

Finally, the administration was aware of a new media context. If the United States launched a war against Iraq, it would be the first competitive twenty-four-hour-news war. During the war in Afghanistan, Fox News Channel and MSNBC had emerged as significant competitors to CNN, and both were likely to be more editorially predisposed to supporting the administration than CNN would be. This gave the administration much broader access to mobilize its base of support if it developed an effective communications strategy.

All of these lessons conveyed to Bush and his staff a sense that, with a carefully crafted and executed public relations campaign, they could mobilize and sustain the necessary public support for taking on Saddam Hussein.

The 2002 State of the Union Address

The first order of business for the hardliners in the war for public opinion was to attack the conventional arguments against regime change in Iraq. Selective engagers and liberals had two principal arguments: that ten years of containment strategies had effectively boxed in Saddam Hussein and that the public would not sustain its support because there was no direct link between Saddam and Al Qaeda.[42]

With these two arguments in mind, Bush's advisors concluded that they needed to develop the link between Iraq and Al Qaeda and demonstrate that containment would not work.[43] They developed a rhetorical attack strategy. Bush's top two speechwriters, David Frum and Michael Gerson, invented the term "axis of evil." It was consciously intended to convey three things. First, "axis" implied that, directly or indirectly, Al Qaeda and Iraq were linked. If not directly connected regarding September 11, they were most certainly linked (and hence, allied) in their desire to harm the United States. Second, "evil" was included to convey that Iraq and groups like Al Qaeda were irrational. Given the core assumption of rationality in deterrence theory, this suggested that containment could not work.[44] And third and perhaps most significantly, the term alluded to a parallel with World War II—total war—and the need for massive commitment. The term made its debut in the 2002 State of the Union Address. When it was delivered, it tied all of these issues together. Bush proclaimed: "The Iraqi regime has plotted to develop anthrax, and nerve gas, and nuclear weapons for over a decade." He added that Iraq, along with Iran and North Korea "and their terrorist allies, constitute an *axis of evil,* arming to threaten the peace of the world"[45]

The speech triggered immediate reactions. Critical news media editorial boards chastised the president for what many referred to as his "belligerent" tone. Others wondered if this signaled that the administration was preparing to fight simultaneous wars in Iraq, Iran, and North Korea. Despite the criticism, the speech did generate a flurry of news television coverage on Iraq and on Saddam Hussein's historical efforts to develop weapons of mass destruction.[46] And, in the following week, newspapers across the country began to follow the news broadcasts with feature stories on Iraq's defiance of United Nations resolutions. Some of the most influential news organizations sided with the hardliners' portrayal of Iraq as the most immediate threat to the United States. The *Washington Post,* for example, warned that "Iraq, busy rebuilding its weapons of mass destruction in the absence of U.N. inspectors, represents the most immediate threat, and the . . . tool of forcible regime change—of military action—must also be considered."[47] Meanwhile, leading members of Congress also increased their support for the president's position. Senators John McCain and Joseph Lieberman, among others, warned that the threat from Saddam was growing each day and that "time is not on our side."[48]

The shift of focus raised concerns, however, within some elements of the administration. Selective engagers and reluctant warriors at the State Department and on the Joint Chiefs found themselves increasingly on the defensive. In a series of testimonies before Congress, Secretary of State Powell sought to downplay the significance of the administration's new tack on Iraq by suggesting that it was more a continuation of a policy dating back to the Clinton era.[49] Towing the administration's broader line, he did not rule out unilateral action: "There may be times when we have to act alone. . . . We can't have our national interest constrained by the views of the coalition."[50] But he stressed the need to act principally in accordance with the widest possible support. The Joint Chiefs' concerns rested on four main points: (1) activating and deploying sufficient forces (draft war plans concluded that more than 200,000 would be needed to conduct the offensive action), (2) the timing and logistics of such a deployment (a major combat operation would require several months of preparations), (3) that Saddam Hussein might unleash his weapons of mass destruction against American forces, (4) trepidation about the post-Iraq situation (who would emerge to lead Iraq and what role would American forces be required to play?).[51]

Slow Shift in Public Support

Throughout the spring, the hardliners continued their rhetorical campaign. In dozens of speeches in dozens of cities around the country they argued that regime change in Iraq was imperative, that the United States could not allow "terror states and their terrorist allies to threaten us with weapons of mass destruction."[52] Bush's advisors chose his commencement speech at the U.S. Military Academy at West Point to introduce a new doctrine (later dubbed the Bush Doctrine) outlining the basic conditions for the preemptive use of force. In this speech, Bush argued that the traditional notions of defense, containment, and deterrence did not make sense in a world in which rogue regimes could acquire and use weapons of mass destruction or hand them off to sinister terrorist organizations. As a result, Bush proclaimed, "our security will require all Americans to be forward-looking and resolute, to be ready for preemptive action, when necessary, to defend our liberty and to defend our lives."[53] His message was clear: new threats required new thinking.

The public and political discourse on Iraq, as anticipated, began to shift from a largely theoretical discussion of attacking Iraq to a more realistic assessment of the likely costs and benefits of actually doing so. As this occurred, public support for invading Iraq began to drop, from its peak of 74 percent in November 2001 to 61 percent in June 2002.[54] Despite this slippage, the administration was effective in setting the agenda and framing the debate. By June, the troika of threats—proliferation of weapons of mass destruction, terrorism, and Iraq—far outpaced all other threats in the international system as the most critical to Americans. Eighty-six percent of Americans polled believed that the threat that Iraq would develop weapons of mass destruction was a "critical" threat to the vital interests of the United States.[55]

In addition, the president's framing of the debate had put political opponents in an awkward position. Selective engagers and liberals expressed concern with the new language and warned against the "rush to war." Nonetheless,

Saddam Hussein's record demonstrated a willingness to use chemical weapons against civilian populations; he had invaded Iran in 1980 and Kuwait in 1990; and he had a record of seeking nuclear capabilities. Those opposed to regime change were left to argue why, in the face of extensive evidence of brutality and potential danger, they supported the continuation of Saddam's rule. Furthermore, the administration continued to refer to regime change as nothing new; they argued that Clinton had first embraced the policy of regime change with his signature on the Iraq Liberation Act of 1998. Thus boxed in, many selective engagers and liberals ultimately acceded to considering regime change in Iraq. For example, Senate Majority Leader Tom Daschle, a long-time critic of the administration's "unilateralist" foreign policy, summed up the position of most liberals: "There is broad support for a regime change in Iraq. The question is, how do we do it and when do we do it?"[56]

The hardliners had framed the analytical narrative on Iraq so as to convey a sense of urgency and threat. They had launched their campaign in January and less than six months later, even liberals were accepting the concept as an appropriate next step in Bush's war on terror. Capitalizing on their success, Bush and his inner circle held regular highly secret meetings in which they began to develop military and diplomatic plans for regime change in Iraq.[57] By the end of July, the question was not whether or not the Bush administration was going to move forward with an effort to remove Saddam Hussein, but how.

Selective Engagers and Liberals Weigh In

By early August, liberals and selective engagers sensed that the hardliners within the administration, and the president himself, were increasingly intent on military action against Iraq. They were principally concerned with what they saw as the "unilateralist" tone and posture of the hardliners. Senate Foreign Relations Committee Chairman Joseph Biden and Senator Daschle both argued that the administration needed to line up allies, and they warned of the dangers, the long-term implications and costs, of unilateral action. Senators Richard Lugar and Chuck Hegel, two highly regarded Republicans, also warned the administration not to press ahead without international support, and without a carefully crafted plan for "winning the peace."

In what was almost certainly an organized campaign, Colin Powell and two of the first President Bush's chief selective engager advisors, Brent Scowcroft and James Baker, weighed in to slow the move toward war. On August 5, Powell pressed for and got a private dinner meeting with President Bush and National Security Advisor Rice. According to *Washington Post* reporter Karen DeYoung's account, Powell argued that if the United States acted without broader international support Bush "would look like a bully, like he didn't care, like the administration was only interested in getting its own way, was not interested in what the rest of the world had to say."[58]

After the meeting, a series of op-ed commentaries by selective engagers appeared warning that the hardliners were dismissing the costs of war. On August 15, Brent Scowcroft wrote in the *Wall Street Journal* that Saddam Hussein did not pose an imminent threat and that war in Iraq would divert resources and international goodwill from the war on terrorism.[59] Former Secretary of State Lawrence Eagleburger was even more alarmist in expressing his concern. Speaking on Fox News Channel about the influence of Paul Wolfowitz, Richard Perle, and other neoconservatives, he said: "I must tell you, I think they're devious. . . . I am scared to death that they are going to convince the president that they can do this overthrow of Saddam on the cheap, and we'll find ourselves in the middle of a swamp because we didn't plan to do it in the right way."[60]

Sensing the shift in the public discourse, Bush sought to mitigate the criticism. After a meeting with his top military and national security advisors on August 21 at his ranch in Crawford, Texas, Bush told reporters, "Listen . . . America needs to know, I'll be making up my mind based upon the latest intelligence and how best to protect our own country plus our friends and allies."[61] The implication was that he had not made up his mind on going to war and that the former advisors did not have access to the same information he had and could not fully understand the threat. Nonetheless, four days later, former Secretary of State James Baker wrote in the *New York Times:* "[Regime change] cannot be done on the cheap. . . . If we are to change the regime in Iraq, we will have to occupy the country militarily. The costs of doing so, politically, economically and in terms of casualties, could be great."[62] He concluded that it would be imperative to develop a broad international coalition for the action.

The hardliners, however, did not sit idle. Vice President Cheney delivered a very hard-hitting speech to the annual convention of the Veterans of Foreign Wars. He warned that the costs of inaction would be much higher than the costs of action: "Simply stated, there is no doubt that Saddam Hussein now has weapons of mass destruction. There is no doubt that he is amassing them to use against our friends, against our allies, and against us." He then attacked the arguments presented by Scowcroft, Baker, and others by suggesting that they counseled "a course of inaction that could have devastating consequences for many nations, including our own." He added that removing Saddam most certainly would not be a distraction from the war on terror. Rather, it would deliver a final blow to Islamic extremists. And "as for the reaction of the Arab 'street,' the Middle East expert Professor Fouad Ajami predicts that after liberation, the streets in Basra and Baghdad are 'sure to erupt in joy in the same way the throngs in Kabul greeted the Americans.' Extremists in the region would have to rethink their strategy of Jihad." His final warning was that Saddam would likely acquire nuclear weapons "fairly soon." He then invoked his long-standing distrust of intelligence analysis: "Just how soon, we cannot really gauge. Intelligence is an uncertain business. . . . Let me give you just one example of what I mean. Prior to the Gulf War, America's top intelligence analysts would come to my office in the Defense Department and tell me that Saddam Hussein was at least five or perhaps even 10 years away from having a nuclear weapon. After the war we learned that he had been much closer than that, perhaps within a year of acquiring such a weapon."[63]

Refocusing the Campaign and Restoring Executive Cohesion

Amid the frenzied public and intra-administration debate during August, public opinion began to shift. In late August, Gallup polling data revealed, support for invading Iraq had dropped to 53 percent, and 41 percent were opposed to it. Also, significant majorities expressed the view that the United States should wait and give the United Nations more time to get weapons inspectors back into Iraq. Powell and Cheney seemed to be openly feuding, and the entry of former President Bush's senior advisors into the fray signaled to many that the White House was in disarray.

Sensing the shift, and with additional polling data suggesting that the president had not done enough to "explain why the U.S. might take action in Iraq,"[64] Bush returned to Washington from a three-week vacation in Texas intending to tighten and refocus his campaign. He had three goals: to restore consensus within his administration, to develop a comprehensive and disciplined plan for selling the administration's case for war, and to develop a strategy that would effectively accommodate and ultimately co-opt the opposition to American action in Iraq.

The first order of business was to get his advisors unified in support of the effort to remove Saddam Hussein. Throughout August, Powell had advocated that the president use his speech before the United Nations General Assembly slated for September 12 to focus on Iraq and to develop broader international support. Cheney and Rumsfeld remained not only skeptical of the United Nations but convinced that deference to an international coalition, and the United Nations in particular, would ultimately harm American interests.[65] Bush resolved the dispute by agreeing to go to the United Nations, but he announced that he would shift the focus to the United Nations and their failure to enforce their own resolutions on Iraq.

On September 7 and 8, British prime minister Tony Blair met with President Bush in Washington and at Camp David to encourage him to proceed via the United Nations. Bush assured Blair that he would go to the United Nations. In exchange, he obtained from Blair a private assurance that regardless of what happened at the UN, Great Britain would join with the United States in the military action—Bush would have a partner.[66] The British position seemed to seal the deal: Bush would accept the Security Council process, as long as any resolution had teeth; Blair's open support mitigated some of Powell's concerns; and while Cheney and Rumsfeld reluctantly acquiesced to the United Nations process for the time being, both were convinced that in the end, the U.S. military would remove Saddam Hussein.

While he was busy building consensus within his administration, President Bush also tasked his key communications staff to develop a comprehensive strategy to sell the administration's case for war and to establish strict "message discipline" on statements coming from the White House. President Bush's chief of staff, Andrew Card, and his staff created the White House Iraq Group to coordinate the "daily message on Iraq."[67] The team produced a Web site, Iraq: A Decade of Deception and Defiance, which was unveiled during Bush's speech at the United Nations. The team also monitored many of the public comments of senior administration officials and worked to keep them in line with the daily message. For example, they pressed Secretary of Defense Rumsfeld to withdraw a 2,300-word article he had written and submitted to the *Washington Post*'s Outlook section. The piece made a pointed case for the right of the United States to conduct a unilateral, preemptive strike against adversaries intent on developing weapons of mass destruction—a line that deviated from the focused message being projected during the run-up to the president's General Assembly speech.[68] Card's team also studied the congressional calendar to determine the best timing for congressional hearings. They reassembled the team of communications experts who had effectively framed the humanitarian dimensions of the war in Afghanistan.[69] In addition, Rumsfeld gathered his own team of public relations specialists, an informal "strategic communications" group that included high-level Republican public relations operatives. According to *PR Week,* Pentagon spokeswoman Victoria Clarke, the former director of Hill and Knowlton's Washington office, brought together "this group of Beltway lobbyists, PR people and Republican insiders."[70] One of their tasks was to review Pentagon efforts to convince the public of direct links between terrorism and rogue states, like Iraq, that harbor terrorism.

The timing of the campaign, set to begin in early September, had been carefully calculated. As Andrew Card said in a candid comment that was later widely criticized, "From a marketing point of view you don't introduce new products in August."[71] Card's strategy was effective. The administration launched its mobilization campaign on the day following Labor Day, timed for the return of members of Congress to Washington. During the first NSC meeting upon Bush's return to Washington, he and his advisors discussed the domestic political angle of heading for war in Iraq. The administration decided that the best way its campaign could erode potential congressional opposition was to press for a formal vote authorizing the president to use force. Cheney believed that the November elections gave the administration a strategic advantage. He felt, according to Bob Woodward's account, that "voters would know before the election where every congressman and senator stood on Saddam Hussein and his dangerous regime."[72]

The first major offensive began on September 8. Bush's principal national security advisors hit the Sunday morning talk shows that day.[73] Their message was clear and disciplined: Saddam Hussein's regime was aggressively pursuing weapons of mass destruction, including nuclear weapons; it had links to international terrorism, and Al Qaeda in particular; and Iraq, along with Al Qaeda, was intent on inflicting harm on the United States. But the most alarming trend, according to the officials, was Iraq's nuclear weapons programs. Cheney stressed that while there were gaps in what the United States knew about Iraq's weapons programs, the intelligence did reveal that "in fact" Saddam Hussein was "aggressively seeking nuclear weapons."[74] The administration argued that it had firm intelligence reports that Iraq had attempted to acquire high-strength aluminum tubes to be used in centrifuges to process enriched uranium. Rice told CNN that such tubes were "only suited" for nuclear weapons development. She added, "We don't want the smoking gun to be a mushroom cloud."[75] Cheney told an audience of Republicans that the United States had "irrefutable evidence" that the tubes were destined for centrifuges. On the CBS News program *Face the Nation* Rumsfeld warned: "Imagine a September 11 with weapons of mass destruction. It's not 3,000; it's tens of thousands of innocent men, women, and children."[76]

What these senior members of the administration failed to disclose, however, was that the end use of the aluminum tubes had been the subject of intensive debate within the U.S. intelligence community for the better part of a year and many of the government's top nuclear scientists "seriously doubted" that the tubes were meant for nuclear weapons production. Instead, both Cheney and Rice were emphatic that all evidence pointed to Saddam Hussein's aggressive efforts to develop nuclear weapons.

While stressing the magnitude of the threat, they also tried to stifle criticism of President Bush by trying to show that he was committed to building an international response to that threat. They all announced that the president would go to the United Nations on September 12 to deliver a speech demanding that the United Nations enforce its many resolutions on Iraq. Furthermore, they added, Bush was now receiving open endorsement for his maneuvers from Prime Minister Tony Blair, who had traveled to Camp David on September 7 and 8 to meet with Bush.

The mobilization campaign was timed to coincide with the first anniversary of the terrorist attacks. On the evening of September 11, President Bush addressed the nation from Ellis Island, with the Statue of Liberty lit in the background. While he did not directly speak to the issue of Iraq, he signaled that he would present a strong case for further action in the war on terror during his speech to the General Assembly the following day.

On September 12, he delivered a major speech to the United Nations General Assembly. He warned that Saddam Hussein was defying the Security Council and that Iraq was intent on developing nuclear weapons, a situation that would dramatically destabilize the Middle East and pose a threat to all other nations. To mollify critics among the selective engagers, he added, "We will work with the U.N. Security Council for the necessary resolutions."[77] But he also warned the body: "We want the United Nations to be effective. We want the resolutions of the world's most important multilateral body to be enforced. And right now those resolutions are being unilaterally subverted by the Iraqi regime."[78] He concluded by warning the United Nations that if it did not protect international security, the United States would.

The speech had its intended effect. Across the country, editorial boards generally endorsed the president's speech. Even those previously skeptical of the administration's position concluded that the pressure was on the United Nations to enforce its existing resolutions. For example, James Baker wrote in the *Washington Post* that the speech had made the case against Iraq: "The question is no longer why the United States believes force is necessary to implement resolutions involving Iraq, but why the United Nations, after years of inaction, does not now agree. . . . The administration's challenge now is to persuade the United Nations to act on its principles."[79]

Over the next several weeks, the administration continued to argue that Saddam Hussein was on the verge of acquiring nuclear weapons. Bush told one reporter: "I would remind you that when the inspectors first went into Iraq and were denied, finally denied access, a report came out of the Atomic—the IAEA—that they were six months away from developing a weapon. I don't know what more evidence we need."[80] Two weeks later, officials at the International Atomic Energy Agency announced that no such report had ever been issued by them.

The Critical Week: September 24–31

The combined effect of the efforts of the first two weeks in September was to slow and then reverse the decline in support for invading Iraq. Gallup polling numbers, which in late August had revealed a drop in support to 53 percent, now rebounded five points to 58 percent. A CBS poll indicated even stronger support, with 68 percent saying they would approve taking military action against Iraq to remove Saddam Hussein from power.[81]

In addition, the residual effect of Vice President Cheney's emphatic declaration about Saddam's military capabilities at the VFW convention in August had triggered extensive news commentary and analysis and precipitated a shift in the number of Americans who believed that Saddam actually possessed weapons of mass destruction. In mid-August before Cheney's speech, a CNN/USA Today/Gallup poll found that 55 percent of those polled believed that Saddam "currently possessed" weapons of mass destruction, while 39 percent thought he was trying to develop them.[82] After the speech, a CBS/New York Times poll reported that 79 percent of Americans believed that Iraq "currently possessed" such weapons.[83] It is perhaps most notable that a survey of registered voters by Fox News reported that 69 percent of those surveyed believed that Saddam Hussein already possessed *nuclear weapons.*[84]

Still, the polling data continued to reflect dual concerns among the public. On the one hand, the public expressed significant concern over the threat emanating from Iraq: nearly 8 out of 10 Americans were convinced that Iraq possessed weapons of mass destruction and 62 percent thought that Iraq was planning to use those weapons against the United States.[85] On the other hand, the polling data showed that the public wanted the administration not only to secure a congressional resolution authorizing the use of force but also to gain support from the country's allies and the United Nations.

Over the next week, the hardliners sought to add a sense of urgency to American and international action. On September 18, Rumsfeld told the House Armed Services Committee, "No terrorist state poses a greater and more immediate threat to the security of our people and the stability of the world than the regime of Saddam Hussein."[86] That was followed the next day by the president's draft resolution to Congress. It stated specifically that September 11 underscored the "threat that Iraq will transfer weapons of mass destruction to international terrorist organizations," and it cited the "high risk that the current Iraqi regime will either employ those weapons to launch a surprise attack against the United States or its armed forces or provide them to international terrorists who would do so."[87]

Perhaps even more significant was that Colin Powell now seemed to be on board with the overall effort. Although Powell had long been battling the hardliners at the Pentagon, after Bush's pledge to secure a UN resolution and after Blair's announcement of firm support for Bush's position, Powell consistently—except for the occasional extemporaneous critical remark—participated in the effort to sell the administration's position. On September 20, Powell appeared before the House International Relations Committee and urged lawmakers to pass the resolution, by arguing that it was imperative the United States present a unified face to the world in order to enlist their support for a showdown with Iraq. Powell was still the most respected figure in the Bush administration; his own popular approval routinely exceeded that of Bush. He used this stature to ease the concerns of moderate Republicans and Democrats that Bush was already set on war. He acknowledged to members of Congress that he had been "known as a reluctant warrior" but said he believed that, for diplomacy to have a chance, "the threat of war has to be there."[88]

Paralleling the administration's blitz was the mobilization of dozens of think tanks and ad hoc collections of commentators sympathetic to the war plans. The Committee for the Liberation of Iraq, the Project for the New American Century, the Washington Institute for Near East Policy, the Hudson Institute, the Middle East Forum, and the American Enterprise Institute either endorsed en mass or included key individuals who supported U.S. military action to remove Saddam Hussein from power. These individuals and groups stepped up their coordinated campaign to sell their ideas. Leading the way was the public relations firm headed by Eleana Benador, which coordinated many of the communication activities.[89] Benador was the agent for Richard Perle, R. James Woolsey, Max Boot, Michael Ledeen, Alexander Haig, Frank Gaffney, Ruth Wedgwood, and Richard Pipes among others. She aggressively pitched her clients to the major news organizations around the country; most of them made routine media appearances, in the run-up to the war in Iraq, on ABC, NBC, CBS, MSNBC, CNN, PBS, and Fox News Channel. The editor of the *Wall Street Journal* noted that Benador called the paper almost daily: "I think it's safe to say we've used everyone on her list."[90]

The Media as Not-So-Independent Brokers

Not only did the news organizations provide ample opportunity for Benador's clients to promote their views; the media frequently reported sympathetically or with uncritical deference to the White House's portrayal of the threat posed by Saddam Hussein. To cite one example, on September 8 the *New York Times* ran a page-one story titled "U.S. Says Hussein Intensifies Quest for A-Bomb Part," written by David Sanger and Judith Miller and relying almost exclusively on administration sources and Iraqi defectors, which stated that Iraq had sought to acquire aluminum tubes to use in centrifuges in its effort to enrich uranium and build nuclear weapons.[91] The headline and the first several paragraphs conveyed a sense of urgency and uncritically transmitted the hardliners' warnings that the "smoking gun" might come in the form of a "mushroom cloud."

Media critic Michael Massing has found consistent and systematic biases, errors, and distortions in the news media's reporting throughout the prewar period. Massing concludes that several factors conspired to create these problems, including that many journalists relied extensively on sources within the administration and were reluctant to jeopardize their access to the White House; that several leading journalists had personal or longstanding ties to Iraqi dissidents and exiles, many of whom had clear agendas and biases that were not fully disclosed; and that editors frequently deferred to the judgment of their reporters concerning the integrity of sources.[92] Furthermore, many journalists, publishers, and broadcasters were caught up in the wave of patriotism that followed the events of September 11, 2001, and were more deferential to the president and his representations of the threats facing the United States than they might have been under other circumstances. The burden of proof, more often than not, was put on people expressing views critical of the administration, who were asked to demonstrate conclusively that the hardliners were wrong.

The Democrats' Dilemma

Meanwhile, as Congress began debate on a resolution authorizing the president to use force to disarm Saddam Hussein, the pressure of election-year politics put many liberals on the defensive. Democrats were well aware that Republicans had a significant advantage over them in the eyes of Americans as to which party could best handle national security matters. Thirty years earlier, Richard Nixon had launched a massive campaign against George McGovern and the "New Left" of the Democratic Party, portraying them as weak on defense and national security. Since then, Republicans have routinely campaigned as the party best able to defend American security. Polling data conducted after September 11, 2001, confirmed that most Americans believed Republicans to be better able to protect national security than Democrats.[93] Within this politicized context, according to a *Washington Post* report, more than a dozen Democrats who opposed the resolution nonetheless concluded that it was better to support the resolution than face a "backlash from voters."[94] Senior Democratic strategists also pointed out that every Democrat facing a tough race in the House of Representatives had lined up in support of the resolution. Clearly Cheney's political timing of the resolution was having its desired effect.

Still, some liberals were less compliant and believed that the war talk was principally motivated by election politics. On September 25, the issue erupted. That morning, the *Washington Post* reported: "Four times in the past two days, Bush has suggested that Democrats do not care about national security. . . . as Bush continues his record-setting fundraising effort, he has shown an eagerness to discuss the topic in political venues as polls show the effort is aiding Republican candidates."[95] The article generated a fiery response from Senate Majority Leader Tom Daschle: "The president is quoted . . . as saying . . . the Democratic-controlled Senate is not interested in the security of the American people. . . . That is outrageous—outrageous. The president ought to apologize."[96] The immediate concern at the White House was that Daschle's anger would stall negotiations over the language of the Iraq resolution in the Senate. Daschle hinted that it would be difficult to patch up differences in language with the White House prior to the October adjournment. Further complicating the picture for the hardliners was that on September 24, the Dow Jones Industrial averages lost 189 points (2.4 percent) in trading—the fourth triple-digit loss in six sessions—and had its lowest closing level (7,683) since October 1, 1998.[97]

This fueled the criticism that the timing of the war resolution was designed to distract the public from the economic situation. Senators Robert Byrd and Ted Kennedy both delivered speeches seeking to reframe the Iraq situation as a crisis fabricated by a shrewd political machine seeking electoral advantage in the mid-term elections by distracting public attention from the economy and the recently revealed cases of scandalous corporate wrong-doing.

The administration's campaign on Iraq was again briefly on the defensive. In response, the hardliners intensified their campaign. After Daschle's speech, they introduced, for first time, the claim that they had "credible evidence" of direct links between Saddam Hussein and Al Qaeda. Condoleezza Rice stated that "high-ranking detainees" captured during the previous year and being held at the United States Naval Station in Guantanamo Bay, Cuba, had told investigators that Al Qaeda had received training from Iraqi officials in developing chemical weapons. Rice concluded, "There clearly are contacts between al-Qaida and Iraq that can be documented."[98] Rumsfeld, speaking at a Chamber of Commerce luncheon in Atlanta, claimed that he had "very reliable" and "credible" reporting that Iraq and Al Qaeda had "discussed safe haven opportunities in Iraq, reciprocal nonaggression discussions . . . and that al Qaeda leaders have sought contacts in Iraq who could help them acquire weapons of mass destruction capabilities." This evidence, he declared, was "bullet-proof." He stressed that senior members of Al Qaeda had been in Baghdad in "recent periods," according to intelligence reports that he called "factual" and "exactly accurate."[99]

Over the next week, administration officials continued to stress those links. The administration's case also received a boost from Prime Minister Tony Blair, who on September 28 released a white paper that cited new information "that Iraq could quickly launch a chemical or biological warhead and that it had sought to acquire uranium in Africa that could be used to make nuclear weapons."[100] And, on October 2, Bush scored a significant victory when the House minority leader and would-be Democratic presidential candidate Dick Gephardt publicly endorsed Bush's resolution. Speaking at a Rose Garden press announcement with Gephardt and more than two dozen other lawmakers behind him, Bush warned that Saddam's regime was "a threat of unique urgency" and proclaimed that Saddam was "a student of Stalin."

Despite all this success, senior administration officials worried that the Senate debate on the resolution might become further bogged down, since leading Senate Democrats were arguing that the administration was motivated by politics. To step up the pressure on the Democrats, President Bush's communication team decided that the president needed once again to talk directly to the nation. They scheduled a presidential address before a live and sympathetic audience in Cincinnati, Ohio, for October 7, having concluded that he was more effective when speaking in such a setting. In his speech, which was drafted almost exclusively by his senior political advisors, Bush outlined in detail the threat posed by Iraq.[101] At no point did he cite an explicit link between Saddam Hussein and the events of September 11—there was none—but the speech carefully and skillfully developed the message that Saddam was intent on forging a direct relationship with Al Qaeda and other terrorist organizations to attack the United States. Bush warned that the Iraqi regime could "have a nuclear weapon in less than a year" and would "be in a position to pass nuclear technology to terrorists." To add greater imagery to the threat Bush added that "facing clear evidence of peril, we cannot wait for the final proof, the smoking gun that could come in the form of a mushroom cloud."[102]

The Cincinnati speech was followed by button-holing of key holdouts in Congress. Powell called Susan Collins of Maine and again stressed that congressional support for the resolution would enhance the administration's ability to secure an international consensus to tighten the noose around Saddam—and thereby be the last best hope to avoid war.

Ultimately, liberals were hampered in their opposition to war by the widespread view that Saddam Hussein possessed weapons of mass destruction. The intelligence community had concluded that he probably had chemical and biological weapons, but they were much less certain of the nature of Iraq's nuclear research program. Still, the administration's firm and confident portrayal of the threat from Iraq was difficult to counter publicly. The administration had long cultivated the message to the intelligence community that any ambiguity in intelligence could only be interpreted in a worst-case scenario.

In response to intelligence reports that Iraq possessed chemical and possibly biological weapons, several Senate Democratic leaders, like Tom Daschle, Joseph Biden, and presidential hopefuls John Kerry, John Edwards, and Bob Graham, signaled that they would endorse the resolution but encouraged the president to develop a broad international coalition before initiating war. Some liberal Democrats—Senators Robert Byrd, Carl Levin, and Ted Kennedy among them—warned that the United States might be embarking on another Vietnam. In the middle, most Democrats supported military action, but only with broad international support. This split and the ensuing internal debates among Democrats triggered a new round of accusations—that the Democratic Party did not have a coherent plan to enhance American security and were otherwise weak on defense. Former Democratic senator Gary Hart, writing for the op-ed page of the *New York Times,* lamented that the Democrats were once again on the defensive on the issue of national security policy.[103]

The Bush campaign that had begun in earnest in early September had already paid off. Public opinion polls revealed overwhelming support for the president. By early October, the Pew Research Center for the People and the Press reported that two-thirds of the American public believed that Saddam Hussein had been involved in the attacks that had happened on September 11 the previous year. More strikingly, 79 percent of Americans believed that Iraq either possessed or was on the verge of acquiring nuclear weapons.[104]

On October 10 and 11, the House of Representatives and then the Senate passed their resolutions authorizing the president to use force if necessary. In just over ten months after the traditional conservative and neoconservative coalition formed in the Bush administration, it had framed the political discourse on Iraq, beginning with the much maligned "axis of evil," creating near consensus in the country on the necessity for immediate regime change in Iraq, and achieving a joint House and Senate resolution authorizing the president to use force to accomplish that goal. The hardliners effectively employed executive branch information, framing, and mobilization advantages to weigh in on the debate and shift and shape the political discourse.

Deciding on a Military Plan and Mollifying the Critics

Following passage of the congressional resolution, Bush decided, in mid-October, on a military plan prepared by General Tommy Franks.[105] Because of the logistical requirements of the plan, sometime in early February would be the earliest the forces would be set to go.

As part of its implicit bargain with Congress and the public during debate on the congressional resolution, the administration had committed itself to seeking a new UN Security Council resolution. Over the course of the next three weeks, Powell pressed the international community for support.[106] On November 8, the Security Council unanimously passed Resolution 1441, which proclaimed that Iraq was in material breach of its disarmament obligations under a series of previous resolutions, called for the immediate and unrestricted access of UN inspectors to facilities in Iraq, and warned the Iraqi government that it would "face serious consequences" if it obstructed inspectors or in any way violated its obligations. The resolution also set up a sixty-day time period for preparation of an initial inspections report to the Security Council and set January 27, 2003, as the due date.

Bush immediately stressed that the international community was in complete agreement that Saddam Hussein's "cooperation must be prompt and unconditional or he will face the severest consequences."[107] In an op-ed piece in the *Washington Post* two days later, Powell also asserted that the UN resolution revealed that most of the world concurred in its demands on Iraq.[108]

Despite these broad statements, Powell's diplomatic efforts ultimately resulted in an ambiguously worded resolution. It did not reveal a consensus. And almost immediately, other Security Council members and the inspection team differed in their interpretation of the intent of Resolution 1441. For example, Hans Blix, chief inspector, sent his advance team to Iraq on November 18 but believed he was to submit an *interim* report by the sixty days specified in Resolution 1441. He thought that after January 27 he would be conducting further inspections, under the auspices of Security Council Resolution 1284, which had established the inspections regime in 1999, and that he would then be submitting a report on March 27 that would identify the "key remaining disarmament tasks."[109] In addition, France, Germany, and Russia demanded that no action be taken in Iraq until the inspectors had issued their report and the Security Council had issued a second resolution.

The hardliners immediately jumped on what they saw as the United Nations balking on its responsibilities and putting its bureaucratic interests ahead of American security. They stressed that Resolution 1441 gave the United States all of the legal basis and political legitimacy necessary to take action. At this point, selective engagers too concluded that the United Nations process—and the positions of France, Germany, and Russia—would only serve to strengthen Iraq's intransigence.

Wavering Public Opinion?

The inspections process triggered its own dynamic with respect to American public opinion. The public was not so much split in its opinion about the resolution and the inspections as it was conflicted in its preferences about the overall situation. On the one hand, most Americans wanted the inspections process to proceed, because they hoped it would avert war. They also desired that the administration continue to work through the United Nations. On the other hand, a majority of Americans also highly approved of President Bush's handling of the situation and expressed confidence in his leadership. Several polls also suggested that, while a majority of Americans wanted the Bush administration to pursue a second UN resolution, they also would support Bush if he chose to go to war without a second resolution.

But Bush was increasingly frustrated with the inspections process and concerned about the sustainability of his public and political support. American troops were shipping out in large numbers to wait at the ready in the middle of the Kuwaiti desert. The health of their morale and that of their families and neighbors most certainly required that they not be stationed there indefinitely merely to contain Saddam. In a meeting with Rice in mid-January, Bush observed, "Time is not on our side here. Probably going to have to—we're going to have to go to war."[110]

As the military finalized its war plans and neared completion of the deployment of its forces for a military offensive, the administration launched a final campaign to rally the country. Bush was still worried that the public case needed to be strengthened. A briefing by CIA officials on December 21 had left him concerned that the available evidence on Saddam Hussein's weapons capability was not sufficient to sway the public. The CIA sent its follow-up case to the White House on January 22, and on January 23 an op-ed article by Condoleezza Rice was published in the *New York Times*. Titled "Why We Know Iraq Is Lying," it argued that the case was "clear and resounding" that Iraq was not voluntarily disarming and that it was treating the UN weapons inspection process as a "game."[111] On January 25, three days before Bush was scheduled to deliver the State of the Union speech, the senior deputies—Cheney's chief of staff Scooter Libby, Condoleezza Rice and her deputy Stephen Hadley, Richard Armitage, Paul Wolfowitz, and the White House political and communication team of Dan Bartlett, Michael Gerson, Karen Hughes, and Karl Rove—assembled to go through the information and package it to sell to the public.[112]

Significant tension developed among the officials over what the intelligence really said. Armitage thought that the neoconservatives—Libby and Wolfowitz in particular—routinely extracted worst-case scenarios out of ambiguous material. Libby cited evidence on connections between Iraq and Al Qaeda, most notably September 11 hijacker Mohammed Atta's alleged meetings with Iraqi intelligence officials in Prague, which Powell and Armitage dismissed. Armitage believed Libby was overstating the case. Despite the tensions, the group unanimously agreed that, overall, the intelligence coupled with Saddam's track record signaled a real danger to the United States.

The information package developed at the January 25 session provided the basis for President Bush's State of the Union Address. In the speech, Bush repeated the long list of dangers that he and the hardline coalition saw in Saddam Hussein's regime. He again posited that Saddam Hussein was aggressively pursuing nuclear weapons. And, as part of this proposition, he repeated that Iraq had attempted to get aluminum tubes to use in development of nuclear weapons. Also included in the speech were the now infamous sixteen words "the British government has learned that Saddam Hussein recently sought significant quantities of uranium from Africa." (Those reports had been deemed unreliable three months earlier by the CIA, which had requested that the citation be dropped from Bush's speech in Cincinnati.) Bush also stressed that secret intelligence evidence revealed that Saddam was aiding and protecting terrorists, including members of Al Qaeda and that he could provide weapons of mass destruction to terrorists without detection. Bush concluded: "If this threat is permitted to fully and suddenly emerge, all actions, all words, and all recriminations would come too late."[113]

The speech was followed by Secretary of State Powell's presentation to the United Nations on February 5. Bush's senior political advisors had suggested that Powell be the one to take the evidence to the United Nations and sell the case to anyone still sitting on the fence. His reputation as a moderate—indeed a reluctant warrior—would give further credibility to those with doubts. Powell was also very articulate and persuasive. In his one-hour presentation, he delivered the strongest case he had so far made for war. With CIA Director George Tenet seated directly behind him, Powell presented what he claimed was conclusive evidence of Iraqi intransigence and violations regarding compliance with the UN resolutions—satellite imagery and communications intercepts of what he reported as secret mobile biological laboratories and Iraqi efforts to relocate banned chemical and biological munitions.

Bush's State of the Union speech and Powell's presentation had the intended effect. The *Washington Post* titled its editorial on February 6 "Irrefutable" and led with "It is hard to imagine how anyone could doubt that Iraq possesses weapons of mass destruction." The editorial said that Powell's talk would "stand as a worthy last effort to engage the United Nations."[114] The *New York Times*, long skeptical of military action in Iraq, concluded that Powell "may not have produced a 'smoking gun,' but he left little question that Mr. Hussein had tried hard to conceal one."[115] Following the presentation, polls showed more than two-thirds of Americans acknowledging that Bush had made a "convincing case."[116] Most notably, a CNN/USA Today/Gallop Poll conducted in early February revealed that 87 percent were either convinced or thought it likely that Iraq had direct ties to Al Qaeda.[117] The numbers also confirmed that there would probably be no major political backlash from a war.

The administration continued to press its case. What neither Bush nor Powell ever mentioned were internal government estimates of the costs of this military action and the risks that could follow defeat of Saddam Hussein's regime. In January, the National Intelligence Council (NIC) prepared two analyses for President Bush which predicted that toppling Saddam Hussein's regime would trigger broader support for Islamic fundamentalism among Iraqis and other Arabs and that there was a real possibility of a coordinated insurgency and guerrilla warfare aimed at American troops.[118] However, because of the highly classified nature of the documents, their circulation was tightly controlled, and opponents and skeptics in Congress and the media were unaware of the NIC's predictions.

The media remained largely hamstrung by its inability to independently confirm or refute much of what the administration reported. Those journalists in Iraq were under strict control by the Iraqi government and unable to do their traditional information collection. Meanwhile, those reporting from Washington and New York were forced to rely extensively on either U.S. government sources or on members of the Iraqi exile and dissident community, all of whom had significant biases in favor of overthrowing Saddam Hussein. Furthermore, as the *New York Times* ombudsman reported fifteen months after the war began, much of the *Times*'s reporting during the prewar period was flawed, because it was premised on unsubstantiated claims by parties with "vested interests" and because reporters were frequently writing with an eye toward "coddling sources" and maintaining access.[119] Even the *Times* editors themselves conceded that several articles ranging from the fall of 2001 through 2003 were based on information that was "controversial" and "insufficiently qualified or allowed to stand unchallenged."[120]

The Bush administration had so effectively sold its agenda that when the antiwar movement did gain momentum in the United States and around the globe and even after an unprecedented global demonstration in hundreds of cities in dozens of countries on February 16, there was no significant shift in

American public or political support for military action. The protest actions came nearly six months after the hardliners in the Bush administration had stepped up their mobilization campaign and directed the political debate in Washington.

Winning the Peace, Discounting the Costs

The only lingering question on the eve of the war remained the potential costs. The last effort by selective engagers and reluctant warriors was to shift the focus from the threat posed by Saddam Hussein to the costs of military action. Army Chief of Staff General Eric Shinseki told a congressional panel in late February that he believed it would take several hundred thousand troops to shore up the security situation in Iraq after the war. The hardliners responded immediately by arguing that such estimates were "wildly off the mark."[121] Paul Wolfowitz, for example, told a congressional hearing that the $95 billion price tag predicted in published reports was certainly too high and did not reflect (1) that the Iraqis would welcome the Americans and greatly assist in Iraq's rebuilding, (2) that those nations opposing the war would certainly sign up to help with the rebuilding, and (3) that Iraq's oil revenues would help defray any costs. He concluded by stating, "To assume we're going to pay for it all is just wrong."

By late February, however, this debate was largely insignificant. The political space for military action was well established. With nearly 200,000 American troops amassed in the deserts of Kuwait, the prevailing view in the public and Congress was essentially, "let's get on with it already." After February 5, any shift in public or political support was not sufficient to dramatically raise the political costs of launching a preventive war. Public opinion polls still revealed that most Americans wanted Bush to secure strong UN approval for any military action, but those polls also suggested that the public would support the president regardless. President Bush was intent on removing Saddam Hussein from power, and he had public and political support. In early March, General Tommy Franks reported that his military preparations were complete and that he was ready to launch his plan. On March 17, President Bush issued one final ultimatum to Saddam Hussein to leave the country or face military attack. Two days later, Bush gave the order for American forces to begin the war.

Summary

The hardliners in the Bush administration came into office in 2001 intent on removing Saddam Hussein from power. They had spent the better part of a decade advocating various strategies to accomplish this goal. They believed that Saddam posed a threat in the Middle East and that, given the opportunity, he would seek to inflict harm on the United States. After September 11, they saw that threat as no longer simply plausible but probable.

Others, such as liberals and selective engagers, were inclined to believe that a robust containment strategy could have been built—especially after September 11—and could have ensured that Saddam posed no significant threat outside of Iraq. Many were also suspicious of the hardliners' claims that he might develop nuclear weapons or biological weapons and then give them to terrorist organizations—especially Al Qaeda. They reasoned that, because he would not be able to control such organizations and they might use those weapons against his own regime, he would not lend them assistance. They argued that the hardliners were both overstating the dangers posed by Iraq and underestimating the potential costs of war.

In the immediate aftermath of the September 11 tragedy, large numbers of Americans already believed that Iraq was a probable threat to the United States. Saddam Hussein routinely had been identified by Republicans and Democrats over the previous decade as a menace and a threat to regional and international security. In addition, Iraq had increasingly become intertwined in the national discourse of the two other major threats—terrorism and proliferation of weapons of mass destruction—that had emerged within the consciousness of the American public.

The Bush administration, nonetheless, concluded that transforming general predispositions into overt support for war would require a carefully constructed campaign to control and manipulate the flow of information, both to convince the public of the necessity of military action and to delegitimize any political opposition. The administration relied on executive privileges in information collection, analysis, and dissemination to emphasize the threat posed by Iraq and to discount the potential costs.

The hardliners took full advantage of the fact that after September 11, 2001, President Bush's popular approval sky-rocketed to levels well above 80 percent. The public, the news media, and even political opponents gave him wide latitude to respond to the terrorist attacks. The hardliners believed, however, that the political space for going to war was limited, that more distance between September 11 and the onset of a war in Iraq would lead to more dissenting voices and an erosion of support. They timed their mobilization campaign for maximal political leverage and to coincide with the military deployment and logistical build-up in the Gulf—all with an eye towards compressing the time frame for action.

In the end, President Bush relied on that public trust and political capital after September 11 to sell the case for war in Iraq. The evidence presented here suggests, however, that President Bush may not only have relied on that trust but may have abused it. The postinvasion evidence revealed that much of the information and assessments of threat used by the Bush administration in their prewar public relations campaign were inflated, distorted, and selectively disclosed to the public. The administration did not simply rely on rhetorical devices, such as invoking rhetorical images of mushroom clouds and the like; it deliberately and selectively used its executive advantages of intelligence collection and analysis to frame a particular version of the threat in order to influence public opinion. When the intelligence reports supported their positions, the hardliners routinely proclaimed them to be "highly credible" or, in the case of Rumsfeld's portrayal of interview data provided by detainees at Guantanamo Bay, as "bullet proof." However, when intelligence reports contradicted or weakened the president's case for war, the administration waged a systematic campaign to discount the integrity of analysis and evidence. This was evident in the administration's portrayal of intelligence analyses that concluded that Iraq was several years away from developing its own nuclear capacity; in response to those assessments, Vice President Cheney and then Bush, Rice, and Rumsfeld all stressed the inherent limitations and "uncertainty" of intelligence analysis.

President Bush and his advisors also released intelligence when it beefed up their case for war. Powell's presentation to the United Nations Security Council in February 2003 included audio tape of highly classified electronic intercepts—an unprecedented disclosure by the United States of its signal intelligence sources and methods. Yet, the National Intelligence Council's predictions on the likely postwar violence and insurgency and other internal analysis on the potential costs were tightly restricted and unknown even to most of Congress.

A second notable factor in this case is that unlike the cases of Somalia and Bosnia presented in Chapter 5, there were few unsanctioned leaks from within the administration. Postwar media reporting has revealed that there was extensive debate and dissent within the administration throughout 2002 and early 2003, especially within the intelligence and scientific bureaucracies, over the way in which the administration represented intelligence reports to Congress and the public. The technical and highly sensitive nature of this intelligence and its extremely high classification may explain much of the reluctance of lower-level government officials to leak the materials or any information about internal debates on the subject. But, it is also clear that senior officials within the White House sought to control all aspects of the public debate on Iraq (even to the extent of compelling Secretary of Defense Rumsfeld to withdraw a 2,300-word opinion piece that he had submitted to the *Washington Post*) and that they were unprepared to tolerate any unsanctioned release of information.

A final interesting element of the sales campaign was the manner in which the administration's campaign was coordinated with, and supported by, the efforts from neoconservative intellectuals outside of the administration. Many of these intellectuals had a direct line to the Office of the Secretary of Defense through Rumsfeld's Defense Policy Review Board. Several of its members, such as Kenneth Adelman, Eliot Cohen, Newt Gingrich, Richard Perle, Ruth Wedgwood, and James Woolsey, were particularly vocal advocates for war. In the age of twenty-four-hour news channels and the corresponding insatiable demand for content in programming, cable news producers routinely called upon these Washington insiders to provide "authoritative" commentary and analysis of the situation regarding Iraq.

Ultimately, the disconnect between the prewar rhetoric and the postinvasion reality, and the ensuing difficulties faced by American troops in Iraq, almost certainly has eroded the long-term political viability of the Bush Doctrine on preemption. Despite categorical statements by the administration and their pro-war allies before the war, the United States has found no weapons of mass destruction and no evidence of prewar direct ties between Saddam Hussein and Al Qaeda. American troops were not, by and large, greeted as liberators; instead American troops saw the emergence of a significant insurgency in the first eighteen months after the invasion, and more than 1,000 Americans soldiers have been killed and more than 7,000 wounded. Furthermore, during the summer of 2004, several polls revealed that a majority of Americans had come to believe the war to have been a mistake.[122] This is reminiscent of the public's eventual reaction to the war in Vietnam, despite the persistent claims by Presidents Johnson and Nixon that the United States would prevail. It is not clear that advocates for the next preemptive war will be able to replicate these strategies to develop and ensure public and political support. Iraq may not ultimately prove to be another Vietnam, but it may have led to a strong resurrection of the Vietnam syndrome and greater public aversion to the use of force in the future.

CHAPTER SEVEN

Conclusion

> When all is said and done, interventions are political decisions and they
> will only become more political.   —BRENT SCOWCROFT

General Findings

One of the great myths in American foreign policy is that politics stops at
the water's edge. There is a dramatic and consistent tendency associated with
American decisions on going to war: American foreign policy elites hold different beliefs about when and where the United States should use force, and
they fight fierce battles for public and political support. Only in those rare
instances when the United States is directly attacked does politics seem to stop
at the water's edge. And, even then it simply quiets down for a short time; it
does not stop. There is also a dramatic and consistent tendency of elites trying
to sell intervention and war to the American public and using all of the resources at their disposal to deliberately control and manipulate information.

Competing Elite Beliefs

A principal conclusion of this book is that competing beliefs by policy elites
exist and they matter. International crises and conflicts, like facts, do not speak
for themselves. Elites perceive and interpret them through their own world

views. We routinely hear debates that force should be used to support American interests or to advance American values, and we also hear debates on the costs of action versus those of inaction. These debates are not simply academic. They reflect fundamental differences of world view. Indeed, understanding these beliefs and the means used to advocate for them is critical to explaining American use of force in the past half-century.

Even during the height of the Cold War—the so-called era of American foreign policy consensus—American foreign policy elites held deeply divided views on the nature of threats to American interests and values and the costs associated with meeting those threats with force. While most foreign policy elites supported versions of the American Cold War containment doctrine, they regularly differed over the way that doctrine should be applied, especially when the use of military force was being considered. Those debates are again raging in regard to the war in Iraq.

The paragraphs below and Table 7.1 summarize where the various foreign policy elites stood on U.S. military intervention in the regional and civil conflicts discussed in this book.

In the case of Indochina in 1954 selective engagers and hardliners believed that a French defeat would be a significant loss to American vital national interests. Indochina possessed strategic resources of rubber and tin. It also possessed a South China Sea coastline conducive to the development of deep-water ports. Because of this strategic importance, hardliners believed it was imperative that the United States take forceful action. Liberals, however saw the French activities as an effort to restore colonial control over the Associated States of Indochina and found this antithetical to American values. As a result, liberals believed that the United States could not (and should not) in good conscience support an effort that would inevitably prop up French colonial rule. Reluctant warriors, meanwhile, saw Indochina as another politically ambiguous situation in which American forces could quickly and easily become bogged down in a protracted land war. They concluded from experience in Korea that U.S. military operations could not be successful unless the United States was truly committed to full mobilization and war—an unlikely prospect in regional conflicts in remote areas of the world.

In Lebanon in 1958 similar divisions existed. Selective engagers and hardliners quickly surmised the geostrategic importance of Lebanon and of America's presence in the Middle East. As the violence erupted in May they asserted that, regardless of the cause of the violence, both Egyptian leader Nasser and

Table 7.1. Preferences of Advocacy Groups regarding Intervention in Various Crises

	Hardliners	Selective Engagers	Liberals	Reluctant Warriors
Indochina 1954				
Favored	+	+		
Supported conditionally				
Opposed			+	+
Lebanon 1958				
Favored	+			
Supported conditionally		+		
Opposed			+	+
Grenada 1983				
Favored	+	+		
Supported conditionally				+
Opposed			+	
Somalia 1992				
Favored			+	
Supported conditionally				
Opposed	+	+		+
Bosnia 1992				
Favored	+		+	
Supported conditionally				
Opposed		+		+
Iraq 2003				
Favored	+			
Supported conditionally		+		
Opposed			+	+

the Soviet Union were likely to exploit it to undermine American influence in Lebanon and, ultimately, throughout the Middle East. Consequently, they concluded that the United States should be prepared to intervene on behalf of Lebanese President Camille Chamoun if he requested U.S. assistance. Liberals, however, remained skeptical of the domestic political shenanigans of Chamoun. They wondered whether or not Chamoun had ignited the crisis by his own extra-constitutional and antidemocratic practices to secure a stronger grip on power.

Scholars, journalists, and commentators routinely cite the trauma of Vietnam as the beginning of the breakdown of national consensus in foreign policy; and, while Vietnam disrupted much of the foreign policy establishment, the basic parameters of foreign policy elite cleavages continued to revolve around the same axes. In Grenada, hardliners saw the 10,000-foot runway under construction at the new Port Salinas airport, in conjunction with the New Jewel Movement's stated Marxist-Leninist principles, as a clear indication of Soviet and Cuban attempts to expand international communism in the Caribbean. For the selective engagers, the willingness of right-wing neighboring Caribbean states to support American military action and the perceived low military costs of rolling back the Marxist influence in Grenada combined to convince them that American military action was appropriate. Liberals, however, saw the crisis in Grenada largely as a domestic crisis that did not warrant American military action. They remained highly suspicious of the hardliners and selective engagers in the Reagan administration and believed that Reagan and his advisors were committed to escalating their hardline anticommunist crusade through the Caribbean and Latin America.

These divisions persisted into the post–Cold War and post–September 11 eras as well. In 1992, the first President Bush and his core selective engager and reluctant warrior advisors adamantly opposed military action in Somalia and Bosnia. They argued that, with the end of the Cold War, the United States simply had no geostrategic interests in either conflict. Liberals, however, concluded that the systematic targeting of civilian populations by combatants in both crises and the magnitude of human suffering warranted quick and decisive American military action. They believed that—especially in the post–Cold War era—the United States, with its global superiority in military capability, had a moral obligation to use this capacity to stop genocide, to prevent gross violations of international humanitarian law, and to alleviate severe human distress. For their part, hardliners concluded that Bosnia and the Balkans remained of U.S. interest. They argued that if violence were to spill over to Kosovo, Macedonia, and even Greece and Turkey it would have serious consequences for American interests throughout all of Europe and the Near East.

As Americans debated war in Iraq, hardliners declared that Saddam Hussein's track record coupled with the terrorist attacks of September 11, 2001, exposed the United States to new and more acute dangers from Iraq. Selective engagers and liberals, however, believed that international sanctions and American and British enforcement of the no-fly zones over northern and southern Iraq were effectively containing Saddam. They did not view the threat emanating from Iraq with the same sense of urgency or as representing the same degree of danger as the hardliners did.

In each case, policy elites held differing views about whether or not the United States should intervene. Furthermore, these differences consistently reflected fundamentally different views about the nature of the dangers facing the United States, the purpose and efficacy of American power, and the costs and consequences of war.

Information and Propaganda Advantages

The second major conclusion of this book is that decisions on military intervention and war are the result of active and aggressive campaigns for or against a particular war. Ultimately, decisions to send American men and women into combat are not made at some level higher than politics. This is not to suggest that intervention decisions are the result of elites pandering to voters with a mind to the next election or in order to distract the public from some other political issue.[1] The argument here is that elites view international crises through the lens of their normative world views. Their beliefs are real. Perhaps it is because they hold their beliefs so firmly that policy elites routinely engage in determined and sophisticated efforts—including the frequent use of information manipulation and distortion—to frame how the public perceives a particular crisis.

The argument developed here has demonstrated that four factors contribute to the success or failure of the information-control and issue-framing advantages necessary for selling war: the role of the presidency and the cohesiveness of the executive branch, the resources of the opposition, the role of the news media, and the duration of the crisis.

Role of the Presidency and Executive Cohesion

One of the most important contributing factors to information and propaganda advantages is the role of the presidency and the degree of cohesion within the executive branch. The president has enormous advantages in early collection and analysis of information on international crises, and because of his role as commander in chief, most Americans show considerable deference to the president on matters of national security. While Congress does maintain some oversight in matters of intelligence and defense, the congressional influence is quite limited, especially with regard to the day-to-day management of international crises. Congress, like the public, has tended to defer to the judgment of the executive branch, and popular presidents are given even more latitude.

The research presented here reveals a variety of ways in which the president can exploit these advantages. Perhaps the most common tool is rhetorical pronouncements and other devices designed to define the nature of the crisis and create political backing for the president's view. In 1954, Eisenhower introduced the "domino theory" by arguing that a communist victory in Indochina would ripple throughout all of Southeast Asia, South Asia, the Middle East, and beyond. In 1958, he repeatedly depicted Lebanese president Camille Chamoun as the victim of ruthless attacks by Egypt and Syria. In March 1983, Ronald Reagan warned a national television audience of the dangers of the new airport construction by fervent Marxists in Grenada. In 1992, George H. W. Bush and his senior advisors dismissed arguments for intervention in Somalia and Bosnia by labeling the conflicts as quagmires fueled by age-old ethnic hatreds. And in 2003, George W. Bush, Richard Cheney, Condoleezza Rice, and Donald Rumsfeld all used the rhetorical images of a "mushroom cloud" to stress their view of the costs of not acting immediately to remove Saddam Hussein from power in Iraq. In each case, presidents and their senior advisors routinely used nationally televised speeches or press conferences in the effort to persuade the public of their position for or against intervention and war.

The research presented here also demonstrates a consistent pattern in the political use and manipulation of intelligence reports and analyses. When it suited his purpose, each president cited and championed intelligence reports that favored his view of the world, while discounting or dismissing intelligence reports that contradicted or weakened his position. So, for example, in April 1954, in a bid to influence Congress to support the administration's position, Secretary of State Dulles introduced "fresh top secret" intelligence that "Red Chinese" forces were aiding the Vietminh surrounding the French forces at Dienbienphu. In 1958, the Eisenhower administration dismissed a UN report that found little if any external infiltration into Lebanon by arguing that the administration possessed much more sophisticated intelligence than the UN had and that it demonstrated clear and serious infiltration by Egypt and Syria. In 1983, President Reagan announced that American intelligence reported that the coup leaders in Grenada were threatening to detain American students. He also spoke of huge "warehouses" full of arms and ammunition that went far beyond "defensive" purposes. And in 2003, Bush administration officials repeatedly cited reports of Iraq's efforts to acquire aluminum tubes and of its contact with members of Al Qaeda as the administration built support for war. In each case, the intelligence reports promoted by the executive were subsequently revealed to be either untrue or significantly embellished.

Interestingly, the "firm" intelligence in each of these cases, with the exception of Dulles's claim during the Dienbienphu crisis, was based on information given by individuals from the country in question who were actively seeking American military intervention: Charles Malik in Lebanon in 1958, Sir Paul Scoon in Grenada in 1983, leading members of the Iraqi National Congress in Iraq in 2003. Each of the reports was proven factually incorrect and subsequently discredited by postintervention investigation.

When information and intelligence concluded something other than the administration's preference, it was routinely discounted or dismissed. In 1992, Assistant Secretary of State Tom Niles told a congressional panel that, while there were intelligence reports on the existence of Bosnian concentration camps, the reports were inconclusive. And in 2003, Vice President Cheney and Condoleezza Rice repeatedly discounted intelligence reports suggesting that Saddam Hussein would need a significant amount of time to acquire nuclear weapons. They each argued that since intelligence was such an "uncertain business" it would not be wise to base a policy of inaction upon it.

Efforts to control perception of a situation were most effective when an administration was united and cohesive in its views. When in addition the administration developed a coordinated and systematic public relations campaign, the administration's analytical narrative of the crisis often prevailed. This was most notably the case regarding Lebanon and Grenada. In those crises, the Eisenhower and Reagan administrations, respectively, controlled the deliberation process to ensure maximum executive cohesion and to protect against undisclosed leaks. Before and during these crises, all internal deliberations were conducted by a very small team of advisors that shared the preference for intervention. With such extensive executive cohesion, the White House produced a unified policy line. And, as a result, each administration was able to present the crisis as a simple good versus evil, right versus wrong dichotomy.

In the case of Iraq, much has been written of a major split within the Bush administration between Powell and the State Department and the hardliners at the Pentagon during prewar policy deliberations. But after it was apparent that President Bush had sided with the hardliners and seemed intent on war, much of the division within the administration on whether or not to go to war disappeared. As he had done in Somalia a decade earlier, Powell shifted gears and supported the decision for war.

When the executive was highly fragmented, the result was institutional confusion, extensive leaks of internal deliberations, and an overall breakdown in message cohesion and discipline. Under these circumstances, advocacy groups outside the executive branch were able to gain access to information that previously had been restricted. Leaks were a consistent problem for Eisenhower in the Indochina crisis. His initial plan to send 200 American technicians to Indochina in late January immediately found its way into the newspapers, significantly reducing his ability to set the agenda and frame the debate.

Opposition Resources, the Media, and Crisis Duration

In the conflicts examined, the resources of opposing views, the role of the media, and the duration of each crisis contributed significantly to determining whether or not a president was able to control the portrayal of the crisis. Crises that lingered enabled groups outside of the executive to develop independent information sources to challenge or verify the administration's point of view. In the case of Indochina, for example, by the time Americans had been bankrolling the French war effort for more than four years, journalists and liberals had established their own presence on the ground, with Christian missionaries and extensive fact-finding trips, and had developed firm conclusions about the crisis there. Indochina became a known entity, and Eisenhower was simply not able to reframe the crisis as part of the global anticommunist struggle. The conflicts in Bosnia and Somalia also lingered for months, compounding the political pressures on the Bush administration. But whereas in Indochina the duration of the crisis constrained the executive in his deliberations on intervention, in 1992, as both humanitarian crises deteriorated, pressure grew on the administration in favor of intervention. Ultimately, the administration's initial framing of the events could not be maintained as journalists and liberal opponents gradually collected their own information and launched more sophisticated advocacy campaigns of their own.

Crises that erupted on short notice gave advantages to the group in control of the executive for a variety of reasons. First, when an issue arose quickly, others who sought to mobilize public opinion did not have time to accomplish their aims. Second, unexpected crises inherently privileged the executive's information advantage—there generally were limited sources of information, that is, few correspondents or independent analysts. Consequently, the media and competing policy groups had to rely on information gathered and disseminated by the administration. This was the case in Lebanon, in which the rapid sequence of events coupled with an insufficient presence on the ground precluded journalists and opponents of intervention from learning the nature of the crisis for themselves. In Grenada, the highly compressed duration of the crisis and the restrictions on access to the island by the PRG government allowed the administration to launch its intervention with almost complete national and international surprise.

The passage of time played an idiosyncratic role in the process of President George W. Bush's decision to intervene in Iraq. In the immediate aftermath of September 11 and with the United States experiencing a heightened sense of vulnerability, the Bush administration's strategy was essentially a race against time. Americans were willing to countenance war in Iraq, but the administration believed that the greater the distance between September 11, 2001, and the onset of war the harder it would be to sustain that support. The administration worked diligently, first to prepare the public for the real prospect of war and then to expedite the planning process and launch the war before it lost support. In short, it sought to compress the time frame in order to maximize the advantage of the residual effect of September 11. The "rush to war" was the only politically viable option for war.

The role of the news media is one of the most complex aspects in the analysis of public opinion and foreign policy. This is particularly so because historically the media has been simultaneously criticized for being overly supportive of administrations' policies and overly combative. The findings here reinforce other studies that have concluded that the media can and frequently does provide means for the collection and dissemination of information that critically assesses the views presented by the administration. However, in less accessible parts of the globe or in countries where media presence and activity were highly restricted, there was limited reporting from the ground, at least initially. Because of a lack of resources, expertise, and access to these crisis areas, the media often focused its early attention on the U.S. policy response and reporting from Washington. Naturally, much of this initial reporting tended to be biased in favor of the analytical portrayal being projected by the administration.

The evidence suggests that the administration's advantages were mitigated in those areas where journalists had preexisting expertise and experience in reporting. In 1954, journalists and other writers had long been in Southeast

Asia. Many had been dispatched to the region to cover postwar Japan or the Korean conflict or the French war in Indochina. Graham Greene's reporting, later depicted in the best-selling novel *The Quiet American,* gave Americans a vivid picture of life in French colonial Saigon.

In cases such as Lebanon and, initially, Bosnia, the combination of limited resources and editorial pressure for stories generated reporting that largely mirrored or propagated the official U.S. government narrative of the crises. In Lebanon, few Americans were based in the country, and the media bias—on the part of both correspondents and their editors—was to publish information from Beirut and only as it pertained to American holdings or citizens. In Bosnia, although initially caught unprepared, as the crisis persisted journalists were able to travel to the conflict zones. And, in doing so they frequently developed alternative analyses of the crises, which were subsequently broadcast and printed. Furthermore, when journalists found a glaring disconnect between the official version of events and their own investigations on the ground, they became even more emboldened and critical in their coverage. In Bosnia, journalists were particularly angered by the Bush administration's efforts to downplay the existence of concentration camp–type detention centers in August 1992. In response, they redoubled their efforts to find evidence and confront the administration with it. That evidence served as the basis for an exponential increase in critical coverage that month.

For years, journalists in Iraq had been restricted in their reporting. From 1998 onward, their principal sources of information had been U.S. government officials and Iraqi defectors or exiles. This situation produced reporting that was insufficiently challenged in its representation of opinion or assertions as fact. To the extent they could, many journalists sought to challenge the administration's assertions, but without much access to either Iraq or sensitive U.S. intelligence, the media was largely hamstrung in its ability to serve as an effective check on official administration framing of the situation.

Latent Public Opinion: Credible Threat and Plausible Theory of Victory

Despite all the effort put into them, not all the executive arguments for or against intervention have worked, even those sold by presidents with strong information advantages. Sometimes they have encountered public opinion that resisted persuasion. In the case of Indochina, for example, Eisenhower was not able to overcome lingering public reluctance to intervene in another war in Asia—especially one to aid French colonialism. The conflict's geographic and temporal proximity to the Korean conflict made the prospect a tough sell. In addition, for most Americans the conflict in Indochina was not against international communism but a nationalist response to French colonialism. Furthermore, judging by the Korean engagement and the French effort itself, any U.S. military involvement would likely be a difficult and highly costly war.

Conversely, in Lebanon and Grenada, Presidents Eisenhower and Reagan found a public that was more accepting of the idea of using military force to project American power. Americans had grown weary after a string of defeats and were prepared to support military interventions that had a prospect of success. Eisenhower found in the wake of Sputnik and anti-American actions from Berlin to Caracas, that Americans wanted to demonstrate U.S. strength and resolve. In that sense, the situation in Lebanon posed a credible threat—Nasser's trip to Moscow greatly helped in that regard—and a clear sense that the Marines would succeed. Grenada, too, emerged within the context of a general feeling of anxiety. The American public had become increasingly frustrated with the malaise of the 1970s and the post-Vietnam era and the perception of an overall decline in America's global position. The proximity to the Iran hostage crisis and the vulnerability of the American medical students conveyed a credible threat, and there was a plausible theory of victory. (It is important to note that in Reagan's efforts in Nicaragua and El Salvador there was not a plausible theory of victory.)

Before the U.S. involvement in Somalia and Bosnia, latent public opinion was mixed on the question of intervention. On the one hand, Americans were marginally opposed to further extending U.S. military commitments across the globe in the post–Cold War era. They tended to sense that the conflicts in Somalia and Bosnia were extremely complex, which would make any military action difficult. On the other hand, public opinion polling routinely revealed that Americans wanted something done. When the crises in Somalia and the former Yugoslavia first surfaced, polling results briefed to the first President Bush and his core advisors revealed these mixed public attitudes. The polls suggested that the public simultaneously was wary of committing U.S. forces in civil conflicts but also supportive of using American forces to alleviate humanitarian crises. In short, in neither Somalia nor Bosnia did the public opinion polling data reveal any firmly entrenched public stance—either for or against military intervention. This led the administration to adopt an initial strategy to do nothing more than manage public opinion and to prevent any shift in public support toward a more interventionist policy approach.

Regarding Iraq the public was highly willing to consider use of force. Saddam Hussein had been part of American lexicon for more than a decade. His actions inside his own country, his attacks on neighboring Iran and Kuwait, albeit ten and twenty years earlier, and the events of September 11, 2001, all enhanced the credibility of the threat posed by his regime. In addition, America's decisive victory over Iraqi forces during the first Gulf War provided Americans with a general sense that another war against Iraq would be winnable within an acceptable range of costs.

The Future of American Military Interventions

Much has been written about how the events of September 11, 2001, and their aftermath brought about a fundamental shift in American foreign policy. To be sure, the United States is in a particularly active phase in the use of military force. Since 1989, the United States has intervened in Panama, Kuwait, northern Iraq, Somalia, Bosnia, Haiti, Kosovo, Afghanistan, and Iraq. And, with the promulgation of the Bush Doctrine and the ongoing war on terror, it appears that the United States is poised to continue its active intervention indefinitely.

While the future is full of uncertainty, the findings presented here do allow for some modest assessments of what we might expect.

Greater or Lesser Concentrations of Information?

In the late 1990s, there were many predictions that our current notion of information and propaganda advantages was likely to become a relic of the past. With dramatic developments in information technologies, nonstate actors now have unprecedented access to information. State monopolies on information appear to be increasingly tenuous. For example, humanitarian organizations now rent commercial satellite capability to collect imagery of current or developing humanitarian tragedies. Human rights organizations are now beginning to use similar technology to monitor and collect evidence of war crimes and atrocities.

To be sure, these processes may bring a leveling of the playing field in the competition between national strategic interests and humanitarian values. And, while we may see a growing marketplace of ideas as a result of these new technologies, we might also see countervailing trends. If nongovernmental organizations and the media can gain more sophisticated strategies for collecting and packaging information, so too can governments. The executive branch itself has continued to refine its strategies for information control, propaganda, and spin.

As the most recent case, Iraq, attests, the president and his staff can still develop significant advantages to frame the nature of a crisis. The president will always have a certain amount of inherent credibility and public trust. The case made for war in Iraq demonstrates how the Bush administration selectively used, and ultimately distorted and manipulated, information and intelligence to mobilize and sustain support. President Bush and his advisors skillfully developed, packaged, and timed their messages for maximum appeal. He used his State of the Union speech in 2002 and again in 2003, and he pointedly chose his most popular and respected cabinet member, Secretary of State Colin Powell, assisted by animated graphics, to present the administration's case on Iraq to the United Nations. The public believed that the information being provided by the administration was truthful and credible. All three speeches led to a jump in public support for war. If Iraq is a guide, when an administration is fully cohesive and aggressively develops message discipline, it no doubt will be able to develop and maintain information and framing advantages.

Additionally, further trends in news coverage may even enhance future presidents' abilities to develop information and framing advantages. Since the end of the Cold War, most news organizations have reduced significantly the number of their foreign-based correspondents.[2] Instead, "celebrity journalists" tend to parachute into the world's hot spots. While these journalists are extremely skilled, they are not likely to have preexisting knowledge or information resources and their learning curves are likely to be steep. This may further bias reporting of regional and civil conflicts toward the analytical narratives produced and disseminated by administration officials, whether they are hardliners, selective engagers, reluctant warriors, or liberals.

The Perils of Politics

Ultimately, however, success for an administration might be fleeting. Because rhetorical campaigns are such an integral part of mobilizing public and political support, there is a tendency to oversell the message. The constant temptation to manipulate and distort information, frequently leads the public to develop unrealistic expectations about the nature or likely cost or efficacy of military intervention. This does not pose a problem if a war turns out to be quick and decisive, as in Lebanon and Grenada, and where there have been few if any casualties, as in Bosnia and Kosovo. The problem, however, is that wars are not sport, and they rarely go according to script; and these unrealistic expectations have profound implications, not only for the intervention itself, but also for the long-term commitment to postwar reconstruction.

In the great U.S. military failures of the twentieth century—the war in the Philippines, the war in Korea, and the war in Vietnam—American presidents argued that the United States would face severe peril if it failed to act. They also proclaimed that the war could be won without great sacrifice. When casualties mounted and the financial costs escalated, Americans turned overwhelmingly against the war. In this regard, it remains to be seen how Iraq will play out and how it will be judged, but the lesson from these experiences is that a president who aggressively oversells the use of force will find it difficult to sustain support if the intervention does not go well, especially if the rationale and arguments made for the war are proven to have been exaggerated.

Furthermore, because the use of force is inherently a political decision and because there is a tendency to oversell it, the search for a uniform grand strategy may be an elusive quest. Americans have—and will always have—competing views on the world, on the nature of the international system, and on the anticipated costs, risks, and benefits associated with war. As a result, grand strategies will be fleeting and American foreign policy is likely to move about in fits and starts. In the early 1980s, the Reagan Doctrine failed to gain traction because the claims made by Reagan and his advisors portraying the Nicaraguan Contras as "freedom fighters" seemed at odds with widespread reports of human rights violations being committed by them. In the 1990s, advocates of the Powell Doctrine routinely opposed intervention for humanitarian purposes. These views, however, seemed too callous in the face of mass starvation, and Powell Doctrine advocates soon found themselves under persistent pressure to intervene and, in the end, were compelled to do so under less than desirable and optimal conditions. More recently, the advocates for the Bush Doctrine argued that the only way to meet emerging threats is through the preemptive use of force. This was the logic used to sell the war in Iraq. However, in light of the evidence that Saddam Hussein did not, in fact, possess weapons of mass destruction nor did he have extensive ties with Al Qaeda, the Bush Doctrine may well have reached the limits of its political viability.

A Final Word

In the United States, the decision to intervene militarily in another country is the product of warring ideas and campaigns to sell the idea to the public. Ideally, we would all like American forces to be deployed only for the purest of reasons. This is rarely the case. Regardless of the merits of any particular war or intervention, Americans are asked to fight, die, and kill on behalf of the state. If we understand the process by which decisions for war are made, we can exercise greater vigilance and scrutiny in the future.

Americans are a discerning and trusting people, but even the founders of this country understood the fallibilities of leaders and institutions regarding decisions for war. In 1798, with the country less than a decade old, James Madison expressed his concerns to Thomas Jefferson: "The management of foreign relations appears to be the most susceptible to abuse of all the trusts committed to a Government, because they can be concealed or disclosed, or disclosed in such parts and at such times as will best suit particular views."[3] Those perceptive and prescient words seem just as relevant today.

Notes

O N E : Liberal Theory and the Politics of Selling War

Epigraphs: Quincy Wright, *A Study of War,* vol. 2 (Chicago: University of Chicago Press, 1942), p. 1085. Walter Lippmann quoted in John R. Zaller, *The Nature and Origins of Mass Opinion* (New York: Cambridge University Press, 1992), p. 14.

1. Steve Crabtree, "Americans See More Military Action Coming," Gallup Poll Tuesday Briefing, June 17, 2003 at www.gallup.com/poll/content/default.aspx?ci-8653 (accessed Oct. 3, 2004).

2. There is an extensive literature on the currying of support. It ranges from radical critiques of American political propaganda to "how to" books and pamphlets designed to help Washington newcomers master the techniques of "spin control." For a bibliography of the radical critiques see James R. Bennett, *Control of Information in the United States: An Annotated Bibliography* (Westport, CT: Meckler, 1987). For general reference see Kenneth W. Thompson, ed., *Three Press Secretaries on the Presidency and the Press: Jody Powell, George Reedy, and Jerry terHorst* (Lanham, MD: University Press of America, 1983); Stephanie Greco Larson, *Creating Consent of the Governed: A Member of Congress and the Local Media* (Carbondale: Southern Illinois University Press, 1992); David Morgan, *The Flacks of Washington: Government Information and the Public Agenda* (Westport, CT: Greenwood Press, 1986); Stephen Hess, *The Government-Press Connection: Press Officers and Their Offices* (Washington, DC: Brookings Institution, 1984); John Anthony Maltese, *Spin Control: The White House Office of Communications and the Management of Presidential News,* 2nd ed. (Chapel Hill: University of North Carolina Press, 1994); and Judson J. Connor, *Meeting the Press: A Media Survival Guide for the Defense Manager* (Washington, DC: National Defense University, 1993).

3. Writing more than sixty years ago, Quincy Wright observed that the nature of warfare makes elite consensus on the use of force unlikely: "The military results to be expected from war are rarely certain, and the eventual economic, political, and cultural consequences can seldom be calculated with any approximation to accuracy. War is a gamble, and, even if calculations are made, there is usually difference of opinion in high quarters and even more among the general population. There is almost never a universal acceptance of any proposition concerning the need or wisdom of a particular war." Quoted in Wright, *Study of War,* vol. 2, pp. 1086–1087.

4. See Andrew Moravcik, "Taking Preferences Seriously: A Liberal Theory of International Politics," *International Organization,* vol. 51, no. 4 (Autumn 1997), pp. 513–554.

5. Ibid.

6. Immanuel Kant, *Perpetual Peace,* ed. Lewis White Beck (Indianapolis: Bobbs-

Merrill Educational Library, 1957). Much of the work in the Democratic peace literature addresses this issue. See Bruce Russett, *Grasping the Democratic Peace: Principles
for a Post–Cold War World* (Princeton: Princeton University Press, 1993); James Lee Ray,
*Democracy and International Conflict: An Evaluation of the Democratic Peace Proposi-
tion* (Columbia: University of South Carolina Press, 1995); and John M. Owen IV, *Liberal Peace, Liberal War: American Politics and International Security* (Ithaca: Cornell
University Press, 1997).

7. Kant, *Perpetual Peace*, pp. 12–13.

8. Owen, *Liberal Peace, Liberal War*, p. 35.

9. Michael W. Doyle, "Liberalism and World Politics," *American Political Science
Review*, vol. 80, no. 4 (December 1986) p. 1161.

10. Kant, *Perpetual Peace*, p. 13. Kant also states: "The state of peace among men
living side by side is not the natural state (*status naturalis*); the natural state is one
of war. This does not always mean open hostilities, but at least an unceasing threat of
war. A state of peace, therefore, must be *established*, for in order to be secured against
hostility it is not sufficient that hostilities simply be not committed; and, unless this
security is pledged to each by his neighbor (a thing that can occur only in a civil state),
each may treat his neighbor, from whom he demands this security, as an enemy"
(p. 10).

11. Owen, *Liberal Peace, Liberal War*, p. 38.

12. Fernando R. Tesón, "Kantian International Liberalism," in David R. Mapel and
Terry Nardin, eds., *International Society: Diverse Ethical Perspectives* (Princeton: Princeton University Press, 1998), p. 111.

13. Doyle, "Liberalism and World Politics," p. 1160.

14. See Ole R. Holsti and James N. Rosenau, *American Leadership in World Affairs:
Vietnam and the Breakdown of Consensus* (Boston: Allen and Unwin, 1984); Eugene R.
Wittkopf, *Faces of Internationalism: Public Opinion and American Foreign Policy* (Durham, NC: Duke University Press, 1990); Michael A. Maggiotto and Eugene R. Wittkopf,
"American Public Attitudes Toward Foreign Policy," *International Studies Quarterly*,
vol. 25, no. 4 (December 1981): 601–631. For discussion of elite attitudes based on historical evaluation see Tony Smith, *America's Mission: The United States and the Worldwide Struggle for Democracy in the Twentieth Century* (Princeton: Princeton University
Press, 1994); and Robert W. Tucker and David C. Hendrickson, *The Imperial Temptation: The New World Order and America's Purpose* (New York: Council on Foreign Relations Press, 1992).

15. Historians also have demonstrated deep cleavages among foreign policy elites
throughout the past century, beginning with the anticolonialist and mugwump movements of the late nineteenth century to the isolationists during the interwar period. See
for example, Robert L. Beisner, *Twelve against Empire: The Anti-Imperialists, 1898–1900*
(New York: McGraw-Hill, 1968); Thomas G. Paterson, ed., *American Imperialism and
Anti-Imperialism* (New York: Crowell, 1973); and Selig Adler, *The Isolationist Impulse:
Its Twentieth-Century Reaction* (New York: Abelard-Schuman, 1957). A number of
scholars argue that, contrary to conventional wisdom, politics were not set aside dur-
ing the early Cold War foreign policy debates. See I. M. Destler, Leslie Gelb, and
Anthony Lake, *Our Own Worst Enemy: The Unmaking of American Foreign Policy,* (New
York: Simon and Schuster, 1984). For example, H. W. Brands argues that bipartisanship
on foreign policy had eroded by 1952, see H. W. Brands, Jr., *Cold Warriors: Eisenhower's*

Generation and American Foreign Policy (New York: Columbia University Press, 1988), p. 9. Ernest R. May and Richard E. Neustadt argue that there was "bitter, partisan, and utterly consensus-free debate about the loss of China, the long-term stationing of troops in Europe, the limiting of warfare in Korea, and whether a new war ought to be risked for Dien Bien Phu, Quemoy, or the Matsus"(*Thinking in Time: The Uses of History for Decision Makers* [New York: Free Press, 1986], pp. 258–259).

16. For an elaboration on selective engagement, see Robert J. Art, "Geopolitics Updates: The Strategy of Selective Engagement," *International Security,* vol. 23, no. 3 (Winter 1998–99), pp. 79–113.

17. Ibid., p. 80.

18. See for example, James A. Baker III, "The Right Way to Change a Regime," *New York Times,* August 25, 2002, sec. 4, p. 9.

19. For a sample of the hardline neoconservative views, see Paul Wolfowitz, "Remembering the Future," *National Interest,* Spring 2000, pp. 35–45; Angelo Codevilla, "Victory: What It Will Take to Win," *Claremont Review of Books,* November 2001; Charles Krauthammer, "The Unipolar Moment Revisited," *National Interest* (Winter 2002–03) pp. 5–17; Lawrence F. Kaplan and William Kristol, *The War Over Iraq: Saddam's Tyranny and America's Mission* (San Francisco: Encounter Books, 2003); and, Eliot A. Cohen, *Supreme Command: Soldiers, Statesmen, and Leadership in Wartime* (New York: Free Press, 2002). For an overview of the traditional conservative views see George H. Nash, *The Conservative Intellectual Movement in America Since 1945* (Wilmington, DE: Intercollegiate Studies Institute, 1998), chap. 4; and Ramesh Ponnuru, "Getting to the Bottom of the 'Neo' Nonsense," *National Review,* June 16, 2003, pp. 29–32. For a debate between traditional conservatives and neoconservatives, see "The Path To Victory: A Symposium on the War with William F. Buckley Jr., Angelo M. Codevilla, Frank Gaffney, Mackubin T. Owens, Norman Podhoretz, and David Tucker," in *Claremont Review of Books,* vol. 2, no. 4, Fall 2002.

20. See, for example, Richard K. Betts, *Soldiers, Statesmen, and Cold War Crises,* 2nd ed. (New York: Columbia University Press, 1991) and Christopher Gacek, *The Logic of Force: The Dilemma of Limited War and American Foreign Policy* (New York: Columbia University Press, 1994).

21. See for example, Patrick J. Buchanan, "Whose War? A Neoconservative Clique Seeks to Ensnare Our Country in a Series of Wars that Are Not in America's Interest," *American Conservative,* March 24, 2003; Patrick J. Buchanan, "America First: And Second, and Third," *National Interest,* no. 19 (Spring 1990), pp. 77–82; Ted Galen Carpenter, "An Independent Course," *National Interest,* no. 21 (Fall 1990), pp. 16–25; Nathan Glazer, "A Time for Modesty," *National Interest,* no. 21 (Fall 1990), pp. 31–35.

22. See Eugene Gholz, Daryl G. Press, and Harvey Sapolsky, "Come Home America." For a review and critique of these arguments see Joshua Muravchik, *The Imperative of American Leadership: A Challenge to Neo-Isolationism* (Washington, DC: American Enterprise Press, 1996).

23. Joseph S. Nye, Jr., *The Paradox of American Power: Why the World's Only Superpower Can't Go It Alone* (New York: Oxford University Press, 2002); Joseph S. Nye, Jr., "Redefining the National Interest," *Foreign Affairs,* vol. 78, no. 4 (July–August 1999); and Strobe Talbott, "Democracy and the National Interest," *Foreign Affairs,* vol. 75, no. 6 (November–December 1996).

24. For a review of humanitarianist advocacy see Samantha Power, "*A Problem From*

Hell": America and the Age of Genocide (New York: Basic Books, 2002); Linda Melvern, *A People Betrayed: The Role of the West in Rwanda's Genocide* (London: Zed Books, 2000); and, Holly Burkhalter, "The Question of Genocide: The Clinton Administration," *World Policy Journal*, vol. 11, no. 4 (Winter 1994): 44–54.

25. According to Ole Holsti, "a finding that major decisions seemed to be correlated with public preferences does not, by itself, establish a causal link." Ole Holsti, "Public Opinion and Foreign Policy: Challenges to the Almond-Lippmann Consensus," *International Studies Quarterly*, vol. 36, p. 453, quoted in Albert S. Yee, "The Effects of Ideas on Policy," *International Organization*, vol. 50, no. 1 (Winter 1996), p. 72.

26. For a discussion of the executive-congressional relationship on use of force, see Francis D. Wormuth and Edwin B. Firmage, *To Chain the Dog of War: The War Power of Congress in History and Law* (Dallas: Southern Methodist University Press, 1986).

27. John E. Mueller, *War, Presidents, and Public Opinion* (New York: John Wiley and Sons, 1973).

28. There is an extensive body of literature on public opinion and American foreign policy, see for example, Bernard C. Cohen, *The Public's Impact on Foreign Policy* (Boston: Little, Brown, 1973); Ole R. Holsti, *Public Opinion and American Foreign Policy* (Ann Arbor: University of Michigan Press, 1996); Benjamin I. Page and Robert Y. Shapiro, *The Rational Public: Fifty Years of Trends in Americans' Policy Preferences* (Chicago: Chicago University Press, 1992), chaps. 5 and 6; Morton Berkowitz, P. G. Bock, and Vincent J. Fuccillo, *The Politics of American Foreign Policy* (Englewood Cliffs, NJ: Prentice-Hall, 1977); and Ronald H. Hinckley, *People, Polls, and Policymakers: American Public Opinion and National Security* (New York: Lexington Books, 1992). While much of this literature concludes that public opinion affects foreign policy decisions in only limited ways, there is more evidence that, in the context of specific decisions to deploy U.S. military force in overseas combat situations, the influence of public opinion is more direct. For a review of recent literature on this topic see Douglas C. Foyle, *Counting the Public In: Presidents, Public Opinion, and Foreign Policy* (New York: Columbia University Press, 1999), pp. 1–9.

29. Philip J. Powlick, "The Attitudinal Bases for Responsiveness to Public Opinion Among American Foreign Policy Officials," *Journal of Conflict Resolution*, vol. 35 (1991), pp. 611–641. See also, Philip J. Powlick and Andrew Z. Katz, "Defining the American Public Opinion–Foreign Policy Nexus," *Mershon International Studies Review*, vol. 42 (1998), pp. 29–61.

30. Hinckley, *People, Polls, and Policymakers*.

31. For bottom-up theories see Page and Shapiro, *The Rational Public*. For top-down theories see Zaller, *The Nature and Origins of Mass Opinion*.

32. Zaller, *The Nature and Origins of Mass Opinion*, chap. 2. See also Harold D. Lasswell, "The Study and Practice of Propaganda," in Harold D. Lasswell, Ralph D. Casey, and Bruce Lannes Smith, *Propaganda and Promotional Activities: An Annotated Bibliography* (Chicago: University of Chicago Press, 1969), pp. 31–42.

33. Page and Shapiro, *The Rational Public*, chap. 5.

34. Zaller, *The Nature and Origins of Mass Opinion*, p. 1.

35. For example, see Edward S. Herman and Noam Chomsky, *Manufacturing Consent* (New York: Pantheon, 1988); Michael Margolis and Gary A. Mauser, eds., *Manipulating Public Opinion: Essays on Public Opinion as a Dependent Variable* (Belmont, CA: Wadsworth, 1989); and John E. Mueller, *Policy and Opinion in the Gulf War* (Chicago:

University of Chicago Press, 1994). For an application of this process to national security decisionmaking see Thomas J. Christensen, *Useful Adversaries: Grand Strategy, Domestic Mobilization, and Sino-American Conflict, 1947–1958* (Princeton: Princeton University Press, 1996).

36. See Jack L. Snyder, *Myths of Empire: Domestic Politics and International Ambition* (Ithaca: Cornell University Press, 1992), chap. 7. See also the theoretical argument developed in Jack Snyder and Karen Ballentine, "Nationalism and the Marketplace of Ideas," *International Security,* vol. 21, no. 2 (Fall 1996), pp. 5–40.

37. Page and Shapiro, *The Rational Public,* p. 372.

38. For extensive discussion of the importance of the presidency, see Richard E. Neustadt, *Presidential Power: The Politics of Leadership* (New York: Wiley, 1980); Samuel Kernell, *Going Public: New Strategies in Presidential Leadership,* (Washington, DC: Congressional Quarterly Press, 1986); Fred Greenstein, *The Hidden-Hand Presidency: Eisenhower as Leader* (New York: Basic Books, 1982); and Alexander George, *Presidential Decisionmaking in Foreign Policy: The Effective Use of Information and Advice* (Boulder: Westview Press, 1980).

39. For a discussion of the "stickiness" of ideas, see Margaret Weir, "Ideas and the Politics of Bounded Innovation," in Sven Steinmo, Kathleen Thelen, and Frank Longstreth, eds., *Structuring Politics: Historical Institutionalism in Comparative Analysis* (New York: Cambridge University Press, 1992), pp. 188–216.

40. James Meernik, "Presidential Decision Making and the Political Use of Military Force," *International Studies Quarterly,* vol. 38 (1994), pp. 121–138; Page and Shapiro, *The Rational Public,* pp. 348–350.

41. See, for example, Margaret E. Keck and Kathryn Sikkink, *Activists beyond Borders: Advocacy Networks in International Politics* (Ithaca: Cornell University Press, 1998), pp. 16–25.

42. See, for example, Bernard Cohen, *The Press and Foreign Policy,* (Princeton: Princeton University Press, 1963); Daniel Hallin, "The Media, the War in Vietnam, and Public Support: A Critique of the Thesis of an Oppositional Media," *Journal of Politics,* vol. 46, no. 1 (February 1984), pp. 2–24; Robert Entman and Benjamin Page, "The Iraq War Debate and the Limits to Media Independence," in W. Lance Bennett and David L. Paletz, eds., *Taken by Storm: The Media, Public Opinion and U.S. Foreign Policy in the Gulf War* (Chicago: University of Chicago Press, 1994); and John Zaller, "Strategic Politicians, Public Opinion, and the Gulf War," also in Bennett and Paletz, *Taken by Storm.*

43. See related discussion in John Zaller and Dennis Chiu, "Government's Little Helper: U.S. Press Coverage of Foreign Policy Crises, 1945–1991." *Political Communication,* vol. 13, no. 4 (December 1996), pp. 385–406.

44. In his extensive survey of *New York Times* reporting of overseas crises, Nicholas O. Berry found that in the early days and weeks of a crisis overseas, the American media has often not been well staffed to report from the region in turmoil. Furthermore, because much of the initial reporting concentrates on the U.S. policy response to the crisis, the media tend to focus on the deliberative process between the president and his national security staff. Berry argues that this is why the media are often criticized as being overly apologetic for the executive in the early days of a crisis. As the crisis persists, the media begin deploying their own resources, to collect an independent base of information. At this point, Berry argues, the media begin to report much more criti-

cally. Nicholas O. Berry, *Foreign Policy and the Press: An Analysis of* The New York Times' *Coverage of U.S. Foreign Policy* (New York: Greenwood Press, 1990).

45. Berry, *Foreign Policy and the Press,* p. xiii.

46. Between 1964 and the end of 1967, most of the television and newspaper coverage of the Vietnam War simply transmitted the official argument that unless communism was checked in Vietnam all of Southeast Asia would fall. See Page and Shapiro, *The Rational Public,* pp. 226–234; Daniel Hallin, *The Uncensored War: The Media and Vietnam* (New York: Oxford University Press, 1986), pp. 114–158; and Zaller, *The Nature and Origins of Mass Opinion,* pp. 329–330.

47. Harry Piotrowski, "The Structure of the International System," in Peter J. Schraeder, ed., *Intervention in the 1980s: U.S. Foreign Policy in the Third World* (Boulder: Lynne Rienner, 1989), p. 177.

48. Page and Shapiro, *The Rational Public,* pp. 226–234.

49. See Zaller and Chiu, "Government's Little Helper" and W. Lance Bennett, "Toward a Theory of Press-State Relations in the United States," *Journal of Communication,* vol. 40 (1990), pp. 103–125.

50. Thomas G. Patterson, *Contesting Castro: The United States and the Triumph of the Cuban Revolution* (New York: Oxford University Press, 1994).

51. Daniel Yankelovich, *Coming to Public Judgment: Making Democracy Work in a Complex World* (Syracuse, NY: Syracuse University Press, 1991).

52. See Alexander George and Timothy McKeown, "Case Studies and Theories of Organizational Decision Making," in Robert Coulam and Richard Smith, eds., *Advances in Information Processing in Organizations,* vol. 2 (Greenwich, CT: JAI Press, 1985), pp. 21–58.

53. B. M. Blechman and S. S. Kaplan, *Force without War: U.S. Armed Forces as a Political Instrument* (Washington, DC: Brookings Institution, 1978), p. 12. Schraeder, *Intervention in the 1980s,* p. 3.

54. While this approach may introduce some selection bias into the results, a far greater bias occurs when the case selection does not allow for variation on the dependent variable. For a discussion on this see Gary King, Robert O. Keohane, and Sidney Verba, *Designing Social Inquiry: Scientific Inference in Qualitative Research* (Princeton: Princeton University Press, 1994), pp. 128–149.

T W O : Saying No to the French at Dienbienphu

Epigraph: All four quotes are extracted from letters to the Senate Armed Services Committee and Senator Saltonstall from constituents and are found in Legislative Archives, RG 46, Records of the U.S. Senate, 83rd Congress, 1st and 2nd sess., Committee on Armed Services: General Correspondences, Indochina, Box #239. National Archives (hereafter NARA), Washington, DC.

1. For example see Ole Holsti and James Rosenau in *American Leadership in World Affairs* and Richard A. Melanson in *Reconstructing Consensus: American Foreign Policy since the Vietnam War* (New York: St. Martin's Press, 1991).

2. Ernest R. May and Richard E. Neustadt argue that there was "bitter, partisan, and utterly consensus-free debate about the loss of China, the long-term stationing of troops in Europe, the limiting of warfare in Korea, and whether a new war ought to be risked for Dien Bien Phu, Quemoy, or the Matsus," in *Thinking in Time* (pp. 258–259).

3. Reprinted in Chalmers M. Roberts, "The Day We Didn't Go to War," *Reporter*, vol. 11, September 14, 1954, pp. 31–35.

4. For a review of the historiography of the Eisenhower administration, see Stephen G. Rabe, "Eisenhower Revisionism: The Scholarly Debate," in Michael J. Hogan, ed., *America in the World: The Historiography of American Foreign Relations since 1941* (Cambridge: Cambridge University Press, 1995), pp. 300–325.

5. George Herring and Richard Immerman conclude that Eisenhower's position on the question of intervention was "characteristically elusive." See George C. Herring and Richard H. Immerman, "Eisenhower, Dulles, and Dienbienphu: 'The Day We Didn't Go to War' Revisited," *Journal of American History*, vol. 72 (September 1984), pp. 343–363.

6. The French government established the Associated States of Indochina in 1946 as a "sovereign" but not independent member of its French Union. The Associated States included Vietnam, Laos, and Cambodia.

7. For an overview of the prevailing foreign policy beliefs within the Eisenhower administration, see Stephen E. Ambrose, *Eisenhower: The President*, vol. 2. (New York: Simon and Schuster, 1984); Robert Cutler, *No Time for Rest* (Boston: Little, Brown, 1965); and, Dwight D. Eisenhower, *Waging Peace* (Garden City, NY: Doubleday, 1963).

8. John Lewis Gaddis, *Strategies of Containment: A Critical Appraisal of Postwar American National Security Policy* (New York: Oxford University Press, 1982), pp. 130–131.

9. Ibid., p. 137.

10. Robert A. Divine, *Eisenhower and the Cold War* (New York: Oxford University Press, 1981), p. 34.

11. Dulles speech to the Council on Foreign Relations, January 12, 1954, *Department of State Bulletin*, January 25, 1954, p. 108.

12. Gaddis, *Strategies of Containment*, pp. 127–163.

13. Quoted in Glenn H. Snyder, "The New Look of 1953," in Warner R. Schilling, Paul Y. Hammond, and Glenn H. Snyder, *Strategy, Politics, and Defense Budgets* (New York: Columbia University Press, 1962), p. 464.

14. Gaddis, *Strategies of Containment*, pp. 127–163.

15. "NSC 124/2," NSC files, Box 53, NARA, College Park, MD.

16. Quoted in Neil Sheehan, *The Pentagon Papers as Published by the New York Times* (New York: Bantam Books, 1971), p. 10.

17. Dwight D. Eisenhower, "Remarks at the Governors' Conference, Seattle, Washington, August 4, 1953," *Public Papers of the Presidents of the United States: Dwight D. Eisenhower*, vol. 1, *1953*. (Washington, DC: U.S. Government Printing Office, 1960), pp. 540–541.

18. *Foreign Relations of the United States* [hereafter *FRUS*], *1952–1954*, vol. 13, p. 782.

19. "NSC 162/2," NSC files, Box 54, NARA, College Park, MD.

20. Quoted in Robert Donovan, *Eisenhower: The Inside Story* (New York: Harper and Brothers, 1956), p. 125.

21. Ibid., p. 126.

22. *The Congressional Record*, March 31, 1954, p. 4208.

23. "Public Opinion on Indochina, Special Report on American Opinion," May 8, 1953, South East Asia, 1953–1961, Box 41, Office of Public Opinion Studies, Record Group 59, NARA, College Park, MD.

24. U.S. Senate, Committee on Foreign Relations, *The Far East and South Asia: Report of Senator H. Alexander Smith on a Study Mission to the Far East,* 83rd Congress, 2nd sess., 1954, p. 15.

25. An illustration of this argument is presented in John F. Kennedy, *The Strategy of Peace,* ed. Allan Nevins (New York: Harper and Row, 1960).

26. See Thomas G. Paterson, *Cold War Critics: Alternatives to American Foreign Policy in the Truman Years* (Chicago: Quadrangle Books, 1971).

27. See U.S. Senate, 80th Congress, Senate Foreign Relations Committee, vol. 157; Assistance to Greece and Turkey, March 25, 26, 27, and 31, 1947. For an excellent discussion on the specific effort of the administration to overcome congressional and public opposition and ambivalence to providing support for Greece and Turkey, see Joseph Jones, *The Fifteen Weeks: February 21–June 5, 1947* (New York: Viking Press, 1955).

28. U.S. Department of State, *Foreign Relations of the United States, 1945: British Commonwealth and Far East,* vol. 6, (Washington, DC: U.S. Government Printing Office, 1969), p. 297. In March 1945, even as the Japanese coup was unfolding, Roosevelt continued to oppose U.S. support for French colonialism. He told General Wedemeyer that he planned "to discontinue colonization of Southeast Asia" and that he was "determined that there would be no military assistance to the French in Indochina." Ronald H. Spector, *Advice and Support: The Early Years, 1941–1960* (Washington, DC: Center of Military History, 1983), p. 32.

29. Gregory A. Olson, *Mansfield and Vietnam: A Study in Rhetorical Adaptation* (East Lansing: Michigan State University Press, 1995), pp. 21–25.

30. A full text of Senator John F. Kennedy's report is reprinted in *The Congressional Record,* April 6, 1954, p. 4673.

31. Ibid.

32. *Christian Science Monitor* editorial quoted in "Current Popular Opinion on Indochina, Special Report on American Opinion," April, 1953, p. 2, South East Asia, 1953–1961, Box 41, Office of Public Opinion Studies, Record Group 59, NARA, College Park, MD.

33. Ibid.

34. David Douglas Duncan, "The Year of the Snake," *Life,* vol. 35, no. 5, August 3, 1953. Henry Luce, the hardliner publisher of *Life* tried to suppress the article because it criticized America's anticommunist policy. According to James R. Arnold, it was "only Duncan's willingness to stand up to the magazine mogul in a face-to-face encounter [that] allowed the article to be published." James R. Arnold, *The First Domino: Eisenhower, the Military, and America's Intervention in Vietnam* (New York: William Morrow, 1991), pp. 122–124.

35. For a discussion of both pragmatic and doctrinaire isolationists, see Ted Galen Carpenter, "The Dissenters: American Isolationists and Foreign Policy, 1945–1954" (Ph.D. diss., University of Texas, 1980). See also George Edward Dyer, "Military Isolation in the United States, 1939–1966" (Ph.D. diss., Texas Tech University, 1967).

36. Justus Doenecke, *Not to the Swift: The Old Isolationists in the Cold War Era* (Lewisburg, PA: Bucknell University Press, 1979), chaps. 10–12.

37. Ibid., chap. 12.

38. For a comprehensive argument on the implications of the Korean conflict and the limited war doctrine see Gacek, *Logic of Force;* see also, Betts, *Soldiers, Statesmen, and Cold War Crises.*

39. For a discussion of the military personnel who opposed intervention see Melanie Billings-Yun, *Decision against War: Eisenhower and Dien Bien Phu, 1954* (New York: Columbia University Press, 1988). See also David Petraeus, "Korea, the Never-Again Club, and Indochina," *Parameters,* vol. 17, December 1987, pp. 59–70; and Betts, *Soldiers, Statesmen, and Cold War Crises.*

40. Doenecke, *Not to the Swift,* p. 239.

41. Gacek, *Logic of Force,* chap. 4.

42. William Duiker, *U.S. Containment Policy and the Conflict in Indochina* (Stanford, CA: Stanford University Press, 1994), p. 140.

43. Hardliners within the Joint Chiefs of Staff were particularly frightened at the prospect of a French compromise in Indochina. At one point they even suggested that the United States tell Paris that a French withdrawal from Indochina "under unsatisfactory conditions would necessitate a review of our overall strategy in regard to NATO, on the assumption that France was no longer a full partner in the Free World coalition." Spector, *Advice and Support,* p. 197.

44. Ibid., p. 196.

45. Ibid., p. 195.

46. Ibid.

47. Douglas Foyle, *Counting the Public In,* pp. 82–88.

48. Memorandum from C. D. Jackson to the President, July 11, 1953, DDE Papers, Administration Series, Box 21, C. D. Jackson 1953 (1), DDE Library.

49. George Gallup, *The Gallup Poll: Public Opinion 1935–1971,* vol. 2: 1949–1958 (New York: Random House, 1972), p. 1146; and "Special Report on American Opinion, Current Popular Opinion of Indochina," November 16, 1953, South East Asia, 1953–1961, Box 41, Office of Public Opinion Studies, Record Group 59, NARA, College Park, MD.

50. Gallup, *The Gallup Poll,* p. 1171 (emphasis added).

51. See, Memorandum from C. D. Jackson to the President, July 11, 1953, DDE Papers, Administration Series, Box 21, C. D. Jackson, 1953 (1), DDE Library.

52. *FRUS, 1952–1954,* vol. 13, p. 428.

53. Ibid., p. 430.

54. Ibid., p. 969.

55. Ibid. (emphasis added).

56. See "Special Reports on American Public Opinion," 1954, South East Asia, 1953–1961, Box 41, Office of Public Opinion Studies, Record Group 59, NARA, College Park, MD.

57. See Robert H. Ferrell, *The Diary of James C. Hagerty* (Bloomington: Indiana University Press, 1983), p. 13.

58. See "Special Reports on American Public Opinion," July 1953, September 1953, and November 1953, South East Asia, 1953–1961, Box 41, Office of Public Opinion Studies, Record Group 59, NARA, College Park, MD.

59. See "One Foot in a New War: U.S. Technicians In Indochina—Volunteers Next? *U.S. News and World Report,* February 12, 1954, editorial, pp. 20–21.

60. "Gloom over Indochina," *Washington Post,* February 5, 1954, editorial, p. 11.

61. Ibid.

62. Foyle, *Counting the Public In,* p. 84.

63. See Ferrell, *Diary of James C. Hagerty,* p. 13.

64. See Robert Cutler, "Memorandum for the President," February 8, 1954, White House Office, National Security Council Staff: Papers, 1948–1961, Executive Secretary's

Subject File Series, Box 17, Special Assistant (Cutler)-Memorandum, 1954 (2), DDE Library.

65. Reference Collection of Miscellaneous Declassified Documents (electrostatic copies), Box 1, Planning Board Notes, NSC Meeting Notes Series, Records of White House Staff Secretary, DDE Library.

66. *FRUS, 1952–1954*, vol. 13, pp. 1015–1016. Nixon's comments and the activity by the Operations Coordinating Board reflect the effort to reframe the emphasis of the war away from one portrayed as a lost cause for French colonialism to one as a free world effort to resist the establishment of "Chinese Communist Imperialism." See related memos in White House Office, National Security Council Staff: Papers, 1948–1961, Box no. 37, OCB 091, Indo-china (File #1), November 1953–July 1954, DDE Library.

67. *FRUS, 1952–1954*, vol. 13, pp. 1015–1016.

68. Carl Marcy, Chief of Staff, Senate Foreign Relations Committee, 1955–1973, Oral History Interviews, September 14–16, 1983, Senate Historical Office, Washington, DC, pp. 60–61.

69. Based on survey of published articles listed in *Readers Guide to Periodical Literature*, 1954.

70. Ibid.

71. Robert H. Ferrell, *The Eisenhower Diaries* (New York: W. W. Norton, 1981), February 8, 1954, p. 275.

72. According to Eisenhower's press secretary, James Hagerty, a routine practice, which was stepped up at this time, was to call news organizations and complain about editorials with which the president disagreed. Hagerty estimated that throughout his tenure as press secretary he had a "50% success ratio—not that the editorial would change, but that by providing additional 'facts' the news organization would not 're-peat the same mistake in the next one.'" James Hagerty Oral History, p. 456, DDE Library. See also, James C. Hagerty, Papers, 1953–1961; Box 2 and 3, DDE Library.

73. See Foyle, *Counting the Public In*, pp. 84–85. For the liberal critique see *The Congressional Record*, Senate, March 9, 1954, pp. 2902–2904; March 15, 1954, pp. 3272–3275. The public relations campaign on Indochina was in many respects no different than other efforts within the administration to beef up its public relations campaigns. For example, Craig Allen demonstrates that from mid-1953 on, Eisenhower became extra-ordinarily attentive to the development of a strong marketing strategy for his presidency. He told his advisors that they should view their jobs as though they were in "advertising and sales" for a larger corporation. He was the first president to regularly consult with Madison Avenue executives on the public perceptions of his presidency. Eisenhower tried to recruit marketing genius Sigmund Larmon to join the White House staff. In late 1953, Eisenhower hired movie and television star Robert Montgomery to serve as his television consultant in order to enhance his ability to convey his message to television audiences. See Craig Allen, *Eisenhower and the Mass Media: Peace, Prosperity, and Prime-Time TV* (Chapel Hill: University of North Carolina Press, 1993), chaps. 1 and 2.

74. John G. Norris, "USAF Adds Men, Bombers in Indochina," *Washington Post*, February 6, 1954, p. 1.

75. "Stennis Says AF Unit in Indochina Perils U.S.," *Washington Post*, February 10, 1954, p. 1.

76. Eisenhower, *Public Papers, 1954*, pp. 250, 253.

77. Ibid., p. 277.

78. *FRUS, 1952–1954,* vol. 13, p. 1114.

79. A number of recent studies demonstrate that Eisenhower was extremely attentive to public opinion research and actively solicited information on and analysis of his popularity. Eisenhower frequently sought advice from George Gallup, Henry Luce, and C. D. Jackson. In addition, he frequently tasked his own staff to produce analysis of public opinion research. For example, in the spring of 1954, Gabriel Hauge, the White House economics advisor, produced a breakdown of trends in Eisenhower's ratings for the prior twelve months. According to Craig Allen, the Eisenhower White House had more research on itself than any previous administration had had. See Allen, *Eisenhower and the Mass Media,* p. 37; and Foyle, *Counting the Public In,* chaps. 2–5.

80. Herring and Immerman, "Eisenhower, Dulles, and Dienbienphu," pp. 343–363.

81. John Prados, *The Sky Would Fall, Operation Vulture: The U.S. Bombing Mission in Indochina, 1954* (New York: Dial Press, 1983), p. 70.

82. Melanie Billings-Yun suggests that Ely was "fatalistic" toward Dienbienphu and was charged by his government to solicit U.S. financial and material support to enable the French to withdraw from Indochina from a position of strength. She argues that "Radford bombarded his guest with high-level meetings aimed at convincing him of the importance the American authorities placed on a victory at Dien Bien Phu and of the optimism they still held out." (*Decision against War,* p. 37.)

83. *FRUS, 1952–1954,* vol. 13, p. 1159.

84. Ibid., p. 1168.

85. Ibid., p. 1165.

86. Ibid., pp. 1163–1168.

87. Ibid., pp. 1165–1166.

88. The administration's strategy was not lost on reporters. According to *New Yorker* reporter Richard Rovere, writing in April 1954, "[the administration] *in the past couple of weeks has been conducting what must undoubtedly be one of the boldest campaigns of political suasion ever undertaken by an American statesman.* Congressmen, political leaders of all shadings of opinion, newspapermen, and radio and television personalities have been rounded up in droves and escorted to lectures and briefings on what the State Department regards as the American stake in Indochina." Richard Rovere, "Letter from Washington," *New Yorker,* April 17, 1954, pp. 71–72 (emphasis added).

89. John Foster Dulles, Telephone Conversation with Secretary Wilson, March 22, 1954, John Foster Dulles Papers, JFD Chronological Series, Box 7, John Foster Dulles Chron, March 1954 (1) Telephone calls, DDE Library.

90. John Foster Dulles Papers, JFD Chronological Series, Box 7, John Foster Dulles Chron, March 1954 (1) Telephone calls, DDE Library.

91. Department of State, *Bulletin,* April 5, 1954, pp. 512–513.

92. Cited from *FRUS, 1952–1954,* vol. 13, p. 1161. For a full text see Eisenhower, *Public Papers, 1954,* pp. 339–349.

93. Prados, *The Sky Would Fall,* p. 81. The record of Dulles's briefings can be found in his conversations with Carl McCardle in John Foster Dulles Papers, JFD Chronological Series, Box 7, John Foster Dulles Chron, March 1954 (1) Telephone calls, DDE Library. Carl McCardle regularly conferred with Dulles, and he wrote the March 29 nationally televised speech on Indochina. See Carl W. McCardle Papers, 1953–57; Series VI; Oral History Transcripts, Box 15, DDE Library.

94. See "Special Reports on American Public Opinion," February 1954, March 1954, April 1954, and May 1954, South East Asia, 1953–1961, Box 41, Office of Public Opinion Studies, Record Group 59, NARA, College Park, MD.

95. Prados, *The Sky Would Fall*, p. 81.

96. Dana Adams Schmidt, "Administration to Tell U.S. West's Stake in Indo-China," *New York Times*, March 29, 1954, p. 1.

97. John Foster Dulles, Telephone Conversation with Mr. McCardle, March 27, 1954, John Foster Dulles Papers, JFD Chronological Series, Box 7, John Foster Dulles Chron, March 1954 (1) Telephone calls, DDE Library.

98. Carl McCardle recalls that during the writing of the speech "it all came out, if I may say so, pure Dulles." Carl W. McCardle Papers, 1953–57; Series VI; Oral History Transcripts, Box 15, p. 33, DDE Library.

99. Dulles speech to overseas writers in New York on March 29, 1954, quoted in Norman A. Graebner, *The New Isolationism: A Study in Politics and Foreign Policy Since 1950* (New York: Ronald Press, 1956), pp. 163–164 (emphasis added).

100. It is further evidence of the deep concern raised by the specter of a French defeat that James Hagerty wrote in his diary that, during a luncheon with Eisenhower and two close friends of the president—both editors at major news organizations—Eisenhower lamented the situation and suggested that "even though he would have to deny it forever, the United States might have to use carrier planes to bomb the area around Dien Bien Phu to prevent it from falling into enemy hands." Quoted in Foyle, *Counting the Public In*, p. 95.

101. *FRUS, 1952–1954*, vol. 13, p. 1224.

102. Gacek, *Logic of Force*, p. 108.

103. Prados, *The Sky Would Fall*, p. 95.

104. Doenecke, *Not to the Swift*, p. 242.

105. *FRUS, 1952–1954*, vol. 13, p. 1224.

106. John Foster Dulles, Telephone Conversation with Admiral Radford, April 5, 1954, John Foster Dulles Papers, 1951–1959, JFD Chronological Series, Box 7, John Foster Dulles Chronological, April 1954 [Telephone Calls], DDE Library.

107. "Dulles Warns Red China Nears Open Aggression in Indo-China; President Cautions on 'Jitters,'" *New York Times*, April 6, 1954, p. 1.

108. For a wide range of the views expressed in Congress, see Doenecke, *Not to the Swift*, pp. 238–243.

109. Senate Armed Services Committee and Senator Saltonstall, Legislative Archives, RG 46, Records of the U.S. Senate, 83rd Congress, 1st and 2nd sess., Committee on Armed Services: General Correspondences, Indochina, Box #239, NARA, Washington, DC.

110. "Dulles's War," *Chicago Tribune*, March 31, 1954, p. 16.

111. Monthly Survey of American Opinion on International Affairs, Public Studies Division, Bureau of Public Affairs, Survey no. 155, March 1954. South East Asia, 1953–1961, Box 41, Office of Public Opinion Studies, Record Group 59, NARA, College Park, MD.

112. Quoted in Doenecke, *Not to the Swift*, p. 240.

113. Ibid.

114. Senate Armed Services Committee and Senator Saltonstall, Legislative Archives, RG 46, Records of the U.S. Senate, 83rd Congress, 1st and 2nd sess. Committee on Armed Services: General Correspondences, Indochina, Box #239, NARA, Washington, DC.

115. Files and Petitions on Indochina, Legislative Archives, Senate Foreign Relations Committee, Uniform folder, Boxes 1–3, 1954, NARA, Washington, DC.

116. Cited in "American Opinion Series Report on American Private Organizations and Groups," South East Asia, 1953–1961, Box 41, Office of Public Opinion Studies, Record Group 59, NARA, College Park, MD.

117. Ibid.

118. U.S. Senate Armed Services Committee, Correspondence File, Box 1, Legislative Archives, NARA, Washington, DC.

119. In public opinion polls taken by the National Opinion Research Council and Gallup Polls in 1953 and 1954, when Americans were asked if they supported providing American troops to support the French in Indochina, between 70 percent and 89 percent expressed their opposition. For a comparative table of these surveys see Wittkopf, *Faces of Internationalism,* p. 187.

120. *Congressional Record,* April 5, 1954, vol. 100, part 3, 83rd Congress, 2nd sess., pp. 4577–4578.

121. Ibid. at April 6, 1954, p. 4673.

122. "Must We Fight in Indo-China?" *New Republic,* May 3, 1954, editorial, pp. 7–8. The editorial ridiculed the administration's effort to frame the Indochina conflict as a struggle against communism rather than a fundamental problem associated with colonialism. "No statement in recent years by a spokesman for the United States bears less relation to military or political realities than this one which places the whole responsibility for the war and the whole burden of concessions on the Communist side."

123. "The War Nobody's Trying to Win: Here's the Real Lowdown on Indochina," *U.S. News and World Report,* March 19, 1954, editorial, pp. 28–32; "How to Win in Indochina," *U.S. News and World Report,* April 2, 1954, editorial, pp. 37–42.

124. Graham Greene, "Indochina," *New Republic,* April 5, 1954, pp. 13–15. See also Graham Greene, "To Hope Till Hope Creates," *New Republic,* April 12, 1954, pp. 11–13.

125. Sherman Adams, *Firsthand Report* (New York: Harpers, 1961), p. 122.

126. *FRUS, 1952–1954,* vol. 13, pp. 1253–1254.

127. Ibid., pp. 1261–1262.

128. David L. Anderson, *Trapped by Success: The Eisenhower Administration and Vietnam, 1953–1961* (New York: Columbia University Press, 1991), pp. 34–35. Anderson also points out that throughout this time period, "the White House staff was on an hour's call to return to Washington because of Indochina."

129. Robert C. Albright, "Senate Told Indo Policy Is Unchanged," *Washington Post,* April 20, 1954, p. 6.

130. Ibid.

131. Graebner, *New Isolationism,* pp. 164–165.

132. Dwight D. Eisenhower, Letter to General Alfred M. Gruenther, April 26, 1954, Dwight D. Eisenhower Papers as President-Whitman File; Administration Files, Box 16, DDE Library.

133. According to Marquis Childs, as reported in Memorandum for the Secretary from Carl McCardle: April 30, 1954, John Foster Dulles Papers, 1951–59: General Correspondence and Memoranda Series, Box 2, Strictly Confidential-C-D (1), DDE Library.

134. Eisenhower was frustrated with the British and said that he "considered writing a note to Churchill suggesting that his government was really promoting a second Munich." Quoted in Gregory Olson, "Eisenhower and the Indochina Problem," in Mar-

tin J. Medhurst, ed., *Eisenhower's War of Words: Rhetoric and Leadership* (East Lansing: Michigan State University, 1994), p. 114.

135. Sheehan, *The Pentagon Papers,* p. 12.

136. Memorandum to the President, May 12, 1954, John Foster Dulles Papers, Subject Series, Indochina, May 1953–May 1954 Box (3), DDE Library. In explaining the rationale for the president's policy, the national security advisor told General Smith on April 30 that the United States needed to coordinate all military activities with a "regional grouping so that it would not appear that the US was acting alone to bale out French colonies and so as to meet Congressional sentiment." Memorandum for General Smith from Robert Cutler, April 30, 1954, White House Office, Office of the Special Assistant for National Security Affairs: Records, 1952–61; NSC Series Briefing Notes Subseries: Box 11, Indochina 1954, DDE Library.

137. Conference with the President, May 5, 1954, White House Office, Office of the Special Assistant for National Security Affairs: Records, 1952–61; NSC Series Briefing Notes Subseries: Box 11, Indochina 1954, DDE Library.

138. White House Office, Office of the Staff Secretary: Legislative Meetings Series, Box 2 L-13 (2) May 3 and 10, 1954, DDE Library.

139. Eisenhower and Dulles still pursued contingency planning in case there was a change of French position. On May 18, Eisenhower authorized various departments and agencies to prepare "with the highest urgency and secrecy" a formal evaluation of U.S. intervention strategies. See *FRUS, 1952–1954,* vol. 13, p. 1581. The full report is found at White House Office, National Security Council Staff Papers, 1948–1961; Disaster File, Box 54 (Indochina 7), DDE Library.

140. Memorandum of Conversation with the President, 19 May 1954, John Foster Dulles, White House Memorandum, Box 1, Folder 3, DDE Library cited in Olson, "Eisenhower and the Indochina Problem," p. 114.

141. See, for example, "Why War Talk Is Fading: Kickback from the Voters Jolted Policy Makers," *U.S. News and World Report,* May 7, 1954, pp. 25–26.

142. Leslie Gelb and Richard Betts, *The Irony of Vietnam: The System Worked* (Washington, DC: Brookings Institution, 1979), p. 60.

143. Billings-Yun, *Decision against War,* p. xii.

144. It would take another year and a half of witnessing battlefield casualties and dramatically escalating deficits to begin to turn liberals against the Vietnam War.

THREE: Intervention in Lebanon

Epigraph: Quoted in Sherman Adams, *Firsthand Report: The Story of the Eisenhower Administration* (New York: Harper and Brothers, 1961), p. 290.

1. Notable exceptions are Erika Alin, *The United States and the 1958 Lebanon Crisis* (Lanham, MD: University Press of America, 1994); Douglas Little, "His Finest Hour? Eisenhower, Lebanon, and the 1958 Middle East Crisis," *Diplomatic History,* vol. 20, no. 1 (Winter 1996); Alan Dowty, *Middle East Crisis: U.S. Decision-Making in 1958, 1970, and 1973* (Berkeley: University of California Press, 1984).

2. For a brief historiography of the Lebanese intervention see Douglas Little, "America and the Middle East since 1945," in Michael Hogan, ed., *America in the World: The Historiography of American Foreign Relations since 1941* (Cambridge: Cambridge University Press, 1995), pp. 488–491.

3. An insightful discussion of the operational problems associated with the Marine landing comes from Roger Spiller, *"Not War, But Like War": The American Intervention in Lebanon* (Fort Leavenworth, KS: Combat Studies Institute, 1984).

4. According to U.S. military reviews of the intervention, the initial landing was replete with logistical and procedural snafus. See Spiller, *"Not War, But Like War"*; and Gary W. Wade, *Rapid Deployment Logistics: Lebanon, 1958* (Fort Leavenworth, KS: U.S. Army Command and General Staff College, 1984).

5. Fahim Qubain, *Crisis in Lebanon* (Washington, DC: Middle East Institute, 1961), p. 116.

6. Charles Thayer, *Diplomat* (New York: Harper, 1959), p. 33.

7. Robert McClintock, *The Meaning of Limited War* (Boston: Houghton Mifflin, 1967), p. 110.

8. For the range of potential military and diplomatic costs estimated before the intervention see Special National Intelligence Estimates on June 4, 1958, and June 14, 1958, in *FRUS, 1958–1960*, vol. 11, pp. 93–98, 120–122.

9. Ibid.

10. See description in Drew Pearson and Jack Anderson, *U.S.A.: Second Class Power* (New York: Simon and Schuster, 1958), pp. 325–328; see also Betts, *Soldiers, Statesmen, and Cold War Crises*, p. 90.

11. *FRUS, 1958–1960*, vol. 11, pp. 244–245.

12. Walid Khalidi, *Conflict and Violence in Lebanon: Confrontation in the Middle East* (Cambridge: Harvard University, Center for International Affairs, 1979), chap. 1.

13. Walid Khalidi suggests that by the mid-1940s this probably did not accurately reflect the true proportion: "it was based on the assumption that the Moslems had acquiesced in this weighting system in favor of the Christians, irrespective of demographic realities, in order to ally Christian minoritarian fears of engulfment by the overall regional Moslem majority." See Khalidi, *Conflict and Violence in Lebanon*, p. 36.

14. Qubain, *Crisis in Lebanon*, p. 18.

15. Little, "His Finest Hour?" p. 33.

16. Qubain, *Crisis in Lebanon*, p. 38.

17. CIA officers converged in Beirut with large sums of cash to funnel to pro-Western politicians. See William Blum, *The CIA, a Forgotten History* (London: Zed Books, 1986), p. 103; Miles Copeland, *The Game of Nations: The Amorality of Power Politics* (New York: Simon and Schuster, 1969), pp. 226–227; David Atlee Phillips, *The Night Watch: 25 Years of Peculiar Service* (New York: Atheneum, 1977), pp. 67–76; and Wilbur Crane Eveland, *Ropes of Sand: America's Failure in the Middle East* (New York: W. W. Norton, 1980), p. 248.

18. This was a point that would later hamper international diplomatic efforts to stabilize the May–June crisis. There simply were no official opposition leaders who could mollify the situation.

19. Ambrose, *Eisenhower: The President*, vol. 2, p. 462.

20. Quoted in Kenneth Kinney, "The Use of Force by the Great Powers," in F. S. Northedge, *The Use of Force in International Relations* (New York: Free Press, 1974), p. 54.

21. Ambrose, *Eisenhower: The President*, vol. 2, p. 464. See also William Stivers, "Eisenhower and the Middle East," in Richard A. Melanson and David Mayers, eds., *Reevaluating Eisenhower: American Foreign Policy in the 1950s* (Urbana: University of

Illinois Press, 1987) and Irene Gendzier, "The United States, the USSR, and the Arab World in NSC Reports of the 1950s," *American-Arab Affairs,* vol. 28 (Spring 1989).

22. Ambassador Robert McClintock, who had served as U.S. chargé d'affaires in Saigon during the Dienbienphu crisis, became U.S. ambassador to Lebanon in early 1958 and quickly concluded that Chamoun and Malik were likely to lead Lebanon into chaos with their claims of external aggression and their desire to rewrite the Lebanese constitution. See *FRUS, 1958–1960,* vol. 11, pp. 3–5.

23. McClintock recommended that the United States support Chamoun because of his Western policy orientation. In a cable to Washington, McClintock also acknowledged, "Of course we could not say this publicly and our official line would be one of assiduous refusal to meddle in Lebanese politics." Embassy in Beirut to Department of State, Telegram 654, May 12, 1958, 783A.00/5-1258, Department of State Central Files, NARA, College Park, MD.

24. Dowty, *Middle East Crisis,* p. 27.

25. For a detailed examination of Senator Fulbright's ideas and beliefs about the use of force and U.S. intervention see Randall Bennett Woods, *Fulbright: A Biography* (Cambridge: Cambridge University Press, 1995). Woods describes Fulbright as "an idealist, one who believed in the efficacy of principles and institutions, who was convinced that the rule of law together with cultural exchange would make the world safe for diversity" (p. 222).

26. Woods, *Fulbright,* p. 221.

27. Walter Johnson, ed., *The Papers of Adlai E. Stevenson: Toward a New America,* vol. 7, *1955–1957* (Boston: Little, Brown, 1976), pp. 402–403.

28. "Survey of American Organizations and International Affairs," November 1957, Middle East, Office of Public Opinion Studies, Record Group 59, NARA, Washington, DC. See also, Charles Chatfield, *The American Peace Movement: Ideals and Activism* (New York: Twayne Publishers, 1992), pp. 104–109.

29. "Survey of American Organizations and International Affairs," November 1957.

30. See David S. Meyer, "Protest Cycles and Political Process: American Peace Movements in the Nuclear Age," *Political Research Quarterly,* vol. 46 (September 1993); Milton S. Katz, *Ban the Bomb, A History of SANE, The Committee for a Sane Nuclear Policy* (New York: Praeger, 1987); and Robert Divine, *Blowing on the Wind: The Nuclear Test Ban Debate, 1954–1960* (New York: Oxford University Press, 1978).

31. Divine, *Blowing on the Wind*; see also, Jeffrey W. Knopf, *Domestic Society and International Cooperation: The Impact of Protest on U.S. Arms Control Policy* (New York: Cambridge University Press, 1998), pp. 112–146.

32. Doenecke, *Not to the Swift.*

33. Dyer, "Military Isolation."

34. Jack Raymond, "Pentagon Opposes Using U.S. Military in Lebanon," *New York Times,* June 26, 1958, p. 1.

35. *FRUS, 1958–1960,* vol. 11, pp. 93–98, 120–122.

36. Raymond, "Pentagon Opposes Using Military in Lebanon," p. 1.

37. In mid-1957, Chamoun rigged parliamentary elections by increasing the size of parliament and creating new districts, in which he was guaranteed to secure a Chamber "overwhelmingly favorable to himself and morally committed to amend the Constitution and reelect him to a second term in 1958." Malcolm Kerr, "Political Decision Making in a Confessional Democracy," in Leonard Binder, ed., *Politics in Lebanon* (New

York: John Wiley and Sons, 1966), p. 206. Chamoun was facilitated in his efforts by covert U.S. action(David Atlee Phillips, *The Night Watch* [New York: Atheneum, 1977]).

38. It is not certain who killed Al Matni, the gunmen were never caught. Nonetheless, it was well known and documented that Al Matni was a vociferous opponent of Chamoun who did not go unnoticed by the Chamoun government. In July 1957 he was arrested and charged with defamation of the president for publishing a report that the UNF was deliberating whether or not to ask parliament to try Chamoun for interference in the 1957 parliamentary elections. He was also charged with defamation of the president in August 1957 for publishing a letter from Chamoun's opponents charging that the government had bought votes during the elections. In November 1957, Al Matni was stabbed outside of his office in Beirut in an assassination attempt. His attackers were never caught. Following his murder, several letters were found in his possession that warned that he would be killed if he did not stop publishing criticisms of Chamoun. Based on Al Matni's storied relationship with the Chamoun government, opposition leaders and the public quickly attributed his murder to pro-Chamoun forces. See Qubain, *Crisis in Lebanon* and Agnes Korbani, *U.S. Intervention in Lebanon, 1958 and 1982* (New York: Praeger, 1991), pp. 35–37.

39. *FRUS, 1958–1960*, vol. 11, pp. 3–48.

40. Little, "His Finest Hour?" p. 39. *FRUS, 1958–1960*, vol. 11, pp. 45–48.

41. *FRUS, 1958–1960*, vol. 11, pp. 45–48.

42. Ibid.

43. Ibid.

44. Dwight D. Eisenhower, *Waging Peace*, pp. 266 and 270.

45. Ibid., p. 270.

46. Alin, *The United States and the 1958 Lebanon Crisis*, p. 78. See also Ambrose, *Eisenhower: The President*, p. 463, and Eisenhower, *Waging Peace*, p. 266.

47. Alin, *The United States and the 1958 Lebanon Crisis*, pp. 81–82.

48. See also Foyle, *Counting the Public In*, chaps. 3 and 4.

49. The results of these polls were not lost on the administration. During the May 13th meeting, both Dulles and Eisenhower lamented the growing domestic and international perception that the administration had not been sufficiently diligent in responding to increasing Soviet agitation around the globe. See *FRUS, 1958–1960*, vol. 11, pp. 45–48, and Alin, *The United States and the 1958 Lebanon Crisis*, p. 79.

50. Andrew Goodpastor, memorandum of conversation, May 15, 1958, Ann Whitman files, DDE Diary Series, box 33, Staff Notes (2), May 1958, DDE Library.

51. *FRUS, 1958–1960*, vol. 11, pp. 45–48; see also, Goodpastor, memorandum of conversation, May 15, 1958.

52. Quoted in Richard Barnett, *Intervention and Revolution: The United States and the Third World* (New York: World Publishing, 1968), p. 143.

53. Eisenhower, *Waging Peace*, p. 266.

54. Alan Dowty argues that, at this point, Eisenhower and Dulles were "careful to prepare the ground legally and constitutionally for any eventuality" (Dowty, *Middle East Crisis*, p. 43).

55. *FRUS, 1958–1960*, vol. 11, pp. 49–50.

56. Ibid., pp. 45–50, see also Goodpastor, memorandum of conversation, May 15, 1958.

57. "Riots in Lebanon Linked to Nasser," *New York Times*, May 13, 1958, p. 5.

58. Dowty, *Middle East Crisis,* fn. 66, p. 43.

59. Controlling leaks and creating a focused message were hallmarks of Eisenhower's administration. See Allen, *Eisenhower and the Mass Media.*

60. For a survey of Eisenhower's thoughts on the strength and influence of these groups see "Letter to Reverend Edward Elson," July 31, 1958, DDE Diary Series, Box 34, DDE Dictation, July 1958, DDE Library.

61. For a discussion among Senate Foreign Relations Committee members on this point see comments made during a committee meeting on June 26, 1958. U.S. Senate, Committee on Foreign Relations Meeting, Thursday, June 26, 1958, *Study of United States Foreign Policy* (Washington, DC: U.S. Government Printing Office), pp. 461–478.

62. Based on survey of *Readers' Guide to Periodical Literature,* 1957 and 1958.

63. For example see Foster Hailey, "U.S. Library Burned in Lebanon in Riot Against Pro-Western Regime," *New York Times,* May 11, 1958, p. 1; and Tom Masterson (AP), "Lebanese Rioters Burn U.S. Library," *Washington Post,* May 11, 1958, p. A1.

64. See for example, Masterson, "Lebanese Rioters Burn U.S. Library," p. A1; (Reuters), "6 More Are Killed in Lebanon Rioting," *The Washington Post,* May 12, 1958, p. A6; Tom Masterson (AP), "Nasserism Sparks Serious Beirut Strife," *Washington Post,* May 12, 1958, p. A6; (UP), "Lebanese Fire Second U.S. Library," *Washington Post,* May 13, 1958, p. A1; Larry Collins (UP), "Mob in Lebanon Tries to Storm U.S. Embassy," *Washington Post,* May 14, 1958, p. A1.

65. Thayer, *Diplomat,* p. 18.

66. Ibid.

67. In a report to Dulles, H. Schuyler Foster concluded that most of the Washington-based national security correspondents were sympathetic to the administration's initial assessments of the crisis in Lebanon. State Department Bureau of Public Opinion, "Monthly Survey of American Opinion on International Affairs," June 3, 1958, no. 206, p. 6, Office of Public Opinion Studies, Record Group 59, NARA, College Park, MD.

68. As early as the beginning of Eisenhower's first term in office, his staff classified American journalists, editors, and columnists according to their degree of influence with the American public and according to their support for the administration's policies. See "Letter to Mrs. Edgar Eisenhower," May 6, 1960, DDE Papers as President, Ann Whitman File, Name Series, 1953–1961, Box 12, Edgar Eisenhower (2) 1959–1960, DDE Library.

69. See for example, "Riots in Lebanon," *New York Times,* May 13, 1958, p. 21; and "Lebanon Aflame," *Washington Post,* May 14, 1958, p. A14.

70. Collins, "Mob in Lebanon Tries to Storm U.S. Embassy," p. A1 (emphasis added).

71. "Embattled Lebanon," *New York Times,* May 20, 1958, p. 32.

72. (Reuters), "6 More Are Killed in Lebanon," p. A6; Masterson, "Nasserism Sparks Serious Beirut Strife," p. A6; (UP), "Lebanese Fire Second U.S. Library," p. A1; Collins, "Mob in Lebanon Tries to Storm U.S. Embassy," p. A1.

73. "Lebanon Aflame," p. A14.

74. See Foster Hailey, "U.S. Library Burned in Lebanon in Riot Against Pro-Western Regime," *New York Times,* May 11, 1958, p. 1; "Riots in Lebanon Linked to Nasser," *New York Times,* May 13, 1958, p. 5; "Beirut, Algiers, and Caracas," *New York Times,* May 14, 1958, p. 32.

75. Warren Rogers, Jr., "Planes to Go to Lebanon, 'If Needed,'" *Washington Post,* May 18, 1958, p. A1.

76. Monthly Survey of American Opinion on International Affairs, June 3, 1958, no. 206, Office of Public Opinion Studies, 1943–1965, Record Group 59, NARA, College Park, MD.

77. Ibid., p. 6.

78. Chalmers M. Roberts, "Mansfield Rejects Dulles' Contention Hill Gave Extra Troop Use 'Mandate,'" *Washington Post*, May 22, 1958, p. A11.

79. Neal Stanford, "Dulles Defies Reds on Aid to Lebanon," *Christian Science Monitor*, May 20, 1958, p. 1.

80. Daily Opinion Summary, no. 3287, Lebanon, May 16, 1958, Office of Public Opinion Studies, 1943–1965, Record Group 59, NARA, College Park, MD.

81. Ibid., no. 3288, Lebanon, May 18, 1958.

82. Monthly Survey, no. 206, June 3, 1958.

83. Ibid.

84. *FRUS, 1958–1960*, vol. 11, p. 77.

85. Ibid., p. 124.

86. Ibid., p. 135.

87. Ibid., p. 135.

88. Little, "His Finest Hour?" p. 41. See also *FRUS, 1958–1960*, vol. 11, p. 137.

89. Ibid., p. 136.

90. Ibid.

91. *FRUS, 1958–1960*, vol. 11, pp. 158–162, 166–168. See also Alin, *The United States and the 1958 Lebanon Crisis*, pp. 88–98.

92. See also *FRUS, 1958–1960*, vol. 11, p. 149, which documents a meeting at the Pentagon between Dulles and NSC officials to discuss the constitutional basis for intervention, the potential congressional response to it, and the need for United Nations approval to make intervention more "palatable." See also Dulles's discussions with his staff and with Lebanese Foreign Minister Charles Malik, on June 30, 1958, and July 2, 1958, respectively in *FRUS, 1958–1960*, vol. 11, pp. 185–190, 194–196.

93. Dwight Eisenhower, "Supplementary Notes, Legislative Leadership Meeting," June 17, 1958, Box 33, June 1958–Staff Notes (3), DDE Diary Series (Ann Whitman Files), DDE Library.

94. U.S. Department of State, Office of Public Communication, Bureau of Public Affairs, *Department of State Bulletin*, July 7, 1958 (Washington, DC: U.S. Government Printing Office).

95. Eisenhower, "Supplementary Notes, Legislative Leadership Meeting," June 17, 1958.

96. Joseph Alsop, "Lebanon Weighs Call for Military Intervention," *Washington Post*, June 19, 1958, p. A4.

97. Chalmers M. Roberts, "Secretary Asserts Troops May Move Without U.N. Call," *Washington Post*, June 18, 1958, pp. A1, A6.

98. Ibid.

99. U.S. Senate Committee on Foreign Relations meeting, Thursday, June 26, 1958, *Study of United States Foreign Policy* (Washington, DC: U.S. Government Printing Office), p. 475.

100. Ibid.

101. Ibid.

102. "Can the U.N. Do the Job," *Washington Post*, June 19, 1958, p. A11; Hanson Bald-

win, "UN and the Crises," *New York Times,* June 20, 1958, p. 2; "Infiltration Increases in Lebanon," *Washington Post,* June 24, 1958, p. A6.

103. "A Time for Patience," *New York Times,* June 16, 1958, p. 22.

104. "Watchdog in Lebanon," *Washington Post,* June 12, 1958, p. A22.

105. "Beirut's Burden," *Washington Post,* June 16, 1958, p. A10.

106. Ibid.

107. Drew Middleton, "Contest for Lebanon Involves Vast Stakes," *New York Times,* June 29, 1958, p. E4.

108. Joseph Alsop, "Munich in Beirut?" *Washington Post,* June 27, 1958, p. A13.

109. "U.N. Chief Sees Little Infiltration," *Washington Post,* July 4, 1958, p. A6.

110. "Lebanon: Mideastern Austria," *New York Times,* July 9, 1958, p. 26.

111. State Department Bureau of Public Opinion, Daily Opinion Summary, July 7, 1958, no. 3321, Office of Public Opinion Studies, Record Group 59, NARA, College Park, MD.

112. For a discussion and analysis of the decision-making process see Korbani, *U.S. Intervention in Lebanon,* pp. 46–50.

113. John Foster Dulles, Memorandum of Conference with the President, July 14, 1958, DDE Diary Box 35, Staff Memos, July 1958 (2); DDE Library; and, Memorandum for the Record: Meeting re Iraq, July 14, 1958; John Foster Dulles Papers, 1951–59; JFD Chronological Series; (John Foster Dulles Chronological), July 1958; DDE Library.

114. Memorandum of Conference, July 14, 1958, White House Office of Staff Secretary, State Department Series, Box 3, State Department, 1958, May–August (4), DDE Library.

115. Ibid.

116. Ibid.

117. Ibid.

118. Draft of letter to Harold Macmillan, DDE Diary, Box 34, DDE Dictation, July 1958, DDE Library. Eisenhower made a similar disclosure on the importance of public opinion and political support in a lengthy personal letter to the Reverend Edward Elson of the National Presbyterian Church, on July 31, 1958. See DDE Diary Series, Box 34, DDE Dictation, July 1958, DDE Library.

119. See Telephone Call from Senator Knowland, July 14, 1958, 6:06 p.m.; Telephone Call from the Vice President, July 15, 1958, 8:46 a.m.; Telephone Call from Senator Knowland, July 15, 1958, 8:55 a.m., all in Dulles Papers, Telephone Calls Series, Memoranda of Telephone Conversations between June 2, 1958, and July 31, 1958 (4), DDE Library.

120. For obvious reasons, no mention was made of Chamoun's extraconstitutional activities, which had precipitated the domestic crisis in Lebanon. For a complete compendium of official statements and documents on the Lebanese crisis see M. S. Agwani, *The Lebanese Crisis, 1958: A Documentary Study* (Bombay: Asia Publishing House, 1965).

121. "Mr. Berding's notes on background press conference," James C. Hagerty Papers, Press Secretary of the President Papers, 1953–1961, Box 7, Mid-East: Lebanon (July 1958), DDE Library.

122. See public opinion data reported in Bruce Russett and Elizabeth Hansen, *Interest and Ideology: The Foreign Policy Beliefs of American Businessmen* (San Francisco: W. H. Freeman, 1975), pp. 198–199.

123. Little, "His Finest Hour?" p. 52.

F O U R : Battling the Vietnam Syndrome in Grenada

Epigraphs: McFarlane quoted in Constantine Menges, *Inside the National Security Council* (New York: Simon and Schuster, 1988), p. 83. Michael K. Deaver with Mickey Herskowitz, *Behind the Scenes* (New York: William Morrow, 1987), p. 147. Ronald Reagan, "Address to the Nation, October 27, 1983," *Weekly Compilation of Presidential Documents* 19 (October 24, 1983), p. 1501.

1. "President's Remarks, October 25, 1983," *Department of State Bulletin 83* (December 1983), p. 67 (emphasis added).

2. For example, Yaacov Vertzberger concludes that "the political risks made a military operation unthinkable without a legitimizing event to justify and trigger intervention." Vertzberger, *Risk Taking and Decisionmaking: Foreign Military Intervention Decisions* (Stanford, CA: Stanford University Press, 1998), p. 178. For traditional views on prospects for an easy victory in Grenada, see discussion in Gregory Sandford and Richard Vigilante, *Grenada: The Untold Story* (New York: Madison Books, 1984); Kai P. Schoenhals and Richard A. Melanson, *Revolution and Intervention in Grenada: The New Jewel Movement, the United States, and the Caribbean* (Boulder: Westview Press, 1985).

3. Brigitte Lebens Nacos, *The Press, Presidents, and Crises* (New York: Columbia University Press, 1990), chap. 6.

4. Schoenhals and Melanson, *Revolution and Intervention in Grenada*, p. 30.

5. Ibid., p. 35.

6. Anthony Payne, Paul Sutton, and Tony Thorndike, *Grenada: Revolution and Invasion* (New York: St. Martin's Press, 1985), pp. 26–31.

7. See, for example, Jeane Kirkpatrick, ed., *Dictatorships and Double Standards: Rationalism and Reason in Politics* (New York: Simon and Schuster, 1982), pp. 47, 54; and Robert Pastor, "U.S. Policy toward the Caribbean: Continuity and Change," in Peter M. Dunn and Bruce W. Watson, eds., *American Intervention in Grenada: The Implications of Operation "Urgent Fury"* (Boulder: Westview Press, 1985), pp. 15–28.

8. Upon learning of the planned covert actions, the Senate Intelligence Committee ordered the CIA to suspend any direct political action in Grenada.

9. William Russel Nylen, "United States–Grenada Relations, 1979–1983: American Foreign Policy towards a 'Backyard' Revolution," *Pew Case Studies in International Affairs,* Case 306, (Washington, DC: Pew Charitable Trusts, 1983), p. 15.

10. Gregory Sandford, *The New Jewel Movement: Grenada's Revolution, 1979–1983* (Washington, DC: Center for the Study of Foreign Affairs, 1995), pp. 98–106.

11. The minutes of an emergency meeting of the Central Committee on August 26, 1983, revealed the situation: "At present the Revolution is facing its worst crisis ever. . . . The mood of the masses is characterized at worst by open dissatisfaction and cynicism, and at best by serious demoralization." Cited in Schoenhals and Melanson, *Revolution and Intervention in Grenada*, p. 61.

12. Payne, Sutton, and Thorndike, *Grenada*, chap. 6.

13. Nylen, "United States–Grenada Relations."

14. The details of this and the sequence of events leading to Bishop's execution are thoroughly described in Schoenhals and Melanson, *Revolution and Intervention in Grenada*, pp. 71–84.

15. Jerel A. Rosati, "The Domestic Environment," in Peter J. Schraeder, ed., *Intervention in the 1980s: U.S. Foreign Policy in the Third World* (Boulder: Lynne Rienner, 1989), p. 154.

16. For an overview of this effort see Jerel A. Rosati, *The Carter Administration's Quest for Global Community;* David Forsythe, *Human Rights and U.S. Foreign Policy: Congress Reconsidered* (Gainesville: University of Florida Press, 1988); and Jimmy Carter, *A Government As Good As Its People* (New York: Simon and Schuster, 1977).

17. Frank J. Smist, Jr., *Congress Oversees the Intelligence Community, 1947–1989* (Knoxville: University of Tennessee Press, 1985) and John M. Oseth, *Regulating U.S. Intelligence Operations* (Lexington: University Press of Kentucky, 1985). See also, U.S. Senate Select Committee to Study Governmental Operations with Respect to Intelligence Activities, *Final Report,* Book I: *Foreign and Military Intelligence,* 94th Congress, 2nd sess., 1976, chap. 8.

18. Berry, *Foreign Policy and the Press;* and Daniel Hallin, "The Media, the War in Vietnam, and Political Support: A Critique of the Thesis of an Oppositional Media," *Journal of Politics* 46 (1984), pp. 2–24.

19. Hallin, *The Uncensored War.*

20. For a review of liberal influence in the Carter administration see, Joshua Moravchik, *The Uncertain Crusade: Jimmy Carter and the Dilemmas of Human Rights Policy* (Washington, DC: American Enterprise Institute, 1988); Gaddis Smith, *Morality, Reason, and Power: American Diplomacy in the Carter Years* (New York: Hill and Wang, 1986); David Skidmore, *Reversing Course: Carter's Foreign Policy, Domestic Politics and the Failure of Reform* (Nashville: Vanderbilt University Press, 1996), chap. 2; and Cyrus Vance, *Hard Choices* (New York: Simon and Schuster, 1983) chaps. 1–3.

21. President Jimmy Carter's Inaugural Address, cited in David F. Schmitz and Vanessa Walker, "Jimmy Carter and the Foreign Policy of Human Rights: The Development of a Post–Cold War Foreign Policy," *Diplomatic History* vol. 28, no. 1 (2004), p. 113.

22. Theodore Draper "Appeasement and Détente," *Commentary,* vol. 61, no. 2 (February 1976). See also Max M. Kampelman, "Introduction," in Charles Tyroler II, ed., *Alerting America: The Papers of the Committee on the Present Danger* (Washington, DC: Pergaman-Brassey's International Defense Publishers, 1984), p. xv.

23. "Is America Becoming Number 2? Current Trends in the U.S.-Soviet Military Balance," in Tyroler, *Alerting America,* pp. 39–93.

24. "Interview with Richard Perle," *Episode 19: The Freeze, CNN Cold War History Project,* at http://www.gwu.edu/nsarchiv/coldwar/interviews/episode-19/perle3.html (accessed August 23, 2003).

25. The most notorious revelation of cleavages within the Carter administration occurred during President Carter's speech at the U.S. Naval Academy on June 7, 1978. The speech began in a liberal tone conciliatory toward the Soviet Union but became highly confrontational (selective engager) by the end. For a discussion of the speech and cleavages in the administration, see Raymond Garthoff, *Détente and Confrontation* (Washington, DC: Brookings Institution, 1985), pp. 600–608.

26. Jeane Kirkpatrick, *The Reagan Phenomenon and Other Speeches on Foreign Policy* (Washington, DC: American Enterprise Institute, 1981), pp. 8–11.

27. Ibid.

28. See Kampelman, "Introduction," ix–xi.

29. Condoleezza Rice, "U.S.-Soviet Relations," in Larry Berman, ed., *Looking Back*

on the Reagan Presidency (Baltimore: Johns Hopkins University Press, 1990), pp. 73–77; and Alexander Haig, Jr., *Caveat: Realism, Reagan, and Foreign Policy* (New York: Macmillan, 1984).

30. Rice, "U.S.-Soviet Relations."

31. Kirkpatrick, *Dictatorships and Double Standards.*

32. Ibid., p. 8.

33. For example, NSDD-32 called for an economic offensive by the United States to neutralize Soviet control over Eastern Europe; NSDD-66 targeted the Soviet economic "strategic triad" of financial credits, high technology, and natural gas; and, NSDD-75 shifted American policy from one of coexistence to the ultimate objective of fundamentally changing the Soviet regime.

34. Menges, *Inside the National Security Council,* p. 99.

35. Tony Thorndike, "Grenada," in Peter J. Schraeder, ed., *Intervention in the 1980s: U.S. Foreign Policy in the Third World* (Boulder: Lynne Rienner, 1989), p. 256.

36. Cited in J. Pearce, *Under the Eagle: U.S. Intervention in Central America and the Caribbean* (London: Latin America Bureau, 1981), p. 240.

37. George Gallup, "2 of 3 in U.S. See El Salvador Becoming 'Another Vietnam,'" *Washington Post,* March 26, 1981.

38. Jonathan Kwitney, "Apparent Errors Cloud U.S. White Paper on Reds in El Salvador," *Wall Street Journal,* June 8, 1981.

39. Edwin Meese III, *With Reagan: The Inside Story* (Washington, DC: Regnery Gateway, 1992), p. 237.

40. Quoted in Cynthia J. Arnson, *Crossroads: Congress, the Reagan Administration, and Central America* (New York: Pantheon, 1989), p. 48.

41. Payne, Sutton, and Thorndike, *Grenada,* p. 62.

42. James McCarthy, "Reagan Decides to Step up Military Presence in Caribbean," *Miami Herald,* January 30, 1982.

43. In Grenada's agreement with Cuba, Bishop announced that Cuba would provide construction equipment and skilled labor. Grenada was responsible for raising more than half the cost of the project. In 1981, the PRG asked the European Community to hold a donors' conference in which the airport could be showcased. In response, the Reagan administration launched a large-scale and successful diplomatic effort to block any European funding of the airport. See Payne, Sutton, and Thorndike, *Grenada,* pp. 61–70.

44. Donald Abelson, *American Think-Tanks and Their Role in U.S. Foreign Policy* (New York: St. Martin's Press, 1996), chap. 4.

45. Pastor, "U.S. Policy toward the Caribbean," p. 23.

46. Ibid., pp. 15–28.

47. Dellums's report was later widely ridiculed when PRG documents collected after the U.S. intervention revealed that Dellums staff member Barbara Lee had presented a draft of the report to the PRG for comment on the facts collected. See, for example, Rowland Evans and Robert Novak, "Grenada and the Black Caucus," *Washington Post,* November 21, 1983, p. A17.

48. Abelson, *American Think-Tanks,* chap. 4.

49. For a review of the nuclear freeze movement see, Douglas C. Waller, *Congress and the Nuclear Freeze Movement: An Inside Look at the Politics of a Mass Movement* (Amherst: University of Massachusetts Press, 1987); David Cortright, *Peace Works: The*

Citizen's Role in Ending the Cold War (Boulder: Westview Press, 1993); and Jeffrey W. Knopf, *Domestic Society and International Cooperation: The Impact of Protest on U.S. Arms Control Policy* (Cambridge: Cambridge University Press, 1998), chap. 7.

50. See Gacek, *The Logic of Force*; Betts, *Soldiers, Statesmen, and Cold War Crises*; and David H. Petraeus, "The American Military and the Lessons of Vietnam" (Ph.D. diss., Princeton University, 1987).

51. Andrew Krepenevich, *The Army in Vietnam* (Baltimore: Johns Hopkins University Press, 1986).

52. Betts, *Soldiers, Statesmen, and Cold War Crises*, p. 214.

53. For a discussion of military attitudes during the early Reagan administration, see Gacek, *Logic of Force*, pp. 250–258; and, David H. Petraeus, "The American Military."

54. Gacek, *Logic of Force*, p. 254.

55. Colin L. Powell with Joseph E. Persico, *My American Journey* (New York: Random House, 1995), pp. 148–149.

56. Menges, *Inside the National Security Council*, p. 61.

57. The quality of the intelligence on this point remains questionable even today. See Gerald Hopple and Cynthia Gilley, "Policy without Intelligence," in Peter M. Dunn and Bruce W. Watson, eds., *American Intervention in Grenada: The Implications of Operation "Urgent Fury"* (Boulder: Westview Press, 1985); Patrick E. Tyler, "The Making of an Invasion," *Washington Post*, October 30, 1983, p. A14; Robert Beck, *The Grenada Invasion: Politics, Law, and Foreign Policy Decisionmaking* (Boulder: Westview Press, 1993), p. 106; Bill Keller, "Reports Cite Lack of Coordination during U.S. Invasion of Grenada," *New York Times*, December 4, 1983, p. 14; Philip Taubman, "Senators Suggest Administration Exaggerated Its Cuba Assessment," *New York Times*, October 30, 1983, p. 22.

58. Hopple and Gilley, "Policy without Intelligence."

59. Beck, *Grenada Invasion*, p. 106.

60. Richard Betts describes how, only under pressure from the hardliners, did the military put together a limited noncombatant evacuation contingency plan. On October 20, the Joint Chiefs were tasked with developing a full-scale invasion force with limited intelligence, a short timetable, and uncertain political and military objectives. See Betts, *Soldiers, Statesmen, and Cold War Crises*, p. 216.

61. Beck, *Grenada Invasion*, p. 107.

62. For a discussion of this suspicion, see Meese, *With Reagan*, p. 102.

63. Larry Speakes and Robert Peck, *Speaking Out: The Reagan Presidency from Inside the White House* (New York: Charles Scribner's Sons, 1988), and interview with Michael Deaver, February 9, 1999.

64. Maltese, *Spin Control*, p. 199.

65. Ibid.

66. Ibid.; Nacos, *The Press, Presidents and Crises*, p. 160.

67. Maltese, *Spin Control*, p. 197.

68. See, for example, S. Steven Powell, *Second Front: Advancing Latin American Revolution in Washington* (Washington, DC: Capital Research Center, 1986); "Political Wreckers: A Radical Think-Tank Is Out to Dismantle the System," *Baron's*, July 28, 1980, p. 7; and Abelson, *American Think-Tanks*, chap. 6.

69. Meese, *With Reagan*, p. 234.

70. Ibid., p. 235.

71. Ibid., p. 107.

72. Meese had persuaded President Reagan to sign a formal order compelling the FBI to administer polygraph examinations to all national security personnel in the White House. The event prompted Secretary of State George Shultz to threaten his resignation if Reagan did not reverse his decision. See discussion in Lou Cannon, *President Reagan: The Role of a Lifetime* (New York: Simon and Schuster, 1991), pp. 423–427.

73. Peter Kornbluh, "Nicaragua," in Peter J. Schraeder, ed., *Intervention in the 1980s: U.S. Foreign Policy in the Third World* (Boulder: Lynne Rienner, 1989), p. 245.

74. See NSDD 77, Management of Public Diplomacy Relative to National Security, January 14, 1983, p. 1.

75. Kornbluh, "Nicaragua," pp. 245–246.

76. Beck, *Grenada Invasion*, pp. 107, 138, 230 n. 39.

77. Ibid., p. 138.

78. Interview with Michael Deaver, February 9, 1999.

79. Citing Jamaican officials, the *Washington Post* reported that "the United States had urged the Caribbean nations to consider action against Grenada" during the OECS conference. See Juan Williams, "Jamaicans Indicate U.S. Signaled Will to Invade," *Washington Post*, October 27, 1983, p. A20; Nylen, "United States–Grenada Relations," p. 34; and Beck, *Grenada Invasion*, p. 110.

80. In each of these four countries, the right-wing leaders faced serious political opposition to intervention on grounds that it would violate Grenadan sovereignty. Each of the leaders used his or her own information advantages to rally domestic support. For example, in Jamaica, Prime Minister Seagaw fabricated a story that a busload of children had been killed by Bishop's executioners and that one child who had managed to get out of the bus alive had his legs blown off as he tried to run away. See Juan Williams, "Jamaicans Indicate U.S. Signaled Will to Invade," p. A20.

81. Nylen, "United States–Grenada Relations," p. 34; Beck, *Grenada Invasion*, pp. 111–113.

82. Following the invasion, State Department spokesman John Hughes explicitly "denied, as other officials had earlier, that the United States had in any way contacted the OECS nations first or suggested that the alliance invite U.S. participation." See "U.S. Saw Uncertain Grenada as 'A Floating Crap Game,'" *Washington Post*, October 27, 1983, p. A9. This directly contradicts the interview evidence presented by Assistant Secretary of State Langhorne Motley and Ambassador Frank McNeil to William Russel Nylen cited in "United States–Grenada Relations." It also directly contradicts the well-documented findings of Beck, published in *Grenada Invasion*.

83. See Beck, *Grenada Invasion*, p. 104. This information is based on Beck's interviews with an unnamed State Department official.

84. Interview with Michael Deaver.

85. Shultz, *Turmoil and Triumph*, pp. 329–330.

86. Speakes and Peck, *Speaking Out*, pp. 151, 155.

87. The emphasis on "equally important" was conveyed by Michael Deaver. Interview with Michael Deaver.

88. Vertzberger, *Risk Taking and Decisionmaking*, p. 185.

89. Ronald Reagan, *An American Life* (New York: Simon and Schuster, 1990), p. 451.

90. Meese, *With Reagan*, p. 217.

91. Shultz, *Turmoil and Triumph*, pp. 344–345.

92. Interview with Michael Deaver. See also, James Wright, *Balance of Power* (Atlanta: Turner Publishing, 1996), pp. 394–395.

93. Interview with Michael Deaver.

94. Ibid.

95. Ibid.

96. Ibid.

97. Ibid.

98. Nacos, *The Press, Presidents and Crises*, chap. 6.

99. Interview with Michael Deaver.

100. Ibid.

101. Meese, *With Reagan*, p. 218.

102. Cannon, *President Reagan*, p. 445.

103. Tip O'Neill with William Novak, *Man of the House: The Life and Political Memoirs of Speaker Tip O'Neill* (New York: Random House, 1987), p. 365.

104. Wright, *Balance of Power*, pp. 394–395.

105. O'Neill, *Man of the House*, pp. 366–367.

106. Up until this moment Speakes and the entire press office had been kept in the dark on the action.

107. Menges, *Inside the National Security Council*, p. 86.

108. Speakes and Peck, *Speaking Out*, p. 161.

109. Within hours of Reagan's address, his assessment of the threat to the American students was challenged by the Chancellor of the St. George's Medical School, who claimed that none of his students was in danger. He would later recant his claim (after he was given a "special briefing" by the CIA and State Department). Nonetheless, from a public relations perspective, his statements encouraged liberals to question the veracity of the administration's claims.

110. Barry Sussman, *What Americans Really Think and Why Our Politicians Pay No Attention* (New York: Pantheon, 1988), pp. 36–37 (emphasis added).

111. "Reagan Aide Says U.S. Invasion Forestalled Cuban Arms Buildup," *New York Times*, October 27, 1983, p. A1. Three days after the invasion, the White House announced it had captured explicit plans that "serious consideration was being given to seizing Americans as hostages and holding them." However, when all the confiscated documents were revealed to the press in the months following the invasion, there were no explicit plans to seize Americans.

112. Speakes and Peck, *Speaking Out*, p. 161.

113. "Grenada: New Colony, New Myth," *Baltimore Sun*, October 24, 1984, p. 11A.

114. Hugh O'Shaughnessy, *Grenada: An Eyewitness Account of the U.S. Invasion and the Caribbean History That Provoked It* (New York: Dodd, Mead, 1981), pp. 169–173.

115. Interview with Michael Deaver; Meese, *With Reagan*, p. 218.

116. Cannon, *President Reagan*, p. 337.

117. Ronald Reagan, Address to the Nation, October 27, 1983. This claim was later contradicted by the findings of journalists during postinvasion reports from Grenada. See Richard Harwood, "Tidy U.S. War Ends: 'We Blew Them Away,'" *Washington Post*, November 6, 1983, p. A1.

118. Beck, *Grenada Invasion*, pp. 57–58.

119. Sussman, *What Americans Really Think*, pp. 36–37; Cannon, *President Reagan*, p. 337.

120. Sussman, *What Americans Really Think*, pp. 36–37.

121. Loren Jenkins, "Grenada Military Base Found Well Stocked: 'Stacked Warehouse' Shelters Vintage Guns," *New York Times*, October 29, 1983, p. A1.

F I V E : Famine in Somalia and Ancient Hatreds in Bosnia

Epigraphs: Quoted from Michael Gordon, "Envoy Asserts Intervention in Somalia Is Risky and Not in Interests of U.S.," *New York Times*, December 6, 1992, p. 14. Quoted in Joshua Muravchik, "The Strange Debate over Bosnia," *Commentary*, vol. 94, no. 5 (November 1992), p. 31.

1. Quoted in John L. Hirsch and Robert B. Oakley, *Somalia and Operation Restore Hope: Reflections on Peacemaking and Peacekeeping* (Washington, DC: United States Institute of Peace, 1995), p. 43.

2. In fact, the option of U.S. military deployment was not even on the agenda for discussion at the November 21 meeting, according to several participants. Author interviews with Adm. David Jeremiah (Oakton, VA, April 29, 1999); Andrew Natsios, then assistant administrator for the U.S. Agency for International Development and president's special representative on Somalia (by telephone, March 29, 1999); Herman Cohen, then assistant secretary of state for African affairs (Arlington, VA, March 30, 1999); James Woods, then deputy assistant secretary of defense for Africa and international security policy (Arlington, VA, March 30, 1999); and Walter Kansteiner, then staff member responsible for Africa on the National Security Council and deputy White House spokesman (Washington, DC, March 29, 1999).

3. Interviews with Kansteiner, Herman Cohen, Natsios, and with James Bishop, who was then acting assistant secretary of state for human rights and humanitarian affairs (Washington, DC, March 29, 1999).

4. U.S. Department of State *Dispatch* Supplement, September 1992, p. 14; interview with Kansteiner.

5. Quoted in Don Oberdorfer, "The Path to Intervention: A Massive Tragedy We Could Do Something About," *Washington Post*, December 6, 1992, p. A1.

6. Hirsch and Oakley, *Somalia and Operation Restore Hope*, p. 42.

7. Colin L. Powell, "U.S. Forces: Challenges Ahead," *Foregin Affairs*, vol. 71, no. 5 (Winter 1992), pp. 32–46.

8. See Mohamed Sahnoun, *Somalia: The Missed Opportunities* (Washington, DC: United States Institute of Peace, 1994).

9. Interview with Natsios.

10. "Emergency Plan of Action: Somalia," International Committee of the Red Cross, Geneva, Switzerland, and Nairobi, Kenya, July 21, 1992.

11. According to James Wood, who served as the assistant secretary of defense for Africa and international security policy, the entire set of political questions concerning the deployment (which included: Who was in charge in Somalia? How could the mission be successfully turned over to a follow-on UN force? Would the famine be mitigated without a comprehensive political solution to Somalia's failed state apparatus?) was relegated to "planning assumptions" to be addressed when the American force was on the ground. (Interview with Woods.) Furthermore, Herman Cohen, then assistant secretary of state for African affairs, recalls, "There wasn't any real planning on this. If you have a Somalia with no institutions—a collapsed state—you want to figure out

how to re-establish some order. You need to do this at a minimum to make the effort worthwhile. There was a lot of technical discussion on the need for police building, municipal services, and how we could harass the UN to do these things. There was also a lot of discussion on the mission—we concluded that we should disarm to the extent it was needed for the success of the mission. But we didn't really know what that meant. Should we send our forces to weapons storage sites? We really weren't sure what we were doing." (Interview with Herman Cohen.)

12. "Into Somalia," *Newsweek,* December 21, 1992, pp. 26–28.

13. Ibid.

14. Quoted in Art Pine, "U.S. Offers GIs to UN for Somalia," *Los Angeles Times,* November 27, 1992, p. A1. Ultimately, it was the issue of disarming the roaming bandits ("technicals") and the lingering threat these technicals posed to UN forces that prompted U.S.-led efforts to locate and arrest tribal leader Mohammed Aideed and to the fateful October 3, 1993, raid in Mogadishu in which eighteen U.S. soldiers were killed. See two-part series by Rick Atkinson, "The Raid that Went Wrong" (*Washington Post,* January 30, 1994, p. A1) and "Night of a Thousand Casualties" (*Washington Post,* January 31, 1994, p. A1).

15. Based on interviews with Bishop, Herman Cohen, Woods, Kansteiner, and the telephone interview with Natsios.

16. Nearly all senior Bush administration officials and outside experts understood that Somalia was a collapsed state and that any lasting food relief and stabilization would require answers to the difficult political questions confronting Somalia. Telephone interview with Natsios and interview with former National Security Advisor Brent Scowcroft, Washington, DC, April 29, 1999. See also Jeffrey Clark, "Debacle in Somalia," *Foreign Affairs,* vol. 72, no. 1 (1993), pp. 109–123.

17. For a discussion of Barre's rise to power see I. M. Lewis, "The Politics of the 1969 Somalia Coup," *Journal of Modern African Studies,* vol. 10 (October 1972), pp. 381–408; and Al Castagno, "Somalia Goes Military," *Africa Report* (February 1970).

18. Walter Clarke, *Somalia: Background Information for Operation Restore Hope, 1992–1993* (Carlisle Barracks, PA: U.S. War College, December 1992), pp. 12–13.

19. Military assistance to Barre was suspended by the U.S. Congress in 1988 and 1989 because of "the extraordinary level of violence against civilians committed by Barre's forces in their counterinsurgency campaign in the north." "Somalia: A Fight to the Death?" *Africa Watch,* vol. 4, no. 2, February 13, 1992, p. 27.

20. Boutros Boutros-Ghali, "The Situation in Somalia," *Report of the United Nations Secretary General,* April 21, 1992.

21. "Somalia: A Fight to the Death?"

22. Estimates made by International Committee of the Red Cross.

23. Cited in Clarke, *Somalia: Background Information.* See also estimates presented in Stephen John Stedman, "Conflict and Conciliation in Sub-Saharan Africa," in Michael E. Brown, ed., *The International Dimensions of Internal Conflict* (Cambridge: MIT Press, 1996), pp. 235–266.

24. Sahnoun, *Somalia: Missed Opportunities,* pp. 15–16.

25. These estimates were made by UN Special Representative Under Secretary Mohamed Sahnoun and French Minister of Health and Humanitarian Action Bernard Kouchner at a press conference on August 3, 1992, following their visit to Somalia.

26. For example, see President [George H. W.] Bush, "Toward a New World Order,"

Address before a joint session of Congress, September 11, 1990, *Dispatch* 1, no. 3 (September 17, 1990), pp. 91–94.

27. Quoted in Robert D. Schulzinger, *U.S. Diplomacy since 1900*, 4th ed. (Oxford: Oxford University Press, 1998), p. 354.

28. For example, see John Mearsheimer, "Back to the Future: Instability in Europe After the Cold War, *International Security*, vol. 15, no. 1 (Summer 1990). According to Walter Kansteiner of the National Security Council staff, Mearsheimer's article captured the attention of many senior decision makers. Interview with Kansteiner.

29. Secretary of State James Baker, "From Points to Pathways of Mutual Advantage: Next Steps in Soviet-American Relations," *Dispatch* 1, no. 8 (October 22, 1990).

30. For an example of the arguments made by selective engagers, see President [George H. W.] Bush, "Operation Desert Storm Launched," January 16, 1991, *Dispatch* 2, no. 3; Secretary of State James Baker, "Why America Is in the Gulf," address before the Los Angeles World Affairs Council, October 29, 1990, *Dispatch* 1, no. 10.

31. Secretary James Baker, "America's Stake in the Persian Gulf," Statement before the House Foreign Affairs Committee, September 4, 1990, *Dispatch* 1, no. 2., p. 69.

32. U.S.-Soviet Defense and Military Relations, NSDD [National Security Decision Directive] 311, July 28, 1988, http://www.fas.org/irp/offdocs/nsdd/23-3163a.gif (accessed August 4, 2003).

33. See Helen Dewar, "Senators Stop Short of INF Vote," *Washington Post*, May 27, 1988, p. A1.

34. Charles Krauthammer, "Too Hungry for START," *Washington Post*, May 27, 1988, p. A19.

35. John H. Cushman, Jr., "Top Arms-Control Official Quits; Criticizes Haste in Seeking Treaty," *New York Times*, November 21, 1987, p. 1.

36. Lawrence Knudson, "Nunn Complains Reduced Military Threat Not Considered in Budget," Associated Press Wire Service, December 12, 1989.

37. *CNN Crossfire*, June 1, 1990 transcript #65.

38. For a sample of the hardliner views, see Elliot Abrams, "Why America Must Lead," *National Interest*, no. 28 (Summer 1992), pp. 56–62; Charles Krauthammer, "Universal Dominion: Toward a Unipolar World," *National Interest*, no. 18 (Winter 1989–1990), pp. 46–49; Charles Krauthammer, "The Unipolar Moment," *Foreign Affairs*, vol. 70, no. 4 (Fall 1991), pp. 23–33; Joshua Muravchik, "The End of the Vietnam Paradigm," *Commentary*, vol. 91, no. 5 (May 1991), pp. 17–23; Joshua Muravchik, "Losing the Peace," *Commentary*, vol. 94, no. 1 (July 1992), pp. 37–42; Robert Jastrow and Max Kampelman, "Why We Still Need SDI," *Commentary*, vol. 94, no. 5. (November 1992), pp. 23–29; and William S. Lind, "Defending Western Culture," *Foreign Policy*, no. 84 (Fall 1991), pp. 40–50.

39. Patrick Tyler, "U.S. Strategy Plan Calls for Insuring No Rivals Develop," *New York Times*, March 8, 1992, p. 1.

40. For an overview of these positions, see Muravchik, "Strange Debate over Bosnia."

41. See for example, Theodore C. Sorensen, "Rethinking National Security," *Foreign Affairs*, vol. 69, no. 3, (Summer 1990), pp. 1–18; Carl Gershman, "Freedom Remains the Touchstone," *National Interest*, no. 19 (Spring 1990), pp. 83–86; Richard Gardner, "The Comeback of Liberal Internationalism," *Washington Quarterly*, vol. 13 (Summer 1990), pp. 23–39; Stanley Kober, "Idealpolitick," *Foreign Policy*, no. 79 (Summer 1990), pp. 3–24; Stanley Hoffmann, "The Case for Leadership," *Foreign Policy*, no. 81 (Winter

1990–91), pp. 3–19; and Stanley Hoffmann, "A New World," *Foreign Affairs,* vol. 69, no. 4 (Fall 1990), pp. 115–122.

42. Betts, *Soldiers, Statesmen, and Cold War Crises,* pp. 213–236.

43. For official statements on Serb aggression, see "First U.S. Report on War Crimes in the Former Yugoslavia," *Dispatch,* vol. 3, no. 39 (September 1992), p. 22. For assessment of the general and publicly proclaimed views of the conflict held by the Bush administration, see Roy Gutman, *A Witness to Genocide* (Shaftesbury, UK: Element, 1993); Leonard J. Cohen, ed., *Broken Bonds: The Disintegration of Yugoslavia* (Boulder: Westview, 1993); and David Gompert, "How to Defeat Serbia," *Foreign Affairs,* vol. 73, no. 4 (July–August 1994), pp. 30–47.

44. "Intervention at the London Conference on the Former Yugoslavia," *Dispatch,* vol. 3, no. 35 (August 31, 1992).

45. See Times Mirror Center for the People and the Press, *News Interest Indexes,* October 1991 and June 1992.

46. Ibid.

47. "Relief: What Is Bush Waiting For?" *Newsweek,* July 6, 1992.

48. Barton Gellman, "Defense Planners Making Case against Intervention in Yugoslavia," *Washington Post,* June 13, 1992, p. A16. See also Eric Schmitt, "Bush Calls Allies on Joint Effort to Help Sarajevo," *New York Times,* June 29, 1992, p. A1; R. W. Apple, "Few Choices, Fewer Hopes: Bush under Pressue," *New York Times,* August 7, 1992, p. A1.

49. Interview with Scowcroft.

50. Interview with a representative from InterAction, Washington, DC, April 14, 1999.

51. See Brent MacGregor, *Live, Direct, and Biased? Making Television News in the Satellite Age* (London: Arnold, 1997), pp. 35–37.

52. Garrick Utley, "The Shrinking of Foreign News: From Broadcast to Narrowcast," *Foreign Affairs,* vol. 76, no. 2 (March–April 1997), pp. 2–10.

53. Only a few of the journalists from the major American national news organizations had ever traveled to or covered Yugoslavia prior to 1992. Blaine Harden of the *Washington Post* was based in Warsaw and his previous assignment was covering Africa. Roger Cohen of the *New York Times* had never traveled to Yugoslavia prior to August 1992. Tom Gjelten of National Public Radio was based in Berlin when the war in Croatia broke out and had never covered Yugoslavia prior to the war. Roy Gutman of *Newsday* had covered Yugoslavia in the early 1970s but had not been to the region since 1974. Telephone interviews with Roger Cohen, May 17, 1999, interview with Tom Gjelten, Washington, DC, March 10, 1999, and interview with Roy Gutman, Washington, DC, March 9, 1999.

54. Telephone interview with Roger Cohen, May 17, 1999, and interview with Gjelten.

55. Interview with Roger Cohen.

56. Ibid.

57. Interview with Gjelten.

58. Ibid.

59. Andrew Kohut and Robert C. Toth, "The People, the Press, and the Use of Force," in Aspen Strategy Group, *The United States and the Use of Force in the Post–Cold War Era* (Queenstown, Md.: Aspen Institute, 1995), p. 149. Many journalists covering the Bosnian conflict at the time expressed bewilderment at the public indifference to the

conflict. Warren Strobel suggests that action in Bosnia was characterized as having such a high degree of futility that most Americans simply did not believe the United States could do anything about the problems there. Warren P. Strobel, *Late-Breaking Foreign Policy: The News Media's Influence on Peace Operations* (Washington, DC: United States Institute of Peace), pp. 143–152.

60. Interview with Kansteiner.

61. Interview with Scowcroft.

62. Don Oberdorfer, "U.S. Took Slow Approach to Somali Crisis," *Washington Post,* August 24, 1992, p. A13.

63. Despite these efforts, however, there was virtually no media coverage of Somalia between January 1992 and mid-July of that year. None of the major U.S. networks or newspapers had reporters assigned specifically to the crisis. Interview with Andrew Natsios, March 29, 1999. See also Oberdorfer, "U.S. Took Slow Approach to Somali Crisis."

64. According to James Bishop, when Secretary of State James Baker found out about this effort, which "had Cohen's fingerprints all over it," he "got really pissed off" and sent the assistant secretary of state for international organizations, John Bolton, to New York to retract the effort. Interview with Bishop.

65. According to James Woods, Baker and his aides did not want to increase UN peacekeeping operations, because "the United States would ultimately be called upon to pay for it." Interview with Woods.

66. Oberdorfer, "U.S. Took Slow Approach to Somali Crisis."

67. Cleavages existed between Natsios, Bishop, and Cohen, all of whom were pressing for active U.S. engagement in Somalia, and Assistant Secretary of State for International Organizations John Bolton, the National Security Council staff, and the Joint Chiefs, all of whom opposed expanding the U.S. role. See Terrence Lyons and Ahmed I. Samatar, *Somalia: State Collapse, Multilateral Intervention, and Strategies for Political Reconstruction* (Washington, DC: Brookings Institution, 1995), p. 88 fn. 27.

68. Lyons and Samatar, *Somalia*, p. 31.

69. Jane Perlez, "Deaths in Somalia Outpace Delivery of Food," *New York Times,* July 19, 1992, p. 1.

70. Seth Faison, "U.N. Head Proposes Expanded Efforts for Somalia Relief," *New York Times,* July 25, 1992, p. 1.

71. Interview with Bishop.

72. Interview with Scowcroft.

73. Ibid.

74. Interview with Kansteiner.

75. Oberdorfer, "U.S. Took Slow Approach to Somali Crisis."

76. Interview with Scowcroft.

77. Adm. David Jeremiah, vice chairman of the Joint Chiefs of Staff, stated that the view of the Joint Chiefs was that the famine in Somalia was caused first and foremost by warring tribes who had been "fighting for centuries." Interview with Adm. David Jeremiah, Oakton, VA, April 29, 1999.

78. Interviews with Bishop, Herman Cohen, Kansteiner, and Woods.

79. Interview with Bishop. In a similar story, James Woods, then deputy assistant secretary of defense for Africa and international affairs, recounts that in the summer of 1992 Fred Cuny, who was very well known in humanitarian relief, came to the Pentagon and briefed a team of officers from U.S. Southern Command (SOCOM) on a "light

option." Under the plan, American troops would be deployed to Somalia in areas outside of Mogadishu to establish security zones for humanitarian relief and distribution. The SOCOM team was very interested in the proposal but the Joint Chiefs' representatives reacted "negatively." When Woods followed up on the idea a few weeks later, the Joint Chiefs "denied the existence of any light option. They said no SOCOM team had been in the building, they were never there, it never happened." Interview with Woods.

80. Interview with Bishop.

81. Interview with Herman Cohen.

82. Interview with Roger Cohen.

83. Tom Gjelten, interviewed by Warren Strobel, quoted in Strobel, *Late-Breaking Foreign Policy,* p. 104.

84. For example, see Patrick Glynn, "Rescue Bosnia," *New Republic,* August 17 and 24, 1992. According to Tom Gjelten, there was a learning curve for most reporters on the scene, because few had had any prior experience in the region: "It took a while for us to figure it out." Author's interview with Gjelten.

85. Department of State Daily Press Briefing, Monday, August 3, 1992.

86. William Hill, director of the Office of East European Analysis in the Bureau of Intelligence and Research, said, "We knew about this stuff going on—it was also a developing story. But we had known about it and had been trying to do something about it for a while within the USG [United States government] and from an international perspective." Interview with William Hill, March 23, 1999.

87. John Fox, responsible for Eastern European affairs on the Policy Planning Staff, called EUR to demand an explanation for the reversal. He was told that Secretary Eagleburger's office had instructed the staff to use the revised language. In a follow-up conversation with Eagleburger's executive assistant, Bill Montgomery, Fox was told, "This is too hot to handle and Larry wants us to get ahead of it. We can't afford to confirm this." Fox immediately went to his boss, Bill Burns, and urged Burns to take the matter up with the secretary, telling Burns, "This is a lie. There is evidence inside this building [that these camps exist]." Interview with Fox.

88. Eagleburger quoted in Strobel, *Late-Breaking Foreign Policy,* p. 150.

89. Zimmerman quoted in ibid. pp. 150–151.

90. Interview with John Fox and James Hooper, March 18, 1999. Furthermore, according to William Hill, who had accompanied Niles to the House Foreign Affairs Committee hearing, "Niles should have slammed his fist down on the table and said this information outraged him and that it was his highest priority to gain access to the camps. Instead, he sat there and tried to deny everything. With the information we had, he should have known he wouldn't get away with this line." Interview with Hill.

91. Clifford Krauss, "U.S. Backs away from Charge of Atrocities in Bosnia Camps," *New York Times,* August 5, 1992, p. 1.

92. Ibid.

93. Interview with Gutman.

94. Quoted in Strobel, *Late-Breaking Foreign Policy,* p. 150.

95. Data from Network Evening News Abstracts, Television News Archives, Vanderbilt University.

96. Gwen Ifill, "The 1992 Campaign: The Democrats, Clinton Counter on Foreign Policy," *New York Times,* July 29, 1992, p. A1.

97. Krauss, "U.S. Backs away from Charge of Atrocities in Bosnia Camps."

98. See, for example, ABC *World News Tonight,* August 8, 9, and 10, 1992; NBC *Nightly News,* August 7, 8, and 10, 1992; and CBS *Evening News,* August 8 and 9, 1992. Television News Archives, Vanderbilt University.

99. "The Ethnic Cleansing of Bosnia-Hercegovina," U.S. Senate, Senate Foreign Relations Committee Report, August 15, 1992 (Washington, DC: U.S. Government Printing Office).

100. See, for example, Margaret Thatcher, "Stop the Excuses. Help Bosnia Now," *New York Times,* August 6, 1992, p. A23.

101. Jim Hoagland, "August Guns: How Sarajevo Will Reshape U.S. Strategy," *Washington Post,* August 9, 1992, p. C1.

102. Leslie H. Gelb, "Foreign Affairs, the West's Scam in Bosnia," *New York Times,* August 9, 1992, p. 17.

103. Interview with Scowcroft.

104. Quoted in Hoagland, "August Guns," *Washington Post,* August 9, 1992, p. C1.

105. Quoted in Strobel, *Late-Breaking Foreign Policy,* p. 148.

106. "Rescue Bosnia," *New Republic,* August 17 and 24, 1992, p. 7.

107. Interview with Scowcroft.

108. Quoted in "Rescue Bosnia," p. 7.

109. Quoted in Michael Gordon, "Conflict in the Balkans; 60,000 needed for Bosnia, a U.S. General Estimates," *New York Times,* August 12, 1992, p. 8.

110. James Gerstanzang and Melissa Healy, "U.S. to Airlift Food to Combat Somali Famine," *Los Angeles Times,* August 15, 1992, p. 1.

111. Strobel, *Late-Breaking Foreign Policy,* p. 132.

112. Herman Cohen, "Intervention in Somalia," in Allen E. Goodman, *The Diplomatic Record: 1992* (Boulder: Westview Press, 1995), p. 60.

113. Quoted from Don Oberdorfer, "The Path to Intervention; A Massive Tragedy 'We Could Do Something About,'" *Washington Post,* December 6, 1992, p. A1.

114. Cohen, "Intervention in Somalia," p. 61.

115. Interview with Herman Cohen. Cohen added that "these guys [senior Bush administration officials] were consummate politicians; they really knew Washington. The campaign was heating up; CNN was all over them. . . . It would have been very rare that they'd make a decision of this magnitude without serious political thinking."

116. Telephone interview with Natsios.

117. Ibid.

118. Interview with Scowcroft.

119. Data from Network Evening News Abstracts, Television News Archives, Vanderbilt University. Also cited in Strobel, *Late-Breaking Foreign Policy,* p. 134.

120. Data from Network Evening News Abstracts, Television News Archives, Vanderbilt University.

121. Powell and Cheney apparently raised numerous concerns about the airlift, fearing that U.S. forces would be targeted. Although the airlift was initially scheduled to begin on August 20, it was delayed another eight days. In the end, the United States agreed to fly without weapons; however, the military remained adamant that its forces would be used only to drop relief aid in remote locations. According to most relief workers on the ground in Somalia, the primary problem was security at the warehouses and other distribution cites and not at the airport. And, even though aid workers identified the core problems as ones of distribution rather than initial delivery, Powell and Cheney

refused to lend any support for U.S. assistance in the distribution of relief by providing security so aid workers could collect and distribute the relief that was dropped. The aid workers' predictions proved all too accurate. In September, the amount of food aid arriving in Somalia increased from 20,000 to 37,000 metric tons, yet the amount actually reaching the hands of famine victims fell by 40 percent. See Jane Perlez, "First of U.S. Relief Planes for Somalia Lands in Kenya," *New York Times,* August 19, 1992, p. A3. Data based on Office of Foreign Disaster Assistance Situation Reports, and cited in Hirsch and Oakley, *Somalia and Operation Restore Hope,* p. 25

122. McNeil/Lehrer NewsHour, transcript 4444, August 28, 1992.

123. Ibid.

124. Cited in Roger Cohen, *Hearts Grown Brutal: Sagas of Sarajevo* (New York: Random House, 1998), p. 220.

125. For example, Secretary of State Lawrence Eagleburger dismissed Kenney's position during an interview on the McNeil/Lehrer NewsHour, proclaiming, "To my mind that young man has never set foot in Yugoslavia" (transcript 4444, August 28, 1992).

126. Interview with Hooper.

127. Ibid.

128. Elaine Sciolino, "Bush Asks France and Britain to Back Force of Monitors in Kosovo," *New York Times,* November 25, 1992, p. A6.

129. Quoted in Michael Gordon, "Winter May Kill 100,000 in Bosnia, the CIA Warns," *New York Times,* September 30, 1992, p. 13.

130. Ibid.

131. Quoted in Michael Gordon, "Powell Delivers a Resounding No on Using Limited Force in Bosnia" *New York Times,* September 28, 1999, p. 1.

132. Interview with Hill.

133. Interview with Zimmerman.

134. Interview with Jeremiah.

135. Quoted in Gordon, "Powell Delivers a Resounding No."

136. Michael Gordon, "Bush Backs a Ban on Combat Flights in Bosnia Airspace," *New York Times,* October 2, 1992, p. 1.

137. Interview with Scowcroft.

138. Quoted in John Goshko, "Bush Urges Flight over Bosnia," *Washington Post,* October 3, 1992, p. A1.

139. Ibid.

140. Interview with Scowcroft.

141. "At Least Slow the Slaughter," *New York Times,* October 4, 1992, p. 16.

142. Colin Powell, "Why Generals Get Nervous," *New York Times,* October 8, 1992, p. 35. He later expanded the *New York Times* op-ed piece and published it in *Foreign Affairs* as "U.S. Forces: Challenges Ahead" (Winter 1992).

143. In mid-October, the NSC began to fear that Serb leaders might attempt a similar campaign of violence and ethnic cleansing in Serbia's province of Kosovo. The American officials believed that any action against ethnic Albanians, the overwhelming majority of Kosovo residents, might easily ignite a wider conflict throughout the Balkans. By early November, a consensus emerged that Kosovo was a "different kettle of fish" than Bosnia and was within U.S. geostrategic interests. The NSC concluded that the United States would have to issue a deliberate warning to Miloševic against taking any action in Kosovo. Powell and Cheney opposed the action, fearing that U.S. forces

would be drawn into the conflict more directly. See Sciolino, "Bush Asks France and Britain to Back Monitors in Kosovo."

144. Interview with Kansteiner.

145. Ibid.

146. Interview with Bishop.

147. Cited in Herman Cohen, "Intervention in Somalia," p. 63.

148. The weekend after the election, Bush invited Powell and his family to Camp David. According to Powell, he was told by Barbara Bush that the president needed his close friends with him at that time. Bush apparently went into a post-election depression, angry that the public had rejected him for Bill Clinton (Powell, *My American Journey* [New York: Random House, 1995], p. 562).

149. Telephone interview with Zimmerman, interviews with Fox, Hooper, and Hill.

150. Interview with John Fox, Eastern European affairs expert on the Policy Planning Staff, March 22, 1999.

151. "West Plans Searches, Force if Needed in Yugoslav Blockade," *Los Angeles Times,* November 18, 1992, p. 1.

152. Powell, *My American Journey,* p. 562.

153. Thomas Friedman, "The Transition: President-Elect Clinton Says Bush Made China Gains," *New York Times,* November 20, 1992, p. 1.

154. Hirsch and Oakley, *Somalia and Operation Restore Hope,* p. 43.

155. Interview with Jeremiah.

156. Ibid.

157. Interview with Herman Cohen.

158. Interview with Jeremiah.

159. Interview with Scowcroft.

160. Ibid.

161. Interview with Kansteiner.

162. Interview with Scowcroft.

s i x : The War over Iraq

Epigraphs: Remarks by Vice President Richard Cheney to the Veterans of Foreign Wars 103rd National Convention, August 26, 2002. U.S. Senator Robert C. Byrd, "The Truth Will Emerge," speech before U.S. Senate, May 21, 2003. Lawrence Eagleburger on FNS, Monday, August 19, 2002. Transcript at http://www.foxnews.com/story/0,2933,60704,00.html.

1. Richard A. Clarke, *Against All Enemies: Inside America's War on Terror* (New York: Free Press, 2004), p. 24.

2. Ibid., p. 32.

3. Bob Woodward, *Bush at War* (New York: Simon and Schuster, 2003), p. 91.

4. Condoleezza Rice, "9/11 for the Record," *Washington Post,* March 22, 2004, p. A21.

5. Woodward, *Bush at War,* p. 99.

6. Samantha Power, *A Problem from Hell: America and the Age of Genocide* (New York: Basic Books, 2003), pp. 351–373.

7. Eric Schmitt, "Panel Says U.S. Faces Risk of a Surprise Missile Attack," *New York Times,* July 16, 1998, p. A26.

8. "Executive Summary of the Report of the Commission to Assess the Ballistic

Missile Threat to the United States," July 15, 1998, p. 1, at http://www.house.gov/hsac/testimony/105thcongress/BMthreat (accessed October 4, 2004).

9. Four years later when the American air war in Kosovo seemed to be stalling, the Balkan Action Council placed a full-page ad in the *New York Times* calling for the immediate deployment of ground forces in Kosovo. Rumsfeld, Wolfowitz, Perle, Kirkpatrick, John O'Sullivan, Eugene V. Rostow, and Max Kampleman and several other hardliners were members of the Balkan Action Council's executive board.

10. Michael R. Gordon and General Bernard E. Trainer, *The Generals' War: The Inside Story of the Conflict in the Gulf* (Boston: Little, Brown, 1995), p. 150.

11. Ibid.

12. Ibid.

13. Ibid., p. 151.

14. See, for example, Paul Wolfowitz, "Rebuilding the Anti-Saddam Coalition," *Wall Street Journal*, November 18, 1997, p. A22.

15. Schmitt, "Panel Says U.S. Faces Risk," p. A26.

16. The letter was sent on January 26, 1998, and can be viewed on the Project for the New American Century Web site at http://www.newamericancentury.org/iraqclintonletter.htm (accessed October 4, 2004).

17. A second open letter was sent to President Clinton on February 19, 1998, similarly calling for military action in support of regime change in Iraq. That letter was signed by the following Bush administration officials: Elliott Abrams (NSC), Richard Armitage (State), John Bolton (State), Doug Feith (Defense), Fred Ikle (Defense Policy Board), Zalmay Khalilzad (White House), Peter Rodman (Defense), Donald Rumsfeld (Secretary of Defense), Paul Wolfowitz (Defense), David Wurmser (State), Dov Zakheim (Defense), and Richard Perle (Defense Policy Board). It was also signed by Robert Kagan, William Kristol, Frank Gaffney (director, Center for Security Policy), Joshua Muravchik (American Enterprise Institute), Martin Peretz (editor-in-chief, *The New Republic*), Leon Wieseltier, (*The New Republic*), former congressman Stephen Solarz. See "Open Letter to the President," February 19, 1998, at http://www.iraqwatch.org/perspectives/rumsfeld-openletter.htm (accessed June 1, 2004).

18. Condoleezza Rice, "Promoting the National Interest," *Foreign Affairs*, vol. 79, no. 1 (January–February 2000), p. 59.

19. Colin L. Powell, "Confirmation Hearing of Colin L. Powell," January 17, 2001, at http://www.state.gov/secretary/rm/2001/443.htm (accessed June 1, 2004).

20. James A. Baker III, "Getting Ready for 'Next Time' in Iraq," *New York Times*, February 27, 1998, p. A25. Following American airstrikes on Iraq, Baker repeated this theme in a follow-up editorial. See James A. Baker III, "Everything in Its Own Time," *New York Times*, December 18, 1998, p. A35.

21. Brent Scowcroft, "Taking Exception: The Power of Containment," *Washington Post*, March 1, 1998, p. C7.

22. "Confronting Saddam Hussein," *Washington Post*, October 28, 1998, p. A18.

23. "Statement by the President in His Address to the Nation," at http://www.whitehouse.gov/news/releases/2001/09/20010911-16.html (accessed June 1, 2004).

24. Woodward, *Bush at War*, p. 49.

25. Ibid., p. 61.

26. See PBS *Frontline*, "The Long Road to War," transcript, at http://www.pbs.org/wgbh/pages/frontline/shows/longroad/etc/script.html (accessed June 1, 2004).

27. Woodward, *Bush at War,* p. 60.

28. Ibid., p. 99.

29. Throughout the first eight months of the Bush administration, it was not uncommon for conservatives and neoconservatives to send the word out to friends and supporters in think tanks and to media pundits to write letters and opinion pieces to aid the hardliners' internal battles in the administration. See Jane Perlez, "Bush Team's Counsel Is Divided on Foreign Policy," *New York Times,* March 27, 2001, p. A1.

30. Elaine Sciolino and Patrick E. Tyler, "Some Pentagon Officials and Advisors Seek to Oust Iraq's Leader in War's Next Phase," *New York Times,* October 12, 2001, p. B6.

31. James Risen, "How Pair's Finding on Terror Led to Clash on Shaping Intelligence," *New York Times,* April 28, 2004. p. A1.

32. Ibid.

33. David W. Moore, "Americans Believe U.S. Participation in Gulf War a Decade Ago Worthwhile," Gallup News Service, February 21, 2001.

34. Eliot A. Cohen, "World War IV," *Wall Street Journal,* November 20, 2001, p. A18.

35. Thomas L. Friedman, "Foreign Affairs: Today's News Quiz," *New York Times,* November 20, 2001, p. A19.

36. Frank Newport, "Overwhelming Support for War Continues," Gallup News Service, November 29, 2001.

37. Bob Woodward, *Plan of Attack* (New York: Simon and Schuster, 2004), p. 3.

38. When Bush returned from Camp David on September 16, he immediately assembled his communications team to develop a strategy for a comprehensive public relations campaign to build and manage public support for the military effort. Woodward, *Bush at War,* pp. 88, 94–97.

39. Ibid., p. 95.

40. The influence of Bush's political advisors Karl Rove and Karen Hughes is recounted by former Bush speechwriter David Frum in *The Right Man: The Surprise Presidency of George W. Bush* (New York: Random House, 2003), esp. chap. 3. See also, Lou Debose, Jan Reid, and Carl M. Cannon, *Boy Genius: Karl Rove, The Brains Behind the Remarkable Political Triumph of George W. Bush* (Public Affairs, 2003) and James Moore and Wayne Slater, *Bush's Brain: How Karl Rove Made George W. Bush Presidential* (Hoboken, NJ: John Wiley and Sons, 2002), especially part 3.

41. Moore and Slater, *Bush's Brain,* pp. 288–291.

42. For example, Baker and Scowcroft emphasized this line in their respective op-ed responses to calls for regime change in 1998. Even Colin Powell suggested during his confirmation hearings that regime change policy had adversely affected Saddam's ability to acquire weapons of mass destruction.

43. According to speechwriter David Frum, Bush "needed something to assert, something that made clear that September 11 and Saddam Hussein were linked after all and that for the safety of the world, Saddam Hussein must be defeated rather than deterred" (Frum, *The Right Man,* p. 233).

44. Karen DeYoung and Dana Millbank, "U.S. Repeats Warnings on Terrorism; Bush Urges Other Nations to 'Get Their House in Order,'" *Washington Post,* February 1, 2002, p. A1.

45. President George W. Bush, State of the Union Speech, January 29, 2002, at http://www.whitehouse.gov/news/releases/2002/01/iraq/20020129-11.html (accessed June 1, 2004) (emphasis added).

46. See transcripts from ABC, CBS, and NBC nightly news broadcasts, Television News Archives, Vanderbilt University.

47. "Yes They Are Evil," *Washington Post*, February 3, 2002, p. B7.

48. Daniel Rubin, "U.S. Warns NATO on Iraq; Allies Urged to Join New War on Terrorism, or America Will Go It Alone," *Pittsburgh Post Gazette*, February 3, 2002, p. A1.

49. Michael R. Gordon and David E. Sanger, "Powell Says U.S. Is Weighing Ways to Topple Hussein," *New York Times*, February 13, 2002, p. A1.

50. David E. Sanger, "U.S. Goal Seems Clear, and the Team Complete," *New York Times*, February 13, 2002, p. A18.

51. Thomas E. Ricks, "Military Bids to Postpone Iraq Invasion; Joint Chiefs See Progress in Swaying Bush, Pentagon," *Washington Post*, May 24, 2002, p. A1.

52. Eric Schmitt, "Cheney, at Marine Base, Reinforces Bush's Stand on War against Terror," *New York Times*, February 18, 2002, p. A10.

53. "Remarks by the President at 2002 Graduation Exercise of the United States Military Academy, West Point, New York," June 1, 2002, at http://www.whitehouse.gov/news/releases/2002/06/20020601-3.html (accessed June 1, 2004).

54. Jeffrey M. Jones, "Removing Saddam Considered an Important Foreign Policy Goal," Gallup News Service, June 21, 2002.

55. "U.S. General Population Topline Report," *WorldViews 2002*, Chicago Council on Foreign Relations and the German Marshall Fund of the United States, October 2002, pp. 89–100.

56. Morton M. Kondrake, "Congress Should Hold Great Debate over Policy on Iraq," *Roll Call*, June 27, 2002.

57. Nicholas Lemann, "How It Came to War," *New Yorker*, March 31, 2002. See also David E. Sanger and Thom Shanker, "Exploring Baghdad Strike as Iraq Option," *New York Times*, July 29, 2002, p. A1; and Eric Schmitt and David E. Sanger, "Bush Has Received Pentagon Options on Attacking Iraq," *New York Times*, September 21, 2002, p. A1.

58. PBS *Frontline*, "The Long Road to War," transcript.

59. Brent Scowcroft, "Don't Attack Saddam," *Wall Street Journal*, August 15, 2002, p. A12.

60. Lawrence Eagleburger on FNS, Monday, August 19, 2002. Transcript at http://www.foxnews.com/story/0,2933,60704,00.html (accessed June 13, 2004).

61. "President Discusses Iraq, the Economy, and Homeland Security," August 16, 2002, at http://www.whitehouse.gov/news/releases/2002/08/iraq/20020816-3.html.

62. James A. Baker III, "The Right Way to Change a Regime," *New York Times*, August 25, 2002, sec. 4, p. 9.

63. "Vice President Speaks at VFW 103rd National Convention," August 26, 2002, at http://www.whitehouse.gov/news/releases/2002/08/iraq/20020826.html.

64. CNN/USA Today/Gallop Poll, September 2002, Polling the Nations Database, http://poll.orspub.com/poll/lpext.dll?f=templates&fn=main-h.htm (accessed October 2, 2004).

65. *Time* magazine, for example, reported that Powell was so "frustrated" that he told his aides he would leave the administration at the end of the current term. See Massimo Calibrisi, "Colin Powell: Planning for an Exit," *Time*, September 9, 2002, p. 14.

66. "Blair's War," PBS *Frontline*, transcript at http://www.pbs.org/wgbh/pages/frontline/shows/blair/etc/script.html (accessed June 1, 2004).

67. Woodward, *Plan of Attack*, p. 172.

68. Karen DeYoung and Mike Allen, "Disarm Iraq Quickly, Bush to Urge U.N.; Failure to Move May Lead to U.S. Action," *Washington Post*, September 7, 2002, p. A1; and David E. Sanger, "Blair, Meeting with Bush, Fully Endorses U.S. Plans for Ending Iraqi Threat," *New York Times*, September 8, 2002, p. 23.

69. According to Martha Brant of *Newsweek*, Dan Bartlett, White House communications chief told a conference call of public relations specialists, "We're getting the band together." The band, reported Brant, was "made up of the people who brought you the war in Afghanistan—or at least the accompanying public-relations campaign. Their greatest hit: exposing the Taliban's treatment of women. . . . They aim to use it against Saddam Hussein, respond to his disinformation and control the message within the administration so no one—not even Vice President Dick Cheney—freelances on Iraq." Cited in Sheldon Rampton and John Stauber, *Weapons of Mass Destruction: The Uses of Propaganda in Bush's War on Iraq* (New York: Jeremy P. Tarcher and Penguin, 2003), pp. 38–39.

70. Douglas Quenqua, "Pentagon Seeks PR Advice Before Diplomatic Attempt," *PR Week*, August 26, 2002, and at http://www.prweek.com/news/news_story.cfm?ID= 156288 2002. Hill and Knowlton had gained considerable notoriety during the first Persian Gulf War.

71. Elisabeth Bumiller, "Bush Aides Set Strategy to Sell Policy on Iraq," *New York Times*, September 7, 2002, p. A1.

72. Woodward, *Plan of Attack*, p. 168.

73. "With Few Variations, Top Bush Advisers Present Their Case Against Iraq," *New York Times*, September 9, 2002, p. A8.

74. Cited in David Barstow, William J. Broad, and Jeff Gerth, "How the White House Embraced Disputed Arms Intelligence," *New York Times*, October 2, 2004, p. 1.

75. Ibid.

76. Todd S. Purdum, "Bush Officials Say Time Has Come for Action on Iraq," *New York Times*, September 9, 2002, p. A1.

77. The line had generated so much consternation for the hardline coalition that they continued to battle against its inclusion. In the end, the line did not make its way onto the teleprompter; but Bush had rehearsed it, and he included it on his own.

78. "President's Remarks at the United Nations General Assembly," New York, September 12, 2002 at http://www.whitehouse.gov/news/releases/2002/09/20020912-1.html (accessed May 31, 2004).

79. James A. Baker III, "The U.N. Route," *Washington Post*, September 15, 2002, p. B7.

80. Joseph Curl, "Agency Disavows Report on Iraq Arms," *Washington Times*, September 27, 2002.

81. CBS News, September 24, 2002, Polling the Nations Database (see n. 64) (accessed October 2, 2004).

82. CNN/USA Today/Gallup Poll, August 23, 2002, Polling the Nations Database (see n. 64) (accessed October 2, 2004).

83. CBS/New York Times, September 7, 2002, Polling the Nations Database (see n. 64) (accessed October 2, 2004).

84. Fox News/Opinion Dynamics Poll, September 12, 2002, Polling the Nations Database (see n. 64) (accessed October 2, 2004).

85. CBS/New York Times, September 7, 2002, Polling the Nations Database (see n. 64) (accessed October 2, 2004).

86. Jim VandeHei and Karen DeYoung, "Bush to Seek Broad Power on Iraq," *Washington Post,* September 19, 2002, p. A1.

87. "Text of Proposed Resolution," *Washington Post,* September 20, 2002, p. A20.

88. Cited in Woodward, *Plan of Attack,* p. 187.

89. Rampton and Stauber, *Weapons of Mass Deception,* pp. 56–60.

90. Ibid., and Joe Hagan, "She's Richard Perle's Oyster," *New York Observer,* April 7, 2003.

91. Michael R. Gordon and Judith Miller, "U.S. Says Hussein Intensifies Quest for A-Bomb Parts, *New York Times,* September 8, 2002, p. 1. For a critical review of this article, see Michael Massing, *Now They Tell Us: The American Press and Iraq* (New York: New York Review of Books, 2004), pp. 29–35; and Barstow, Broad, and Gerth, "How the White House Embraced Disputed Arms Intelligence," p. 1.

92. Massing, *Now They Tell Us.*

93. "Support for Potential Military Action Slips to 55%: Party Images Unchanged with a Week to Go," Pew Research Center for the People and the Press, October 30, 2002.

94. Jim VandeHei, "Daschle Angered by Bush Statement; President 'Politicizing' Security Issue, He Says," *Washington Post,* September 26, 2002, p. A1.

95. Dana Milbank, "In President's Speeches, Iraq Dominates, Economy Fades," *Washington Post,* September 25, 2002, p. A1.

96. VandeHei, "Daschle Angered by Bush Statement," p. A1.

97. "Dow Drops 189; Hits 4-Year Low," *Washington Post,* September 25, 2002, p. E3.

98. Margaret Warner interview with Condoleezza Rice, Transcript #7463, *The NewsHour with Jim Lehrer,* September 25, 2002.

99. Eric Schmitt, "Rumsfeld Says U.S. Has 'Bulletproof' Evidence of Iraq's Links to Al Qaeda," *New York Times,* September 27, 2002, p. A9.

100. Warren Hoge, "Blair Says Iraqis Could Launch Chemical Warheads in Minutes," *New York Times,* September 25, 2002, p. A1.

101. Elisabeth Bumiller, "Still Advising From Afar and Near," *New York Times,* October 21, 2002, p. A12.

102. "President Bush Outlines Iraqi Threat, Remarks by the President on Iraq," Cincinnati, Ohio, October 7, 2002, at http://www.whitehouse.gov/news/releases/2002/10/iraq/20021007-8.html (accessed June 1, 2004).

103. Gary Hart, "Note to Democrats: Get a Defense Policy," *New York Times,* October 3, 2002, p. A27.

104. "Americans Thinking about Iraq, but Focused on the Economy: Midterm Election Preview," Pew Research Center for the People and the Press, October 10, 2002, at http://people-press.org/reports/display.php3?ReportID=162 (accessed June 1, 2004).

105. David E. Sanger, Eric Schmitt, and Thom Shanker, "War Plan for Iraq Calls for Big Force and Quick Strike," *New York Times,* November 10, 2002, p. A1.

106. For a description of Powell's diplomatic efforts see Woodward, *Plan of Attack,* pp. 220–227.

107. Colum Lynch, "Security Council Resolution Tells Iraq It Must Disarm; Baghdad Ordered to Admit Inspectors or Face Consequences," *Washington Post,* November 10, 2002, p. A26.

108. Colin L. Powell, "Baghdad's Moment of Truth," *Washington Post,* November 10, 2002, B7.

109. Karen DeYoung and Walter Pincus, "Iraq Hunt to Extend to March, Blix Says; Arms Search Timetable Complicates U.S. Plans," *Washington Post*, January 14, 2003, p. A1.

110. Woodward, *Plan of Attack*, p. 254.

111. Condoleezza Rice, "Why We Know Iraq Is Lying," *New York Times*, January 23, 2003, p. A25.

112. This discussion is drawn from Woodward, *Plan of Attack*, pp. 288–292.

113. "President Delivers State of the Union Address, January 28, 2003," at http://www.whitehouse.gov/news/releases/2003/01/iraq/20030128-19.html.

114. "Irrefutable," *Washington Post*, February 6, 2003, p. A36.

115. "The Case against Iraq," *New York Times*, February 6, 2003, p. A38.

116. CNN/USA Today/Gallup Poll, January 31, 2003, Polling the Nations Database (see n. 64) (accessed October 2, 2004).

117. CNN/USA Today/Gallup Poll, February 5, 2003, Polling the Nations Database (see n. 64) (accessed October 2, 2004).

118. Douglas Jehl and David E. Sanger, "Prewar Assessment on Iraq Saw Chance of Strong Divisions," *New York Times*, September 28, 2004, p. 1.

119. Daniel Okrent, "Weapons of Mass Destruction? Or Mass Distraction?" *New York Times*, May 30, 2004.

120. "The Times and Iraq," *New York Times*, May 26, 2004, p. 6.

121. Eric Schmitt, "Pentagon Contradicts General on Iraq Occupation Force's Size," *New York Times*, February 28, 2003, p. A1.

122. Joseph Carroll, "American Public Opinion About the Situation in Iraq," Gallup News Service, June 29, 2004.

SEVEN: Conclusion

Epigraph: Interview with Brent Scowcroft.

1. For example, contrary to the one-line explanation in the movie *Wag the Dog*, that the American intervention in Grenada was to divert the public's attention away from the attack on U.S. service personnel in Lebanon, Chapter 4 above demonstrates that much of the critical decision making on Grenada actually preceded the events in Lebanon.

2. See, for example, Garrick Utley, "The Shrinking of Foreign News."

3. Letter to Thomas Jefferson, May 13, 1798, in Saul K. Padover, ed., *The Complete Madison* (New York: Harper and Brothers, 1953), p. 257.

Bibliography

MANUSCRIPT COLLECTIONS

Dwight D. Eisenhower Presidential Library, Abeline, KS

John Foster Dulles Papers (JFD Papers)
   JFD Chronological Series
   Subject Series
   Telephone Calls Series
   White House Memoranda Series

Dwight D. Eisenhower: Papers as President of the United States, 1953–1961 (Ann
      Whitman File) (DDE Papers)
   Administrative Series
   Ann Whitman Diary Series
   DDE Diaries Series
   Dulles-Herter Series
   Legislative Meetings Series
   Miscellaneous Series
   Name Series
   National Security Council (NSC) Series
   Press Conference Series

James C. Hagerty Papers
Bryce Harlow Records
C. D. Jackson Papers
National Security Council Staff Papers, 1948–1961
   Executive Secretary's Subject File Series

Office of the Special Assistant for National Security Affairs Records, 1952–1961
   NSC Series, Administration Subseries
   NSC Series, Briefing Notes Subseries
   NSC Series, Subject Subseries
   Special Assistant Series, Subject Subseries

Office of the Staff Secretary (OSS) Records, 1952–1961
   Cabinet Series
   Legislative Meetings Series
   L. Arthur Minnich Series

Subject Series, Alphabetical Subseries
Subject Series, DOD Subseries

Oral Histories
Dwight D. Eisenhower
Andrew Goodpaster
James C. Hagerty
Carl McCardle

National Archives, Washington, DC

Diplomatic Branch
General Records of the Department of State, Record Group 59
Office of Public Opinion Studies, 1943–1965, Record Group 59

Modern Military Records Branch
Joint Chiefs of Staff Records, Record Group 218
Geographic File, 1954–1956
Geographic File, 1956–1958
Records of the Chairman, Arthur Radford

INTERVIEWS

Ambassador James Bishop, Washington, DC, March 29, 1999
Ambassador Herman Cohen, Arlington, VA, March 30, 1999
Roger Cohen, May 17, 1999 (by telephone)
Michael Deaver, Washington, DC, February 9, 1999
John Fox, Washington, DC, March 22, 1999
Tom Gjelten, Washington, DC, March 10, 1999
Roy Gutman, Washington, DC, March 9, 1999
William Hill, Washington, DC, March 23, 1999
James Hooper, Washington, DC, March 24, 1999
Admiral David Jeremiah (USN Ret.), Oakton, VA, April 29, 1999
Walter Kansteiner, Washington, DC, March 29, 1999
Andrew Natsios, March 29, 1999 (by telephone)
General Brent Scowcroft (USA Ret.), Washington, DC, April 29, 1999
James Woods, Arlington, VA, March 30, 1999
Ambassador Warren Zimmerman, March 24, 1999 (by telephone)

BOOKS AND ARTICLES

Abelson, Donald. *American Think Tanks and Their Role in U.S. Foreign Policy.* New York: St. Martin's Press, 1996.
Abrams, Elliot. "Why America Must Lead." *National Interest,* no. 28 (Summer 1992).
Adams, Sherman. *Firsthand Report.* New York: Harper, 1961.
Adelman, Jonathan, ed. *Superpowers and Revolution.* New York: Praeger, 1986.
Adler, Selig. *The Isolationist Impulse: Its Twentieth-Century Reaction.* New York: Abelard-Schuman, 1957.

Agwani, M. S., ed. *The Lebanese Crisis, 1958: A Documentary Study*. New York: Asia Publishing House, 1965.

Alexander, Charles C. *Holding the Line: The Eisenhower Era, 1952–1961*. Bloomington: Indiana University Press, 1975.

Alin, Erika G. *The United States and the 1958 Lebanon Crisis*. Lanham, MD: University Press of America, 1994.

Allen, Craig. *Eisenhower and the Mass Media: Peace, Prosperity, and Prime-Time TV*. Chapel Hill: University of North Carolina Press, 1993.

Ambrose, Stephen E. *Eisenhower: The President*. Vol. 2. New York: Simon and Schuster, 1984.

Anderson, David L. *Trapped by Success: The Eisenhower Administration and Vietnam, 1953–1961*. New York: Columbia University Press, 1991.

Arnold, James R. *The First Domino: Eisenhower, the Military, and America's Intervention in Vietnam*. New York: William Morrow, 1991.

Aron, Raymond. "What Is a Theory of International Relations." *Journal of International Affairs*, vol. 21, no. 2 (1967), 185–206.

Aspen Institute. *The United States and the Use of Force in the Post–Cold War Era*. Queenstown, MD: Aspen Institute, 1995.

Baldwin, David. *Paradoxes of Power*. New York: Basil Blackwell, 1989.

Baldwin, David. "Security Studies and the End of the Cold War." *World Politics*, vol. 48 no. 1 (October 1995), 117–141.

Barnet, Richard J. *Intervention and Revolution: The United States in the Third World*. New York: World Publishing, 1968.

Beck, Robert. *The Grenada Invasion: Politics, Law, and Foreign Policy Decisionmaking*. Boulder: Westview Press, 1993.

Beisner, Robert L. *Twelve against Empire: The Anti-Imperialists, 1898–1900*. New York: McGraw-Hill, 1968.

Bennett, James R. *Control of Information in the United States: An Annotated Bibliography*. Westport, CT: Meckler, 1987.

Bennett, W. Lance. "Toward a Theory of Press-State Relations in the United States." *Journal of Communication*, vol. 40, (1990), 103–125.

Bennett, W. Lance, and David L. Paletz, eds. *Taken by Storm: The Media, Public Opinion, and U.S. Foreign Policy in the Gulf War*. Chicago: University of Chicago Press, 1994.

Berkowitz, Morton, P. G. Bock, and Vincent J. Fuccillo. *The Politics of American Foreign Policy*. Englewood Cliffs, NJ: Prentice-Hall, 1977.

Berman, Larry, ed. *Looking Back on the Reagan Presidency*. Baltimore: Johns Hopkins University Press, 1990.

Berry, Nicholas O. *Foreign Policy and the Press: An Analysis of* The New York Times' *Coverage of U.S. Foreign Policy*. New York: Greenwood Press, 1990.

Beschloss, Michael R., and Strobe Talbott. *At the Highest Levels: The Inside Story of the End of the Cold War*. Boston: Little, Brown, 1993.

Betts, Richard. "The Delusion of Impartial Intervention." *Foreign Affairs*, vol. 73, no. 6, (November–December 1994): 20–33.

Betts, Richard. *Soldiers, Statesmen, and Cold War Crises*, 2nd ed. New York: Columbia University Press, 1991.

Billings-Yun, Melanie. *Decision against War: Eisenhower and Dien Bien Phu, 1954.* New York: Columbia University Press, 1988.

Binder, Leonard, ed. *Politics in Lebanon.* New York: John Wiley and Sons, 1966.

Blechman, B. M., and S. S. Kaplan. *Force without War: U.S. Armed Forces as a Political Instrument.* Washington, DC: Brookings Institution, 1978.

Blum, William. *The CIA, a Forgotten History: U.S. Global Interventions since World War 2.* London: Zed Books, 1986.

Boutros Ghali, Boutros. "The Situation in Somalia." *Report of the United Nations Secretary General.* April 21, 1992.

Brands, H. W., Jr. *Cold Warriors: Eisenhower's Generation and American Foreign Policy.* New York: Columbia University Press, 1988.

Briggs, Philip J. *Making American Foreign Policy: President-Congress Relations from the Second World War to the Post–Cold War Era,* 2nd ed. Lanham, MD: Rowman and Littlefield, 1994.

Brzezinski, Zbigniew. "Selective Global Commitment." *Foreign Affairs,* vol. 70, no. 4 (Fall 1991): 1–20.

Buchanan, Patrick J. "America First: And Second, and Third." *National Interest,* no. 19 (Spring 1990): 77–82.

Cannon, Lou. *President Reagan: The Role of a Lifetime.* New York: Simon and Schuster, 1991.

Capitanchik, David. *The Eisenhower Presidency and American Foreign Policy.* London: Routledge and Kegan Paul, 1969.

Carpenter, Ted Galen. *The Captive Press: Foreign Policy Crises and the First Amendment.* Washington, DC: Cato Institute, 1995.

Carpenter, Ted Galen. "The Dissenters: American Isolationists and Foreign Policy, 1945–1954." Ph.D. diss., University of Texas, 1980.

Carpenter, Ted Galen. "An Independent Course." *National Interest,* no. 21 (Fall 1990): 28–31.

Carter, Jimmy. *A Government As Good As Its People.* Simon and Schuster, 1977.

Castagno, Al. "Somalia Goes Military." *Africa Report* (February 1970).

Chatfield, Charles. *The American Peace Movement: Ideals and Activism.* New York: Twayne Publishers, 1992.

Christensen, Thomas J. *Useful Adversaries: Grand Strategy, Domestic Mobilization, and Sino-American Conflict, 1947–1958.* Princeton: Princeton University Press, 1996.

Clark, Jeffrey. "Debacle in Somalia." *Foreign Affairs,* vol. 72, no. 1 (1993): 109–123.

Clarke, Walter. *Somalia: Background Information for Operation Restore Hope, 1992–1993.* Carlisle Barracks, PA: U.S. War College, December 1992.

Cohen, Bernard. *The Press and Foreign Policy.* Princeton: Princeton University Press, 1963.

Cohen, Bernard. *The Public's Impact on Foreign Policy.* Boston: Little, Brown, 1973.

Cohen, Eliot A. "The Future of Force." *National Interest,* no. 21 (Fall 1990): 3–15.

Cohen, Eliot A. *Supreme Command: Soldiers, Statesmen and Leadership in Wartime.* New York: Free Press, 2002.

Cohen, Roger. *Hearts Grown Brutal: Sagas of Sarajevo.* New York: Random House, 1998.

Connor, Judson J. *Meeting the Press: A Media Survival Guide for the Defense Manager.* Washington, DC: National Defense University, 1993.

Copeland, Miles. *The Game of Nations: The Amorality of Power Politics*. London: Weidenfeld and Nicolson, 1969.

Cortright, David. *Peace Works: The Citizen's Role in Ending the Cold War*. Boulder: Westview Press, 1993.

Crocker, Chester A., Fen Osler Hampson, and Pamela Aall, eds. *Managing Global Chaos: Sources of and Responses to International Conflict*. Washington, DC: United States Institute of Peace, 1996.

Cumings, Bruce. *The Origins of the Korean War,* vol. 2. Princeton: Princeton University Press, 1990.

Cutler, Robert. *No Time for Rest*. Boston: Little, Brown, 1965.

Daalder, Ivo H., and James M. Lindsay. *America Unbound: The Bush Revolution in Foreign Policy*. Washington, DC: Brookings Institution, 2003.

Daggett, Stephen, and Nina Serafino. "The Use of Force: Key Contemporary Documents." *Report to Congress*. Congressional Research Service. October 17, 1994.

Dagne, Theodros. "Somalia: War and Famine." *Report to Congress*. Congressional Research Service. December 23, 1992.

Dahl, Robert A. *Modern Political Analysis,* 5th ed. Englewood Cliffs, NJ: Prentice Hall, 1991.

Dallek, Robert. *The American Style of Foreign Policy: Cultural Politics and Foreign Affairs*. New York: Knopf, 1983.

Damrosch, Lori, ed. *Enforcing Restraint: Collective Intervention in Internal Conflicts*. New York: Council on Foreign Relations, 1993.

David, Paul T., and David H. Everson, eds. *The Presidential Election and Transition, 1980–81*. Carbondale: Southern Illinois University Press, 1983.

Davidson, Scott. *Grenada: A Study in Politics and the Limits of International Law*. Brookfield, VT: Gower, 1987.

Deaver, Michael K., with Mickey Herskowitz. *Behind the Scenes*. New York: William Morrow, 1987.

Debose, Lou, Jan Reid, and Carl M. Cannon. *Boy Genius: Karl Rove, the Brains Behind the Remarkable Political Triumph of George W. Bush*. New York: Public Affairs, 2003.

Destler, I. M., Leslie Gelb, and Anthony Lake. *Our Own Worst Enemy: The Unmaking of American Foreign Policy*. New York: Simon and Schuster, 1984.

Divine, Robert A. *Blowing on the Wind: The Nuclear Test Ban Debate, 1954–1960*. New York: Oxford University Press, 1978.

Divine, Robert A. *Eisenhower and the Cold War*. New York: Oxford University Press, 1981.

Dobbs, Charles M. *The Unwanted Symbol: American Foreign Policy, the Cold War, and Korea, 1945–1950*. Kent, OH: Kent State University Press, 1981.

Doenecke, Justus D. *Not to the Swift: The Old Isolationists in the Cold War Era*. Lewisburg, PA: Bucknell University Press, 1979.

Donovan, Robert J. *Eisenhower: The Inside Story*. New York: Harper, 1956.

Dowty, Alan. *Middle East Crisis: U.S. Decision-Making in 1958, 1970, and 1973*. Berkeley: University of California Press, 1984.

Doyle, Michael W. "Liberation and World Politics." *American Political Science Review*, vol. 80, no. 4 (December 1986): 1151–1169.

Drew, Elizabeth. *Portrait of an Election: The 1980 Presidential Campaign*. New York: Simon and Schuster, 1981.

Duiker, William J., *U.S. Containment Policy and the Conflict in Indochina.* Stanford, CA: Stanford University Press, 1994.

Dunn, Peter M., and Bruce Watson, eds. *American Intervention in Grenada: The Implications of Operation "Urgent Fury."* Boulder: Westview Press, 1985.

Dyer, George Edward. "Military Isolation in the United States, 1939–1966." Ph.D. diss., Texas Tech University, 1967.

Eisenhower, Dwight D. *Public Papers of the Presidents of the United States: Dwight D. Eisenhower.* Vol. 1, *1953.* Washington, DC: U.S. Government Printing Office, 1960.

Eisenhower, Dwight D. *Waging Peace, 1956–1961: The White House Years.* Garden City, NY: Doubleday, 1965.

Elman, Colin. "Horses for Courses: Why Not Neorealist Theories of Foreign Policy?" *Security Studies,* vol. 6, no. 1 (1996): 7–53.

Eveland, Wilbur Crane. *Ropes of Sand: America's Failure in the Middle East.* New York: W. W. Norton, 1980.

Ewald, William Bragg, Jr. *Eisenhower the President: Crucial Days, 1951–1960.* Englewood Cliffs, NJ: Prentice Hall, 1981.

Ferrell, Robert H. *The Diary of James C. Hagerty.* Bloomington: Indiana University Press, 1983.

Ferrell, Robert H. *The Eisenhower Diaries.* New York: W. W. Norton, 1981.

Finnemore, Martha. *National Interests in International Society.* Ithaca, NY: Cornell University Press, 1996.

Forsythe, David P. *Human Rights and U.S. Foreign Policy: Congress Reconsidered.* Gainesville: University of Florida Press, 1988.

Foyle, Douglas C. *Counting the Public In: Presidents, Public Opinion, and Foreign Policy.* New York: Columbia University Press, 1999.

Frieden, David A. *Debt, Development, and Democracy.* Princeton: Princeton University Press, 1991.

Friedman, Edward, and Mark Selden, eds. *America's Asia: Dissenting Essays on Asian-American Relations.* New York: Pantheon, 1971.

Frum, David. *The Right Man: The Surprise Presidency of George W. Bush.* New York: Random House, 2003.

Frum, David, and Richard Perle. *An End to Evil: How to Win the War on Terror.* New York: Random House, 2003.

Gacek, Christopher M.. *The Logic of Force: The Dilemma of Limited War in American Foreign Policy.* New York: Columbia University Press, 1994.

Gaddis, John Lewis. *Strategies of Containment: A Critical Appraisal of Postwar American National Security Policy.* New York: Oxford University Press, 1982.

Gaddis, John Lewis. *The United States and the Origins of the Cold War, 1941–1947.* New York: Columbia University Press, 1972.

Gallup, George. *The Gallup Poll: Public Opinion, 1935–1971.* Vol. 2: *1949–1958.* New York: Random House, 1972.

Gardner, Richard. "The Comeback of Liberal Internationalism." *Washington Quarterly,* vol. 13 (Summer 1990): 23–39.

Garthoff, Raymond. *Détente and Confrontation.* Washington, DC: Brookings Institution, 1985.

Gelb, Leslie, and Richard Betts. *The Irony of Vietnam: The System Worked.* Washington, DC: Brookings Institution, 1979.

Gendzier, Irene. "The United States, the USSR and the Arab World in NSC Reports of the 1950s." *American-Arab Affairs*, vol. 28 (Spring 1989).

George, Alexander. *Presidential Decisionmaking in Foreign Policy: The Effective Use of Information and Advice*. Boulder: Westview Press, 1980.

George, Alexander, and Timothy McKeown. "Case Studies and Theories of Organizational Decision Making." In *Advances in Information Processing in Organizations*. Ed. Robert Coulam and Richard Smith. Vol. 2, pp. 21–58. Greenwich, CT: JAI Press, 1985.

Gershman, Carl. "Freedom Remains the Touchstone." *National Interest*, no. 19 (Spring 1990): 83–86.

Gholz, Eugene, Daryl G. Press, and Harvey Sapolsky. "Come Home America: The Strategy of Restraint in the Face of Temptation." *International Security*, vol. 21, no. 4 (Spring 1997).

Glazer, Nathan. "A Time for Modesty." *National Interest*, no. 21 (Fall 1990): 31–35.

Goldstein, Judith. *Ideas, Interests, and American Trade Policy*. Ithaca, NY: Cornell University Press, 1993.

Goldstein, Judith, and Robert O. Keohane, eds. *Ideas and Foreign Policy: Beliefs, Institutions, and Political Change*. Ithaca, NY: Cornell University Press, 1993.

Goodman, Allen E. *The Diplomatic Record: 1992*. Boulder: Westview Press, 1995.

Gordon, Michael R., and Bernard E. Trainer. *The General's War: The Inside Story of the Conflict in the Gulf*. Boston: Little, Brown, 1995.

Gourevitch, Peter. *Politics in Hard Times: Comparative Responses to International Economic Crises*. Ithaca, NY: Cornell University Press, 1986.

Graebner, Norman A. *The New Isolationism: A Study in Politics and Foreign Policy since 1950*. New York: Ronald Press, 1956.

Greenstein, Fred. *The Hidden-Hand Presidency: Eisenhower as Leader*. New York: Basic Books, 1982.

Greenstein, Fred, and John P. Burke. *How Presidents Test Reality: Decisions on Vietnam 1954 and 1965*. San Francisco: Russell Sage Foundation, 1989.

Haas, Peter. "Introduction: Epistemic Communities and International Policy Coordination." *International Organization*, vol. 46, no. 2 (1992): 1–37.

Haass, Richard N. *Intervention: The Use of American Military Power in the Post–Cold War World*. Washington, DC: Carnegie Endowment for International Peace, 1994.

Haass, Richard N. *Conflicts Unending: The United States and Regional Disputes*. New Haven: Yale University Press, 1990.

Habermas, Jürgen. "Towards a Theory of Communicative Competence." *Inquiry*, vol. 13, no. 4 (Winter 1970): 360–375.

Hahn, Peter L. *United States, Great Britain, and Egypt, 1945, 1956: Strategy and Diplomacy in the Early Cold War*. Chapel Hill: University of North Carolina Press, 1991.

Haig, Alexander M., Jr. *Caveat: Realism, Reagan and Foreign Policy*. New York: Macmillan, 1984.

Halberstam, David. *The Best and the Brightest*. New York: Random House, 1972.

Hall, Peter A., ed. *The Political Power of Economic Ideas: Keynesianism across Nations*. Princeton: Princeton University Press, 1989.

Hallin, Daniel C. *The Uncensored War: The Media and Vietnam*. New York: Oxford University Press, 1986.

Hallin, Daniel C. "The Media, the War in Vietnam, and Public Support: A Critique of the Thesis of an Oppositional Media." *Journal of Politics*, vol. 46, no. 1 (February 1984): 2–24.

Hartz, Louis. *The Liberal Tradition in America*. San Diego: Harcourt Brace Jovanovich, 1991.

Hayter, Teresa. *Aid as Imperialism*. Harmondsworth, England: Penguin, 1971.

Held, David. *Models of Democracy*. 2nd ed. Stanford, CA: Stanford University Press, 1996.

Herman, Edward S., and Noam Chomsky. *Manufacturing Consent: The Political Economy of the Mass Media*. New York: Pantheon, 1988.

Herring, George. *America's Longest War: The United States and Vietnam, 1950–1975*, 3rd ed. New York: McGraw-Hill, 1996.

Herring, George C., and Richard H. Immerman. "Eisenhower, Dulles, and Dienbienphu: 'The Day We Didn't Go to War' Revisited." *Journal of American History*, vol. 72 (September 1984): 343–363.

Hess, Stephen. *The Government-Press Connection: Press Officers and Their Offices*. Washington, DC: Brookings Institution, 1984.

Hinckley, Ronald H. *People, Polls, and Policymakers: American Public Opinion and National Security*. New York: Lexington Books, 1992.

Hirsch, John L., and Robert B. Oakley. *Operation Restore Hope: Reflections on Peacemaking and Peacekeeping*. Washington, DC: United States Institute of Peace, 1995.

Hoffmann, Stanley. "The Case for Leadership." *Foreign Policy*, no. 81 (Winter 1990/91): 3–19.

Hoffmann, Stanley. "A New World and Its Troubles." *Foreign Affairs*, vol. 69, no. 4 (Fall 1990): 115–122.

Hoffmann, Stanley. *Gulliver's Troubles: The Setting of American Foreign Policy*. New York: McGraw-Hill, 1968.

Hogan, Michael J., ed. *America in the World: The Historiography of American Foreign Relations since 1941*. Cambridge: Cambridge University Press, 1995.

Hogan, Michael J., ed. *The End of the Cold War: Its Meanings and Implications*. New York: Cambridge University Press, 1992.

Holsti, Ole R. *Public Opinion and American Foreign Policy*. Ann Arbor: University of Michigan Press, 1996.

Holsti, Ole R. and James N. Rosenau. *American Leadership in World Affairs: Vietnam and the Breakdown of Consensus*. Boston: Allen and Unwin, 1984.

Hoopes, Townsend. *The Devil and John Foster Dulles*. Boston: Little, Brown, 1973.

Hoopes, Townsend. *The Limits of Intervention*. New York: McKay, 1969.

Houghton, Neal D., ed. *Struggle Against History: U.S. Foreign Policy in an Age of Revolution*. New York: Simon and Schuster, 1968.

Hughes, Thomas L. "The Crack Up." *Foreign Policy*, vol. 40 (1980): 52–53.

Hunt, Michael. *Ideology and American Foreign Policy*. New Haven: Yale University Press, 1987.

Ikenberry, G. John, David A. Lake, and Michael Mastanduno, eds. *The State and American Foreign Economic Policy*. Ithaca, NY: Cornell University Press, 1988.

Immerman, Richard. *The CIA in Guatemala: The Foreign Policy of Intervention*. Austin: University of Texas Press, 1982.

Immerman, Richard H. "The United States and the Geneva Conference of 1954: A New Look." *Diplomatic History*, vol. 14, no. 1 (Winter 1990): 46–66.

Jastrow, Robert, and Max Kampelman. "Why We Still Need SDI." *Commentary,* vol. 94, no. 5. (November 1992): 23–29.

Jentleson, Bruce. "The Pretty Prudent Public: Post Post-Vietnam American Opinion on the Use of Military Force." *International Studies Quarterly,* vol. 36 (1992): 49–74.

Jervis, Robert. *Perception and Misperception in International Politics.* Princeton, NJ: Princeton University Press, 1976.

Jervis, Robert, Richard Ned Lebow, and Janice Gross Stein, eds. *Psychology and Deterrence.* Baltimore, MD: Johns Hopkins University Press, 1985.

Johnson, Walter, ed. *The Papers of Adlai E. Stevenson: Toward a New America, 1955–1957.* 8 vols. Boston: Little, Brown, 1976. Vol. 6.

Jones, Joseph. *The Fifteen Weeks: February 21–June 5, 1947.* New York: Viking Press, 1955.

Kant, Immanuel. *Perpetual Peace.* Ed. Lewis White Beck. Indianapolis: Bobbs-Merrill Educational Library, 1957.

Kanter, Arnold, and Linton Brooks, eds. *U.S. Intervention Policy for the Post–Cold War World: New Challenges and New Responses.* New York: W. W. Norton, 1994.

Kaplan, Lawrence F., and William Kristol. *The War Over Iraq: Saddam's Tyranny and America's Mission.* San Francisco: Encounter Books, 2003.

Katz, Milton S. *Ban the Bomb, A History of SANE, The Committee for a Sane Nuclear Policy.* Westport, CT: Greenwood Press, 1986.

Katzenstein, Peter J., ed. *Between Power and Plenty: Foreign Economic Policies of Advanced Industrialized States.* Madison: University of Wisconsin Press, 1978.

Kaufman, Burton I. *The Korean War: Challenge in Crisis, Credibility, and Command.* Philadelphia: Temple University Press, 1986.

Keck, Margaret E., and Kathryn Sikkink. *Activists beyond Borders: Advocacy Networks in International Politics.* Ithaca, NY: Cornell University Press, 1998.

Kegley, Charles W., Jr. "The Neoidealist Moment in International Studies? Realist Myths and the New International Realities." *International Studies Quarterly,* vol. 37, no. 2 (June 1993): 131–146.

Kennedy, John F. *The Strategy of Peace.* Ed. Allan Nevins. New York: Harper and Row, 1960.

Kernell, Samuel. *Going Public: New Strategies in Presidential Leadership.* Washington, DC: Congressional Quarterly Press, 1986.

Khalidi, Walid. *Conflict and Violence in Lebanon: Confrontation in the Middle East.* Cambridge: Harvard University, Center for International Affairs, 1979.

Khong, Yuen Foong. *Analogies at War: Korea, Munich, Dien Bien Phu and the Vietnam Decisions of 1965.* Princeton: Princeton University Press, 1992.

King, Gary, Robert O. Keohane, and Sidney Verba. *Designing Social Inquiry: Scientific Inference in Qualitative Research.* Princeton: Princeton University Press, 1994.

Kirkpatrick, Jeane J. *Dictatorships and Double Standards: Rationalism and Reason in Politics.* New York: Simon and Schuster, 1982.

Kirkpatrick, Jeane J. *The Reagan Phenomenon and Other Speeches on Foreign Policy.* Washington, DC: American Enterprise Institute for Public Policy Research, 1983.

Klare, Michael T. *War Without End: American Planning for the Next Vietnams.* New York: Knopf, 1972.

Klarevus, Louis. "The 'Essential Domino' of Military Operations: American Public Opinion and the Use of Force." *International Studies Perspectives* (November 2002): 417–437.

Knopf, Jeffrey W. *Domestic Society and International Cooperation: The Impact of Protest on U.S. Arms Control Policy*. New York: Cambridge University Press, 1998.

Kober, Stanley. "Idealpolitik." *Foreign Policy*, no. 79 (Summer 1990): 3–24.

Kohut, Andrew, and Robert C. Toth. "Arms and the People." *Foreign Affairs*, vol. 73, no. 6 (November–December 1994): 47–61.

Kolko, Gabriel. *Anatomy of a War: Vietnam, the United States, and the Modern Historical Experience*. New York: Pantheon Books, 1985.

Kolko, Gabriel. *Confronting the Third World: United States Foreign Policy, 1945–1980*. New York: Pantheon, 1988.

Kolko, Gabriel. *The Politics of War: The World and United States Foreign Policy, 1943–1945*. New York: Random House, 1968.

Korbani, Agnes G. *U.S. Intervention in Lebanon, 1958 and 1982*. New York: Praeger, 1991.

Krauthammer, Charles. "The Unipolar Moment." *Foreign Affairs*, vol. 70, no. 1 (1990–1991): 23–33.

Krauthammer, Charles. "Universal Dominion: Toward a Unipolar World." *The National Interest*, no. 18 (Winter 1989–1990): 46–49.

Krehbiel, Keith. *Information and Legislative Organization*. Ann Arbor: University of Michigan Press, 1991.

Krepenevich, Andrew F., Jr. *The Army and Vietnam*. Baltimore: Johns Hopkins University Press, 1986.

Kristol, Irving. "Defining Our National Interest." *National Interest*, no. 21 (Fall 1990): 16–25.

Kull, Steven. "What the Public Knows that Washington Doesn't." *Foreign Policy*, vol. 101 (Winter 1995): 102–115.

Lake, David A., and Donald S. Rothchild, eds. *The International Spread of Ethnic Conflict: Fear, Diffusion, and Escalation*. Princeton: Princeton University Press, 1998.

Larson, Deborah Welch. *Origins of Containment: A Psychological Explanation*. Princeton, NJ: Princeton University Press, 1985.

Larson, Eric. *Casualties and Consensus: The Historical Role of Casualties in Domestic Support for U.S. Military Operations*. Santa Monica, CA: RAND, 1996.

Larson, Stephanie Greco. *Creating Consent of the Governed: A Member of Congress and the Local Media*. Carbondale: Southern Illinois University Press, 1992.

Lasswell, Harold D., Ralph D. Casey, and Bruce Lannes Smith. *Propaganda and Promotional Activities: An Annotated Bibliography*. Chicago: University of Chicago Press, 1969.

Lebow, Richard Ned, and Thomas Risse-Kappen, eds. *International Relations Theory and the End of the Cold War*. New York: Columbia University Press, 1995.

Lewis, I. M. "The Politics of the 1969 Somalia Coup." *Journal of Modern African Studies*, vol. 10, no. 3 (October 1972): 383–408.

Licklider, Roy, ed. *Stopping the Killing: How Civil Wars End*. New York: New York University Press, 1993.

Lind, William S. "Defending Western Culture." *Foreign Policy*, no. 84 (Fall 1991): 40–50.

Lippmann, Walter. *Public Opinion*. New York: Free Press, 1997.

Little, Douglas. "His Finest Hour? Eisenhower, Lebanon, and the 1958 Middle East Crisis." *Diplomatic History*, vol. 20, no. 1 (Winter 1996): 27–54.

Lomperis, Timothy J. *The War Everyone Lost—And Won: America's Intervention in Viet Nam's Twin Struggles*. Baton Rouge: Louisiana State University Press, 1984.

Lyon, Peter. *Eisenhower: Portrait of the Hero*. Boston: Little, Brown, 1974.

Lyons, Gene, and Michael Mastanduno, eds. *Beyond Westphalia? National Sovereignty and International Intervention*. Baltimore: Johns Hopkins University Press, 1995.

Lyons, Terrence, and Ahmed I. Samatar. *Somalia: State Collapse, Multilateral Intervention, and Strategies for Political Reconstruction*. Washington, DC: Brookings Institution, 1995.

MacDonald, Douglas J. *Adventures in Chaos: American Intervention for Reform in the Third World*. Cambridge: Harvard University Press, 1992.

MacKinnon, Michael G. *The Evolution of U.S. Peacekeeping Policy Under Clinton: A Fairweather Friend?* London: Frank Cass, 2000.

Maggiotto, Michael A., and Eugene Wittkopf "American Public Attitudes Toward Foreign Policy" *International Studies Quarterly*, vol. 25, no.4, (December 1981): 601–631.

Maltese, John Anthony. *Spin Control: The White House Office of Communications and the Management of Presidential News*. 2nd ed. Chapel Hill: University of North Carolina Press, 1994.

Mapel, David R., and Terry Nardin, eds. *International Society: Diverse Ethical Perspectives*. Princeton: Princeton University Press, 1998.

Margolis, Michael, and Gary A. Mauser, eds. *Manipulating Public Opinion: Essays on Public Opinion as a Dependent Variable*. Belmont, CA: Wadsworth, 1989.

Mastanduno, Michael. "Preserving the Unipolar Moment: Realist Theories and U.S. Grand Strategy After the Cold War." *International Security*, vol. 21, no. 4 (Spring 1997): 49–88.

Mauer, John H., and Richard H. Porth. *Military Intervention in the Third World: Threats, Constraints, and Options*. New York: Praeger, 1984.

May, Ernest R., and Richard E. Neustadt. *Thinking in Time: The Uses of History for Decision Makers*. New York: Free Press, 1986.

Maynes, Charles William. "America Without the Cold War." *Foreign Policy*, no. 78 (Spring 1990): 3–25.

McClintock, Robert. *The Meaning of Limited War*. Boston: Houghton Mifflin, 1967.

McNeil, Frank. *War and Peace in Central America: Reality and Illusion*. New York: Charles Scribner's Sons, 1988.

McPherson, Harry. *A Political Education*. Boston: Little, Brown, 1972.

Mearsheimer, John. "Back to the Future: Instability in Europe After the Cold War." *International Security*, vol. 15, no. 1 (Summer 1990): 5–56.

Medhurst, Martin J., ed. *Eisenhower's War of Words: Rhetoric and Leadership*. East Lansing: Michigan State University, 1994.

Meernik, James. "Presidential Decision Making and the Political Use of Military Force." *International Studies Quarterly*, vol. 38 (1994): 121–138.

Meese, Edwin, III. *With Reagan: The Inside Story*. Washington, DC: Regnery Gateway, 1992.

Melanson, Richard A. *Reconstructing Consensus: American Foreign Policy since the Vietnam War*. New York: St. Martin's Press, 1991.

Melanson, Richard A., and David Mayers, eds. *Reevaluating Eisenhower: American Foreign Policy in the 1950s*. Urbana: University of Illinois Press, 1987.

Melvern, Linda. *A People Betrayed: The Role of the West in the Rwandan Genocide*. London: Zed Books, 2000.

Menges, Constantine C. *Inside the National Security Council: The True Story of the Making and Unmaking of Reagan's Foreign Policy*. New York: Simon and Schuster, 1988.

Merrill, John. *Korea: The Peninsular Origins of the War*. Newark: University of Delaware Press, 1989.

Meyer, David S. "Protest Cycles and Political Process: American Peace Movements in the Nuclear Age." *Political Research Quarterly*, vol. 46 (September 1993): 451–479.

Milner, Helen. *Resisting Protectionism: Global Industries and the Politics of International Trade*. Princeton: Princeton University Press, 1988.

Minear, Larry, Colin Scott, and Thomas G. Weiss, eds. *The News Media, Civil Wars and Humanitarian Action*. Boulder: Lynne Rienner, 1996.

Moore, James, and Wayne Slater. *Bush's Brain: How Karl Rove Made George W. Bush Presidential*. Hoboken, NJ: John Wiley and Sons, 2003.

Moravcik, Andrew. "Taking Preferences Seriously: A Liberal Theory of International Politics." *International Organization*, vol. 51, no. 4 (Autumn 1997): 513–554.

Morgan, David. *The Flacks of Washington: Government Information and the Public Agenda*. Westport, CT: Greenwood Press, 1986.

Morgenthau, Hans J. *Politics among Nations: The Struggle for Power and Peace*. 4th ed. New York: Alfred A. Knopf, 1967.

Morgenthau, Hans J. *Truth and Power: Essays of a Decade, 1960–1970*. New York: Praeger, 1970.

Morley, Morris H. *Imperial State and Revolution: The United States and Cuba, 1952–1986*. Cambridge: Cambridge University Press, 1987.

Morley, Morris H. *Washington, Somoza and the Sandinistas: State and Regime in U.S. Policy toward Nicaragua, 1969–1981*. Cambridge: Cambridge University Press, 1994.

Mower, A. Glenn, Jr. *Human Rights and American Foreign Policy: The Carter and Reagan Experiences*. New York: Greenwood Press, 1987.

Mueller, John E. *Policy and Opinion in the Gulf War*. Chicago: University of Chicago Press, 1994.

Mueller, John E. *War, Presidents, and Public Opinion*. New York: John Wiley and Sons, 1973.

Muravchik, Joshua. "The End of the Vietnam Paradigm." *Commentary*, vol. 91, no. 5 (May 1991): 17–23.

Muravchik, Joshua. *The Imperative of American Leadership: A Challenge to Neo-Isolationism*. Washington, DC: American Enterprise Press, 1996.

Muravchik, Joshua. "Losing the Peace." *Commentary*, vol. 94, no. 1 (July 1992): 37–42.

Muravchik, Joshua. "The Strange Debate Over Bosnia." *Commentary*, vol. 94, no. 5 (November 1992): 30–37.

Muravchik, Joshua. *The Uncertain Crusade: Jimmy Carter and the Dilemmas of Human Rights Policy*. Lanham, MD: Hamilton Press, 1986.

Nacos, Brigitte Lebens. *The Press, Presidents, and Crises*. New York: Columbia University Press, 1990.

Nagai, Yonosake, and Akira Iriye, eds. *The Origins of the Cold War in Asia*. New York: Columbia University Press, 1977.

Nash, George H. *The Conservative Intellectual Movement in America since 1945*. Wilmington, DE: Intercollegiate Studies Institute, 1998.

Neff, Donald. *Warriors at Suez: Eisenhower Takes America into the Middle East*. New York: Simon and Schuster, 1981.

Neustadt, Richard E. *Presidential Power: The Politics of Leadership from FDR to Carter.* New York: Wiley, 1980.

Northedge, F. S., ed. *The Use of Force in International Relations.* New York: Free Press, 1974.

Nye, Joseph S., Jr. *The Paradox of American Power: Why the World's Only Superpower Can't Go It Alone.* New York: Oxford University Press, 2002.

Nylen, William Russell. "United States–Grenada Relations, 1979–1983: American Foreign Policy towards a 'Backyard' Revolution." *Pew Case Studies in International Affairs,* Case 306. Pew Charitable Trusts, 1983.

Oglesby, Carl, and Richard Shaull. *Containment and Change.* New York: Macmillan, 1967.

Olson, Gregory A. *Mansfield and Vietnam: A Study in Rhetorical Adaptation.* East Lansing: Michigan State University Press, 1995.

O'Neill, Tip, with William Novak. *Man of the House: The Life and Political Memoirs of Speaker Tip O'Neill.* New York: Random House, 1987.

Ornstein, Norman J. "Foreign Policy and the 1992 Election." *Foreign Affairs,* vol. 71, no. 3 (Summer 1992): 1–16.

Oseth, John M. *Regulating U.S. Intelligence Operations.* Lexington: University Press of Kentucky, 1985.

O'Shaughnessy, Hugh. *Grenada: Revolution, Invasion and Aftermath.* London: Hamish Hamilton, 1984.

Ottosen, Rune. "Media and War Reporting: Public Relations vs. Journalism." *International Peace Research Institute, Oslo Report,* no. 5. October 1992.

Owen, John M., IV. *Liberal Peace, Liberal War: American Politics and International Security.* Ithaca, NY: Cornell University Press, 1997.

Oye, Kenneth A., Robert J. Lieber, and Donald Rothchild, eds. *Eagle in a New World: American Grand Strategy in the Post–Cold War World.* New York: Harper Collins, 1992.

Padover, Saul K., ed. *The Complete Madison: His Basic Writings.* New York: Harper and Brothers, 1953.

Page, Benjamin I., and Robert Y. Shapiro. *The Rational Public: Fifty Years of Trends in Americans' Policy Preferences.* Chicago: University of Chicago Press, 1992.

Parmet, Herbert S. *Eisenhower and the American Crusades.* New York: Macmillan, 1972.

Parmet, Herbert S. *J.F.K.: The Presidency of John F. Kennedy.* New York: Dial Press, 1983.

Paterson, Thomas G., ed. *American Imperialism and Anti-Imperialism.* New York: Crowell, 1973.

Paterson, Thomas G., ed. *Cold War Critics: Alternatives to American Foreign Policy in the Truman Years.* Chicago: Quadrangle Books, 1971.

Paterson, Thomas G. *Contesting Castro: The United States and the Triumph of the Cuban Revolution.* New York: Oxford University Press, 1994.

Payne, Anthony, Paul Sutton, and Tony Thorndike. *Grenada: Revolution and Invasion.* New York: St. Martin's Press, 1984.

Pearce, Jenny. *Under the Eagle: U.S. Intervention in Central America and the Caribbean.* Boston: South End Press, 1982.

Petraeus, David H. "The American Military and the Lessons of Vietnam." Ph.D. diss., Princeton University, 1987.

Petraeus, David. "Korea, the Never-Again Club, and Indochina." *Parameters*, vol. 17 (December 1987): 59–70.

Phillips, David Atlee. *The Night Watch*. New York: Atheneum, 1977.

Powell, Colin L. "U.S. Forces: Challenges Ahead." *Foreign Affairs*, vol. 71, no. 5 (Winter 1992): 32–46.

Powell, Colin L., with Joseph E. Persico. *My American Journey: An Autobiography*. New York: Random House, 1995.

Powell, S. Steven. *Second Front: Advancing Latin American Revolution in Washington*. Washington, DC: Capital Research Center, 1986.

Power, Samantha. *A Problem from Hell: America and the Age of Genocide*. New York: Basic Books, 2002.

Powlick, Philip J. "The Attitudinal Bases for Responsiveness to Public Opinion Among American Foreign Policy Officials." *Journal of Conflict Resolution*, vol. 35 (December 1991): 611–641.

Powlick, Philip J., and Andrew Z. Katz. "Defining the American Public Opinion–Foreign Policy Nexus." *Mershon International Studies Review*, vol. 42 (May 1998): 29–61.

Prados, John. *The Sky Would Fall, Operation Vulture: The U.S. Bombing Mission in Indochina, 1954*. New York: Dial Press, 1983.

Qubain, Fahim. *Crisis in Lebanon*. Washington, DC: Middle East Institute, 1961.

Quigley, John. *The Ruses for War: American Interventionism since World War II*. Buffalo, NY: Prometheus Books, 1992.

Rampton, Sheldon, and John Stauber. *Weapons of Mass Deception: The Uses of Propaganda in Bush's War on Iraq*. New York: Jeremy P. Tarcher/Penguin, 2003.

Ramsbotham, Oliver, and Tom Woodhouse. *Humanitarian Intervention in Contemporary Conflict*. Cambridge, MA: Polity Press, 1996.

Ray, James Lee. *Democracy and International Conflict: An Evaluation of the Democratic Peace Proposition*. Columbia: University of South Carolina Press, 1995.

Reagan, Ronald. *An American Life*. New York: Simon and Schuster, 1990.

Reed, Laura, and Carl Kaysen, eds. *Emerging Norms of Justified Intervention*. Cambridge: American Academy of Arts and Sciences, 1993.

Ripley, Randall B., and James M. Lindsay, eds. *Congress Resurgent: Foreign and Defense Policy on Capitol Hill*. Ann Arbor: University of Michigan Press, 1993.

Risse-Kappen, Thomas. *Cooperation among Democracies: The European Influence on U.S. Foreign Policy*. Princeton: Princeton University Press, 1995.

Risse-Kappen, Thomas. "Public Opinion, Domestic Structure, and Foreign Policy in Liberal Democracies." *World Politics*, vol. 43 (July 1991): 479–512.

Roberts, Chalmers M. "The Day We Didn't Go to War." *Reporter*, vol. 11, September 14, 1954.

Rodley, Nigel S., ed. *To Loose the Bands of Wickedness: International Intervention in Defence of Human Rights*. London: Brassey's, 1992.

Rosati, Jerel A. *The Carter Administration's Quest for Global Community*. Columbia: University of South Carolina Press, 1987.

Rosenberg, Emily S. *Spreading the American Dream: American Economic and Cultural Expansion, 1890–1945*. New York: Hill and Wang, 1982.

Rostow, W. W. *The Diffusion of Power*. New York: Macmillan, 1972.

Russett, Bruce. *Grasping the Democratic Peace: Principles for a Post–Cold War World*. Princeton: Princeton University Press, 1993.

Russett, Bruce, and Elizabeth Hanson. *Interests and Ideology: The Foreign Policy Beliefs of American Businessmen*. San Francisco: W. H. Freeman, 1975.

Russett, Bruce, and Miroslav Nincic. "American Opinion on Use of Military Force Abroad." *Political Science Quarterly*, vol. 91, no. 3 (1976): 411–431.

Sahnoun, Mohamed. *Somalia: The Missed Opportunities*. Washington, DC: United States Institute of Peace, 1994.

Sandford, Gregory. *The New Jewel Movement: Grenada's Revolution, 1979–1983*. Washington, DC: Center for the Study of Foreign Affairs, 1985.

Sandford, Gregory, and Richard Vigilante. *Grenada: The Untold Story*. New York: Madison Books, 1984.

Schilling, Warner R., Paul Y. Hammond, and Glenn H. Snyder. *Strategy, Politics, and Defense Budgets*. New York: Columbia University Press, 1962.

Schlesinger, Arthur M., Jr. *A Thousand Days: John F. Kennedy in the White House*. Boston: Houghton Mifflin, 1965.

Schoenhals, Kai P., and Richard A. Melanson. *Revolution and Intervention in Grenada: The New Jewel Movement, the United States, and the Caribbean*. Boulder: Westview Press, 1985.

Schraeder, Peter J., ed. *Intervention in the 1980s: U.S. Foreign Policy in the Third World*. Boulder: Lynne Rienner, 1989.

Schulzinger, Robert D. *U.S. Diplomacy since 1900*. 4th ed. New York: Oxford University Press, 1998.

Sheehan, Neil. *A Bright Shining Lie: John Paul Vann and America in Vietnam*. New York: Random House, 1988.

Sheehan, Neil. *The Pentagon Papers, as Published by the New York Times*. New York: Bantam Books, 1971.

Shimko, Keith. "Realism, Neorealism, and American Liberalism." *Review of Politics*, vol. 54, no. 2 (Spring 1992): 281–301.

Shulimson, Jack. *Marines in Lebanon: 1958*. Washington, DC: U.S. Marine Corps, 1966.

Shultz, George P. *Turmoil and Triumph: My Years as Secretary of State*. New York: Scribners, 1993.

Sikkink, Kathryn. *Ideas and Institutions: Developmentalism in Brazil and Argentina*. Ithaca, NY: Cornell University Press, 1991.

Skidmore, David. *Reversing Course: Carter's Foreign Policy, Domestic Politics and the Failure of Reform*. Nashville: Vanderbilt University Press, 1996.

Smist, Frank J., Jr. *Congress Oversees the Intelligence Community, 1947–1989*. Knoxville: University of Tennessee Press, 1985.

Smith, Gaddis. *Morality, Reason, and Power: American Diplomacy in the Carter Years*. New York: Hill and Wang, 1986.

Smith, R. B. *An International History of the Vietnam War*, vol. 3, *The Making of a Limited War, 1965–66*. New York: St. Martin's Press, 1991.

Smith, Tony. *America's Mission: The United States and the Worldwide Struggle for Democracy in the Twentieth Century*. Princeton: Princeton University Press, 1994.

Snyder, Jack. *Myths of Empire: Domestic Politics and International Ambition*. Ithaca, NY: Cornell University Press, 1991.

Snyder, Jack, and Karen Ballentine. "Nationalism and the Marketplace of Ideas." *International Security*, vol. 21, no. 2 (Fall 1996): 5–40.

Sorenson, Theodore C. *Kennedy*. New York: Harper and Row, 1965.

Sorenson, Theodore C. "Rethinking National Security." *Foreign Affairs*, vol. 69, no. 3 (Summer 1990): 1–18.

Speakes, Larry, with Robert Peck. *Speaking Out: The Reagan Presidency from Inside the White House*. New York: Charles Scribner's Sons, 1988.

Spector, Ronald H. *Advice and Support: The Early Years, 1941–1960*. Washington, DC: Center of Military History, 1983.

Spiller, Roger J. *"Not War, But Like War": The American Intervention in Lebanon*. Fort Leavenworth, KS: Combat Studies Institute, 1981.

Steinmo, Sven, Kathleen Thelen, and Frank Longstreth, eds. *Structuring Politics: Historical Institutionalism in Comparative Analysis*. Cambridge: Cambridge University Press, 1992.

Stinchcombe, Arthur L. *Constructing Social Theories*. Chicago: University of Chicago, 1968.

Strobel, Warren P. *Late-Breaking Foreign Policy: The News Media's Influence on Peace Operations*. Washington, DC: United States Institute of Peace, 1997.

Stueck, William Whitney, Jr. *The Road to Confrontation: American Foreign Policy toward China and Korea, 1947–1950*. Chapel Hill: University of North Carolina Press, 1981.

Stueck, William. *The Korean War: An International History*. Princeton: Princeton University Press, 1995.

Sulzberger, C. L. "Foreign Affairs: The Nutcracker Suite." *New York Times*. April 10, 1966, sec. E, p. 8.

Sussman, Barry. *What Americans Really Think and Why Our Politicians Pay No Attention*. New York: Pantheon, 1988.

Tarrow, Sydney. *Power in Movement: Social Movements, Collective Action and Politics*. Cambridge: Cambridge University Press, 1994.

Thayer, Charles W. *Diplomat*. New York: Harper, 1959.

Thompson, Kenneth W., ed. *Three Press Secretaries on the Presidency and the Press: Jody Powell, George Reedy, and Jerry terHorst*. Lanham, MD: University Press of America, 1983.

Tucker, Robert W., and David C. Hendrickson. *The Imperial Temptation: The New World Order and America's Purpose*. New York: Council on Foreign Relations Press, 1992.

Turner, Kathleen J. *Lyndon Johnson's Dual War: Vietnam and the Press*. Chicago: University of Chicago Press, 1985.

U.S. Department of Defense. *U.S.-Vietnam Relations, 1945–1967: A Study Prepared by the Department of Defense*. Vol. 1, part 3. Washington, DC: U.S. Government Printing Office, 1971.

U.S. Department of State. *Foregin Relations of the United States, 1945, British Commonwealth and Far East*. Vol. 6. Washington, DC: U.S. Government Printing Office, 1969.

U.S. Department of State. *Foreign Relations of the United States, 1952–1954*. Vol. 13. Washington, DC: U.S. Government Printing Office.

U.S. Department of State. *Foreign Relations of the United States, 1958–1960*. Vol. 11. Washington, DC: U.S. Government Printing Office.

U.S. Senate, Committee on Foreign Relations. *The Far East and South Asia: Report of Senator H. Alexander Smith on a Study Mission to the Far East*. 83rd Congress., 2nd sess. 1954.

U. S. Senate, Committee on Foreign Relations Meeting, Thursday, June 26, 1958. *Study of United States Foreign Policy*. Washington, DC: U.S. Government Printing Office.

U.S. Senate, Select Committee to Study Governmental Operations with Respect to Intelligence Activities. *Final Report*. Book 1: *Foreign and Military Intelligence*. 94th Congress, 2nd sess. 1976.

Utley, Garrick. "The Shrinking of Foreign News: From Broadcast to Narrowcast." *Foreign Affairs*, vol. 76, no. 2 (March–April 1997): 2–10.

Vance, Cyrus R. *Hard Choices: Critical Years in America's Foreign Policy*. New York: Simon and Schuster, 1983.

Vertzberger, Yaacov Y. I. *Risk Taking and Decisionmaking: Foreign Military Intervention Decisions*. Stanford, CA: Stanford University Press, 1998.

Wade, Gary H. *Rapid Deployment Logistics: Lebanon, 1958*. Fort Leavenworth, KS: U.S. Army Command and General Staff College, 1985.

Walker, Jack L., Jr. *Mobilizing Interest Groups in America: Patrons, Professions, and Social Movements*. Ann Arbor: University of Michigan Press, 1991.

Waller, Douglas C. *Congress and the Nuclear Freeze Movement: An Inside Look at the Politics of a Mass Movement*. Amherst: University of Massachusetts Press, 1987.

Walt, Stephen M. *The Origins of Alliances*. Ithaca, NY: Cornell University Press, 1991.

Walter, Barbara. "The Critical Barrier to Civil War Settlement." *International Organization*, vol. 51, no. 3 (Summer 1997): 335–364.

Waltz, Kenneth N. *Theory of International Politics*. Reading, MA: Addison-Wesley, 1979.

Warshaw, Shirley Anne, ed. *Reexamining the Eisenhower Presidency*. Westport, CT: Greenwood Press, 1993.

Weinberger, Caspar W. *Fighting for Peace: Seven Critical Years in the Pentagon*. New York: Warner Books, 1990.

Weiss, Thomas G., and Larry Minear, eds. *Humanitarianism Across Borders: Sustaining Civilians in Times of War*. Boulder: Lynne Rienner, 1992.

Wendt, Alex. "Anarchy Is What States Make of It: The Social Construction of Power Politics." *International Organization*, vol. 46, no. 2 (Spring 1992): 391–425.

Williams, William A. *The Tragedy of American Diplomacy*. 2nd ed. New York: Dell Publishing, 1972.

Wittkopf, Eugene R. *Faces of Internationalism: Public Opinion and American Foreign Policy*. Durham, NC: Duke University Press, 1990.

Wolfers, Arnold. "'National Security' as an Ambiguous Symbol." *Political Science Quarterly*, vol. 67 (December 1952): 481–502.

Woods, Randall Bennett. *Fulbright: A Biography*. Cambridge: Cambridge University Press, 1995.

Woodward, Bob. *Bush at War*. New York: Simon and Schuster, 2002.

Woodward, Bob. *Plan of Attack*. New York: Simon and Schuster, 2004.

Wormuth, Francis D., and Edwin B. Firmage. *To Chain the Dog of War: The War Power of Congress in History and Law*. Dallas: Southern Methodist University Press, 1986.

Wright, Jim. *Balance of Power: Presidents and Congress from the Era of McCarthy to the Age of Gingrich*. Atlanta: Turner Publishing, 1996.

Wright, Quincy. *A Study of War*. Vol. 2. Chicago: University of Chicago Press, 1942.

Wurmser, David. *Tyranny's Ally: America's Failure to Defeat Saddam Hussein*. Washington, DC: American Enterprise Institute, 1999.

Yankelovich, Daniel. *Coming to Public Judgment: Making Democracy Work in a Complex World*. Syracuse, NY: Syracuse University Press, 1991.

Yee, Albert S. "The Effects of Ideas on Policy." *International Organization*, vol. 50, no. 1 (1996): 69–108.

Zagoria, Donald S. *Vietnam Triangle: Moscow, Peking, Hanoi*. New York: Pegasus, 1967.

Zaller, John R. *The Nature and Origins of Mass Opinion*. New York: Cambridge University Press, 1992.

Zaller, John, and Dennis Chiu. "Government's Little Helper: U.S. Press Coverage of Foreign Policy Crises, 1945–1991." *Political Communication*, vol. 13, no. 4 (1996): 385–406.

Index